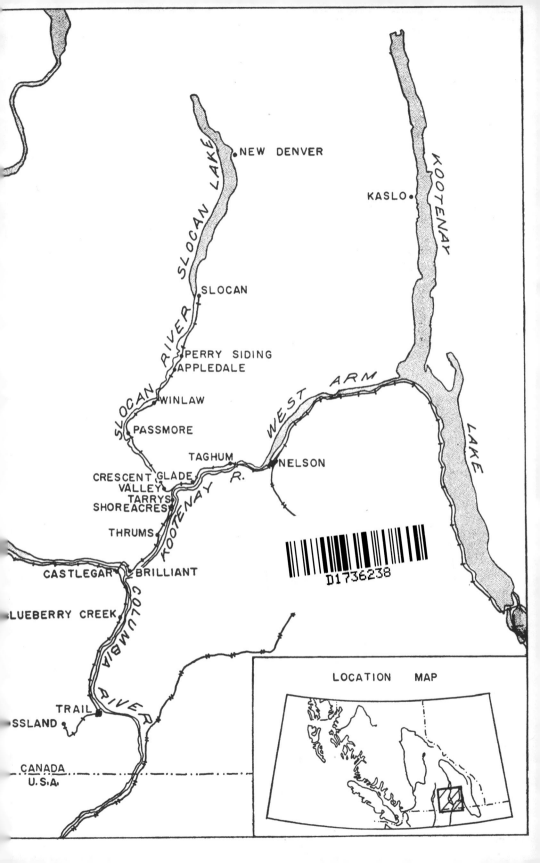

NEW DENVER

KASLO

SLOCAN LAKE

KOOTENAY

SLOCAN

PERRY SIDING
APPLEDALE

WEST ARM

WINLAW

SLOCAN RIVER

PASSMORE

LAKE

TAGHUM

NELSON

CRESCENT GLADE
VALLEY
TARRYS
SHOREACRES

KOOTENAY R.

THRUMS

D1736238

CASTLEGAR BRILLIANT

COLUMBIA

BLUEBERRY CREEK

RIVER

LOCATION MAP

TRAIL

ROSSLAND

CANADA
U.S.A.

THE DOUKHOBORS OF BRITISH COLUMBIA

Doukhobor Research Committee.

BX
7433
D65
1980

The
Doukhobors
of
British Columbia

HARRY B. HAWTHORN
EDITOR

GREENWOOD PRESS, PUBLISHERS
WESTPORT, CONNECTICUT

20704

LIBRARY
Fresno WITHDRAWN Seminary
Fresno, Calif. 93702

Library of Congress Cataloging in Publication Data

Doukhobor Research Committee.
  The Doukhobors of British Columbia.

  "Based on the Report of the Doukhobor Research
Committee ... presented to the Government of British
Columbia in 1952."
  Reprint of the ed. published by University of
British Columbia, Vancouver.
  Includes index.
  1. Dukhobors--British Columbia. 2. British
Columbia--Church history. I. Hawthorn, Harry
Bertram, 1910-   II.   Title.
[BX7433.D65 1980]   289.9   79-8711
ISBN 0-313-20652-X

Copyright 1955 by the University of British Columbia

No part of this book may be reproduced in any form without
permission in writing from the publisher, except by a reviewer who
wishes to quote brief passages in connection with a review written
for inclusion in a magazine, newspaper or radio broadcast.

Reprinted with the permission of Harry B. Hawthorn.

Reprinted in 1980 by Greenwood Press, a division of Congressional
Information Service, Inc., 51 Riverside Avenue, Westport,
Connecticut 06880

Printed in the United States of America

10 9 8 7 6 5 4 3 2 1

FOREWORD

THIS BOOK is based on the *Report of the Doukhobor Research Committee* which was presented to the Government of British Columbia in 1952. The past two years have made it possible to add some new facts, and the different purpose of this book has occasioned some revision. With some pride the authors allow the body of the work to stand largely unaltered, for the events of a lively two years have only confirmed the earlier findings.

A chapter on Religion has been added, new data are incorporated into the chapter on Soils, Agriculture, and Rehabilitation, with comments on recent legislation in the chapter on Public Administration and the Community. The Appendix has been extensively revised, with the inclusion of some Doukhobor statements of faith and principle. The fine photographs by Ben Hill-Tout and A. Stevens illustrate some of the points made by the authors.

The recommendations of the earlier *Report* are presented again without alteration but with comment in the appropriate chapters where some relevant action has already been taken. Two Provincial elections in two years have led to some turmoil where calm and balance were most needed as a background for constructive action. A new Government has understandably required time to make up its mind on policy.

The need for constructive action is no less acute than in 1952. A record number of depredations in 1953 was accompanied by the imprisonment of a large number of Doukhobors once again for nudism.

Yet some legislative and administrative action has reflected the findings of the *Report* and is a move in the direction of the recommended programme. Recognition has been given to Doukhobor marriage, a new "Elections Act" has dropped the provisions excluding Doukhobors from voting, and an imminent revision of the Criminal Code indicates the opinion of the Federal Government that the three-year penalty for nudism should be dropped. The proposed comprehensive survey of the Kootenay area for soils and irrigation, as a preliminary to planning for its development as a region including both Doukhobor and non-Doukhobor lands, has been carried forward. A more detailed inquiry into the allotment of Doukhobor lands has been foreshadowed by an Act and the appointment of a Commission. Advances in the administration of Doukhobor affairs have been made with the formation of three governmental committees.

Yet it cannot be stated that the net result is a clear advance. There ordinated and far greater effort. Minor and piecemeal changes, how-can be no confident expectation of improvement without a more co-ever well-meant, will not add up to a major forward move. The earlier *Report* and the present book document that thesis. For example, the apprehension and institutional care of a few Sons of Freedom children do not rehabilitate the sect. It will be a tragedy if once again piecemeal changes are put forward in place of a comprehensive programme.

HARRY B. HAWTHORN, *Chairman,*

Doukhobor Research Committee,
University of British Columbia.

MEMBERS
OF THE
RESEARCH COMMITTEE

HARRY B. HAWTHORN, *Chairman*, Professor of Anthropology,
The University of British Columbia.

WILLIAM G. DIXON, Associate Professor of Social Work,
The University of British Columbia.

CHARLES W. HARWOOD, Teaching Fellow, Department of Psychology,
University of Washington.

RAYMOND G. HERBERT, Lecturer in Law,
The University of British Columbia.

HUGH HERBISON, Consultative Committee.

GORDON HIRABAYASHI, Assistant Professor of Sociology,
American University, Beirut.

STUART JAMIESON, Associate Professor of Economics,
The University of British Columbia.

CLAUDIA LEWIS, Research Associate, Bank Street College of
Education, New York.

MALCOLM M. MACINTYRE, Professor of Law,
The University of British Columbia.

CHARLES A. ROWLES, Associate Professor of Soils,
The University of British Columbia.

ALFRED SHULMAN, Resident Psychiatrist,
The Seton Institute, Baltimore.

EDRO SIGNORI, Associate Professor of Psychology,
The University of British Columbia.

ALEXANDER W. WAINMAN, Assistant Professor of Slavonic Studies,
The University of British Columbia.

vii

CONTENTS

Appendix. Page 253.

OVER A NUMBER of years it became increasingly evident to some of the authors of this *Report* that the study would eventually have to be made. The growing intensity of the fifty-year old problem of Doukhobor adjustment to life in British Columbia refused to remain ignored. Instead of adjusting over the years, a large minority of the Doukhobors have come into increased conflict with the law. The Sons of Freedom have returned to the jails in larger numbers for arson, dynamiting, nudism and negation of government regulations relating to taxes and schools. The briefest glance shows the possibility of a sympathetic spread of their movement to include other Doukhobors, and the unpalatable likelihood of the rise of vigilantism among the incensed people of the West Kootenay.

A catalytic process, instituting the research which it was hoped would lead to the discovery of ways to lessen the danger, was initiated by Colonel F. J. Mead, who was asked by the Federal Government to act as their observer. Colonel Mead, who has a record of long distinguished service with the Royal Canadian Mounted Police and of sympathetic, capable action in connection with the relocation of the Japanese in World War II, concluded that this was not primarily a police problem, but one which should be studied first by scientists to see what sort of a problem it was, and the authors were eventually induced to undertake the task. They would like to record here the contribution which Colonel Mead has made through his selfless, intelligent and always humanitarian actions.

In the spring of 1950 a request was made by G. S. Wismer, Attorney-General of the Province of British Columbia, to Dr. N. A. M. MacKenzie, President of the University of British Columbia, to appoint a group to carry out research aimed at understanding the situation and at making recommendations for improvement.

The contributors to the study were drawn together, Dr. H. B. Hawthorn being appointed director of the research project and editor of the *Report*. Work commenced late in the summer of 1950 and continued through 1951. The research staff carried on with their normal occupations as well as they could and fitted the work of the project into vacations or limited leaves of absence. Were the study being made again, an endeavour would be made to allow those working upon it to devote their full time to it. The advantage of having one and a half years to work upon the problem has been outweighed by the disadvantages of double work and delayed recommendations.

The inquiry was not given Royal Commission status, with powers to demand information, nor would the research group have accepted such a role. Doukhobors testifying formally on their life and its beliefs can use words in waterfall proportions, which, however honestly intended, do not give the hearer much information about Doukhobor action. The research staff, with their experience in clinical work, studies of primitive cultures, inquiries into labour economics and into various involved, hidden and sensitive areas of human life, assumed at the outset that it was better to go among the Doukhobors, question, listen, observe and where possible take part in their life. Living in the houses of those kind enough to issue invitations, seeing what went on in everyday action, they could form judgments of the background of the actions which were of concern to government and Doukhobor alike. The staff assumed furthermore that some of the Doukhobors— even a few of the Sons of Freedom, who cannot help but feel they are wrongfully blamed and punished and who therefore fall into self-justification more readily than self-explanation—would perceive the problem sufficiently to want to receive aid. This assumption proved correct, and if aid does come to the Doukhobors as a result of this study and the application of its recommendations, many of them can feel they have helped to bring it, by playing host to the research staff (one researcher wrote: "with my snoopy wife and nosey child") and by providing information.

It is very clear to the research staff, however, that few Doukhobors will like this study. For that, no excuse is given. To be of any use the *Report* had to be as objective as care could make it. If a sound programme is to be constructed for a Doukhobor future relatively free from its recent pain and stress, it can only be on the basis of substantially correct knowledge. No person finds that the objective view of his life accords with the way he wants it to be seen, nor does any group escape from this divergence. For correct therapy it was necessary that a correct diagnosis be made, and that has been essayed.

This is not to claim that error has been avoided in the study nor in its summation in the *Report*. Undoubtedly it contains errors, certainly ones of omission; but it is hoped that they are not of major size, and for this hope the contributors find sustenance in the consistency of their reporting, although they worked from backgrounds of different sciences and different ways of approaching the study. It has been gratifying to see a portrayal of the general shape of Doukhobor culture and character forming from the diverse approaches and to realize that the findings are free from major contradictions. With agreement on essentials, some difference of opinion has been allowed

2

to stand in the various chapters of the *Report* in the expectation that they will aid understanding rather than confuse it.

The body of the *Report* is arranged in chapters, each attributed to its main author. The phrase "main author" is used advisedly; in every instance some of the insights and some of the data have come from the joint effort of several people. For reasons of tidiness, however, specific reference to such joint effort is ordinarily omitted.

In the summer of 1950, with more than 400 Doukhobors—many of them breadwinners—in jail, there was need for immediate action. The research staff could not promise a final *Report* before the spring of 1952. Established government agencies looked to them for guidance in policy, which their initial knowledge was hardly adequate to provide. In addition, if the pressures of action had descended prematurely on the research staff, their primary function of research could not have been carried out.

Dean G. C. Andrew, Deputy to the President of the University of British Columbia, devised a compromise which formed a link between the agencies of government which could take action, the various bodies of Doukhobors, the sections of the public most interested and the research staff. A Consultative Committee was formed under his chairmanship to initiate action in the areas of greatest urgency and to function until an administration following from the recommendations of the *Report* could be set up. It was joined from the outset by Emmett Gulley of the American Society of Friends; later R. J. Mawer and H. Herbison were added to its staff. The immediate question of imprisoned Doukhobors was faced and a screening of prisoners was begun with the intention of recommending release of those who gave promise of peaceful behaviour. A more tangled problem was introduced by the request of the Sons of Freedom that they be assisted to leave Canada or to relocate elsewhere inside the country if emigration proved impossible. Welfare assistance for families, particularly for those of prisoners, was needed but it was unacceptable to Sons of Freedom if it involved the usual forms of registration and signing of receipts.

In none of the problem areas could successful action be taken without considerable knowledge of Doukhobor life and needs. But something had to be done immediately. To try to bridge the gap, a number of interim research projects were begun, aimed at limited objectives. Dr. C. A. Rowles investigated the potentialities of a number of sites considered worth studying for resettlement; Dr. Signori and Dr. Shulman aided in the screening of prisoners; Professor Dixon helped to draw up plans for acceptable welfare assistance. To some extent these projects were a burden on an already overloaded research staff and reduced the time available for the basic and long-range study. Yet they did assist the research in a number of ways.

The immediate application of the findings tested how well the staff's developing ideas accorded with reality; the changing situation allowed a study of the forces which were changing it.

The results of the work of the Consultative Committee have been very real and are not to be measured in terms of the success or failure of any one of its various plans. This second committee operated in an exploratory fashion at a time when that was the most constructive thing to do. Its achievements in the matter of the release of prisoners were very real and probably avoided the incarceration of a larger number of sympathy protesters. Its greatest value has lain, however, in allowing the public, the government agencies concerned and above all the many Doukhobors who have attended its meetings to explore the problems in a co-operative way. Doukhobors from all divisions of the group have made submissions to it, given information and participated in a process of government which was plainly neither coercive or exploitative.

In formulating the programme for the Research Committee and assembling the team of workers, the principle was adopted from the first that a combined approach by specialists in several disciplines would be most profitable. To understand the problems besetting the Doukhobors, it was necessary to find out how individual motivation, the cultural tradition and contemporary economic, social and governmental situations contributed to them. No single scientist and indeed no single science could have covered all the aspects which the research team came to know as relevant. The frustrations of joint work have been more than counter-balanced by the strength of an interlocking analysis made from many viewpoints.

The first summer was largely exploratory. Miss Claudia Lewis, Dr. Stuart Jamieson and Professor W. Dixon commenced work. Dr. Jamieson had previously taken part in scientific teamwork with sociologists at McGill University and had later made a difficult and very successful study of migratory agricultural labour in the United States. Assisting him were P. Fogarty and C. K. Toren, graduate students in the social sciences. Miss Lewis was engaged during the academic year in teaching and research in the field of child study at the Bank Street College of Education, New York, and had published a widely used report on children in Tennessee, reflecting situations which were in some respects similar to those in the Kootenays. Professor Dixon combined specialization in municipal government and a detailed knowledge of Provincial affairs with wide experience in welfare programmes.

During the first summer everyone was well received and information was gathered readily. Miss Lewis was fortunate in obtaining Geraldine Kanigan, graduate student, as an assistant, fluent in Russian and with relatives among the Doukhobors. They were guests in a

4

number of homes, and in order to recompense their hosts, who would not accept money, took part in the daily work of the households.

Statistical data were not readily available and most of the existing statistics were admittedly guesswork. Valuable information was forthcoming from the Unemployment Insurance Offices, and Dr. Jamieson and Mr. Fogarty collected more from a questionnaire circulated among employers of the area.

In the late fall of 1950 Dr. Shulman obtained a leave of absence and spent several months in the Kootenays, conducting a number of extended interviews. Dr. Shulman had previously worked with Doukhobor patients at Essondale Mental Hospital in Vancouver, had studied many case-records and the rapidly growing mass of research findings, and had formulated a number of hypotheses relating to Doukhobor character and culture which he was able to test in house to house visits. His wife, Leah Shulman, a graduate in anthropology and psychology, accompanied him and aided in the acquisition of a major amount of material from interview, test and observation.

Dr. Rowles from time to time conducted parties of Sons of Freedom to inspect sites on which he had gathered data for possible resettlement. The Sons of Freedom had failed to obtain permission to enter any of the countries suggested, and consequently British Columbia was combed for suitable areas.

In addition, Dr. Rowles, with the assistance of Albert Van Ryswick, and the co-operation of Neil Drewry of the Department of Lands and Forests, initiated a survey of the Doukhobor lands in the Kootenays, with a view to enabling them to be used more effectively when ownership is restored.

During the fall and winter, meetings of the research group were held by the members who were in Vancouver. This provided opportunity to cross-check data and ideas and discover gaps in knowledge. Participants who were not in Vancouver were retained within a committee of correspondence.

A review of the work of the first summer indicated some areas in which further research was wanted. Dr Shulman felt it would be helpful if a check on some findings could be made with the methods of the social psychologist. It had become apparent that it would be necessary to learn a great deal more about the structuring of Doukhobor society, the methods of communication, the lines of authority. Consequently, Charles Harwood and Gordon Hirabayashi, doctoral candidates in social psychology and sociology at the University of Washington, were invited to take part in the second summer's work. Professor M. M. MacIntyre and Professor R. Herbert undertook to explore some of the ways in which the Doukhobors were entangled with the law. Hugh Herbison, graduate in History and in Theology, and a member of the Wider Quaker Fellowship, was submerged in

5

the work of the Consultative Committee during the initial period of the research but was able to write a section drawing from his knowledge of Doukhobor religious experience and belief.

A number of consultants assisted throughout the project. Foremost are Dr. E. Signori and Professor A. Wainman. From Dr. Signori's participation in the work of screening the prisoners for release, and from visits to the Kootenays, he has contributed many insights; the pressure of his other work kept him from writing part of the *Report*. Professor Wainman, fluent in Russian, has been of the greatest assistance from the beginning; his first-hand knowledge of Russian rural society provided a useful comparison.

Tribute is also due to those who had studied part of the problem earlier, and whose written works were consulted and used. It is not possible, after all the millions of words which have been exchanged and written during the course of the study, to cite every instance where opinion was first formed or fact discovered by authors like J. F. C. Wright. His work *Slava Bohu* was the first required reading for all members of the research staff and probably saved them from taking months longer in their study. Similar though not equally great use has been made of the valuable master's theses of R. H. C. Hooper, E. P. Reid, H. Trevor, and J. P. Zubek.

The assistance given by many specialists in Provincial Government departments in the Kootenays and in Victoria has been of great value. Mention of a few out of the many is perhaps invidious, but the names of I. Spielmans, Lands Inspector, and C. E. Clay, Inspector of Schools, cannot be omitted. The Chairman of the Research Committee trusts that the many others who have helped with this or that point will bear with a blanket acknowledgment of indebtedness. The same acknowledgment and apology for its diffuseness is offered to the employers in the Kootenays who supplied data.

The secretarial work of Kathleen Stanford was a main reason the *Report* reached its final form in readable condition. Mrs. Shirley Suttles, with talents in anthropology and authorship, has contributed grammar and ideas as assistant in the editorial work. Frances McCubbin, a graduate in sociology and anthropology, was the able secretary and research assistant for the first year. Phyllis Dover and Milena Nastich turned over a mountain of newspapers and documents in compiling a record of the earlier phases of Doukhobor life. Mrs. Edna Parnall and Mrs. Faith Mawhinney unwaveringly guided the *Report* through its later stages.

Above all, the research staff wishes to recognize the part the Doukhobors have played in formulating the study. If self-knowledge is of value, benefit has already accrued to the courageous individuals who contributed facts to the *Report*.

May, 1952   H. B. HAWTHORN

I

THE CONTEMPORARY PICTURE

Harry B. Hawthorn

THE DOUKHOBORS emerged in Russia as a sect of dissident peasants separating themselves during the eighteenth century from the Orthodox Church. Throughout the nineteenth century their actions and beliefs led to intermittent conflict with state and clerical authorities and to persecution and exile, until humanitarians in England and Russia sought a land to which they could emigrate.

In brief, their beliefs centred on direct revelation and guidance, which denied the need for a church organization and by extension included a denial of governmental authority and of the right of anyone to use force in human affairs. The attempt to construct complete and logical systems of belief took them even further, and the translation of belief into action was pursued without the compromises which are usually labelled "common sense." In order to protect their existence, however, they developed ways to evade, mislead, and passively resist the inquiries and requirements of the authorities.

Welcomed by a government which wanted settlers, the first groups of Doukhobors arrived in Canada in 1899, some 7,427 in number. They were followed from 1900 to 1920 by smaller numbers of liberated exiles and their families, totalling 417 in all. In 1927 one small additional group arrived with Peter Petrovich Verigin, son of the man who had been the Doukhobors' first leader in Canada.

They were seeking land and freedom, on their own terms. In their negotiations they were represented by Aylmer Maude, of the English Society of Friends, two Doukhobor delegates, and others. The Doukhobor understanding of the terms of entry and settlement almost certainly lacked clarity. They had in the first place fixed ideas of their goal, which included freedom from the control of any government, and they failed to consider its unattainability. Decisions and communication were hopelessly bogged down, until they had to be made by Maude and the other representatives without the group's full understanding simply because full understanding could not be achieved. Something of the nature of their own governmental processes was shown by the fact that none of the representatives was properly invested with power to negotiate for them. Possibly, aware of the difficulties in the way of reaching and abiding by such agreements, some Doukhobors saw an advantage in being represented by negotiators whose bargains could be repudiated.

Conflict and misunderstanding arising from this early confusion continue today. Yet they were at the outset surmounted to the extent that Doukhobor settlement as homesteaders took place on three blocks of land in Saskatchewan, then Northwest Territories. There, in accordance with their beliefs, they tried variations of communal life, some villages operating as separate co-operative units, and other groups of villages operating with a central administration. In sharp contrast, from the beginning an ever increasing number of farmers worked their land as individuals and set their sights at individual ownership, feeling there was no essential conflict between Doukhoborism and life in Canada.

In 1908 a pioneer group left to start the development of land they had purchased in British Columbia. Within the next five years they were followed by nearly six thousand others. Their reasons for the westward move were not entirely unlike those of some other pioneers; they wished to escape from what they felt to be the constraints of government and the corrupting influences of their Canadian neighbours. Purchasing the land in place of homesteading obviated the need to take an oath of allegiance. The move was precipitated by the stated intention of the Saskatchewan Government to open schools throughout the settlements.

The westward movement of Doukhobors continued through the twenties and thirties, its most recent push the foundation of the small colony at Hilliers on Vancouver Island. There was one major eastward flow to form a settlement in Alberta in 1924. The present urge for migration or relocation is in part similar to the restlessness of earlier decades which impelled the westward drives; some of the recent proposals for relocation are directed northward because a western frontier no longer exists.

In the Appendix to this chapter are historical outlines indicating the sequence of events in various aspects of Doukhobor life in Russia and Canada.

RECOGNITION OF THE GROUP

In Russia the Doukhobors had been known as a reformist peasant sect, challenging the organized church and its ritual, their essential conflict with the government arising over service in the army.

In Canada they were officially recognized for their pacifist beliefs by an Order in Council of 1898, which, with its subsequent revisions, grants exemption from military service to the migrants of 1899 and their descendants who have lived continuously in Canada. To claim this exemption, a Doukhobor obtains certification from one of the various organizations—the Union of Doukhobors of Canada, the Union of Spiritual Communities of Christ, the Named Doukhobors of Canada, the Society of Independent Doukhobors, or the Christian Community and Brotherhood of Reformed Doukhobors.

To their neighbours in British Columbia, to whom they usually refer as "English," they are most often known as "Douks," which is in ordinary speech distinguished from "Canadians."

In addition they are set off from their neighbours by real distinctions of religion, language, economy, food, dress, social life, recreation, and a number of intensely held beliefs. These points of distinctiveness and separateness in their culture have contributed to their conflict with governments and to the difficulties of adjustment to the life of their neighbours.

Their conflict with government has been so violent that it has led to a number of government-appointed studies and judicial inquiries. The first of those in British Columbia commenced a brief four years after their arrival in this Province, while the latest one, prior to the inception of the present study, concluded its work in 1948.

NUMBERS AND LOCALITIES

The total number of the survivors of the original migrants and of their descendants cannot be given with certainty, as an unknown number have left the communities and severed all ties. The guess of the research staff would give around twenty thousand, about half of whom live in British Columbia.

In this Province one estimate gives a Doukhobor population of 11,759. This figure results from detailed investigation, but is thought to be from ten to twenty per cent too high by other observers. The 1951 Census reports a total of 8,170 which is certainly more nearly correct. The main concentration is within the Kootenay and Grand Forks area, with the largest settlements, in descending order, around Grand Forks, Krestova, Slocan Valley, Glade, Ooteshenie, Pass Creek, Castlegar and Shoreacres. More detailed figures are given in the Appendix.

Today, these settlements can be called communities in the sense that people live in close propinquity, hold religious meetings, use a common language, enjoy some joint recreation and see one another in frequent face-to-face relationships. They retain next to nothing of their former arrangements for joint labour and direction of economic interests, except at Hilliers. A few large community houses remain, though even in them the arrangements for living, cooking and eating have long been carried out separately by the individual families; many of the community houses have been burned down, acts possibly motivated in part by the frustrations involved in undirected joint living.

9

MAJOR DIVISIONS OF DOUKHOBORS

Three divisions stand out as important in British Columbia; in addition to these there are national organizations with their present centre of operations in Saskatchewan. The pattern is complicated by changes which are currently taking place in the existing groups.

The Union of Spiritual Communities of Christ, 3,563 in number in 1941, came into being as the successor to the Christian Community of Universal Brotherhood Limited, which was formed before arrival in Canada and incorporated in 1917. Its secretary is John J. Verigin. Local operations are conducted by a trustee in each village and seven districts elect an executive committee. It issues a weekly publication, *Iskra* (The Spark). Ten schools are conducted in the Russian language for the purpose of teaching religion and literacy in that language to pupils of Provincial schools and to some adults, and the organization also undertakes a Youth Movement for those between sixteen and forty. In spite of the name of the organization and the nature of its predecessor, the members of the USCC are independent wage earners and proprietors, the majority of them still residing on the former community lands and paying rent to the Land Settlement Board.

A Society of Independents, with P. P. Abrossimoff as chairman, has existed for about ten years, co-operating closely with the USCC on issues of military exemption. There is some divergence of attitude on the value of community life, which the USCC has not officially or generally disavowed, and on the belief in a divinely inspired leadership.

The main bodies of the third sect, the Sons of Freedom, live at Krestova, Gilpin, Slocan, Glade and Thrums. As individuals, in unascertainable numbers, they live in most of the villages. Their total numbers are estimated at from two to three thousand. There is no hard and fast dividing line of belief or of behaviour between them and the others, and even membership and support are drifting categories. Yet they show in general the most intense reaction to the processes of adjustment to Canadian life, which operate on them as on the others, and the firmest belief in the necessary conflict between good and government.

Many of them have now accepted as leader a newcomer, S. Sorokin, a recent immigrant who has lived in Uruguay for the past two years, purportedly looking for land. They have formed, under Sorokin's direction, a new group, the Christian Community and Brotherhood of Reformed Doukhobors, which is confined to his followers. No new term for the remaining Sons of Freedom has yet arisen.

A small group at Hilliers were until recently living a full community life, largely on the economic basis of old age pensions and children's allowances. They have now scattered as individuals among the other communities, after stating their adherence to the CCBRD mentioned above.

DEGREES AND DIRECTIONS OF DOUKHOBOR CHANGE

The recurring difficulties experienced by agencies of government tend to obscure the fact that the Doukhobors have rapidly adopted and adjusted to Canadian ways. Economic independence, new occupations, dual language, increased literacy, heightened standard and altered manner of living, are all indices of the amount of acculturation which has occurred in Canada. Indeed, the rapidity of this change, and the social and psychological disturbance it inevitably brings, has been a main cause of the reaction of the Sons of Freedom, whose most intense effort is directed toward opposing it.

None of the Doukhobors in Canada now live in a self-sustaining co-operating community. Every individual either works at an outside job, farms or conducts his profession or business as an individual, or is dependent on the earnings of those who do and on government welfare aid. Yet there is a continuing interest in the community idea. Some former community members still believe that joint ownership and communal life are morally preferable. Most Sons of Freedom wish to rebuild a community with all its meaning of religious direction and complete economic sharing, in spite of the fact that they are the group least capable of carrying out such a project.

The great majority of Doukhobors can speak English, nearly all can speak Russian, and most people under 50 years of age are now bilingual. Only in some isolated Sons of Freedom communities are children found who cannot speak English. Elsewhere the lack of English is confined to the older people, though some of the younger women, who meet the outside world less than do the men, use it but little.

It is much the same with literacy, which is generally desired by the Doukhobors, though Sons of Freedom statements often inveigh against it. Even most of the Sons of Freedom express a desire for literacy, at least in Russian, though in Krestova their school in this language teaches only hymns and catechism because of the opposition of the extremists. Increasingly, however, the comics and pulp fiction are exerting their attractions; they and the movies are an irresistible force operating on the young.

The levels of living have risen fairly steadily for most Doukhobors since 1940. This is more true in Saskatchewan and Alberta, where wheat farmers, proprietors, wage earners and professional men have gained from the general rise. In British Columbia there is a much larger depressed group, and also wider variation, and the discontent even of those who disavow any desire for material progress seems re-

11

lated to this. Few are really well-to-do. Perhaps a quarter of the Independents and a smaller proportion of the USCC members maintain the average standards of non-Doukhobors around them. The majority are semi-skilled or unskilled wage earners, who until recently were insecure and enjoyed less than average income. New automobiles are impressive to the casual observer at any Doukhobor meeting, but the proportionate registration is below the average of the districts where they live.

OCCUPATIONS

The occupational picture shows a nearly universal change in patterns of livelihood.

There is a handful of professional men of Doukhobor background, and some merchants and contractors, proprietors and sawmill operators. The numbers in these categories, even allowing for those who have moved away from the locality and have given up their identification with the group, are much smaller than in Saskatchewan.

Others work in several categories of skilled and unskilled labour, crowding into two or three occupations, which makes for economic insecurity and minimizes contact with non-Doukhobors. There are few full-time farmers, though many get some subsistence from their fields and gardens. The former community lands have deteriorated, the orchards are diseased and crowded, the irrigation systems have broken down. The gardens, hayfields and the few head of stock are now used merely to supplement wages and other outside earnings.

There was until recently a general lack of participation in union organizations, with some indication of exclusion from some of those and other business and professional groupings.

The data on employment and skills have a pointed relevance for the relocation desired by, and for, some of the Sons of Freedom. At the first meeting with public representatives, government officials and other members of the Consultative Committee, where relocation was brought up as their desire, Sons of Freedom representatives insisted that they were all farmers, a claim inspired largely by the mystic virtue which they attribute to the simple life. The fact that they all now earn part of their livelihood in other ways demanded the search for a locality where such earning would continue to be possible.

LEVELS OF LIVING

The levels of comfort and the cost of the furnishings and equipment of the Doukhobor house are generally lower than those of other rural Canadians of the area, though the range is roughly the same.

It is difficult to arrive at an accurate statement of the levels of eating. There is a wide range. Many homes have well-balanced,

12

regular meals; in others the normally scanty and irregular meals provide a great contrast to the richness of the guest table. Perhaps this wide variation is usual and derives from the traditional background. It has been noted that in any case the nature of the vegetarian diet adopted by them enforces the average consumption of a very large quantity of starchy foods.

In the consumption of food as well as of other goods there is often a quite human contradiction between the Doukhobors' professed values of simplicity and poverty and what is in fact eaten and used. Violations of these beliefs are shown in the indulgence of children in candy, toys and finery, in the drinking of many of the men, in the scarcely hidden enjoyment of such luxury items as smart clothes and new cars. Although many Doukhobors recognize this contradiction between belief and action to be a usual and natural one, it does often leave a residue of guilt. It is, therefore, one of the targets and also a motivating force of the Sons of Freedom.

RECREATION, ARTS, NON-COMMERCIAL CRAFTS

Most of the recreations which might be enjoyed are frowned upon, hence few opportunities arise to take advantage of the release which could be afforded by games or the creativity of the arts.

Choral singing seems to be a notable exception. Important as is this avenue of expression, it is only available to the ordinary person at the weekly meetings. The singing of the stricter Sons of Freedom is confined to hymns and narratives of Doukhobor history. The others, with choirs in each district, have a lengthy repertoire of folk song in addition, which they sing with enjoyment of the humour and the dramatic qualities, at times enacting parts with vigour. Along with new hymns, new secular songs are still being composed; these are entirely in Russian, as are the older songs. Instruments as well as notation are scorned; in fact, they are definitely tinged with evil in the regard of the older and more puritanical.

There is little inventiveness and creativeness in women's needlework, nor is it very apparent in the crafts of the younger men's cabinet-making, the older men's carving. As a hobby, men in the penitentiary took up wood-carving, but the results were described as stereotyped, uninventive and limited.

Dancing is condemned because, as one of the Sons of Freedom leaders put it, people think of dancing as inevitably linked to Salome and the fate of John the Baptist. This leader told them, however, that they would be less likely to lose their heads if they did dance now and then. There is no folk dancing and ballroom dancing is regarded as immoral and as linked with drinking; yet the young men in particular throng the public dance halls near the communities.

13

Organized competitive games suffer a lesser condemnation. Held in poor regard by some of the older and the more puritanical, they are played by the younger. The extent to which the desire for games should be recognized and how to allow for it is a delicate point of some importance for the Youth Movement to decide.

RELATIONS WITH OTHER CANADIANS

Actual contacts with other Canadians result in a great variety of relationships, differing in number, intensity and meaning. Yet both sides tend to be prejudiced, classifying the relationships in simple and sweeping terms rather than regarding them as differing individually. If individuals do not fit into the group judgment, they are regarded as exceptions, and the judgment stands unchallenged.

In this manner non-Doukhobors regard the Doukhobors as immoral, clannish, unreliable, hypocritical and antagonistic. These are quite usual judgments which any group is likely to make of the stranger; here they are intensified by the real fear which non-Doukhobors of the area may have. Fortified by these sentiments, they accord the Doukhobors a less than even break, in courtesy and in business. Newspaper reporting and other formal treatment of the situation act to support these opinions.

In their turn most Doukhobors regard the non-Doukhobors as immoral, self-indulgent, addled by learning, fuddled by high living, headed individually and collectively down the path to war, and clannish—that is, unfair to Doukhobors. The judgments are intensified by the combined values of communal life and puritanism.

Partly because of their minority position, but even more because of their lesser ability to be assertive, most Doukhobors give less open expression to their opinions than do non-Doukhobors. The usual demeanour of meeting is one of passivity, even smiling politeness. Comparatively few, as individuals, are able to show their disapproval and hostility, whereas nearly every Doukhobor has experienced the name-calling of the street-corner gang. The boldness of the Sons of Freedom therefore wins some admiration from otherwise unsympathetic Doukhobors who have always suffered in silence.

On the one hand, these attitudes of prejudice and rejection have contributed to the frustrations of those Doukhobors who have tendencies to move toward Canadianization, and who have in some numbers been thrown back to become the most aggressive members of the Sons of Freedom; the attitudes serve as justification for the general demand for unequal treatment of the Doukhobors before the law. On the other hand, they are used by the Doukhobors to illustrate their belief that government is essentially evil, and, for the Sons of Freedom, that the Governments of Canada and British Columbia

14

are the most evil of all. Because the women have fewer outside contacts than do the men, they get to know fewer non-Doukhobors as individuals and are less able to soften their judgments by their knowledge of the individual exceptions. For these and other reasons as well, it is usual to find the women more assertive and aggressive, more hostile to other Canadians and condemnatory in their judgments, and more stubbornly conservative in their opposition to the changes which nevertheless continue to affect their lives.

Contacts with non-Doukhobors are too frequent and necessary for any Doukhobor to be able to escape them. He meets the outsider as customer, wage-earner, patient and client, pupil, contributor of taxes and payer of licence fees, as recipient of welfare, and when he incurs police, judicial or penal action. He is subjected to pressures and demands for some change in his ways in every formal and informal contact.

In addition, there are a large number of passer-by contacts, many of which exacerbate relations. All non-Doukhobors in the area have witnessed Sons of Freedom protest gatherings, perhaps nude marching or burning. The large numbers of Doukhobors in a small town on Saturday night, congregating on the sidewalk and talking in Russian, give rise to some feeling that the town has been taken over by them.

There are comparatively few inter-group friendships which become more than superficial pleasant acquaintanceships. Moreover, as mentioned earlier, there have been few instances of joint participation in fraternal, union, business or religious organizations. Schools, in places where they are attended jointly, make for generally good relationships among the children and in the lower grades seem to show friendship based on individual qualities, and an absence of group prejudice. It has been reported, however, that in the higher grades there is an increase of prejudice and an approach to something like the adult judgments.

In Saskatchewan more intermingling in schools has occurred, with friendships more commonly being formed on an individual basis and continuing afterwards. It has been stated that the better acceptance of schooling in that Province has resulted from the longer experience of its Government in dealing with minorities and its more patient and conciliatory policy. It must also be kept in mind, however, that the individuals who migrated to British Columbia were those who decided against the inducement and pressures of Canadian life.

CONFLICTS WITH LAW AND GOVERNMENT

Religious and ethnic minorities live in Canada without persecution or, with the general exception of the Indians, special position before

15

the law. There are few parallels to the discriminatory legislation and the constant clamour and conflict of Doukhobor-Government relations. Beyond the discovery and reporting of fact, this study aims to explore the ways in which this minority can be given freedom to develop its own culture without harming neighbours or nation.

Most of the formal relationships of the Doukhobors with the Governments of Canada and British Columbia have been accompanied by conflict: over land and its laws of registration and ownership; over citizenship and its privileges and obligations; over education and the receipt of other forms of welfare; and over taxation. The conflicts have led to refusal, avoidance, illegal protest and violence. Gradually, the Sons of Freedom protests have gained the additional aim of wanting to provoke the Canadian Government into taking deportation proceedings, ignoring the fact that the consent of two nations is required for a deportation.

As interpreted by some Doukhobors, the pattern of protest in Russia and in Canada has been threefold, first directed against an organized church, next against war, while the last and present stage is still unclear in its purpose. Statements made at the time of recent protests have given their motivation somewhat differently, however, as being against land ownership, education, war, imprisonment of protesters and so on. The psychological backgrounds of protest, as well as its relation to religion, social organization and leadership, are presented in following chapters, and show greater complexity than is presented here.

To these refusals, conflicts and protests the governments have responded in varying fashion. There have been attempts to understand the Doukhobors; attempts to meet their wishes; unreasonable faith and at times disillusioned distrust; discriminatory legislation, with harsh and uncalculated action; forgiving mildness; and attempts to enlist the aid of commissions and extra-governmental bodies in the solution of the problems. The very considerable governmental forbearance and benevolence has often been spoiled by inconsistency, ignorance and mis-direction.

Arson, dynamiting and nudity are the actions which draw most violently the attention of other Canadians and the Governments. However, the most frequent violations of the law are associated with registration, schools, taxation and similar matters, and the clashes which have had most influence on Doukhobor life have been over land and the regulations relating to ownership.

In British Columbia since 1924 over 400 instances of arson or dynamiting have occurred, the majority, though not all, involving Doukhobor property only. In some measure the disastrous decline and bankruptcy of the Christian Community of Universal Brotherhood were due to the actual losses and especially the discouragement resulting from these fires, which in lessened number continue today. The obvious violence and hostility of arson, in contradiction to Sons of Freedom claims that it is a pacifist protest, are emphasized by its increased occurrence during periods of economic insecurity for the Doukhobor wage earner and by its link with the frustrations inherent in the way the CCUB operated. One of the recent resurgences of dynamiting and arson has been directed against the railroads in the area.

Nudity is a more passive protest, though also an amply hostile one. Again the motivation is complex. Its suggestions of holy simplicity appeal to many who are otherwise made anxious by its use. It still occurs at many meetings attended by non-Doukhobors, and at present it is aimed most of all at them, and is employed by a dwindling minority consisting of older women and a few of the older men. Like arson, it remains a potential weapon in the Sons of Freedom arsenal, and could revive to have greater significance yet.

Weighty problems lie in the fields of welfare, education, taxation, registration. To a certain extent tolerance, ingenuity and an alteration of programmes, as outlined later, should make these governmental functions more acceptable to the Sons of Freedom. Most of the Doukhobors already accept the welfare and educational programmes of the Provincial Government, along with the implication that registration is needed for their proper administration and that taxation is needed to support the burden. Yet it is apparent that the worst threat to the extreme conservatives among the Sons of Freedom is that very acceptance, and their hostile reaction must be anticipated in the degree to which the others accept the proffered compromises. Consequently, plans for the general improvement of relations must also envisage some constraint of the most intransigent opponents of improved relations.

LAND: OCCUPATION, TENURE AND USE

The great bulk of the lands now occupied by the Doukhobors in British Columbia, some twenty thousand acres in all, was purchased by the Christian Community of Universal Brotherhood, and lost to that organization by mortgage foreclosure in 1938. To prevent wholesale eviction, the Provincial Government took over the land, paid that portion of the indebtedness which attached to the land, and since then has endeavoured to collect rent for occupation and use. It is clear that the major intention of the Government was to assume the role of trustee, though it is also clear from the present nearly complete deterioration of the buildings and irrigation systems and orchards, and the minimal use made of the land today, that the move had a very limited success. In Doukhobor eyes, however, the Gov-

17

ernment emerges as pure villain; the facts of dispossession and ruin are interpreted as seizure by the Government and as the granting of official aid to the mortgage companies, the receiver and other dimly glimpsed agents. The facts that assets which originally cost three or more million dollars were sold by the receivers for less than a million, to meet a debt of half a million, and that the costs of foreclosure and realization have left a balance of only about $140,000, are not interpreted as being part of the wasteful tragedy of the depression so much as a product of the malevolence of government and the financial world. Moreover, the usual beliefs hold no place for the findings of mismanagement by the CCUB and for the many other internal factors which led to bankruptcy.

Many of the past members of the Christian Community of Universal Brotherhood, most of them now members of the Union of Spiritual Communities of Christ, live on the lands formerly owned by the Community. In these lands the Government of the Province has an interest because of the money paid to the mortgagees and the costs it has incurred, and the members of the CCUB hold an equity of redemption in them. Any settlement involves establishing the amounts of these claims, and making recommendations for the disposal of the lands. Because of the magnitude this issue has assumed in the Doukhobor viewpoint, the recommendations to be presented below advise reckoning the equity of every individual in the lands, and making them available for purchase or rent in proportionate amount.

This procedure is suggested although little farming is now carried on. A few of the former CCUB communities continue to operate in the sense that there is a periodic reallotment of land occasioned by migration or changes in size of family, but the plots from which hay is cut or which are put into garden are worked individually. The present obvious dilapidation of the properties which formerly impressed so many observers is perhaps not such a complete change from past perfection to present decay as it might seem; the close study made by Trevor twenty years ago concluded that the farms and orchards were operated quite inefficiently at that time. At present, however, even the appearance of productivity and efficiency is gone.

It is felt, therefore, that the outcome will not be the establishment of a much larger number of farmers. Farming will continue to be a part-time occupation for many, and it is likely that a number will take advantage of present higher prices of land and sell. Some may wish to pool their holdings, in spite of past experience, and venture once again to live in a co-operative community.

In general, the Sons of Freedom cultivate and occupy less land than do the others, continuing a situation of inequality which made its appearance soon after arrival in Canada. Many of them are virtually landless, some of those in Krestova, for example, lacking enough adequately watered land even for a home garden.

Part of the philosophy of resettlement stated here aims at the provision of land which will allow farming, at least as a small-scale and part-time occupation. Enough Sons of Freedom insist on the wickedness of private ownership to make it necessary to allow co-operative holding in any scheme of relocation, even though they probably cannot successfully continue a co-operative enterprise.

SCHOOLING

The attempts of the Provincial Government to operate schools for the children of the Doukhobors in British Columbia have been marked by a long record of opposition and conflict, with, however, steadily increasing compliance, during the past decade, among the Union of Spiritual Communities of Christ and the Independents. The conflict has seen the burning of schools, the intimidation of teachers, and the retreat of Sons of Freedom to places of isolation like Krestova, where it is felt that the educational arm of the Government will not reach. In an attempt to ensure the attendance of children, the Government has enacted special legislation, and as a measure of protection has supplied some schools with armed guards.

The results of schooling under these circumstances have not been impressive. A majority of the young men and women have hardly gone beyond bare literacy in English. Few in the past have attended high school, though it is now becoming usual for Doukhobor children to continue to that level along with their fellow pupils. Fewer yet have gained any job-qualifying attainment from school. A handful have proceeded to university.

The opposition to schooling is composed in part of objections to education in any form, and in part of objections to the Canadianizing influence of public schools. The major grounds of conflict are presented in more detail in later chapters, particularly in Chapter IV.

In reality, the problem with the USCC and Independent families resolves itself into meeting whatever is valid in their objections to schooling and paying attention to their pacifist beliefs. All of their children now attend, and the great majority merely want the schools to be the best possible, having in mind much the same standards as are held by other parents in the Province.

With the Sons of Freedom, the problem varies according to the intensity of their adherence to Sons of Freedom values. With the extreme fringe no compromise agreement can be reached at present. Schooling will meet with opposition from them to the extent that it is effective in doing anything at all beyond teaching the Doukhobor catechism and psalms. With most of them, however, it is likely that

19

manual and technical training will be welcome. Acceptable programmes will have to take much of their content from these areas, using visual aid, practical demonstration and participation as much as possible so as to avoid the appearance of the formal class instruction and book knowledge which they fear. Work camps, adapted from the types developed by the Quakers in Mexico and elsewhere, might supplement any other programmes.

None of the major Doukhobor groups is today tightly organized, closely directed, and fully represented by its leadership. Growing economic individualism has accompanied a breakdown or loosening of the other bonds which held the communities together.

One overall organization, the Union of Doukhobors in Canada, now has its headquarters and main concentration in Saskatchewan. Essentially it is a very loose society of Doukhobors with the purpose of looking after some common interests such as the protection of their pacifist status. Its affiliations with most of the British Columbia groups and individuals are not close, and it excludes the Sons of Freedom.

The Society of Independent Doukhobors expresses the uncertain and variable status of many of these individuals in this Province. It has been in existence about ten years and is indefinite about its aims. Once it held separate religious meetings, but the house in which they took place was burned down, and members now attend the religious meetings of the Union of Spiritual Communities of Christ. The only dependable difference between the members of these two groups is that the Independents now own their own land instead of renting it from the Land Settlement Board as do most of the USCC members. The chairman of the Independents commented that the Independents in British Columbia differ from those in Saskatchewan, where they tend to be so independent and so removed from the group that they do not even want to affiliate with a Society of Independents.

It should not be forgotten that the characteristics of individuals in the various groups cover a wide range, and only by treating the facts very freely can a statement be made of "average" belief or behaviour. For fuller understanding it is important to note many sub-types within the groups. Within the Doukhobors classed as Independents, for example, there appear to be three main subdivisions: a number of people who are veering away from all Doukhobor ties; those who are extremely ambivalent to acculturation, antagonistic to both the Society of Independents and the Union of Spiritual Communities of Christ, and the actual members of the Society of Independents, rather few in number.

The local organizations of the Union of Spiritual Communities of

20

Christ ("Orthodox") are hardly operative in any formal sense. They consist of the remnants of the Hundreds, the communities of the now inoperative Christian Community of Universal Brotherhood. A trustee in each village is given the duty of looking after community property, and seven districts elect an executive committee. In actual operations, an informal gathering of adults decides what to do.

The greatest single influence exerted on this group comes from its secretary, J. J. Verigin, who has specific duties of secular management. Because of his descent and name and the generally hereditary principle of the past theocratic leadership, he is granted a considerable degree of religious leadership, but his position is less certain because of the possible existence of his uncle in Russia, a personage whose role is already deeply embedded in mythology and revelation although he has been lost from sight for many years. On this account, and also because general trends are now weighing against hereditary religious leadership, there is some doubt and dissension, and considerable cloudiness regarding the present meaning of leadership and the rightful incumbent. There is, however, universal support of Mr. Verigin among members of the USCC for his able dealing with the non-Doukhobors.

The Sons of Freedom, separated from the others more by the others' choice, have until recently laid claim to the name Spiritual Community of Christ, incensing the members of the USCC, the Union of Spiritual Communities of Christ. The new name for part of the Sons of Freedom group, the Christian Community and Brotherhood of Reformed Doukhobors, reaches into the attic of Doukhobor organizations and pulls out key words from various past groupings.

Just as the Independents covered too wide a range of belief and characteristics to pass over without comment, so the adherents to the Sons of Freedom include people who are attracted for a variety of reasons. A central core of Sons of Freedom clings to traditional Doukhobor beliefs and desperately strives for consistency in them and resistance to external change. Around these are a number who show greater readiness for compromise, and some who would give up their resistance if it became more uncomfortable. Many other Doukhobors who have recently flocked around the Sons of Freedom do so because their more frequent meetings provide the "ceremonial feeling" noted by Miss Lewis; and they would be likely to return to the Union of Spiritual Communities of Christ if it had a religious revival.

In general the Sons of Freedom express most intensely the belief that guidance comes to the individual Doukhobor from within, and accordingly they have had no formal organization until recently. In apparent contradiction to this condition of political vacuum, however, they have been vulnerable to control and extortion by any individual manipulating the symbols of their belief. One partly successful at-

21

tempt at gaining leadership was made by a man who posed as the representative of the missing Verigin from Russia, and extorted money and terrorized families with the aid of a small gang of hooded followers from the Sons of Freedom. Other manipulations, less clearly directed, have inspired some of the protest actions of the Sons of Freedom. While no one assumes responsibility, and no one achieves recognition as a leader, it is still open to every individual who can write or talk to present the cues which can lead to such action.

The open acceptance of Sorokin by the Sons of Freedom even though he was not a Doukhobor, marked a change, as did the formation of an executive committee. Should this committee grow into a democratically responsible and capable executive, which is yet not at all certain, it could form a foundation for the successful rehabilitation of this group.

II
BACKGROUNDS OF THE PROBLEMS AND RECOMMENDATIONS
Harry B. Hawthorn

THERE IS A clear continuity in Doukhobor belief going back to the seventeenth or eighteenth century in Russia, where it emerged from peasant attitudes towards authority, ritual and communal life. In similar fashion, the high value now placed on communal life by the Sons of Freedom in particular has its ultimate roots in the village life of the peasant before, during and after serfdom, with the intimate direction of work, family life, property, religion, and recreation by the *mir* or village group. At that time, communal life was merely the traditional way; it is only in recent decades that it has been elevated to the status of a holy aim.

Around the time of their origin, the Doukhobors were far from being unique. Dissension and schism were made possible by the partial independence of the village in rural Russia, and by intertwined illiteracy and self-reliance in philosophy and religion. Here, in their history as many Doukhobors see it, there appears a continuity which is in large part fictional. The Sons of Freedom see their opposition to authority as identical with that of the peasant against the despot of his time; they view the dream of a revived communal life as a bulwark against all threats, and see the Canadian Government as operating like the czars, hand in hand with corrupt officials and clergy. Most clearly they see their partial illiteracy and isolation as a protection against these threats.

The strength of the village society, self-reliance in religious matters, and opposition to authority led to the formation of many peasant reformist sects, the Doukhobors becoming noteworthy because of the effective simplicity of their religious and philosophical system, and because of the steadfastness with which they stood by it. Their own conflict with the Russian Orthodox Church becomes nearly lost to view in the many conflicts of the sort from the seventeenth century on, and the relative ineffectiveness of that body in impressing its doctrine on the large number and variety of dissenters in spite of persecution, which at times was harshly oppressive. The conflict with government came into greater prominence through the Doukhobor denial of the right of government to rule. Governments naturally objected to this doctrine and took repressive measures in reprisal, measures which still live in Doukhobor oral history, hymn and thought. Imprisonment, flogging, death, exile and military service were used as punishments for failure to recant. The last measure furnished an ineffective addition to the armed forces of the nation, as the Doukhobor soldier is said to have thrown down his arms at the last moment, before going into action, and to have persuaded others to adopt his refusal to kill.

This is a thumb-nail sketch of the background of exile. Doukhobor colonies were dispersed to various parts of Russia, from the Ukraine to settlements near the Sea of Azof, from there to Transcaucasia. In dispersion, they continued to offend in the old ways and developed new ones. The Russian Government complied with their emigration request at the end of the nineteenth century.

In exile, under real and imagined threats to existence, life was organized in various closely knit units, to which the individual was tied with bonds of belief and custom. Almost as firmly as before, these beliefs and customs reflected their suspicion of the outer world. Yet that the bonds were not permanent nor the life in the communities completely satisfactory has been demonstrated in startling fashion by continued schisms and defections.

Within the Doukhobor community seventy years ago the individual found his friends, his work and subsistence, his family life, the answers to all questions of justice, meaning and value, and direction for even the details of his existence. Hostility against outsiders had been acquired, though the ability to be assertive in dealings with them had been checked; the community gave protection in the ensuing condition of helplessness. It further made up for these inadequacies and for difficulties in its internal operations by endowing its members with a strong belief in moral superiority. Illiteracy also safeguarded against change, as did the development of a protective shell of evasion in dealing with the queries and conversation of non-Doukhobors. The development of sectarian education divided members and outsiders. In addition, in this earlier period when the *mir* supplied all needs, there was no satisfactory life for an individual leaving the sect, no role or occupation, no niche for a displaced individual.

Yet the historical fact is that the communities have disintegrated. In Russia they split several times on issues of principle as well as on disputes over leadership. In Canada they have dwindled by the defection of individuals until no communities in the former sense remain. Among the causes of this disintegration are the inducements offered by life in Canada. Added to these are the pressures of arbitrary personal leadership, of social suffocation by neighbours who feel called on to pry and control as well as aid—pressures tolerated when the alternative is fearful but unbearable when there is no threat from the outside. The inducements to leave community life include the picture of relative economic independence, life under generally impartial and temperate law, the greater comforts and more varied achievements that could be aspired to, the wide range of recreations, the choice of occupations, plus the possibility of maintaining most Doukhobor beliefs. It is small wonder that the extreme die-hards of the Sons of Freedom paint this as a blacker threat than any of the past. The effectiveness of such inducements was shown in the first years in Canada, with the splitting-off of independents, and is now shown in the fact that of all the Doukhobors in Canada only some two or three thousand are insistent on a return to a communal life, which none are actually living. It was also shown through the years in the formation of the many new groupings, The Christian Community of Universal Brotherhood, the Named Doukhobors, the Society of Independent Doukhobors, the Union of Spiritual Communities of Christ, the Sons of Freedom, the Union of Doukhobors of Canada, and now the Christian Community and Brotherhood of Reformed Doukhobors, groups which retain in common only the essential points of principle related to pacifism, a few attitudes to be specified later and some problems in relation to their neighbours.

Even were there adequate moral basis for attempting to enforce a general change of the Doukhobors, change in particular of the Sons of Freedom further toward economic individualism, this review should indicate its uselessness. From all practical considerations, the will of some of the Sons of Freedom to attempt to live in a community should be accepted by the Government, and they should be given what reasonable aid they would receive in rehabilitation as individuals in any case. It is perhaps necessary to add that on equally solid grounds the partial community life of other Doukhobors should also be accepted, even aided. This will involve some continuing separation from their neighbours, less in socio-economic terms than in religion and language. It it is compatible with the maintenance of peaceful relations with their neighbours, this partial community life should be allowed to continue as long as the Doukhobors maintain it. The amount of aid, if any, which should be given to it, perhaps in the form of assistance to the Russian language schools, is another matter. Financial support of these is not sought by the Doukhobors, nor is it the policy of the Provincial Government to aid such schools. To the extent that private individuals and organizations are invited to help these schools, however, it is important that such aid should not be disguised pressure to accept citizenship. No school or other group should push for an assimilation policy framed in those terms, acceptable to immigrants of other backgrounds; such pressures will inevitably engender future Sons of Freedom. Past experience in this situation and in many parallel ones in and out of Canada indicates that effective policy towards realizing an increased Doukhobor contribution to Canada will be in the nature of steps lessening prejudice, increasing opportunity, and perhaps discovering elements of Doukhobor thought and life which will contribute to the richness of Canadian culture.

A further argument for accepting the wish of the Sons of Freedom to achieve stronger community integration lies in the promise it holds of peace with their neighbours. The record does show that, however stressful and changeable, community life has been peaceful as far as relations with outsiders are concerned. Notwithstanding the general difference in temperament among the Sons of Freedom that writers of later chapters indicate, it is certain that community life for them could induce greater peace with their neighbours than has their semi-independent life of the past twenty-five years. Their lawlessness from the first has been associated wth their being outcasts from the communities. Moreover, the use of force against the idea of community life, or the denial of reasonable aid to it, will not make them into good Canadians but will augment their fear and hostility. The choice for a good number of them is whether they will try community life outside jail or inside.

There are a number of conditions which must be made more detailed if relocation, one of a number of possible rehabilitative measures, develops. There will be a need to safeguard the individual's freedom to leave the community if he makes his decision to live as an independent outside it. There will also be a need to safeguard some essentials of individual liberty within the Sons of Freedom communities, and to ensure their self-protection against the racketeering, extortion and hoodlumism to which they have been subject from a few of their own members. While denying the necessity of a clearly structured society, the Sons of Freedom nevertheless feel as sharply as others—perhaps more sharply—the frustration of arbitrary or uncertain community government.

A suggestion has been offered that the Sons of Freedom be scattered across Canada as individuals or single families. It does not need to be stressed that this is impractical as a compulsory measure, lacking present legal basis, expensive, provocative and impossible of maintenance. Yet it does raise the question concerning the treatment of a residue of the Sons of Freedom who might continue their hostile acts against their neighbours—a residue for whose treatment Professor Dixon later outlines a policy.

DEVELOPMENT OF RELIGIOUS AND POLITICAL VALUES

The search for an understanding of Doukhobor action leads to an examination of the beliefs which underlie it. These show differing characteristics of persistence, adaptability and intensity, and in a general way may be ranked in the degree to which they have been amenable to change or compromise. Of course these beliefs do not operate alone in guiding action or in giving rise to it. There are many other guides and motivations, some of them hidden and others more obvious. Those which could be perceived by the research team are set out in later chapters, in the analysis of characters given by Dr. Shulman, of family life by Miss Lewis, and of economic behaviour by Dr. Jamieson.

The belief in individual guidance by divine revelation, and the belief that external authority lacks the necessary religious sanction or wisdom to direct anyone's life, seem to have been the first to arise. Today these remain within the central core of beliefs, the ones which are most resistant to change, which are most widely held and carry out a fundamental role in sanctioning action. Also within this central core are some which appeared later in the development of Doukhobor philosophy: the attitude toward war and killing, attitudes revolving around dependence on the group as a source of strength and a centre of action, and hostility to competition and the use of physical force.

Some of these beliefs have correlates, which are almost equally important. The rejection of the out-group, the non-Doukhobors, is linked to the dependence placed by the Doukhobor on his community. The rejection of ritual, of the written word and the sacraments, follows the denial of the authority of an organized church. The contradiction between rejecting human authority on the one hand and dependency and need of authority on the other has been partially resolved by crediting Doukhobor leadership with an extra endowment of the divine inspiration which is each man's possession.

These are the beliefs which seem least amenable to alteration or compromise. They have been embedded in tradition, are learned in childhood from endless repetition and illustration and are linked with action in every group enterprise.

Related to this core of beliefs are many which seem to be more peripheral. They have arisen as responses to specific situations; repetition of the situation has given them some persistence, but they do not possess the lasting qualities of the above. Of this sort are the beliefs related to protests, demonstrations, arson. These are maintained by the fear and frustration present in Doukhobor lives and would lose their main reason for existence if the emotional states could be altered. In like manner, the paranoid quality of Doukhobor attitudes toward outsiders could not be maintained indefinitely if it were given little to feed on. A decade of official policy and action which avoided giving cause for suspicion and fear and which consistently showed goodwill would work wonders.

Other beliefs of a peripheral and relatively changeable nature are those which centre around self-enhancement through education, development of the arts, acquisition of individual forms of self-expression. These appear to Doukhobors as leading to competitiveness and self-assertiveness, in contrast to which self-denial is sought. In like manner, those concerning schools, statistics and registration are extensions of some of the more central ones. Together with beliefs concerning communal property, puritanism, celibacy, sexual freedom, poverty, return to a Garden of Eden existence, vegetarianism, refusal to exploit animals, prohibition of intoxicating liquors and tobacco, they have at one time or another been followed or advocated by part of the group.

In spite of its disjointed appearance when presented in this fashion, there is a very great degree of consistency within this system of belief. It does possess contradictions, but these are few and minor compared to the contradictions which obtain within the framework of beliefs in most human societies. Indeed its very consistency and logicality constitute much of the basis for conflict between the Doukhobors and the society which is their host. To be effectively linked to action and reality, beliefs must be adaptable to a greater degree than holds within the Doukhobor system. The process of adjustment almost always involves inconsistency, which most people and systems accept without being aware of contradiction. When the constant scrutiny of their own belief by the Doukhobors reveals contradictions, being unable to admit change or accept some inconsistency on a commonsense basis, they engage instead in frantic attempts to hold back the tide. The difference between the various Doukhobor sects lies to a large extent in this. The devouter ones among the Sons of Freedom grow anxious at any perceived contradiction in their beliefs and lead the movement of opposition to the change which they hold to have caused it.

Historically, the growth of the Doukhobor system of belief commenced with the anti-authoritarianism of the peasant, opposed to direction by officials of church and state, and assuming the common divinity of man and direction by the Christ within. The rejection of the ritual of the church and of literacy and the written word, the opposition to war and force, the separation of the sect from others were protective devices whereby the fundamental beliefs were safeguarded. Then in their turn the peripheral beliefs developed, as groups and individuals pondered over their life and religion and strove for consistency and progress.

There seems to be a loose correlation between the length of time Doukhobor beliefs have existed and the depth to which they are held today. The beliefs and attitudes of one of the reformist sects of the seventeenth century, preceding and perhaps influencing the emergence of the Doukhobors, included anti-authoritarianism, puritanism,

28

a desire for ritual freedom and aims for the reorganization of family life. Doukhobor belief itself was not recorded in detail until 1832 and then mainly in terms of the core of religion and opposition to government. Because of the techniques of evasion which were necessary for survival and already developed at that time, it is likely that other values relating to other parts of the culture were also elaborated but not revealed to outsiders. It was not until the time of the contributions made by Tolstoy, Tchertkoff, Bodiansky, and others that some of these came to light. From the time of migration to Canada, there sprang the full growth of the ideas of natural goodness and simplicity, of detailed opposition to the requirements of government departments, and rejection of material advance and science.

Tolstoy would have been more than human had he not tried to influence these protagonists of ideas something like his own. The close and able observer Maude wrote that similar personal reasons motivated Bodiansky to crystallize their ideas on the iniquity of private ownership of land. To the present day the Doukhobors have a fateful attraction for individuals with a social idea or a belief or a system to sell. To the extent that the proffered article seems to fit in the Doukhobor belief system, it is heeded, and may have effect.

The developments listed have been ones which tended to increase the distance between Doukhobor beliefs and those held by other Canadians. Yet not all the changes have been of this nature. Some have been adjustments toward increased compatibility. Even in Russia the Doukhobor culture was adaptive to outer circumstances, particularly in regard to the values belonging in the peripheral stratum. The most readily noticed changes occurred within the group of puritanical beliefs, which at various times relaxed to allow meat-eating, drinking and so on; and which now allow the great majority of Doukhobors in Canada to work for wages, be proprietors, save money, accumulate possessions, and partake of the ordinary amusements of the life around them.

More important from the point of view of peaceful adjustment to this country, however, are the widespread alterations of attitudes toward government. While most Doukhobors still follow the doctrine that they cannot vote and hence share responsibility for a government, yet they also show an increasing acceptance of the idea that a government is an organization made for and responsive to the general welfare. This change in belief underlies the willingness of the majority of Doukhobors to register, send children to school and pay taxes. The continuing divergence in outlook on this point between the Doukhobors of the Prairie Provinces and those of British Columbia is due to the sense of grievance felt by even the Independents in this Province over the land for which they feel they worked so long and concerning which they still distrust the intention of the Government.

This very adaptability of the majority has been one of the motivating forces in the rise of the Sons of Freedom. Their mission, they have felt, has been to recall the majority to the path of true doctrine. In human fashion, they have continued to overlook the fact that they themselves are not fully consistent, and have also changed; in so far as this is felt, the resulting guilt spurs on their missionary work. They clamour for government aid, as do others; they demand the aid of medical science; and those in prison for arson and related disturbances complained about the housing condition of their families, crowded into the remaining unburned dwellings. It is, of course, possible to call this hypocrisy, but it is more helpful when thinking of corrective measures to recognize its universality. Compromise and inconsistency have existed in Doukhobor life from the time it became history, when the anti-authoritarians submitted to a strict theocratic rule. These qualities will no doubt continue to exist, making for some future philosophic turmoil but giving the possibility of change even among the Sons of Freedom. The contradictions in belief should be allowed to continue and wear slowly against facts and against one another. Misapplied force and tenacious argument will not accomplish helpful changes; they will most certainly delay them.

In spite of the attempt made by many Sons of Freedom to fit the practice of nudity in with the striving for natural simplicity, and that or arson with the opposition to materialism and with the pacifism of the historical burning of the arms on St. Peter's Day, 1895, nudity and arson are motivated primarily by hostility, to the non-Doukhobors or to the other Doukhobors who have been the chief losers of property. A brief summary of a few of the conclusions later presented fully by Dr. Shulman is worth repeating when considering these practices and possible change, therapy or punishment. The hostility which underlies them can be lessened only by removing some of its causes and by refusing to step into the complementary role which the Sons of Freedom behaviour calls for. It can be given better avenues of expression, as the means of communication improve. The related feelings of helplessness and dependency and guilt can be mitigated, and the lives of the Sons of Freedom enriched in some ways so as to withdraw the support for such behaviour which comes from the poverty of expression, of creativity, and of other avenues of excitement.

Acting on the principle that the manner and the form of government administration be adapted to this design, the Consultative Committee during its three years of activity from 1950 to 1953 moved in this direction and assisted in lessening the illegal and destructive protest by aiding the processes of communication. Protests were directed through ordinary, effective, legally correct channels, and an endeavour was made to set out government requirements in a clarifying and non-threatening manner. The fact that the protests continue, or at times even seem to increase, that they are still often couched in the tangled and threatening forms the Sons of Freedom use, does not belie the improvement made in three years. This should not be allowed to obscure the likelihood, however, that a failure to make sufficient gains by these methods of predominantly legal protests will be followed by a reversion to the earlier forms of mass parades and arson.

Yet it is not to be expected that these moves of trying to give reasonable satisfaction to Doukhobor needs or of amending legislation, or any other moves, will entirely eliminate the protests. Their simplicity and effectiveness, as indicated in later chapters, are such that both arson and nudity will continue, though lessening in the degree that any programmes are successful. There will remain some incompatibility between Sons of Freedom values and those of other Canadians; harmony with the Government would suit neither some parts of Sons of Freedom belief nor the psychological needs of some individuals. There will be a continuing necessity, therefore, for the Government to restrain by non-provocative measures the more destructive protests.

OPERATION OF THE COMMUNITIES IN CANADA

Influenced both by the communal background of life for the Russian peasant with the *mir* organization, and by his Tolstoyan ideas which erected this once-customary state of affairs into a virtue, the exiled leader, Peter Vasilivich Verigin, advocated a communal basis for life in Canada. A complex variety of reasons led to early partial failure, and out of the resulting frustrations and differences the forerunners of the Sons of Freedom appeared, first in 1902. The allegations heard until recent years, that the Sons of Freedom have been used at times as a stalking-horse to distract the Government's attention, probably have a partial truth. The Sons of Freedom have obvious value as a threat, implying: That is what all Doukhobors will become if not treated right; and as an explanation, that these are the incredible difficulties with which the good Doukhobors have to contend. Moreover, in contrast with the extreme opposition of the Sons of Freedom to the law, the moderate opposition of the others might on many occasions have seemed reasonable or have escaped notice altogether. Yet this does not contradict the destructive influence of the Sons of Freedom on the communities themselves. From the beginning the integrity of the communities was threatened by the attacks of the Sons of Freedom within the ranks and by the strains produced by the success of the Independents; the new environment contributed to these threats by its hardships and the opportunities of individual

31

success. Already by 1900 Bonch-Bruevich stated that there were 2,000 people living on individual farms and 5,000 in communities, two-thirds of whom wanted to become individual farmers.

In Canada the social structure of the communities and the motivations of individuals proved unequal to the stress of continued sharing. This is in part explained by the absence of any external threats such as existed in Russia and which might have held them together. Suspicion, echoes of which can still be heard, was directed against those who were in a position to avoid a full contribution of work or earnings or to claim a greater reward. Men were sent to work outside the community, and were assessed dues amounting in the early years of stress to the full sum of their earnings. Later the difference between their earnings and those of men who worked within the community and received only a small net return for such labour gave rise to feelings of injustice, which have now risen again to trouble the settlement of the affairs of the bankrupt Christian Community of Universal Brotherhood.

This roughening of human relations in field, mill and orchard, and in business, was accompanied by dissension in the community houses, by bad neighbourly relations and by a large amount of gossip and backbiting. These tensions are observable today, probably heightened by the absence of effective leadership. As noted earlier, single families live under very unsatisfactory conditions in the few community houses which remain. Internal discord can be seen externally in the patchwork repair on the roofs of some of these houses; a new patch is sometimes put on by the occupant directly underneath it, to shelter only his rooms.

The basic personality type—those attributes of Doukhobor personality which arise from the general conditioning given by the culture and which are held by the majority—may be searched for explanations of this lack of ability to run community affairs. It is remarked in a later chapter that few can assert themselves to the point of grasping a complex social situation clearly enough to take appropriate action. The resultant helplessness and misunderstanding foster suspicion and hostility, two qualities which stand out in their community life. Among the Sons of Freedom, in place of rationally directed action there is a tendency to substitute a practice like nudity.

Yet these attributes, which in varying degrees are common human ones, find meaning only in a certain social setting; their full results are realized where the social setting fosters uncertainty and confusion. The internal government of the communities has had an insufficiently clear structure; it has lacked any clear specification of functions and responsibilities. In contrast, indeed, there has been a long-fostered denial that a governmental structure exists. Thus the autocratic leaders in Russia and in Canada denied their role at times of conflict with the outside world, and Hooper records that the children of the parents imprisoned on Piers Island, themselves in the Industrial School, maintained their own autocratic direction but never admitted to its existence. The denial and the dissembling were brought about in an earlier century by needs of survival, but the resulting inner uncertainty in the workings of the community organization, has produced confusion, hostility and suspicion.

Another troublesome legacy has been inherited, this time from the self-government of the *mir*: a pattern of self-government in which unanimous consent had to be sought and which in its ideal form could not countenance the suppression of a dissident minority. It is obvious that such a pattern would be fully operative only with the existence of a great degree of rationality and self-confidence and flexibility. Yet the task was made harder by the inheritance of still another tradition from the same organization, that no permanent laws exist, that conscience is the guide.

Such a structure was the one least likely to maintain integration in Doukhobor communities. Coupled with the specifically Doukhobor belief in the existence of divinity in each man and the power of individual revelation, it ensured that every man could be a one-man minority, potentially a hold-out minority on whom no effective control could be brought to bear. Moreover, each man had a strong antagonism to rank, authority, and direct orders and yet could not express that opposition openly. From all this, and from the mystical nature of Doukhobor political thought arises the incredible confusion in the interpretation of command and of other communication.

In the midst of the mystical thought surrounding government, special qualities of leadership and the means of conducting it did nevertheless develop a partial effectiveness. If commands were going to be interpreted by each man as his inner voice guided, a command could be successful if it employed the cues and symbols of his mainsprings of action. A career for a semanticist lies in perusing and interpreting the letters and other communications which have been taken as messages of command. The first reaction to the message from a leader had to be: What does it really mean? But the exegesis was carried out separately by every individual and every group, with no way of arriving at a consensus when the differing conclusions were reached.

Divine sanction was attributed to the most successful of the leaders in the belief that he possessed, usually by inheritance, a greater endowment of the Christ within, though the careful hiding from outsiders of the theocratic reality hindered it from its fullest operation within the community. Factors of striking personal endowment stand out in the accounts of the direction of community affairs by Peter Vasilivich Verigin and Peter Petrovich Verigin. Great dramatic ability, many-sided personalities, supported their positions; in addition, in the periods of inevitable breakdown of operations, they could and did use physical violence to get things going again.

With a recent past of this nature, what is the possibility of an internal democracy—in the sense of being able to find an adequate consensus of opinion and of enjoying freedom from arbitrary constraints—forming in a Sons of Freedom community? The changes in individuals may grow as they form a different view of power-relations, and see the possibility of mutual existence without exploitative dominance. But these changes can be realized only if the structure fosters them from the beginning. Not only will it be necessary to safeguard community members from hidden authoritarian control, which is a form of government to which they lean, but it will be necessary to see in a positive complementary way that they set up a fully representative system of internal government, with clear allotment of work and responsibility, and with rational and adequate social controls.

GOVERNMENT AND THE DOUKHOBORS

As stated earlier, the hand of the past lies heavily over the Governments of Canada and British Columbia in their relations with the Doukhobors in this Province.

Peasant hostility to government found expression in a doctrine denying the right of governments to exist. Their sole purpose, it was held, is to dominate for the purpose of exploitation, their sole basis of operation is brute force. The only authority recognized by the Doukhobor peasant in Russia stemmed from divine revelation within each man, the collective wisdom or revelation of the group of believers, or, occasionally, from an individual in their midst who had a greater share of divinity. Later elaborations equated the source of revelation with the "unspoiled impulses of natural man."

This doctrinal denial has been supplemented in early and recent times by an impressive battery of techniques for thwarting government. Relatively ineffective have been the outright refusals to render government its due; the resulting exile, imprisonment or comparable punishment also disrupted the operation of the community. More effective have been the techniques of peaceful non-cooperation and non-compliance, of concealing the community leadership, the operation of its treasury and other essentials, and of evading taxes by omission and excuse.

Some adjustment in the attitudes toward government has taken place by now, though there is still much ambivalence. Even the Sons of Freedom demand all sorts of welfare and governmental care while denying that government can serve any useful purpose and

34

refusing the registration that could enable welfare to be given equitably. (It might be pointed out that they avoid recognizing this contradiction by the claim that they have been cheated of the results of their toil by the Government.) The communities have long sought state protection from the arsonists even while failing, until recently, to produce information against them that must have been available. On the whole, however, it seems that most Doukhobors, certainly all the USCC and Independents, will now accept the welfare, protective and liberating functions of state agencies, and will increasingly co-operate in their support. The possibility of a more complete change of this nature hinges largely on the spirit and form of administrative action.

Of key importance is the requirement that overall policy and the details of administration, as well as the officials involved, accept the right of the Doukhobors to hold to the non-destructive portion of their values. Moreover the policy must be unequivocal, giving no grounds for the easily-aroused suspicions of these long-time foes of government. It must be just and, at the present time, in order to help heal the past, generous a little beyond what may be their mere due.

Force should not be overestimated as a way of securing compliance with law in this situation; indeed, it would take a wilful denial of the facts of recent history to justify it as the main recourse. The effectiveness of force depends on the existence of a wish to avoid suffering, and it is ineffective if there is a strong drive to martyrdom and strong belief in the virtue of resistance and in the ennobling effect of punishment. Many Sons of Freedom and a few others now regard prison as a place for the virtuous. Instead of bringing social condemnation down on the head of the convict, punishment meted out by the Government now brings social approval in its train. This does not suggest, however, the abnegation of the use of the judicial process along with the constraints of prison or corrective institutions. There is a necessity for the understanding and calculated use of legal restraint, with perhaps the devising of a specially suited system of detention for those whose inner compulsion will force them to con-tinue on the violent path they have been following.

THE POSSIBILITY OF DOUKHOBOR CHANGE

In later chapters some difference of opinion appears in the esti-mates of the ease, rapidity and modes of change in Doukhobor cul-ture, that is, the complex of beliefs, social organization, economic life, and other parts of their human environment. Dr. Rowles, Dr. Jamieson and Professor Dixon have set out programmes based on the expectation that the Doukhobors can start benefitting from them immediately. Emphasizing the linkages between personality and culture and concentrating his attention on the formation of Doukhobor personality, Dr. Shulman sees the need for the Doukhobors to change their own personality type before major improvements can be made in their situation. The often observed difficulty of effecting constructive changes in a culture, the countless instances of the failure, misdirection or slowness of plans of cultural change give support to his thesis.

Yet history records extensive and continuing changes and adjustments among the Doukhobors. Nothing of their life, indeed, has been left unchanged over a century, although there is persistence of some personality traits, there is repetitiveness in the situations of stress and problem, and there is a partial continuity in belief and forms of action. For the majority of Doukhobors the changes in language, standards of living and economic independence over the past fifty years have been an ameliorative adjustment in their relationships with Canadian society.

The difference in opinion among members of the research group on the possibilities of change results from the difference in their methods and interests. On their part, the social scientists are interested in the general run of belief and action and the ways in which these are related to such systems as the production or consumption of goods, the operation of authority and social relationships, or the workings of a religion. Causal processes and related sequences of events can be set out within these boundaries. For example, the growth of the Doukhobor system of belief is described as a development understandable largely in terms of the demands of logical consistency and extension; the secretive, hidden structure of leadership as an invention in response to certain forms of oppression; the present breakdown of agriculture as a result of the depression of the 1930's, of CCUB mismanagement, of inefficient operation, lack of secure tenure to-day and lack of protection from the Sons of Freedom. It is true that much more, some of it psychological in nature, can be added to these analyses and result in their enrichment. But as expanded in a later chapter by Dr. Jamieson, it is adequate for present requirements to account for the state of Doukhobor farming, for instance, in that way. The accounting is reasonably complete, objectively sustainable and indicates a line of corrective action. There is no need to reduce to psychological factors all these phenomena in order to understand and deal with them.

On the other hand, an integration of view-points and techniques including some psychological ones has been the aim of the research group from the beginning. The value of adding the dimension of the psychologist's analysis was shown in many instances where the problem just could not be explained satisfactorily by other techniques. In illustration, the complicated Doukhobor attitudes to property may be approached in a number of non-psychological ways. The observed vigour and constructiveness of much of Doukhobor work, contrasted with the destructiveness of Sons of Freedom depredations; the repeated statements on the wrongfulness of private property, as against the indications that property and comfort are nevertheless enjoyed and desired—these present obvious contradictions although they co-exist not only in the culture, but even in a single Son of Freedom. Such a tangle invites several approaches. Some meaning can be given to it by recalling the contradictory traditions concerning property which derive from the different phases of Doukhobor history. But it requires the psychological exposition of hostility, of its genesis in the experience of most Doukhobors and of the devious support of its permitted forms of expression to give the needed touch of life and detail to the long causal sequence.

The differences in view-point and method among the various sciences thus contribute to a richer understanding, but at the same time produce the slight divergence in conclusions mentioned at the beginning of this section. Some further light is thrown on this divergence in the estimates of the possibilities of Doukhobor change by considering the concept of basic personality type.

Just as the anthropologist, economist, sociologist, and other social scientists deal with abstracted averages or modes of behaviour, units called by such terms as custom or institution, so the psychologist who is studying culture employs abstractions from his observations. Such a concept is basic personality type, which, in Dr. Shulman's words, is yielded by abstracting "from the entire population certain traits which are held more or less in common." The processes of socialization, operating throughout life with a number of shared experiences, produce common elements in the personalities of a large proportion of Doukhobors. Beyond these common elements there may be a wide variation. The nature of the shared elements of the basic personality type and of the range of variation means also that there is considerable overlapping between Doukhobor and non-Doukhobor personality. People with Doukhobor-like personalities are living in other segments of Canadian society, while within the Doukhobor group there are people who vary quite widely from the basic personality type postulated for the group. The existence in other Canadian communities of people who possess characteristics of the Doukhobor basic personality type does not create there the sort of problem which besets the Doukhobors and their neighbours. The situation becomes special in Doukhobor communities because of the frequency and intensity of these characteristics, and becomes unique because of their linked forms of cultural expression. The nature of the problem there is determined by the co-existence of several factors. Among them are: a large number of Doukhobors with these aspects of personality; a social structure which compounds the stress through its manner of operation; and, within the Sons of Freedom, traditional forms of violent behaviour in response to intense stress, anxiety, and frustration.

An addition to the understanding of the nature of the problem and of the possibility of change is given by noting how a minority, variant from the basic personality type, contributes to the present situation. Some who are capable of more assertiveness and open aggressiveness than the average find satisfying roles in guiding or even instigating the protest behaviour of the Sons of Freedom. The vague, secretive patterns of leadership within the social structure, admitting authority if it can be viewed as theocratic and making no demands for formal discharge of the responsibility of office, have enabled individuals of such nature from time to time to attain effective direction of these traditional protests. Without such direction, more of the Sons of Freedom would bear their anxieties and their stresses in quiet passivity after the manner of the USCC members. In contradistinction to this, quite different roles, consciously included in the programme for cultural change, might elicit the participation of still other minority personality types, with results of a positive and constructive nature.

The desirability of constructing and administering programmes so as to create rewarding roles for selected individuals is supported by experience. Successful results of this procedure could be documented from some instances of rapid cultural change among primitive peoples. The workings of the Consultative Committee provide some further support for this suggestion. The opening-up of roles for responsible representation from the Sons of Freedom, with recognition as the main reward, has started a new process of selection; there is a growing prominence of men who are co-operative and reasonable beyond the average. The next stage may show the men in these roles guiding the general behaviour of the group, within the limits set by the basic personality type.

From one viewpoint, therefore, it is Doukhobor culture which is unfit; it fails to furnish these constructive roles, and denies the opportunity to develop and to attain goals which are conceivably within the reach of the people. To that extent, concentrating on the culture rather than on personality, new patterns of social and economic life can be instituted which even if used alone might bring some improvement, at least sufficient to meet the demands of neighbourly peace. Coupled with related changes in Doukhobor personality, improvement would be more rapid and solid. The combined process need not concentrate primarily on the child, since socialization is a process continuing through life. A programme for changing the culture should select new traits for reward, offer new constructive roles, ignore or punish undesired traits, and constrain destructive individuals.

38

This would be only a specialized form of a universal process of history; everywhere the changing cultures of the world emphasize, reward, punish or ignore some personality patterns in each phase of their alteration.

To be at all effective, any programme must be planned and operated with a knowledge of the nature and variety of Doukhobor personality. It will move toward its goal as it affects in a positive way some of the traits and patterning of this personality; it will founder where further conflict and anxiety is created by going counter to these principles.

PRINCIPLES OF ACTION ON THE PROBLEMS

It is generally taken for granted today that social problems have solutions which, if discovered, can be reached through legislative or other social action. This belief is as common now as it has been rare in past centuries. The persons given the task of prescribing for a problem must scrutinize this assumption, however, and ask: can society take effective action in this instance? The query is a most practical one, as is that which follows it; if effective action can be taken, what action?

The research group concluded that a number of courses are open to improve the situation of the Doukhobors in British Columbia, although there is no cure-all. Moreover, there is no "solution" in the sense of a course of action which will promise perfect harmony and stability.

Following a well tried form of analysis, it can be stated that the violent and illegal protests of the Sons of Freedom result from the stress acting on the individual and his culture. The form of this protest behaviour is related to the sorts of stress and the nature of the culture. The public reaction and the impact of law enforcement bear heavily on the problem. The stress, the culture, the protest behaviour and law enforcement are intertwined and affect one another.

Action aimed at making an improvement in the situation could be taken at any point of the problem. Programmes could be aimed at alleviating the stress under which the Doukhobor group is suffering, at altering their society and its culture, at doing something about the protests themselves, or at changing the impact of law on the situation. In this *Report* some action is recommended in each of these areas; something can be done in each, differing in degree of desirability and feasibility.

The impact of the laws and their enforcement on the Sons of Freedom protest is theoretically amenable to change in many ways. The existing laws might be enforced more strictly or their enforcement might be relaxed. The relevant laws can be repealed, altered, or new ones enacted. Such action should be evaluated while keeping in mind that the special legislation already affecting the Doukhobors is related quite directly to some of the social and psychological stress they are now experiencing, and that any change in this area is bound to have effects elsewhere in this enmeshed system of actions and results. It is recommended that one alteration to the Criminal Code be made: the law bearing on Sons of Freedom nudity is held to be unduly punitive, the penalty seems out of line with the gravity of the offence and its application is provocative where martyrdom is sometimes courted. Changes are also recommended in legislation relating to the franchise and the registration of vital statistics.

There are many ways in which programmes could be made to impinge directly on the group and its culture. The group could be removed or isolated, among other possibilities. Modified isolation has been exhaustively considered for the Sons of Freedom. Its use to relieve the pressure which they are under, and which in their turn they exert on others in the Kootenays, is recommended. Stricter isolation, in special prisons, must be held a possibility for those who persist in conceiving that their mission is to threaten and destroy. To assist the emigration they so much desire to a country where the stress is likely to be less severe or the protest behaviour less noticeable is also recommended, if such a country can be found. All nations so far approached on their behalf have refused to entertain the idea. (This is the only apparently unattainable course of action recommended in this *Report*, and is also the only one on which few words of dissent are likely to be heard from anyone in Canada.)

Alteration of the culture of the Sons of Freedom can be approached in a number of ways. The assumption that it can be altered has been examined, with the conclusion that it can. The moral principle that it should be altered at least enough to avoid criminal acts has also been accepted by the research group, although primarily it is not their responsibility to make that decision. They also reached the conclusion that it is desirable to make some changes in the actions and institutions of the non-Doukhobor people of the Province as they affect the Doukhobors.

The recommendations for rehabilitation, for economic support, for development of leadership and greater effectiveness in community operation, for assistance to their own educational programmes and some special adaptation of the Provincial schools are in line with the belief that Doukhobor culture can and should be altered in some degree.

It is of some importance to consider whether changes can be effected in the protest behaviour itself. Other individuals and groups from time to time suffer comparable stress which results in different action. Only some of the Sons of Freedom strip, burn and dynamite

40

as a protest; the majority do not. Can other techniques for expressing grievance be fostered? This calls less for legislative change than for the attention of administrators. In past decades it took a violation of the law by the Sons of Freedom to bring about any government action. A development started by the Consultative Committee was to secure prompt hearing for any grievance which aided in strengthening legitimate and more effective expression of needs.

Finally, some examination should be given to the stresses they live under and their cause. Some of these are internal and their analysis leads to recommendations for the encouragement of changes in Doukhobor life. Other stress results from contact with non-Doukhobors and the larger society. Various courses and kinds of action are indicated, including guides to administrative policy and to private behaviour. Rehabilitation programmes could lessen this internal stress, other government action in fields like vital statistics could reduce it by slight changes of policy. Private citizens whose prejudiced actions now place all Doukhobors under stress should undertake self-education. It is not uncommon today for the majority of citizens in a nation to change parts of their behaviour which are harmful to a minority.

This outlines the way in which the research group conceived of the problem and of the action which might be taken in regard to it. Subsequent chapters discuss the analysis of the problem and the different kinds of action in greater detail. The conclusion of the discussion in these introductory chapters, anticipatory of the more detailed exposition, is that a multiple and complete approach to the problems besetting the Doukhobors and the Province, taken with these principles and relationships in mind, will be effective in the long run. Partial or lopsided action might still be of help, though it cannot be presumed that it will. If expediency compels the adoption of only a partial programme, careful consideration should be given to the effects of its lack of balance.

OUTLINE OF PROPOSALS

The major proposals which are outlined here are set out in later chapters and summarized in Chapter IX. Within these major proposals are a number which have more or less separate status.

1. *An Administration for Doukhobor Affairs.*—This recommendation, discussed by Professor Dixon, is seen as carrying further the action started with the formation of the Consultative Committee; this Committee, representative of groups with an interest in this problem, is envisaged as continuing its operation and holding representation on a Commission of Doukhobor Affairs. The Commission, operating under an appropriate Minister of the Provincial Government, would

41

be charged with assisting the functions entailed in recommendations 2 and 3 below, and with the co-ordination of other relevant action by the different branches of government. This agency should have maximum flexibility and be able to call upon the highly specialized techniques and knowledge needed for successful operation at this stage. It should also aim to put itself out of business. Improvement would be measured by the extent to which existing agencies of government could take over, and the Commission should operate so as to bring about new helpful relations between them and the Doukhobors.

2. *Allotment of the Former CCUB Lands.*—This is a more detailed scheme for implementing the intention of the Government of the Province when it prevented the eviction of the community members following bankruptcy and foreclosure. The purpose of this operation is to offer an entitled Doukhobor the opportunity to purchase a usable parcel of land. With the completion of a necessary minimum of the survey of soils and uses of the lands, the process of subdivision can be started. Subdivision and allotment should operate under an allotment organization, which should be constituted to investigate the equity of each claimant to the lands of the bankrupt community.

It would then be open to any who might wish to try rebuilding a co-operative community to pool their lands for that purpose, or to others who wished to sell their lands to dispose of them in that way.

The background of this recommendation is given in the chapters by Dr. Rowles and Dr. Jamieson.

3. *The Resettlement of Some Sons of Freedom.*—This is called for in part by the fact that at Krestova and Gilpin at present there is insufficient watered land even for garden use. A place for resettlement would need to have sources of support other than farming, and there would be some advantage for the members of the USCC and the Independents if it were distant from their localities. A study of resettlement was made by Dr. Rowles and is reported in a later chapter.

Migration or change of locality is not ordinarily an advantage in itself in cases of social or individual problem; instead, it is often an attempted flight which make a solution even more difficult of attainment. In this case, however, it is held that some move, voluntary and perhaps partial, would be justified by the removal of pressure on other Doukhobors and the breaking of the painful and guilty associations which their home localities now have for some Sons of Freedom. Furthermore, it is hoped that the challenge and excitement of the rebuilding and pioneering which are associated with a move would occupy minds and energies constructively for a time at least, giving opportunity for other influences to work.

But relocation is recommended only if an objective evaluation of a proposed new situation should show the resources of land and

42

employment to be suitable. It is not recommended that relocation be undertaken to a place unfit on these grounds, however enthusiastically it might be acclaimed as a Promised Land by the Sons of Freedom. There is a very real danger of this; if not avoided, it will end in compounding the present difficulties.

4. *Welfare and Education.*—Some changes in administrative procedure in these fields are suggested by Miss Lewis and Professor Dixon.

5. *Franchise and Vital Statistics.*—In Professor Dixon's chapter recognition of Doukhobor marriage custom is advocated, as are some changes in the policy of vital statistics registration and the removal of the barriers to exercising the franchise by those who want it.

6. *Criminal Code and Penal Institutions.*—Set out by Professors MacIntyre, Herbert and Dixon, an alteration recommended in the Criminal Code is the repeal of the section on nudity, which with related offences can be dealt with by other legislation. Professor Dixon recommends special prison arrangements to reduce the harmful, negative effects of the present ones. He further recommends cancelling exemption from military service in cases of conviction for a criminal offence.

43

III

ECONOMIC AND SOCIAL LIFE

Stuart Jamieson

THE UNSATISFACTORY economic position of the Doukhobors, and their economic activities and relationships with others, form one highly important aspect of their problem. This aspect cannot, however, be analyzed by itself, in a separate and distinct compartment. The economic activities of individuals and groups are not merely responses to their own material self-interest however that may be defined. People are also motivated in economic as in other activities by a wide variety of culturally derived attitudes and values. Any attempt at an analysis of Doukhobor economic life is complicated by the fact that their attitudes and values derive from two different and, at many points, conflicting cultures. To understand the economic and social situation of the Doukhobors and the special problems they face today, therefore, requires a study of their cultural history through a half-century of contact with the Canadian environment.

From the circumstances of their origin the Doukhobors derived basic conflicts in social structure, in traditions and in motivations— conflicts which over the centuries have come to extend into almost every aspect of their existence, as much into economic activities as into any other. These conflicts have created serious problems, not only within their own group, but even more in their relationships with others. On the one hand, prolonged oppression by and resistance to the established church, state and aristocracy instilled traditions of opposition to authority in general, to wealth and privilege and, indeed, to virtually all activities that contribute to wealth. These traditions were fortified by the religious beliefs that "one does as the Spirit moves" and "we do not recognize man-made laws, only God's laws." On the other hand, the break from the feudal system entailed considerable carry-over of attitudes of submissiveness and subservience to authority instilled by generations of serfdom without, however, a corresponding carry-over of the feudal class structure into Doukhobor society. The result was some inconsistency and lack of integration. In principle the Doukhobor community in Russia was one of free and equal individuals who obeyed only the dictates of their own consciences and who functioned on a basis of voluntary co-operation. In fact it became a highly centralized theocracy, characterized by an extreme submissiveness to and dependence upon the authority of certain leaders. Such authority was at the same time

44

always vulnerable to opposition and attack from dissident individuals and factions.

Geographic isolation from other groups helped to hold the Doukhobors together. During the early nineteenth century the Doukhobors were banished into a sparsely settled region in the Southern Caucasus where, in comparative isolation from the main body of Russians for several decades, they developed an economic and social system which was more or less in line with, though at the same time it modified and was modified by, their religious and ethical traditions. As a peasant people with limited capital and technical knowledge, the Doukhobors were forced for their own survival to rely upon a simple, relatively self-sufficient economy based upon diversified agriculture and the supplementary trades of a peasant village community.

From such conditions arose the almost mystical role that land, and farming as an occupation, play in the traditional Doukhobor culture. The role derives not only from the peasant's "love of the soil." For the Doukhobors, land suitable for diversified, self-sufficient farming has been necessary to maintain the existence of the sect itself. It has enabled some of them to continue to the present day to live separately from other groups and to remain relatively independent of government—free from the need for education, maintenance of law and order, and other governmental services, and free, accordingly, from the need to pay taxes or other governmental levies to support such services.

Out of these circumstances there developed a distinct economic philosophy and a system of values and motivations which became incorporated into Doukhobor religious belief. A general shortage of capital and resources, coupled with limited education and technical knowledge in a simple agricultural economy, left little room for the individual to advance himself, to experiment in new or different types of enterprises, or to accumulate much wealth. And the absence in Doukhobor society of an established class structure—a priesthood, bureaucracy or aristocracy, or separate classes of businessmen, professionals or skilled tradesmen—tended to limit sharply the range of economic ambitions and goals. The individual's prestige and social status were not determined primarily by education, wealth, income, or position in an official hierarchy. Indeed, executive, professional and white-collar occupations came to have a low status in Doukhobor culture, and to be viewed as useless or parasitic compared to farming and other manual labour. Social status depended instead upon such factors as family, land ownership and skill in farming and related pursuits, age and experience, and loyalty toward the main articles of Doukhobor faith.

Doukhobor religion idealized the simple life and limited the range of economic incentives, thus fortifying the self-sufficient peasant econ-

45

omy. Private wealth, it was argued, excites envy and greed in others. The owner of wealth must protect his property by force if necessary. Then the whole apparatus of government—its maintenance of police, armed forces and repressive laws—comes into play. From a condemnation of human avarice and wealth, Doukhobor beliefs grew to include a denial of virtually all forms of competition and self-assertiveness and even creative endeavour as such.

Their beliefs were unable to crush all the qualities highly developed by their peasant culture: the urge to accumulate money and goods; handiwork and creativeness in embroidery, in woodworking and other arts; self-indulgence in food, liquor and sex.

And on occasion the Doukhobors have directed economic aggressiveness against others, a behaviour pattern common to many insecure and oppressed minorities. Sharp practices frowned upon within the group have been directed against the alien outsider. This aspect of their behaviour has appeared on a number of occasions during the history of the Doukhobors, in their commercial relationships with other ethnic groups in the Southern Caucasus and in their relationships with others in Canada. Where economic aggressiveness is sanctioned and practised against outsiders for any long period of time, sooner or later it enters into relationships among members within the group and thus undermines its unity.

Doukhobor beliefs, while in some respects inhibiting economic drive and aggressiveness among its members, in other respects may have accentuated this side of their character. For one thing, the deep inhibitions imposed by pacifism, outward submissiveness and lack of self-assertiveness, and the general abhorrence of physical aggressiveness or violence, can lead to diversion of activity into other types of behaviour. Potentially important as such an outlet is economic activity—devoting oneself to one's work in order to accumulate substance and get ahead of one's fellows, "beating the other fellow in a deal", and so on.

The organization of economic activities in Doukhobor communities in the Southern Caucasus, so far as one can judge from the available evidence, likewise reflected certain inner inconsistencies. In principle, Doukhobor beliefs condemned private ownership and individual economic activities motivated by self-interest. There was apparently little effort earlier in their history, however, to plan and organize economic activities along closely integrated communal lines. Like most peasant economies, the system apparently was one of loose informal co-operation in some activities, coupled with a considerable measure of individual ownership and operation in farming, handicraft, industry, and in trade. The *mir* system of land distribution was carried over from the Russian village. Various amounts of land of different grades, fruit trees and other resources were allotted to each

46

family in the village according to its size. Periodic redistribution allowed for changes in number and size of families. As in any pioneer settlement, mutual aid was needed in erecting houses and other buildings, in tilling the soil, and in defending the community from bandits. There was little evidence of co-operative or communal enterprise beyond this, in housing, in farming, in industrial undertakings, or in ownership and distribution of crops.

The conflicts in attitude and motivation tended to create somewhat erratic and unpredictable patterns of behaviour. A high centralized system of leadership was not enough by itself to prevent disintegration in a period of fundamental economic and social change. Means of compulsion along vigilante lines were employed. In this respect intimidation of a type later developed by the Sons of Freedom was perhaps inherent in the Doukhobor culture from its very beginnings.

In the earlier period of settlement in the Southern Caucasus, the Doukhobor community was not faced with such crises. A simple self-sufficient agricultural economy provided little to stimulate strong individualistic economic drives. The inner conflicts were held in check. Towards the end of the nineteenth century, however, the Doukhobors came into increasing contact with other peoples as the Southern Caucasus became more thickly settled. There they prospered due to their superior agriculture and their growing trade with others. Differences in character and ability led to widening economic inequalities among families and villages. The social organization was not sufficiently strong to prevent such inequalities developing, nor to prevent these having a disintegrating effect upon the Doukhobor community.

There is some indication that Doukhobor leaders, in order to combat the threat of disintegration, took steps to bring the Doukhobors again into conflict with the Government. They also elaborated and defined the Doukhobor creed and customs more rigidly in order to create social isolation from other groups, as a substitute for the geographic isolation that had been lost. Such were the strictures of Peter Vasilivich Verigin regarding such questions as vegetarianism, sex, the use of liquor and tobacco, payment of taxes, the burning of arms, attendance of children at school, and, especially, communal living and the communal organization of economic activities.

Verigin's policy was partially successful. It united a solid bloc of Doukhobors who sought to obey his directives with fanatical devotion. In doing so they were subjected to increasingly severe persecution from the Russian Government, which culminated in their mass emigration to Canada. But Verigin's policy also caused further stresses, and created divisions within the sect that were to re-emerge among those who settled in Canada. His directives, stemming from his contacts with followers of Tolstoy, were only partially adaptable to the peasant and Doukhobor traditions of his followers. His ideas were accepted, not on the basis of conscious, rational decision, but because of his strong moral position as a martyred leader exiled by the Government.

THE DOUKHOBORS IN CANADA

The Canadian environment on the whole has not alleviated the individual and group conflicts among the Doukhobors, and the trend toward disintegration has accelerated. Persecution in Russia, coupled with isolation, strengthened the sect. The relatively sparse economic environment of rural Russia, where the standard of living in most cases was probably below their own, offered few attractions to leave the Doukhobor communities. Their position was stabilized over a a long period of time. Their world fitted their preconceptions. The Government played the role of oppressor, and the necessities of survival made it practical on the whole to follow the traditional Doukhobor precepts regarding the virtues of simplicity, manual labour, co-operation and mutual aid. In Canada, however, the Doukhobor community has been torn by a broad three-way conflict: between Russian peasant tradition, Doukhobor religion, and forces emanating from the Canadian environment.

The main attraction of Canadian society to the Doukhobors has lain in its manifold economic opportunities and benefits, which appealed to their latent but strong materialistic drives. Traditions of individual initiative and free enterprise put few formal restrictions on the economic activities of individuals. For many years land was easily acquired for individual ownership at low cost. Outside employment has been available at rates of pay high by Russian or Doukhobor standards. The technologically advanced Canadian economy has tempted the Doukhobors with a wide range of careers and of capital and consumer goods—clothes, cars, machinery, gadgets, commercialized recreation and luxuries of all kinds—far beyond anything the Russian peasant environment could afford. The strong outward attraction which the Canadian economy has exerted upon the Doukhobors has destroyed their economic self-sufficiency, weakened their community ties and thus undermined the whole culture and the strength of their traditions.

The nature of government in Canada also has been such as further to undermine Doukhobor beliefs. Doukhobor society has lacked sufficient inner cohesion to hold together without external pressure in the form of persecution from the state. Such pressure has been lessened in Canada with its long-established traditions of democracy, of individual and group liberties and of freedom from tyrannical oppression. Hence the Doukhobors themselves have felt a need to create issues with governments in order to provoke conflict and force them into the oppressive role which they play in Doukhobor tradition.

The outside social environment in Canada has served at the same time to provide a measure of external pressure that has slowed the process of disintegration and helped maintain the Doukhobors as a separate and distinct group. While Doukhobors have been drawn toward Canadian society by the economic opportunities and benefits that it offers, they have been rejected to a considerable degree by that society.

This combination of circumstances has created an atmosphere of extreme uncertainty and insecurity for many Doukhobors. They have become dependent upon the outside Canadian society for satisfaction of their economic needs, but the social accompaniments of Canadian economic life have been in part denied to them. They have been thrown back upon their own community and their own beliefs for security and acceptance. But there is limited satisfaction to be derived from this retreat because the Doukhobor communities themselves have become divided and disorganized.

This three-way cultural conflict thus creates more serious stresses among Doukhobors than among most immigrant groups, and one result is deep and pervasive guilt. They have become more materialistic than before, and at the same time inwardly more aware and ashamed of it. In extreme cases, again among the Sons of Freedom, this inner conflict creates a need for self-punishment, shown in a compulsion to bring hardship and economic ruin upon themselves by going to jail, by burning their houses and belongings (or allowing others to do it), by donating large sums of money for dubious causes, by suffering physical violence at the hands of others, and by stripping.

SASKATCHEWAN

Factionalism and disorganization arising from such conflicts appeared almost from the beginning of Doukhobor settlement in Saskatchewan in 1898. The first villages were established and run on communal lines, as directed in letters written by Peter Vasilivich Verigin while still in Siberia. Communal houses and dining halls were built (though many settlers lived in their own individual dwellings). The land, acquired in several large blocks from the Dominion Government under the Homestead Act, was owned and worked co-operatively, as were most stores, livestock, machinery and other facilities. Wages received from outside employment were (in principle if not always in practice) pooled in the general earnings of the community.

Wide and growing economic inequalities among families and villages created friction and helped frustrate the communal undertakings. Some Doukhobors had brought over from Europe personal property in the form of gold coins, paper roubles or Turkish rugs that could be turned into useful wealth in Canada. They were well dressed and lived in good houses, while at the other extreme were Doukhobors so poor that they were reported to be "dressed in rags" and living in "holes in the ground." Some rich Doukhobors lent money to their less fortunate neighbours at high rates of interest. The well-to-do on the whole opposed communal ownership and operation because they stood to lose. Growing numbers of them, as time went on, withdrew from their village communities to become individual operators. The beginnings of the Sons of Freedom, with their protest movements and demonstrations, were associated with the breakdown of community life. They appear to have been concentrated among the poorer and less successful members, who felt that the future of the sect itself was being jeopardized by the growing individualism of the well-to-do.

Verigin attempted to consolidate and extend the communal organization of the Doukhobors' economic and social life when he arrived in Canada in 1903 to resume active leadership. His most significant move in this direction was to persuade his people to refuse to register for individual titles to their land, as required under the Homestead Act. A substantial number refused to follow Verigin's advice and did assume individual title to their holdings. The majority, however, followed him and thereby lost tens of thousands of acres which they had staked out since 1898.

This development was to have lasting effect on the attitudes of Doukhobors in Canada. From Verigin's point of view it served a double purpose. First, it separated the wheat from the chaff, the lukewarm independent elements from the more orthodox and the zealots. And second, it created an issue that for the time being united the majority of Doukhobors in opposition to the Government.

DOUKHOBORS IN BRITISH COLUMBIA

The main body of Doukhobors, under the leadership of Verigin, had already formed themselves into an organization known as the Christian Community of Universal Brotherhood (CCUB). Their next move was a large-scale resettlement in the West Kootenay region of British Columbia, a project that extended over several years prior to and during World War I. To finance the undertaking, they raised several hundred thousand dollars among themselves and borrowed additional hundreds of thousands from mortgage and loan companies, pledging for collateral community-held land in Saskatchewan as well as newly acquired land and other assets in British Columbia. As early as 1910 they were reported by an official of the Dominion Department of the Interior to have purchased some 8,800 acres of land in the Grand Forks, Brilliant and Slocan junction districts, to have built roads and bridges, sawmills, concrete reservoirs and irrigation facilities, and to have planted tens of thousands of fruit trees. By the outbreak of World War I the Christian Community of Universal Brotherhood had purchased 14,403 acres for a total outlay of $646,007, of which $324,928 was paid up and $321,079 was still owing.

Virtually the entire undertaking was organized and operated on an integrated communal basis under the close supervision of Peter Verigin. The typical unit of settlement was a village composed of two large community houses for each hundred acres of land, with additional dwellings and other farm buildings adjoining them. The community houses were each designed to accommodate thirty-five to fifty persons. Farm land, orchards and other facilities were worked jointly by the occupants of each village. Sawmills, brick plants, stores and other industrial or commercial undertakings were financed and supervised by the central CCUB executive. As in the earlier Saskatchewan settlements, earnings from outside employment were in principle pooled in the general earnings of the community. This system was later supplanted by one of flat annual assessments levied on each adult male of the village. Each village in turn was responsible for raising its quota of money for the over-all operations of the CCUB.

The CCUB expanded and prospered during World War I and afterwards, up to the mid-1920's. In 1917 it was established as a Dominion incorporated company. It was capitalized at $1,000,000, though its total assets were estimated as several times that figure. Peter Verigin issued the shares to himself and thirteen other executive directors of the enterprise. Wartime shortages and high prices provided profitable markets for wheat, lumber, bricks, fruit and other output of CCUB Ltd. enterprises, while plentiful jobs for its members at high wages provided further sources of cash income. Additional acreage was purchased by the CCUB, not only in British Columbia but also in Saskatchewan, Alberta and Manitoba. New industrial enterprises were established, including the jam factory at Brilliant. Verigin as leader of the community imposed a rigid "austerity programme" on himself and his followers in order to reduce consumer expenditures to the minimum and devote the largest possible part of the community's income to paying off the debt and expanding capital assets.

DECLINE AND DISINTEGRATION OF THE CCUB

The CCUB began to decline rapidly after the death of Peter Vasilivich Verigin and the accession of his son, Peter Petrovich Verigin, to leadership. During the interim the executive board of the CCUB, in order to consolidate the company's accounts, borrowed $350,000 from the Bank of Commerce, secured by bonds held by the National Trust Company. After Peter Petrovich Verigin assumed office as president of the CCUB, it went further into debt, and finally into complete bankruptcy in 1937.

There have been many reasons offered to explain this catastrophic reversal in the fortunes of the Doukhobors' major communal undertaking. Much has been spoken and written about Peter Petrovich Verigin's spectacular mismanagement and alleged misappropriation of many hundred thousand dollars of CCUB funds. This could not have been, however, the sole or even the major cause of the CCUB's failure. Fundamentally it rested in the conflicts inherent among the Doukhobors themselves and in their inability to maintain their distinct economic organization intact in the Canadian environment. From the time they first settled in Saskatchewan they had clearly shown themselves incapable of living and working together effectively in closely integrated communal undertakings. The CCUB represented the superimposition upon the Doukhobors, by fiat, of Peter Vasilivich Verigin's rather unrealistic social and economic concepts, which were only partially adaptable to the traditions and attitudes of his followers. The experiment prospered as long as he personally supervised its operations and ruled with an iron hand. Under the erratic and inefficient leadership of his son, the CCUB became torn increasingly by factionalism. Even in the general prosperity of the later 1920's its membership was declining steadily in numbers and morale, and its source of income was shrinking. The severe depression and unemployment of the 1930's merely accelerated the process.

Growing numbers of Independents, whose main careers lay outside the CCUB, found the restrictions of community life irksome. They ceased to contribute to communal undertakings, moved out of the villages and established separate residences on their own farms or in nearby cities and towns. Included among them were some of the ablest members of the Doukhobor community—one skilled administrator, for instance, who had managed the Community's lumbering operations, left to build a prosperous lumber business of his own. In a sense the very size to which the CCUB had grown by the 1920's was its own undoing. Ambitious undertakings such as lumber and sawmilling plants, the jam factory at Brilliant and the cooperative stores at Brilliant and Grand Forks required special skill and training that were not fostered in the traditional Doukhobor culture. The CCUB thus developed a special elite of skilled business executives and administrators who did not have the status within the Doukhobor community that such qualifications usually command. Such skilled personnel, however, had an outside market. Individuals having sufficient ambition and industry to climb to the rank of executive or manager in the CCUB hierarchy, as well as many others, could find greater rewards within the non-Doukhobor community.

At the other extreme, the Sons of Freedom were winning converts and growing in numbers and influence. They became increasingly hostile toward the CCUB leadership during the 1920's and 1930's, and helped to undermine the morale of the whole organization. Their growth was fostered by discouragement over the financial set-backs of the CCUB after years of frugality and effort on the part of the members, and by rising opposition to continued payments of principal and interest at high rates on loans from banks and mortgage companies. Increasing numbers of the Sons of Freedom refused to pay their annual assessments, and community property estimated in 1937 as worth $437,143.12 was burned or destroyed by them. The CCUB leadership attempted to meet the problem of the Sons of Freedom by exerting pressure or outright force to uproot them from the main villages and isolate them in one separate community, that of Krestova. That was the immediate circumstance that provoked the outbreaks of 1932, culminating in the mass imprisonment of the Sons of Freedom on Piers Island.

The whole burden of carrying on the CCUB, and particularly its large overhead of fixed annual payments of principal and interest on its debts, thus fell upon a shrinking membership. At the height of its operations the organization had close to 8,000 members. By 1928 the number had fallen to 5,485. Ten years later there were only 3,103, of whom scarcely more than 2,000 were fully paid-up members. This trend forced higher individual assessments on each remaining member as time went on. The industrial undertakings of the CCUB were operating at a loss from 1928 on, and the Saskatchewan branches fell behind in their assessments. Depression and unemployment during the 1930's reduced the outside incomes and at the same time placed additional burdens on the Community for relief and social welfare on behalf of its destitute members. Finally, in 1937, the CCUB went bankrupt. Foreclosure proceedings were instituted in 1938.

BANKRUPTCY AND FORECLOSURE

By the time the CCUB became bankrupt it had paid off by far the major part of its obligations. Its main financial outlays from 1928 to 1938 were as follows:

Principal paid on loans and mortgages, 1928-38....	$ 704,243.75
Total interest paid, 1928-38	543,661.21
Total taxes paid, 1928-38	301,949.29
Erection of buildings, 1928-33	221,671.29
Purchase of lands, 1928-33	161,839.04
Clearing of lands, 1928-33	220,147.08
Total	$2,153,511.66

Between 1928 and 1938, as the table above shows, the CCUB had paid out a total of $2,153,511.66 in principal and interest on loans and mortgages, on taxes, erection of new buildings, and clearing and purchase of lands. In addition to these outlays, up to 1937 the Community had paid $202,264.55 for construction of roads, bridges, and ferries, and had lost a total of $437,143.12 from incendiarism and fires of unknown origin.

The principal owing by the CCUB on loans, mortgages, and other debts at the time of foreclosure in 1938 was as follows:—

Canadian Bank of Commerce (handled by National Trust Company)	$168,283.12
Sun Life Assurance Company—Vancouver	192,297.51
Sun Life Assurance Company—Regina	80,902.70
Great West Life Assurance Company, Winnipeg	56,717.66
Departments of Lands, Winnipeg	20,852.28
Other creditors[1]	75,663.42
Total	$594,716.69

The $80,902.70 owing to the Sun Life Assurance Company in Regina and the $56,717.66 owing to the Great West Life Assurance Company in Winnipeg were paid off through the sale of certain CCUB Ltd. lands in Saskatchewan to individuals (Doukhobors and others) on agreements for sale. Foreclosure action was taken in British Columbia against the CCUB by the National Trust Company (on behalf of the Canadian Bank of Commerce) and by the Sun Life Assurance Company, for the indebtedness of $168,283.12 and $192,-297.51 respectively. The Sun Life Assurance Company's claims, including accrued interest, taxes, insurance and other costs, were settled by a payment from the Provincial Government of $207,500 (see below). The National Trust Company received $89,000 from the Provincial Government, and the receiver appointed under Court orders disposed of most of the remaining assets of the CCUB to collect the balance owing to its client. Its receivership was taken over in 1945 by the Toronto General Trust Company in Saskatchewan.

The main foreclosure proceedings, undertaken by the receiver appointed by the National Trust Company and later by the Toronto General Trust Company, involved the disposition of CCUB Ltd. assets in all four Western Provinces. Only a fraction of the original value of the assets was realized. They were sold by the receiver, for the most part at knock-down prices. The costs of carrying out the receivership operations over the seven-year-period 1938-45 were very heavy. In the end, a small surplus of only $142,111.07 was left for

[1]These do not include individual members of the CCUB who had (and presumably still have) judgments totalling $205,026.02 against the CCUB but who did not collect their claims in the receivership operations described below.

54

the remaining creditors or "legal heirs" of the CCUB Ltd., after the millions of dollars and untold time, effort and hardship which its Doukhobor members had invested in the enterprise.

The financial statements may be summed up as follows:

Gross receipts from sale of assets

British Columbia
—National Trust Company..............	$286,970.03	
—Sun Life Assurance Company....	207,500.00	$ 494,470.03

Alberta
—National Trust Company..............		91,665.00

Saskatchewan and Manitoba
—National Trust Company..............	150,039.24	
—Toronto General Trust Co.............	198,811.93	
—Sun Life Assurance Company......	80,902.70	
—Great West Life Assurance Co.....	56,717.66	486,471.53

Total........		$1,072,606.56

Liabilities paid, including accrued interest
Canadian Bank of Commerce........	200,241.05	
Sun Life Assurance Company		
—British Columbia........................	207,500.00	
—Saskatchewan	80,902.70	
Great West Life Assurance Co.......	56,717.66	
Others (Toronto General Trust Co.)	78.650.95	
	624,012.36	
Expenses and write-offs............................	306,483.13	930,495.49

Surplus........		$ 142,111.07

The "Doukhobor problem" apparently was settled satisfactorily in Alberta and Saskatchewan, where the CCUB Ltd. lands were sold by the insurance and trust companies to individual Doukhobors and others, mostly CCUB members, on individual agreements for sale. In that way the Community members in those Provinces were able to retain interest in the properties which they developed.

It was found impossible to dispose of the CCUB Ltd. assets in British Columbia in this fashion. The large industrial and commercial units in this Province would have been difficult, if not impossible, to dispose of to former members in individual agreements for sale. According to spokesmen of the mortgage and trust companies, the Community members were afraid to purchase the land because of threats and intimidation from the Sons of Freedom. The latter were fanatically opposed to breaking up the Community lands and properties into individually owned units. The general uncertainty and turmoil of the 1930's, the demonstrations and outrages on the part of the Sons of Freedom, the demoralization of the CCUB leadership in this Province, and the discouragement of the membership militated against an orderly settlement of the problem.

Moreover, the executive apparently hoped to retain the CCUB Ltd. as an integrated enterprise on a reduced scale. It was confidently expected that the sale of Community lands and properties in Alberta and Saskatchewan would suffice to pay off the major part of the indebtedness. Then the main tracts of farm land, the jam factory, sawmills and stores of the CCUB in British Columbia could be maintained intact and be reorganized on a sounder financial basis.

This hoped-for solution likewise proved to be impractical. In 1938, when foreclosure action was begun, farm land in Alberta and Saskatchewan was difficult to sell even at extremely low prices. It is doubtful whether it could have brought in enough money at that time to pay off more than a small fraction of the mortgage indebtedness. Moreover, selling the land in individual agreements for sale meant that the moneys took years to collect, and some $15,252.32 was still owing in 1951 from purchasers in Saskatchewan. The Canadian Bank of Commerce was demanding immediate repayment of its loan to the CCUB, and the National Trust Company as its agent and the appointed receiver were required to sell a major part of the Community assets in British Columbia for cash, and at knock-down prices.

THE PROVINCIAL GOVERNMENT AND THE LAND QUESTION

In the course of the foreclosure proceedings, the Sun Life Assurance Company and the National Trust Company in 1939 took steps to sell the land in British Columbia. Fearing that this would create a major problem in uprooting and dispossessing thousands of Doukhobors, the Provincial Government took emergency measures to forestall the threatened eviction. Under a special Statute, negotiations were begun in 1939 and finally completed in 1942 to meet the mortgage claims against the Community lands. The Sun Life Assurance Company's claims were paid in full, to the amount of $207,500, comprising the following:—

Principal owing on mortgage	$145,369.53
Interest owing on mortgage	49,081.70
Advances (for taxes, fire insurance and foreclosure costs)	13,048.77
Total	$207,500.00

The National Trust Company's claims on behalf of the Canadian

Bank of Commerce were met only in part, through the net payment by the Government of $89,000 to cover land and buildings (including the jam factory) which had been pledged as collateral. The remaining indebtedness was finally paid through sale of other assets by the receiver in British Columbia, Alberta, Saskatchewan and Manitoba.

In this way the Provincial Government assumed trusteeship over some 19,000 acres of land, together with buildings and other facilities formerly owned by the CCUB Ltd. From one point of view this was a humanitarian gesture on the part of the Provincial Government. It prevented wholesale dispossession of the Doukhobors. They have been allowed to continue occupying the land and buildings, and have been charged very moderate rentals. Many have paid no rent at all. The total collected, amounting to a few thousand dollars a year, probably does not even cover the costs of administration by the Land Settlement Board, let alone provide a reasonable rate of interest on the Government's initial investment of $296,500 or reimbursement for the tax revenues that have been sacrificed.

From another point of view, however, the Provincial Government put itself in a dubious position which has greatly complicated the problem of its relationships with the Doukhobors. There is the legal aspect, for one thing. Under foreclosure action, land and other assets are supposed to be sold at public auction after due notice has been given. The Government forestalled this action and took over the land and buildings for a lump sum well under the probable return from auction sales in individual parcels. Or, to put it another way, the Provincial Government, for the sum of $296,500, acquired title to land and buildings in which the Doukhobors had invested millions of dollars plus work. Despite the considerable deterioration in land and buildings that has occurred during and since the 1930's, at present prices these assets would probably be worth well over a million dollars.

The main problem arising out of this situation lies in its effects upon the attitudes of the Doukhobors themselves. Not only is there widespread apathy and discouragement as a result of the collapse and liquidation of their great communal enterprise. There is also a widespread suspicion, which a mere presentation of the facts alone will not dispel, that they were defrauded by the mortgage and trust companies and by the Provincial Government. At the time of foreclosure they had repaid in interest and principal the major part of their indebtedness. Not knowing the technical details and costs involved in the foreclosure proceedings, many suspect that the creditors collected far more from the sale of CCUB assets than was owing to them, and many likewise feel that the Provincial Government tricked the Doukhobors in gaining control of some 19,000 acres of land and buildings for less than $300,000.

57

Partly because of their insecure position as tenants and squatters, the Doukhobor occupants have been unwilling to maintain and improve the land, buildings and other facilities. Large tracts are remaining uncultivated. Houses and other buildings, irrigation facilities, and the like are being allowed to deteriorate or break down entirely. To an increasing degree since the final collapse and liquidation of the CCUB Ltd., Doukhobors have been abandoning farming and have been working at other employments. This has brought a corresponding tendency toward dependence upon city or town for recreational life.

WORLD WAR II AND THE DOUKHOBORS

Canada's entrance into World War II added new complications to the Doukhobor problem. It came in the midst of foreclosure proceedings against the CCUB and the Provincial Government's assumption of trusteeship over CCUB land and buildings in the West Kootenays. In some respects the various factions of Doukhobors drew together in the face of outside hostility and the dangers of war, but in other respects the war-time situation sharpened existing antagonisms and conflicts.

NATIONAL REGISTRATION

The first major wartime difficulty to arise with the Doukhobors was that of registration. Large numbers refused to register as required under the National Registration Act of 1940, and a considerable number were committed to jail at one time or another during the war. Most of these have been identified as Sons of Freedom, but it is quite likely that a number of USCC and Independent Doukhobors were converted to the ranks of the Sons of Freedom by this very issue.

The Federal Government endeavoured to come to some clear understanding with the Doukhobors on the matter of registration. The exemption from military service of the original Order in Council of 1898, was renewed. Evidence was required of "good standing"; i.e., of practising the Doukhobor religious faith and being a member of a recognized Doukhobor organization. Many Doukhobors joined the USCC and paid their dues of $25 a year in order to be sure of exemption.

The USCC executive encouraged the Doukhobors to register as required by law, or at least did not actually oppose registration. Some Sons of Freedom and some others, however, refused to register and suffered in varying degrees thereby. There was a good deal of resentment on the part of those who refused, who felt that the USCC had "sold out" and "compromised with evil." Those who registered gained definite benefits. They avoided jail, they qualified for better-paid jobs than they had enjoyed before, and they were able to get ration books. The Sons of Freedom did not enjoy these privileges. Their privations in food were not as serious, however, as might have been expected. Meat, butter, and sugar were rationed, but meat was not a regular part of their diet; a number had cows, so could make butter for themselves and neighbours, and most of them apparently managed to get sugar from friends and relatives among the registered Doukhobors. The victory signified by non-registration outweighed the real losses of that course of action; antagonism was engendered among the Sons of Freedom toward other Doukhobors, and accounts for some of the postwar attacks against the latter.

SELECTIVE SERVICE

Major difficulties arose from the Selective Service and Mobilization programme launched by the Federal Government in 1943. Little or no effort was taken to prepare the ground, to explain the programme to the Doukhobors beforehand and to enlist their cooperation on a voluntary basis. Public relations were handled clumsily, and widespread opposition was aroused even before the programme was launched. Doukhobors, however, were badly needed for work on a wide variety of vital projects, because of the drastic labour shortage in the region. They could not, however, be effectively forced to work. Hence, government officials avoided an attempt at rigid enforcement.

In principle the Selective Service programme required that every applicant for employment register with the local office of the National Employment Service and be certified as unfit for or exempt from military service, in order to take a job. Seven days' notice to the employer, as well as permission from the employment office, was required by law to quit a job or transfer to other employment. In certain occupations, considered of special importance and suffering critical labour shortages, workers were frozen to their jobs.

The Alternative Service programme was designed specifically for conscientious objectors, including entire groups such as the Doukhobors. In principle this programme authorized the Government to draft conscientious objectors for designated non-military employment and to deduct earnings above the military rate of pay for the support of such organizations as the Red Cross. The Doukhobors, however, (including the leaders of the USCC) felt that the programme was imposed arbitrarily upon them, and for the most part did not accept it. The Government, on its part, apparently did not attempt to enforce it.

Other difficulties were encountered under Selective Service. At one point in 1943, hundreds of Doukhobor carpenters and other construction workers quit their jobs in the midst of erecting the new dam at Brilliant—a project of major wartime importance, needed to increase the output of hydro-electric power for use particularly in the Consolidated Mining and Smelting Company plants at Trail. The district office of Selective Service had to recruit new workers as far east as Quebec to replace the Doukhobor workers. Great difficulty was encountered also in keeping badly needed Doukhobor workers at their jobs in section gangs and maintenance crews on the railways. The former Director of Selective Service states that he had to make numerous trips up and down the CPR tracks in a special speeder to explain the Selective Service regulations to Doukhobor workers and persuade them to stay at their jobs.

The main difficulty seemed to lie in the seven days' notice provision of Selective Service, together with the job-freeze in certain occupations. Doukhobors, as noted below, are concentrated in the ranks of casual workers. They show a strong preference for jobs of short duration, so as to be free to quit when weather conditions require that they look after their farms and gardens. Selective Service officials had to be flexible in their interpretation and enforcement of the regulations to allow for this factor and thus encourage Doukhobors to enter and stay in the labour market.

Large numbers of Sons of Freedom ignored Selective Service regulations entirely, as they had ignored national registration. Many of them avoided registered wage employment and went to work on their own, at construction, and cutting logs or poles on a contract basis, and there was no way to check on them effectively. Many others worked illegally for logging and sawmilling companies. They were employed and paid by these concerns without having previously registered with the employment office, and their names were not entered on the companies' books. An official of one prominent lumber company in Nelson, for instance, tells of its operations near Krestova during 1944 and 1945. All parties kept a sharp eye open for Selective Service investigators and other Government officials. When such an official was seen approaching, the unregistered Sons of Freedom employees would disappear, returning to work when the coast was clear. Another company was more open about its infractions along this line, and paid fines on several occasions. Authorities tended to close their eyes to the situation and accept the inevitable. Lumber was a scarce and critically needed material during the war, and Doukhobors were almost the only workers available. Where the Sons of Freedom were adamant in their refusal to register for employment, it was expedient to ignore it rather than attempt to enforce the law and have to keep them in jail. But, as the former Director of Selective Service observes, "How can we expect such people as the Sons of Freedom to respect the law when several leading citizens of Nelson were aiding and encouraging them to flout it?"

ECONOMIC AND SOCIAL CHANGES IN WARTIME

World War II greatly improved the economic status of the Doukhobors. But in the process of improvement it also added to their demoralization in some respects and accentuated certain conflicts both within their ranks and with other groups. Coming after the disastrous collapse and liquidation of the CCUB, the war led to further disintegration of Doukhobor communities. Opportunities for steady and continuous employment at unprecedented wages drew an increasing number out of their home communities, away from farming and into other employment. With more spending money than ever before, and more contact with the outside, it was inevitable that more would be inculcated with non-Doukhobor motivations and values. They desired increasingly the goods, services and luxuries available in urban communities. In this respect the wartime situation tended to draw the Doukhobors into our society and hasten their acculturation.

On the other hand, the relationship between Doukhobors and the English-speaking residents of Nelson, Trail and other centres became more strained. There was greater resentment against the Doukhobors because their young and able-bodied men were exempt from military service while "our boys are overseas," and because Doukhobors in general were earning higher wages and maintaining a more lavish scale of expenditure than ever before, by virtue of being exempt from military service. There was more openly expressed hostility—pointed remarks aimed at Doukhobors, occasional jostling of them in the streets, and so on. Some of the younger Doukhobors, in response to such treatment, adopted attitudes of defiance. With more money than before, with jobs for the asking and employers clamouring for their services, some became arrogant or posed as being so.

There is still a residue of widespread resentment, prejudice, and discrimination against Doukhobors in Nelson and other communities arising out of the wartime situation. One important manifestation of this is discrimination against Doukhobor workers by employers and other workers in numerous industries and trades. Employment statistics indicate that Doukhobors, whether by choice or otherwise, have not on the average had as many months of employment per annum since the war as they had during the war. Many Doukhobors complain that they are "last hired and first fired."

The fear of government regimentation during wartime, coupled with greater hostility from other groups, threw the Doukhobors back upon themselves and strengthened their pacifism and their opposition to government. For many individual Doukhobors this has meant

61

inner conflict, with feelings of guilt for violating certain articles of faith and for succumbing to various material and other temptations of the outside world. This is an important factor contributing to the postwar depredations of the Sons of Freedom. Outbursts of nudism and arson are designed in part to repudiate the larger society, to unite all Doukhobors in the ranks of the Sons of Freedom, and to isolate them socially from other groups.

PRESENT ECONOMIC STATUS OF DOUKHOBORS IN BRITISH COLUMBIA

To the outside observer, not given to scrutinizing his own inconsistencies, Doukhobor economic behaviour appears as a mass of contradictions. Superficially they appear to violate their faith in such diverse matters as their consumption of meat and alcohol, their individualism in economic behaviour, and their inability or unwillingness to cooperate effectively in projects for their common welfare. They appear to be preoccupied with immediate gain, yet many have shown a willingness to sacrifice their careers or see their property destroyed in the pursuit of a religious ideal. They have a reputation for acquisitiveness and sharp bargaining coupled with a reputation for hospitality, and for gullibility in losing their money in dubious projects.

The casual dismissal of the Doukhobors as hypocrites merely begs the question. A more adequate explanation derives from their deep-seated and intense three-way cultural conflict, between their religious doctrines, their Russian peasant traditions and attributes, and the attractions of the Canadian social and economic environment. This conflict has become more intense in recent years as the stresses of depression followed by World War II broke down their older community organization without at the same time enabling them to fit easily into the Anglo-Canadian culture.

In this situation of continuing change it is exceedingly difficult to evaluate the economic position of the Doukhobors in British Columbia, to sort out and analyze their economic motivations and characteristics. The pattern of inner conflict is such that an individual may be governed by contrasting motivations. And there is an almost infinite variation in the degree to which different individuals are inculcated with motivations from one or another of the cultural patterns.

OCCUPATIONAL DISTRIBUTION

The majority of Doukhobors in the West Kootenay region at present occupy the land formerly owned by the CCUB Ltd., now held in trust by the Provincial Government. They are no longer a predominantly farming people. They depend primarily upon wage employment in other areas for their main livelihood, while cultivating small tracts or garden plots for part of their food needs or to supple-

62

ment their cash income. Most of the farm work is carried on by the women and children. Many men take leave from their outside employment to help in the work of cultivating, planting, and harvesting.

It has not proved possible to get a full statistical picture of the number of Doukhobors and their geographic and occupational distribution in British Columbia. Large numbers of them have steadfastly refused to register with and give vital statistics about themselves to public or private agencies. The decennial census has not so far provided information about them as a separate and distinct group. Data concerning them in other local or district offices of various Federal and Provincial Government departments are fragmentary and incomplete.

The data collected by the district offices in Nelson and Trail of the National Employment Service of the Unemployment Insurance Commission form an exception. Unemployment insurance has been a special boon to the Doukhobors because of their concentration in casual and seasonal jobs, characterized by frequent periods of unemployment during the year. Although there was widespread reluctance among them to register with the National Employment Service for several years after it was established in 1940, the obvious benefits of unemployment insurance in time overcame their traditional opposition. Beginning in 1947 and 1948, large and increasing numbers, including most of the Sons of Freedom, qualified to receive unemployment insurance and registered with the National Employment Service offices in Nelson and Trail. In doing so they provided information about themselves on such questions as age, education, marriage status, number of dependents, community of residence, job and community in which last employed, occupation or trade, months of employment, rates of pay, and trade-union membership.

The data that follow regarding the economic and occupational status of Doukhobors in the West Kootenay region have been drawn mainly from the files of Doukhobor workers registered in the district offices of the National Employment Service in Nelson and Trail, supplemented with information gained through personal interviews and written questionnaires directed to the major employers in this region. In addition, the Employment Service provided a list of employers, with information about location, type of business and number of employees.

The employment statistics provided by the National Employment Service, while giving the most comprehensive picture of the Doukhobors that we have to date, unfortunately are not complete. There is a sizeable but unknown number of workers who do not qualify for unemployment insurance, most of whom, therefore, have not registered with the Employment Service offices in Nelson and Trail. Among these are higher salaried employees, full-time farmers, other proprietors or self-employed persons, and farm workers. A considerable number of Doukhobors—perhaps several hundred all told—may be included in these categories.

In addition, there are some workers who have not been unemployed, or have not changed their jobs, for several years. While registered for and qualified to receive unemployment insurance, they have had no occasion to register for employment with the district offices of the National Employment Service, so that the current data about them are lacking. This explains the apparent discrepancy in the fact that the total number of workers in the current files of the Trail National Employment Service office, as shown in Table II, is only 2,224, while the Consolidated Mining and Smelting Company alone employs over 4,000 workers. Comparatively few Doukhobors, however, for reasons mentioned later, are in this category.

Another sizeable group that possibly has not been included in the statistical survey which follows comprises a number of Sons of Freedom who were in jail at the time this study was being undertaken. That would explain, for instance, the unduly small number of workers listed in Table I as residing in Crescent Valley (in which Krestova is located). As these Sons of Freedom in many cases had not been in the labour market for several months due to their incarceration, a considerable number probably were not registered in the current "live" file of the National Employment Service. Unfortunately, the widespread similarity and duplication of names among Doukhobors, and the inadequacy of the data about Sons of Freedom in police and court records regarding such questions as age, number of dependents, occupation and area of residence, made it impossible to compare them with the records of workers registered with the National Employment Service and thus find out which, and how many, were included or excluded.

Despite these shortcomings, it is safe to say that the statistical information that follows, derived mainly from the National Employment Service files, covers the majority of Doukhobors residing in the West Kootenay region and provides a realistic picture of their occupational and economic status.

MOBILITY

An outstanding characteristic of the Doukhobors as workers is their extreme mobility. This arises from the fact that the majority continue to live in small farms and villages, while their main sources of employment are in non-farming industries and trades located in the larger cities and towns and, to a lesser extent, in more distant logging camps and mining towns.

This is brought out graphically in Table I, which shows the areas of residence and of employment for a sample of 1,437 Doukhobors registered with the district offices of the National Employment Service in Nelson and Trail. These workers reside in some thirty-seven communities. The majority of these are scattered along both sides of the Kootenay and Columbia Rivers between Nelson and Trail. A number are also scattered along a 30- or 40-mile stretch of the Slocan Valley, between South Slocan and New Denver. The largest single concentration of Doukhobors is in the Grand Forks district, separated from the others by a 50-mile stretch of tortuous mountain highway.

The main areas of employment, of course, are the industrial centres of Trail and Nelson, though it is to be noted that hardly more than one-third of the 1,437 Doukhobor workers in the sample were employed in these two cities at the time this survey was made. A sizeable number, comprising almost one-third of the total, were em-

TABLE I.—SPATIAL DISTRIBUTION AND MOBILITY OF 1,437 DOUKHOBOR WORKERS

COMMUNITY	NUMBER RESIDING	NUMBER EMPLOYED
Grand Forks	201	133
Brilliant	170	22
Castlegar	139	93
Shoreacres	131	1
Crescent Valley	129	7
West Grand Forks	124	5
Winlaw	59	3
Nelson	57	348
Salmo	57	53
Thrums	53	1
Slocan Park	39	1
Blewett	31	6
Taghum	31	9
Appledale	29	--
Trail	26	249
Blueberry Creek	21	12
Rosebery	21	14
Glade	20	2
Perry Siding	15	--
Robson	13	11
Kinnaird	12	1
South Slocan	10	44
Passmore	9	17
Vallican	8	5
Fruitvale	6	3
Beaton	5	41
Rossland	4	51
Okanagan	4	3
Slocan	4	

TABLE I.—SPATIAL DISTRIBUTION AND MOBILITY OF 1,437
DOUKHOBOR WORKERS—(*Continued*)

COMMUNITY	NUMBER RESIDING	NUMBER EMPLOYED
West Coast	3	69
Nakusp	3	12
Bonnington Falls	2	2
Crawford Bay	2	1
Procter	1	1
Makinson Landing	1	--
Waneta	1	--
Saskatchewan	1	4
Alberta	--	10
Champion Creek	--	1
East Kootenay	--	17
Fernie	--	1
Fife	--	10
Golden	--	1
Greenwood	--	3
Kaleden	--	1
Kamloops	--	2
Kaslo	--	2
Kimberley	--	5
Midway	--	109
Needles	--	4
Revelstoke	--	1
Sheep Creek	--	6
Silverton	--	5
Washington	--	2
Westbridge	--	3
Unknown	15	30
Totals (55)	1,457	1,437

ployed in the four smaller industrial centres—133 in Grand Forks, 109 in Midway, 53 in Salmo, and 93 in Castlegar. Other main groups were employed in more distant areas, including 69 on the Pacific Coast and 51 in the Okanagan.

It is evident from this survey that most Doukhobors have to travel several miles a day to and from work. Car or truck pools are the common arrangement. Another large minority (particularly in Grand Forks) work in towns or communities, like Trail and Midway, that are too distant for daily commuting, so are able to see their families only at week-ends or during slack periods between jobs. A third minority of some size comprises workers who leave their families for weeks or even months at a time to work at seasonal jobs in still more distant areas, such as the Okanagan and the Coast.

Even Table I does not give the full picture of mobility. In the majority of cases only a fraction of those residing in any community work there. In looking at the individual case-histories, one is amazed at the extent of cross-traffic. Numbers of Nelson residents, for instance, are working in Trail while Trail residents are working in Nelson.

EMPLOYMENT DISTRIBUTION

A further and perhaps more important employment characteristic of the Doukhobors, as may be seen from Tables II and III, is their extreme concentration in a few industries and trades. Of the male workers listed in the Nelson and Trail district offices of the National Employment Service, almost 43 per cent are concentrated in two fields alone; namely, carpentry and lumber products. By far the major portion of the 655 listed as unskilled are in the category of general construction labour. Only a small fraction are in the "white collar" positions classified as "managerial," "professional," "sales," and "clerical." Doukhobors likewise comprise only a small fraction (less than ten per cent on the average) of the workers employed in construction trades other than carpentry, in service trades, metal and mechanical trades, manufacturing, mining, and miscellaneous trades.

TABLE II.—OCCUPATIONAL DISTRIBUTION OF MALE
DOUKHOBOR WORKERS

OCCUPATION	NELSON DISTRICT		TRAIL DISTRICT	
	Total Workers	*Number of Doukhobor Workers*	*Total Workers*	*Number of Doukhobor Workers*
Managerial, professional and sales	70	3	73	4
Clerical	45	3	30	–
Service trades	83	9	71	5
Construction,				
Carpenters	266	189	220	71
Others	32	16	87	1
Lumber products	355	202	258	181
Metal and mechanical trades	27	5	94	–
Mining	124	4	46	–
Transportation and communication	463	147	285	6
Manufacturing	--	--	82	–
Miscellaneous trades	17	--	13	–
General and unskilled	768	372	965	283
Totals	2,250	950*	2,224	551†
	*Doukhobors, 42.2 per cent		†Doukhobors, 25 per cent	

A somewhat larger proportion is employed in transportation and communication. Most of the 153 in this field are employed in section gangs on the railroads, although five are railroad firemen.

A smaller proportion of women among the Doukhobors than among the rest of the population seeks employment outside the home, as may be gauged from Table III. Doukhobor women comprise only a

TABLE III—OCCUPATIONAL DISTRIBUTON OF WOMEN
DOUKHOBOR WORKERS

OCCUPATION	NELSON DISTRICT	TRAIL DISTRICT
Professional and semi-professional	--	1
Book-keepers	--	1
Secretaries, stenographers, and typists	1	--
General office-workers	1	2
Sales clerks	6	6
Cooks, waitresses, and kitchen-workers	17	9
Domestic, personal and protective service	8	4
Building service work	3	--
Laundry, cleaning and pressing	3	1
Food-workers (mostly fruit harvesting and packing	24	29
Factory work (sawmill and box, stone, glass and clay, textiles)	1	8
Totals	64	61

little over six per cent of all registered Doukhobor workers, as compared to more than twenty per cent women among non-Doukhobor workers in this region. As may be seen from the table, a large proportion is concentrated in the category of "food-workers" (almost entirely fruit-packers and harvest-hands employed seasonally in the Okanagan). The other main fields of employment for Doukhobor women are those of cooks and waitresses and domestic service. Again, few (though proportionately more than Doukhobor men) are in "white collar" or office jobs.

There is a similar concentration among the comparatively small number of Doukhobor employers, as may be seen from Table IV. Almost eighty per cent are in the two fields of lumbering and construction alone.

At first glance the position of the Doukhobors in the labour market seems very marginal and insecure. True enough, the men are not concentrated at the bottom of the occupational ladder, in the jobs of lowest pay or lowest status. The proportion of Doukhobors in the ranks of "unskilled" (i.e., 37 per cent) is only slightly higher than the proportion of Doukhobors to all registered workers (i.e., 34 per cent).

As a matter of fact, the jobs in which they specialize—logging, saw-milling, and construction (though not railway maintenance)—pay on the average fairly high hourly rates. The Doukhobors' insecurity lies in the fact that these fields of employment are essentially casual by nature, and particularly vulnerable to seasonal and cyclical unemployment. Comparatively few Doukhobors are employed in the more secure positions, as in white collar and service trades, or in skilled manual trades other than carpentry. Most striking in this regard is the fact that so few Doukhobors are employed in the most important single field of industry and employment in the West Kootenay—that of mining and smelting. Ten leading firms in this field—including the huge Consolidated Mining and Smelting Company of Trail, with over 4,000 workers—employ altogether only eighty-four Doukhobors.

There are several related reasons for this extreme specialization in employment among the Doukhobors. To a considerable degree, as brought out again later, it appears to be due to discrimination by employers and, to a lesser extent, by other workers. This is most apparent in the case of industries and trades in which the typical unit is the small owner-operated enterprise, as in most lines of retail and wholesale trade, local service trades, metal and mechanical trades, and certain building trades. In such cases the personal attitudes of the employer play a more direct role in hiring and firing policy. In many larger companies, particularly in fields—such as saw-milling—where Doukhobors comprise a major part of the labour force, labour-employer relationships are more impersonal, and the skill or availability of Doukhobor workers appears to prevail over any prejudice against them on the part of employers.

Trade-unions with closed shop and apprenticeship regulations have tended to restrict the employment of Doukhobors in certain trades, as in building construction, metal and mechanical trades, and certain fields of transportation. That appears to be one important reason, among others, for the smaller number and proportion of Doukhobors among carpenters and other construction tradesmen in Trail (23.4 per cent) as compared to Nelson (68.8 per cent). Unions in these trades are much more effectively organized in the former city than in the latter.

To a great extent, however, the high concentration of Doukhobors in casual or seasonal jobs appears to be a matter of preference on their part. In fact, the preference on one side and the prejudice on the other are inseparable attitudes in many cases.

The small number of Doukhobors employed in managerial, professional, sales and clerical jobs is related to the low status which white collar jobs have in the Doukhobor scale of values. The long opposition to education, resulting in a low average level of literacy, limits the number entering these fields. Educational requirements also limit the employment of Doukhobors in skilled manual trades.

The fact that most Doukhobors are still tied to the land, continue to reside in their rural villages, and derive part of their livelihood from small-scale subsistence farming prevents many or most of them from getting and keeping stable full-time jobs. They prefer casual or intermittent employment which they can leave temporarily to plant and harvest their crops during short periods of the spring and summer. Their small farms and garden plots, together with unemployment insurance, provide a cushion against unemployment and thus render them less dependent upon full-time employment. This work pattern in turn makes Doukhobors rather undesirable workers from the point of view of employers who prefer stable employees who can be depended upon to stay on the job. This seems to be the main factor accounting for the exceedingly small number of Doukhobors employed by the Consolidated Mining and Smelting Company, for instance.

The small number of Doukhobors employed in mining itself is not difficult to explain. It is a field which is relatively easy to enter, as witness the large proportion of workers who are of first- or second-generation immigrant stock, particularly of Slavic background. Much of the employment is casual or intermittent, and the degree of mobility and rate of labour turnover are traditionally high. The explanation given in numerous personal interviews with Doukhobors is that, as a people having a long peasant tradition in which farming has a particularly high status, they prefer outdoor work. Many actively dislike mining and related trades, particularly when they involve working underground.

Logging and sawmilling, carpentry and woodworking generally, by

TABLE IV.—DOUKHOBOR EMPLOYERS

INDUSTRY OR TYPE OF BUSINESS	NELSON		TRAIL	
	Number of Employers	Number of Employees	Number of Employers	Number of Employees
Logging and lumbering	15	81	21	94
Construction	5	22	8	38
Brush-clearing	1	5	--	--
Sash and door	1	4	--	--
Truck and haulage	2	2	1	1
General store	2	2	3	5
Garage	--	--	1	6
Dry cleaning	--	--	1	1
Grocery	--	--	1	1
Totals	26	116	36	146

contrast, are trades which appear to have a positive attraction for Doukhobors. Such fields of employment have long been supplementary to farming in the traditional Doukhobor economy, both in Russia and Canada. Logging and sawmilling were the first major fields of employment for Doukhobors upon their arrival in Canada, cutting and hauling logs for railway ties as well as for their own dwellings and farm buildings. The CCUB's extensive logging and sawmilling enterprises, as pointed out before, provided a training-ground for large numbers of Doukhobors, executives as well as workers. World War II and the postwar boom accentuated the trend toward this specialization, due to the inflated demand for and price of lumber, the serious labour shortages, and the many job opportunities available to Doukhobors at unprecedented wages. By and large, the most successful individual careers among Doukhobors have been made in this industry. As may be seen from Table IV, the majority of Doukhobor employers (including the largest) are in this industry. So are most of the few Doukhobors who occupy executive positions, including the general manager of one large lumber company and the plant superintendent of another. A considerable number of Doukhobor workers in logging and related fields are also self-employed, working singly or in groups on contract for lumber companies and other customers.

Much the same pattern applies to carpentry and general construction labour. There were training and practice for large numbers in the ambitious construction programmes of the CCUB in the Prairie Provinces and in British Columbia—such projects as the construction of concrete dams and reservoirs, brick-kilns and sawmills, community houses and other buildings. Moreover, the Doukhobors, like other immigrants, specialized in construction labour and were employed in considerable numbers during the construction boom of the 1920's in particular, in Trail, Nelson, and other urban centres. The typical system was for one of the group to act as spokesman or contractor in negotiating with the employer.

The construction boom of World War II and the postwar period, with the characteristic housing shortage, inflated prices and plentiful supply of jobs at high wages, accelerated the trend toward specialization on the part of Doukhobors. It enabled large numbers to learn on the job. Most were in the category of "rough" carpenters, lacking proper apprenticeship training and capable of doing only semi-skilled hammer-and-saw work on such projects as building the Brilliant Dam. Because of the continued high demand for carpenters, coupled with the limited organization and jurisdiction of the Brotherhood of Carpenters and Joiners in the Nelson district, many "rough" carpenters were able to register as fully qualified tradesmen and take advantage of the higher rates of pay.

71

The construction industry ranks next to logging and sawmilling as a field for successful individual careers among Doukhobors. As Table IV shows, it is the other main field in which Doukhobor employers and proprietors are concentrated. And, as in logging and sawmilling, a sizeable but unknown number of Doukhobors are self-employed in contractor groups whose earnings are taken in the form of shares of the contract price rather than in wages paid by the hour.

The relatively small number of Doukhobors in other building trades (plumbers, electricians, plasterers and cement finishers, painters, decorators and paperhangers) is explained in part by their lack of previous experience. Most buildings erected in the settlements established by the CCUB did not have modern plumbing or electrical facilities, or finished plaster walls, so did not provide the opportunities to acquire these and comparable skills to the same extent as in carpentering. And in the main urban centres these trades have tended to be more effectively controlled by trade-unions having closed shop and apprenticeship regulations, which have prevented Doukhobors from competing with established tradesmen.

OWNERSHIP STATUS: GOALS AND INCENTIVES

After several decades in British Columbia the Doukhobors appear to be occupying a very marginal economic position. They are concentrated in highly seasonal occupations, characterized by short duration and relatively low annual incomes. Very few have managed to climb to positions of higher or more secure economic or social status, and few appear to have accumulated great wealth.

This is due partly to external factors that have operated to their disadvantage, particularly the huge losses they suffered through the collapse and liquidation of the CCUB, and the prejudice and discrimination against them in many fields of employment. But fully as important are the limited motivations inculcated by their culture, coupled with the attitudes and behaviour patterns common to the occupations in which they specialize. As a number of special studies have brought out, casual workers may form a distinct cultural group in terms of attitudes and motivations that diverge rather widely at some points from the accepted norm of other occupational groups. Extreme insecurity and intermittency of employment in themselves discourage habits of thrift and stability on the job. Long range ambitions and goals are discouraged, and the individual is preoccupied with short range, immediately realizable objectives.

The most pronounced aspect of this picture is the relatively high rate of labour turnover and the generally short duration of jobs among Doukhobors. Like many a logger on the Coast, as well as the native worker in many areas, the Doukhobor has a reputation in the

West Kootenay for being "shiftless" and "unreliable." He reputedly works for a while until he has made a "stake," when he quits and goes back to his village shack and garden patch, returning to work only after he has used up his money and exhausted his unemployment insurance benefits.

This is not the whole picture, however. Doukhobors generally have lower costs of living than other wage earners, a fact which has enabled many of them to achieve a more substantial position than most casual workers enjoy. Other workers living in Nelson or Trail have to pay city rents and inflated prices for food. Most Doukhobors living in their villages pay annual rents to the Provincial Government of only $30 to $60 for the quarters they occupy, and many Sons of Freedom pay nothing at all. They grow a large part of their food on their own small farms or garden plots. Because of these advantages it is widely said that Doukhobors are generally better off and have more "spending money" than other workers doing the same type of work and earning comparable rates of pay. There is the rather widespread view that Doukhobors are able to save larger sums of money and at the same time spend more on such items as clothes, alcoholic beverages and automobiles.

These opinions are impossible to prove one way or the other. Doukhobors are secretive about money matters, even among themselves, and few keep their money in bank accounts. Nevertheless, there is a good deal in the way of personal observation and eyewitness accounts to support such views.

One indication is that many Doukhobors do have large sums of cash. Reports from storekeepers, car dealers, real estate and insurance salesmen, and the like, are sufficiently frequent and factual in nature to establish this. There is also the undeniable ability of Doukhobors collectively to raise large amounts of money when the occasion demands. Peter Petrovich Verigin raised loans amounting to almost half a million dollars during the latter 1920's, including individual contributions of tens of thousands of dollars in some cases. Again, even such a depressed group as the Sons of Freedom can on short notice raise enough money to buy their leader a new automobile or contribute considerable sums for welfare and other services for indigent members.

While the Doukhobors as a whole thus seem to have a greater ability and propensity to save than have others in the same occupational or income classes, they appear in certain respects to have a lower propensity to invest. This applies not only to business or industrial capital but also to certain durable consumer goods of the type that establishes status in the North American community. Here again there is a divergence in standards of living between Doukhobors and other groups which helps to account for differences in economic incentives and goals and in employment characteristics.

In the American and Anglo-Canadian middle-class the home plays a vital role in determining work habits and motivations. To be accepted and have status among his peers, one must first live in a home in the "right" neighbourhood, furnished with proper taste, in accordance with the standards of the occupational or income classes with which one identifies oneself. These standards usually require that an employee seek at all times to please his employer, stay at his job and strive constantly to get ahead and improve his earnings. Immigrant groups acquire these standards, motivations and behaviour patterns as they become assimilated.

The home does not rank as highly as this in the standard of living of most Doukhobors. Their houses are generally poor, unpainted and sparsely furnished, and are not located in the more "desirable" residential areas. Even well-paid and well-to-do Doukhobors seem to have homes, furniture and appliances well below a standard they could afford. The individual Doukhobor can enjoy acceptance and status among his own group, and in his own community, without having to meet Anglo-Canadian standards in home and furnishings. To that degree he is free from the compulsion to "stay at the job," "please the boss," and "get ahead." And he may also have more money to spend on other things.

The automobile, on the other hand, seems to represent as important an item in the Doukhobors' standard of living as it does among Canadians generally. Other groups in the West Kootenay, however, tend to have exaggerated ideas as to the extent to which Doukhobors own automobiles and trucks. A study of the registration rolls in the Nelson district, for instance, shows that the combined ownership of cars and trucks among Doukhobors is proportionately less than for the rest of the population. In 1951, Doukhobors owned 341 out of the 2,271 registered passenger-cars and 369 out of 1,322 trucks. Ownership of automobiles, however, is still concentrated to a large extent among middle- and upper-income classes, whereas Doukhobors are predominantly in the low and lower-middle wage-earning groups. Within this class they appear to have more and newer cars and trucks than have other elements.

The widespread ownership of cars and trucks among Doukhobors is often taken as another indication that they have more spending money than others in the same occupational or income classes. It may also represent the beginning of a tendency among Doukhobors, common to many minorities, to invest in the types of goods which give the owner a special status in the eyes of the majority group. Their cars, however, probably have more utilitarian than prestige value to them, as indicated by the high proportion of trucks. For people who live in rural communities and must commute long dis-

74

tances to work, cars and trucks are in many cases necessary capital investments. As a type of investment second in size only to houses for most people, ownership of cars and trucks might be expected in time to induce longer range goals and more stable and industrious work habits among Doukhobors. On the other hand, it also increases their mobility and thus enables them to continue living in their farms and villages while earning their livelihood in other communities. The effects of this upon their employment and work habits have been described earlier. In this respect it is arguable that the automobile may impede assimilation and enable the Doukobors to remain a separate and distinct cultural group.

As a third major field of personal investment, many Doukhobors show a relatively high propensity to own land. This is in line, of course, with the historic role of land as a source of security and livelihood. Despite opposition in principle to private property, the vast majority of Doukhobors in the Prairie Provinces have become landowners. In British Columbia also, individuals continue today, as they did while the CCUB was a going concern, to buy land and establish their own separate residences outside the exclusively Doukhobor village communities. Today there are some 1,170 Doukhobor property-owners and taxpayers in the West Kootenays and, as Table V shows, many own more than one holding.

This trend seems to indicate that the vast majority of Doukhobors in the West Kootenays would become land-owners and taxpayers if the Provincial Government were to carry out an adequate programme

TABLE V.—INDIVIDUAL PROPERTY HOLDINGS OF DOUKHOBORS

NUMBER OF HOLDINGS	NUMBER OF OWNERS	NUMBER OF PROPERTIES
Less than 1*	188	91
1	752	752
2	155	260
3	48	99
4	17	38
5	3	15
6	2	12
7	2	14
8	--	--
9	1	9
10	2	20
Totals	1,170	1,310

* Shared by one or more owners.

The figures in this table were obtained from the 1951 Index of Taxpayers in the Tax Assessment Offices in Nelson and Penticton. Unfortunately, they do not show the size or the value of individual holdings.

for selling back to them, in individual parcels and at reasonable terms, the land it now holds as trustee.

The most important single factor serving to discourage greater willingness on the part of Doukhobors to invest in land and other fixed assets, and adapt their economic philosophy, may have been the disastrous failure of the CCUB Ltd., together with the constant threat of the Sons of Freedom. The Doukhobors in Saskatchewan and Alberta who acquired title to land and other assets formerly belonging to the CCUB Ltd. has become, on the whole, an industrious and prosperous group. The majority in British Columbia might conceivably do the same if they could acquire individual title to the land they now occupy and at the same time be protected from depredations at the hands of the Sons of Freedom.

As things stand now, many Doukhobors in British Columbia represent a self-perpetuating economic problem. Their feelings of insecurity, their apathy and limited drive, and their continued ties with their village communities all combine to give them certain unsatisfactory characteristics as employees. Employers and others consequently are inclined to discriminate against them. This, together with attitudes and values in their own culture, attracts them to and keeps them in casual and seasonal occupations such as logging, sawmilling, construction and railway-maintenance work. They remain a marginal group, subject to frequent unemployment and low annual incomes, and are continually thrown back upon their own communities and their traditional Doukhobor standards and beliefs. These provide an alternative type of emotional and economic security, as well as a rationalization for failure to get ahead in the Anglo-Canadian economy. The Sons of Freedom, with their more depressed economic position and negative attitudes toward almost every aspect of outside society, represent the ultimate product of this process.

ECONOMIC RELATIONSHIPS

Of great importance in the economic relationships of the Doukhobors among themselves and with others, as neighbours, buyers and sellers, workers and employers, are the ways in which these relationships are defined. The definitions are part of the belief systems of Doukhobor and non-Doukhobor. They may be more or less remote from reality. Yet they influence the way people regard each other, and they affect their actions. Consequently, along with facts on economic behaviour and relationships, it has been thought necessary to report belief and rumour. The facts themselves and the beliefs about the facts play an intertwined part in determining the economic situation.

Acquisitiveness.—Doukhobors are widely pictured by others

(employers, workers, and government officials alike) as acquisitive and materialistic. "You can't get them to do anything unless they see something in it for *them!*" This is almost the direct antithesis of the Doukhobors' own picture of themselves as without personal greed and avarice.

Evidence given to substantiate this view is, however, somewhat contradictory. On the one hand, Doukhobors are constantly accused by other workers and employers of "scabbing," price-cutting, and working for lower wages. During the prosperous war and postwar years, on the other hand, they have been just as widely accused of taking advantage of the tight labour market and "charging what the traffic will bear."

Again, it is frequently pointed out that the Doukhobors' traditional antipathy to Government regulations and restrictions has disappeared in those cases where there is a clear gain in dollars and cents. It is true that the only branch of Government in which any large number of Doukhobors have registered and provided vital statistics and other information about themselves is the employment office; this entitles them to unemployment insurance benefits in slack times.

But it can be noted here that this generalization is not true in every case. During the depression of the 1930's, for example, a much smaller proportion of Doukhobors than of other groups were on relief. A sample check of the relief rolls in the Nelson district for the fiscal years 1933-34 and 1937-38 shows that a little over four per cent of all recipients of relief checks were Doukhobors. And today some of the most destitute Doukhobor families, particularly among the Sons of Freedom, refuse to register for family allowances and social welfare grants.

Business Ethics.—In line with their reputation as acquisitive, Doukhobors are accused of sharp practices and hard bargains in business deals. One constantly hears the statement, "You've got to watch them or they'll put something over on you."

As an example they are widely accused of bribery—of police, other Government officials and employers. Much of their famous hospitality seems aimed in this way at softening up the enemy or prospective benefactor. One hears about bribery of foremen on the larger projects, for the purpose of getting jobs or being shifted from one job to another more desirable one. "A bottle of whisky a month is the standard price." In the opinion of some executives, bribery is an important factor accounting for the generally poor reputation of Doukhobors as workers. Acceptance of a bribe weakens the authority of a foreman or other official and lessens his ability to command respect and good performance.

There is considerably less agreement as to the degree in which Doukhobors are actually dishonest. Some, while acknowledging their

77

shrewdness, laud the Doukhobors for their honesty and reliability in a deal, for keeping their word and always paying their debts. Others testify to the opposite. The managers of some stores, for instance, instruct their sales clerks to be on the alert whenever Doukhobors are in their stores, because of their reputation for shop-lifting (though some state that this is much less common now than it was earlier, particularly among the "old women with the shopping-bags"). On the matter of Doukhobors keeping their word and paying their debts, there is the widest discrepancy in beliefs. At the one extreme there are storekeepers who assert that they have been doing business with Doukhobors for twenty years or more and have never lost a cent through unpaid debts. A number of such proprietors relate how Sons of Freedom settled all their bills before going to prison for long terms. At the other extreme are those who refuse to sell goods on instalment to Doukhobors on the ground that they are too unreliable.

Perhaps the safest generalization on this point is that the experience with Doukhobors depends to a large extent on the businessmen's own attitudes and policies toward them. Small grocers and proprietors of general stores whose customers are mainly Doukhobors, in small rural communities like Thrums or Winlaw, have found them most trustworthy, while the more impersonal or less friendly proprietors and managers of larger stores in Nelson and Trail find them otherwise. Thievery or other dishonesty may be a technique of hostility and attack, like nudism and arson.

Individualism.—Doukhobors have not shown a great capacity for organizing cooperative projects. The failure of their major communal enterprises in Saskatchewan and later in British Columbia is a case in point. Smaller cooperatives with more limited objectives have met with little success. Another example is the unwillingness or inability of Doukhobors to organize effectively into trade-unions or trade associations, among themselves or with others, in order to strengthen their bargaining power and economic status.

Their individualism is shown perhaps most clearly as wage-earners. The trend in most occupations (particularly under trade-union pressure) is toward wages paid by the hour rather than by piece-rates. This is in part an attempt by wage-earners to enhance their economic and emotional security through restricting individual competition among themselves. Informal group sentiments and ties, the individual's emotional need to be accepted by other men on the job, and so on, all work to this end. Doukhobors, by contrast, seem to prefer piece-rates. In the logging and sawmilling industry, companies generally find that they get better results from Doukhobors working on their own, as "contractors."

The preference for piece-rates may be derived from their dislike of authority and supervision, their preference for working on their own, at their own speed; or again, it may be an expression of their competitive relationship with other workers, as well as among themselves.

Labour-Employer Relations.—In the West Kootenay region, Doukhbors present a special problem of industrial relations. It is not so much that of strikes and lockouts or other such manifestations of labour-employer conflict; these, in fact, are notably few compared to most regions of this Province. The problem is rather one concerning attitudes and policies on the part of both employers and workers, Doukhobor and non-Doukhobor, which give rise to latent tension and conflict. These contribute to further problems, such as high labour turnover and absenteeism, unconsciously or deliberately slow or inefficient work, job discrimination and under-employment, and the like, all of which keep the Doukhobors as a whole in a somewhat marginal and insecure economic status.

Surprisingly, Doukhobor workers have more overt disputes with Doukhobor than with non-Doukhobor employers, according to the local Inspector of the British Columbia Department of Labour in Nelson. There seem to be several allied reasons for this. Due perhaps to Doukhobor tradition itself, there is resentment on the part of many Doukhobors toward those of their group who become employers. More important perhaps is the tendency for Doukhobor employers to haggle over terms and seek to drive hard bargains. Other operators, whether storekeepers or employers, usually set their prices and stick to them. As employers, non-Doukhobors usually maintain the minimum conditions required by law. Each employer is under pressure to meet at least the minimum standards required to keep his labour force and avoid violating the strong code and sentiment against "chiselling." Doukhobor employers generally are not governed by such standards to the same degree. They are more likely to haggle with each worker, to get him at lower than the standard wage, or at longer hours, or to change the wages or other terms of employment after a worker has been hired. The result has been numerous complaints before the Labour Inspector on the part of individual Doukhobor workers against their Doukhobor employers.

Among other employers there is fairly widespread discrimination against Doukhobors. Many employers compare them unfavourably with others. Part of this arises from Doukhobor characteristics, attitudes and practices which have nothing to do directly with the character and capacities of Doukhobor as workers; for example, their pacifistic beliefs and their exemption from military service during both world wars; their past opposition to sending their children to school and paying taxes; and the behaviour of the Sons of Freedom, which has reacted unfavourably upon other Doukhobors. Most of the prejudice against them on the part of employers, however, arises

79

from what are considered to be unsatisfactory characteristics as workers. Table VI, for instance, indicates the opinions expressed by seventy-four employers replying to a written questionnaire. Only a fraction of several hundred employers to whom questionnaires were sent actually replied. Of those who did, giving factual data regarding numbers of Doukhobors employed in different types of jobs and the like, a number expressed no opinion one way or the other about Doukhobor characteristics and qualities as employees. The opinions that were expressed are listed and classified in Table VI.

It will be seen that the total number of firms listed in Table VI

TABLE VI.—ATTITUDES OF SEVENTY-FOUR RESPONDING EMPLOYERS
IN THE WEST KOOTENAYS TOWARDS DOUKHOBORS AS
WORKERS AND EMPLOYEES

FAVOURABLE

OPINIONS ABOUT DOUKHOBOR WORKERS	NO. OF FIRMS
Steady and reliable	7
Hard-working and industrious	4
Honest	4
Efficient	2
Cooperative	2
Ambitious	2
Total number of firms predominantly favourable	5

Neutral

No preference, or no difference from other workers	21
Work best by themselves, in separate Doukhobor groups	3
Work best as individuals when mixed with other workers	2
Do not trust employers—fear of being cheated	1
Total number of firms neutral, or no opinion expressed	44

UNFAVOURABLE

Unreliable	15
Inefficient, or less efficient than other workers	7
Irresponsible	6
Dishonest	6
Don't mix well with other workers	5
Won't stay at the job	4
Tactless, and objectionable manners	4
Need more supervision	4
Distrusted and feared as fanatics	4
Slow and plodding	3
Sly and underhanded	2
Lacking in ambition	2
Objected to by other workers	2
Uncooperative	1
Total number of firms predominantly unfavourable	25

as "predominantly favourable," "predominantly unfavourable," and "neutral" does not correspond with the total number of firms giving each of the opinions listed. The reason is that a firm "predominantly favourable" may nevertheless give a number of unfavourable opinions, and vice versa.

This survey indicates a wide variety of attitudes among employers. As regards such characteristics as reliability, efficiency, honesty and cooperativeness, some employers express directly opposite views about the Doukhobors, for reasons that will be discussed later. Certain patterns, however, do stand out.

One of the most widely held opinions among employers answering this questionnaire, substantiated by numerous personal interviews, concerns the alleged "unreliability" and "irresponsibility" of Doukhobor workers, their "unwillingness to stay on the job," their "lack of ambition," and their "uncooperative" attitudes. Their special shortcoming along this line is their high rate of turnover, their tendency to quit jobs at any time and for no apparent reason. This pattern of behaviour may be partially explained by the limited ambition instilled by the Doukhobor culture; the continued residence in and emotional ties with home village and farm or garden-plot, which many Doukhobors have managed to retain; and the habits and attitudes that tend to develop among workers specializing in casual jobs.

There are possibly additional reasons. High labour turnover is often the unorganized workers' means of protesting, or at least one of them. It may also be derived partly from the religious emphasis upon following the dictates of one's own conscience, together with the traditionally ambivalent attitude of submissiveness and antipathy to authority. Latent hostility on the part of Doukhobor employees is further generated by their awareness of prejudice and discrimination as well as their marginal position as "last hired and first fired."

Another indication lies in the numerous complaints of employers about the Doukhobors' "inefficiency," their "slow and plodding work," and their special need for supervision. Such complaints are common, of course, about any immigrants who are inexperienced in the ways of modern industry and commerce, and who have not as yet acquired the techniques and know-how necessary for fast and efficient work. This does not appear to offer an adequate explanation for the Doukhobors, however. In the early days of their settlement in British Columbia, they showed on the whole considerable skill and industry in the operation of such undertakings as sawmills, brick-works and jam-factories. Most Doukhobors in British Columbia today are second or third-generation residents, and have had fairly long experience in various types of enterprises of the very kind from which many of the employer complaints have come. And, as indicated in the questionnaire and borne out by personal interview and observation, in a

81

few enterprises Doukhobors have proven to be remarkably steady, hard-working and efficient.

Again, slowness and inefficiency on the job, like high turnover and absenteeism, appear to be a product of the Doukhobor culture that comes into force only in certain circumstances, particularly where there is latent conflict with employers or with other workers. And it seems to arise primarily as a more or less concerted reaction where Doukhobors are employed in groups. A representative of a prominent mining company near Salmo, for instance, writes: "If working alone or with another worker (other than another Doukhobor), their work appears to be quite satisfactory. However, if two or more Doukhobors work together it seems that they do not accomplish as much work as they could." Another employer states: "In groups they tend to slow down. As individuals or working with other nationalities they do quite well."

It is in groups that the somewhat negative or hostile attitudes are "talked up" and come into play as another weapon, a sort of concerted slow-down or passive resistance on the job. It is provoked in some cases by friction with other workers, and in other cases by conscious or unconscious opposition to the employer. It is perhaps another manifestation of the problem that Dr. Shulman has pointed out elsewhere—the difficulties that Doukhobors face in communication with others, and particularly the inhibitions which they have against reacting in kind to aggressiveness or hostility.

The problem of the Doukhobors' relationships with other workers draws a good deal of attention. A number of employers have stressed that Doukhobors do not work well with others, and that other workers do not like to work with them. This appears to depend primarily upon how, and in what proportions, they are mixed with other workers. One employer states: "Best results from Doukhobor workers are obtained by having them at all times in a minority among the crew. Otherwise, absenteeism and slow-downs are certain to be a problem. On the other hand, individuals working with Canadians create few unusual conditions."

In direct contradiction to this view, however, a foreman in a large sawmill who has had notably good results with a predominantly Doukhobor crew has this to say: "I've found that if you have them divided about fifty-fifty (i.e., Doukhobors and others), or if the Douks are in the minority, then you'll have trouble. The others 'ride' the Douks; they're down their necks all the time. Then the Douks bunch up and make with the passive resistance." The foreman also finds that an individual non-Doukhobor cannot be put to work in a Doukhobor crew. The Doukhobors isolate him, and they "gang up on him" one way or another, and he cannot last. There should be at least two such workers in a crew, to give one another support.

On the other hand, as some of the quoted statements indicate, most employers seem to find that if Doukhobors are employed as separate individuals among predominantly non-Doukhobor crews, they are as satisfactory as any other workers, and frequently more so. This would depend, of course, on the individual—how acculturated he is, to what degree he is accepted by the other workers, and in general how secure, emotionally and economically, he feels. In some cases a good deal of tension and insecurity may arise. One hears numerous instances of an apparently successful and well-adjusted Doukhobor with a good job and promising career throwing everything up, joining a Sons of Freedom group in a nudist demonstration, and going to jail.

The Sons of Freedom often constitute a special problem in labour relations, according to numerous employers, and special effort has been made in some cases to weed them out. The spokesman of one mining company states in a questionnaire: "Sons of Freedom try more tricks to stall or get out of work, and are more clannish, will speak their own language on the job, and so on." And the sawmill foreman quoted earlier claims that Sons of Freedom often do not work very well with the USCC and Independent Doukhobors. They tend to proselytize and "needle" the others, with the result that arguments flare up and operations are disrupted. He has dismissed a number of them over a period of years. On the other hand, he, like a number of other employers and plant or company officials, includes some Sons of Freedom members among his most able and dependable workers.

In general, Doukhobors seem to function most efficiently in small-scale operations where they can be on their own or in small contractor teams, as in logging and house-building. In large-scale operations the efficiency and dependability of Doukhobors as employees seem to depend primarily upon the efficiency and understanding of management in dealing with them. Their history has been one of extreme dependence upon a strong leadership that had a clear-cut policy, one that could chart the course for them and keep them at it. In the early days of settlement in British Columbia, as we have seen, the CCUB was a healthy going concern. Peter Vasilivich Verigin laid out clearly defined goals for the community and ruled with an iron hand. When the leadership and direction of the CCUB became erratic and inefficient under Peter Petrovich Verigin, the whole enterprise rapidly disintegrated.

In one large sawmill near Nelson, virtually all the employees are Doukhobors, except for some of the office staff and a few key men in the production line. The mill has one of the lowest rates of labour turnover and one of the highest rates of output per man-hour in the region, and the foreman (quoted earlier) with good reason has acquired a reputation for knowing how to handle Doukhobors. One of his cardinal tenets is to deal with them at all times as individuals, never in groups. "As individuals they are distinct personalities; in a group they're all the same—just a bunch of Douks, and you can't do a thing with them." Handling them as individuals includes taking account of their personal needs, such as allowing time off to get the hay in on the farm.

Participation in Trade-unions and Business Organizations.—As might be expected from the preceding analysis, there has been until recently a striking lack of participation on the part of Doukhobors in trade-unions and in business or trade organizations, service clubs, and other organizations that are important in establishing the economic and social status of individuals in urban communities. The Doukhobors definitely are not "joiners" of organizations in which other groups comprise the majority of participants.

The Associated Boards of Trade of the West Kootenay region count only a handful of Doukhobors among the more than 700 members. In the City of Grand Forks—a centre of Doukhobor population, with a sizeable number of Doukhobor-owned and -operated enterprises— only three persons of this group belong to the Board of Trade. In Trail also there are only three, and in Nelson only one. Comparably few belong to service clubs. The reasons for this lack of participation seem fairly obvious. The Doukhobors are concentrated in the ranks of casual manual labour and their economic and social status as a group in the region is based primarily upon this fact. Most of their businessmen have become established only recently, as a result of the wartime and postwar boom. The members of business organizations and service clubs are, in the majority of cases, the more long-established residents of the community who have built up a solid and successful business or status. Hence, even though the formal rules and practices of a business organization or service club may not exclude Doukhobors, the informal attitudes and actions of the members may.

More difficult to explain is the lack of participation on the part of Doukhobors in trade-unions, particularly as they are concentrated in the ranks of wage-earners. In other parts of the Province, unions are well organized in the very trades in which Doukhobors specialize to the greatest degree, namely, logging and sawmilling, carpentry and other building trades and, to a lesser extent, certain railway trades. In the West Kootenay region, unions have managed to maintain only a precarious foothold because of the dominance of Doukhobors in such trades and their apathy or opposition to unionism.

There seem to be a number of reasons for this, some of which have been dealt with earlier in other contexts. Doukhobors live, for the most part, in scattered farms and villages; in many cases they have to travel long distances to and from their jobs; there is the friction with and mutual dislike of other workers on the same types of jobs; they are concentrated in highly seasonal and intermittent types of employment; in some cases their short-run economic interest lies in competing with trade-unions rather than in participating in or cooperating with them; and, finally, there are the differences in cultural backgrounds and standards of living between Doukhobors and other workers in the same occupations.

The trade-union in western society has been the wage-earner's main means of protesting against the industrial system that employs him, and the means by which he organizes with his fellow-workers to achieve improvements that enable him to adjust to his job. Perhaps the most important goal of the trade-union from the point of view of the worker is security: economic security, in the sense of job tenure at an assured rate of pay, because he lacks an alternative source of livelihood; and security in personal or social relationships with other workers. Industrialization and urbanization have tended to weaken and destroy the old ties of family and village life and neighbourliness that once bound people together. Workers seek to re-establish such ties in a new form through the trade-union.

The trade-union does not offer such goals and attractions to the Doukhobors to the same degree. They are not as yet a predominantly urban industrial people. They still reside, for the most part, in their rural villages, where they can raise a large part of their food as well as meet some of their cash needs from garden-plots and farms. Their emotional identification is with their village neighbours, friends and relations, rather than with other workers in the occupations in which they are employed. And their method of protest against employers, as pointed out before, is through high labour turnover and passive resistance on the job, rather than through organized strikes and other formal trade-union action.

The Brotherhood of Carpenters and Joiners in the Nelson district perhaps best illustrates the vulnerable position of trade-unions in this region. In most cities or towns this union has organized all, or practically all, carpenters and has agreements with all builders and contractors establishing closed shop and apprenticeship regulations as well as standard wages and working conditions for various categories of jobs. In the Nelson district, however, this union has managed to organize less than one-third of the Doukhobor carpenters, who comprise by far the majority in the trade in that area. In the union itself they are considered to be rather apathetic members. They are more lax than other members in such matters as attending meetings, participating in elections or other business, and paying their dues. Despite the fact that Doukhobors comprise the majority of members in the Nelson local itself, all the union officers are of Anglo-Canadian background. In Nelson City proper, the carpenters' union has agreements with all resident builders and contractors (including two Doukhobor enterprises) that hire carpenters by the hour, with the exception of a

ECONOMIC AND SOCIAL LIFE

sash and door company owned and operated by Doukhobors which, union officials claim, is paying its workers far below the union scale.

The union's main weakness lies in the fact that the majority of carpenters employed in Nelson and other smaller centres in the district are Doukhobors who commute from farms and villages in the surrounding countryside. As they are more scattered and mobile, and work at a wider range of jobs during the course of the year, they are more difficult to organize and keep organized than are the more stable and settled Anglo-Canadian or other workers in the same trade. Furthermore, from the short-run economic point of view most Doukhobors probably feel they stand to gain by remaining outside union ranks. Because of its weakness and limited membership and jurisdiction, the union has not been able to enforce the apprenticeship rules, minimum standards of competency and workmanship, and rates of pay that apply in most industrial communities. This has enabled many Doukhobor "rough" carpenters to claim the status (and in many cases the pay) of fully qualified carpenters. And it has enabled them to compete with increasing success with established contractors hiring their men by the hour. Growing numbers of Doukhobors have formed crews of contractors who take their wages in the form of shares out of the full contract payment rather than in payment by the hour. By accepting payment in shares that amount to less than the union's hourly rates, such crews are in many cases able to underbid established contractors using hired crews.

The Brotherhood of Carpenters and Joiners and other unions are better organized in Trail and vicinity, and a larger proportion of Doukhobor carpenters belongs to the union. The main reason appears to be that in that area Doukhobors are a minority of all carpenters, and the others are thus able to exert more effective pressure upon them to join the union and live up to its standards.

The situation has changed considerably during the past three years, as the Brotherhood of Carpenters and other building trade-unions have been carrying out more intensive organizing campaigns throughout British Columbia. In 1952 the various locals of the Carpenters' Union throughout the Province were brought together into a newly formed "Provincial Council," to launch a co-ordinated drive for higher rates of pay and for a closer approach to equality in wages and working conditions. As one by-product of this campaign, Carpenters' Union locals in the West Kootenays expanded their membership, particularly among Doukhobors, and carried out strikes for wage increases and other goals.

An even greater lack of organization in the West Kootenay region applied for a long time in the logging and lumber industry. In most regions of this Province the International Woodworkers of America (CIO-CCL) has enrolled the majority of loggers. In the Nelson and Trail districts, however, they were practically untouched, although in recent years the union has been undertaking an ambitious organizing campaign among the Doukhobors. The most important factor, again, appears to be the competition of Doukhobor contractor crews. Under this system, as in building construction, the w ers receive their wages as shares of the full contract payment. In other cases, the Doukhobors who get the contracts from lumber companies hire the workers and pay them by the hour or on a piece-work basis. In any case, the major lumber companies have found it more economical to obtain their main pole and log supplies from contractors than to establish their own logging camps.

The IWA did not have much more success until recently in organizing the more stably employed sawmill and planing mill workers, the majority of whom are also Doukhobors. Up to 1954 in the Nelson district, for instance, the union had an agreement covering the workers in only one plant, the sawmill of the Glacier Lumber Company, and this local was virtually inactive for several years. The Trail district was similarly unorganized.

The IWA, like the Carpenters' Union, has been carrying out an intensive organizing campaign in the northern and southern interior regions of British Columbia during the past two years, with the objective of bringing wages and working conditions in those areas up to the standards applying on the coast. According to union spokesmen, the IWA has been notably successful in enrolling hitherto unorganized Doukhobor workers in the West Kootenays. This campaign culminated in the bitter and long-drawn-out strike in the interior lumber industry during the fall and winter of 1953. Doukhobors, from all accounts, participated as fully as did others in this dispute, although their role appeared to be more passive. Whether or not the union can continue to maintain their interest and support remains to be seen.

The most important union in the West Kootenays—until recently at least—has been the International Mine Mill and Smelter Workers, with its large membership base of 3,000 to 4,000 in the Consolidated Mining and Smelting Company plants at Trail, as well as workers in smaller mines in nearby districts. An intense struggle for jurisdiction raged for several years between the rival United Steel Workers (CIO-CCL) on the one hand, and the IMM & SW, which has been expelled from the CIO and CCL, on the other. This struggle ended in victory for the IMM & SW in 1953. In a survey made in 1950 of the total 4,000-plus members in the two unions, 72 were found to be Doukhobors—19 in the USW and 53 in the IMM & SW. In contrast to the other trades listed above, practically all Doukhobor employees of the CM and S were and are union members. The explanation here lies, of course, in the fact that they are such a small minority among the other workers in this company, and have been subjected to intense pressure in the course of rival union campaigns.

THE PRESENT PROBLEM

Economic and social security in the traditional Doukhobor community required self-sufficiency on the land and strong leadership. The Doukhobors in British Columbia today are virtually both landless and leaderless. Only a minority enjoy clear title to their land. No one leader is accepted widely enough to unify them.

It is generally acknowledged that the Provincial Government's policy with regard to the Doukhobor lands was one of expediency when it was first adopted in 1939. Today, some fifteen years later, it is increasingly unsatisfactory. The Doukhobors feel their tenure to be very insecure; they are never sure that the Government will not "sell the land out from under them." Hence they fail to use it efficiently. They do not invest enough in it even to maintain the present facilities, let alone to put in new and much needed improvements. The productivity of the land is declining and the scale of farming carried on by the occupants has been reduced to the point where it no longer provides a livelihood for more than a few. The vast majority, therefore, must depend upon outside employment, in which their position is marginal and insecure. They face widespread discrimination, due partly to work habits arising from their combined attachment to land and village, and partly to other factors in their cultural background. They are highly concentrated in the casual or seasonal types of jobs, and are vulnerable to frequent and extended periods of unemployment. They are in the larger Canadian society, but not of it. They have to depend upon it for their livelihood, but are not entirely accepted by other groups. They remain a separate and distinct element and are unable or unwilling to participate with other groups in social organizations and activities that would assure them acceptance and higher status.

Yet their own community life has all but disintegrated. The organization of major economic activities under the CCUB Ltd. appears to have been the main factor that held Doukhobor village communities together. Since its collapse and liquidation, nothing else has provided an adequately functioning social organization. Their villages are communities only in the sense that they are clusters of dwellings in which people reside, and, at that, increasing numbers of dwellings are becoming uninhabitable. With the widespread and growing use of automobiles and trucks, the Doukhobors are no longer tied to the village as they were once, and depend increasingly upon outside wage employment for their livelihood and upon outside communities for their recreation. Numbers of them every year buy individual lots and live in their own houses, outside the exclusively Doukhobor communities.

Thus, the USCC Doukhobors are becoming a group of people held together only by the bond of a particular set of religious beliefs that have very little to do directly with their day-to-day economic, social, and recreational life.

The situation has its dangers. The breakdown of USCC community life and the insecure position of many Doukhobors with regard both to land tenure and to their relationships with other groups in the West Kootenay region render them vulnerable to the influence of the Sons of Freedom. Perhaps the main attraction which the Sons of Freedom exerts over other Doukhobors is that they seem to provide an alternative form of brotherhood and an intense community life, of a sort, in place of that which for the USCC element has broken down.

One of the first and most vitally needed steps to deal with the problem of the USCC Doukhobors, then, is a suitable programme to enable them to consolidate their position of growing economic individualism. They should as soon as possible be enabled to acquire individual title to the lands they now occupy under Government trusteeship. This programme would have to take account of a number of factors, such as the investment which the Provincial Government already has in these lands, together with unpaid taxes and administrative expenses since the assumption of the trusteeship; disposition of the surplus funds now available in Saskatchewan after final liquidation of the CCUB Ltd. assets; the decision on qualifications of those entitled to buy land; the size of the parcels available to purchasers; and the conditions of purchase.

The experience of Saskatchewan and Alberta suggests that a settlement of the land problem should bring a measurable improvement in the morale of the Doukhobors and in their relationships with other elements in the population of the West Kootenays as well as with the Government. In the short run, perhaps, it might have the effect of reducing the number of Doukhobors available for wage employment in other industries, in so far as a number of them might become full-time farmers. And there is the possibility that for others their farming interests might compete more than they do now with their job requirements. In the long run, however, they should participate in industry more satisfactorily once the land problem is settled. For with a definite and secure interest in the community, they would have a greater propensity to invest and their economic incentives would be more long range and ambitious.

Any such programme for the USCC Doukhobors, however, cannot be considered separately from the problems presented by the Sons of Freedom. The latter, as pointed out before, helped prevent the sale of land and buildings to individual members of the CCUB when that enterprise went bankrupt. They could probably sabotage any similar programme today just as effectively. As long as the Sons of Freedom threaten the USCC element, the latter will be reluctant to buy land and invest in houses and other improvements.

It is more difficult to devise a programme for improving the condition of the Sons of Freedom. This group comprises, on the whole, the most marginal of Doukhobors. They are subject even more than the others to job discrimination and unemployment, they live in more isolated communities, their housing conditions are rougher, and their general standard of living is lower. They are caught, in a sense, in a self-perpetuating poverty cycle. Their depressed economic position creates feelings of frustration and resentment against injustices, real or imagined. This is part of the reason for their intense hostility to, and attacks upon, the Government and other outside agencies or groups. Retaliatory measures against them, such as jail sentences and job discrimination, help to keep them economically depressed.

If it could be assumed that the major problems of the Sons of Freedom are thus primarily economic in character, then presumably a programme similar to that proposed above for the USCC would be appropriate for them, too. Indeed, a certain number of individual Sons of Freedom might be qualified to participate in plans for buying tracts of land formerly owned by the CCUB Ltd.

A programme for economic rehabilitation of the Sons of Freedom would not in itself be enough, however. The primary motivating goal of most Sons of Freedom is not essentially economic in character. A prominent minority of the Sons of Freedom is now in the category of skilled and well-paid workers, or of substantial farmers and property-owners. A dominant goal of the Sons of Freedom as a whole is that of survival as a separate and distinct sectarian group, even if that means sacrificing all the economic and other benefits that Canadian society has to offer.

For such reasons, relocation of the Sons of Freedom in some other part of the Province has its attractions. Such a move is advisable in order to deal not only with the problems of the Sons of Freedom themselves, but also with those of other Doukhobors. It might be accompanied by the rehabilitation of those who do not wish to leave their present localities. A programme of relocation in an area with adequate land and timber resources, by removing the less successful and the more intransigent Sons of Freedom from the West Kootenays, would eliminate much of the compulsion and intimidation that have held the more economically successful members to the movement. It would provide a source of subsistence from the land for the Sons of Freedom as individuals. The clearing and cultivating of farm land, the building of houses and other structures, would supply a creative satisfaction and meet their need to acquire and accumulate material substance. Such activities might, for a few years at least, eliminate one source of frustration of the Sons of Freedom and provide the opportunity for rehabilitation meanwhile. Locating them in a separate area would also meet their demands for survival as a group, while at

90

the same time some of the need for aggression against others would thereby be removed.

The main issues likely to arise with regard to any proposed settlement of the former CCUB Ltd. lands are:—

(1) Division of the land and buildings for sale to qualified Doukhobors in individual parcels.

(2) Criteria for determining the entitlement of present occupants and other Doukhobors to buy land.

(3) Claims of the Provincial Government against the lands and buildings, comprising the following:—

(a) Net mortgage investment of $268,482.89.

(b) Accrued taxes on the land and buildings since 1942.

(c) Accrued costs of administration through the Land Settlement Board.

(d) Estimated costs of carrying out and administering the proposed allotment.

(4) Disposition of the $142,111.07 surplus left over from sale of other CCUB assets, and payment of other claims against these assets, in Saskatchewan and Manitoba.

(5) Claims of individual Doukhobor creditors of the CCUB recognized in Court judgments in 1938, amounting to more than $290,000.

While the assets of the Christian Community of Universal Brotherhood Ltd. were being liquidated during 1938-45 to pay the mortgage claims of the National Trust Company and the Sun Life Assurance Company, the Provincial Government took steps to prevent the Doukhobor occupants from being displaced from their houses and lands. In 1942 the Government concluded a cash settlement with the two companies, whereby with a net payment of $296,500 it assumed as trustee the title to the land and dwellings formerly owned by the CCUB. Since then the Provincial Government, through its Land Settlement Board, has administered these assets. The former occupants have been allowed to continue occupying the houses and communal dwellings and using the land and buildings. Each family is assessed a rent of between $30 and $60 a year, though a number of occupants—Sons of Freedom and their sympathizers—have refused to pay.

Some of the land has subsequently been sold by the Land Settlement Board, and the Government's claim has been correspondingly reduced by the amounts received from the sales. Its net investment at present amounts to $268,482.89.

It has become generally recognized that the present situation is unsatisfactory in a number of respects dealt with earlier in the *Report*. The usual problem of relationship with Government is complicated and worsened when the Province plays the role of landlord and the Doukhobor that of tenant. Meanwhile the cost has been heavy to the Government and therefore to the taxpaying public. The annual rentals do not even represent the going rate of interest on the mortgage investment in the lands and buildings. Added to this, the Government collects no taxes from these assets, and has to incur costs of administration. All concerned—the occupants, the Government, the taxpayer and the resident non-Doukhobor population of the West Kootenay region—are now losing.

The best way out seems to lie in selling the land and buildings back to the present occupants and to other Doukhobors who may be deemed qualified to purchase. There is some opinion among the present occupants that they would prefer to purchase and use the land on a cooperative basis. This, however, seems to represent a statement of orthodox belief rather than a practical policy. Members of the CCUB in Saskatchewan and Alberta readily bought land and buildings on the basis of individual agreements for sale when these were made available to them by the mortgage companies. Individual purchase has been advocated by some of the present occupants and is likely to be accepted in British Columbia if the Provincial Government should offer the land on this basis. The present occupants have shown little or no inclination to operate their holdings on a cooperative basis since the CCUB collapsed, and at present the relationships among them are often individualistic in the extreme. They have neither the organization nor sufficient inclination for any general programme of cooperative purchase and use of the former CCUB assets now being held by the Government.

The most appropriate policy, then, would be to divide the land and buildings into allotments comparable on the basis of soil quality and other factors, and to sell a lot to each individual entitled to buy. Any individuals wishing to do so could form cooperatives to operate their holdings. In some cases it might be found impossible or uneconomic to divide land and certain buildings into individual holdings, and these might have to be disposed of as integrated units to cooperative or corporate groups of some kind. Some submarginal land might well be left as community pasture or wood-lot.

CLAIMS OF THE PROVINCIAL GOVERNMENT

Any settlement in terms of selling the land and buildings back to the present occupants and other Doukhobors must take account of the Provincial Government's claims against the assets. These comprise the following:—

(1) The net mortgage investment of $268,482.89.

(2) Unpaid taxes accruing from 1942.

(3) Accrued cost of administration of the former CCUB lands and buildings by the Provincial Land Settlement Board.

In addition to these claims, there will be further expenses from carrying out the proposed allotment of land and buildings. These would include such items as the following:—

(1) Costs of surveying the land and subdividing it.

(2) The cost of a Doukhobor lands allotment organization which should be established to settle claims.

(3) Cost of necessary dismantling or moving of houses and other buildings.

DOUKHOBOR CREDITS AND CLAIMS

Allowances would have to be made at the same time for the credits and claims of the present occupants and other Doukhobors. These comprise the following:—

1. The accrued annual rentals paid to the Land Settlement Board. These amount, to date, to approximately $70,000 and would approximately equal the accrued taxes noted as a claim against the assets.

2. A sum of money amounting to $142,111.07 left over after the final liquidation of CCUB assets in British Columbia, Alberta, Saskatchewan, and Manitoba, and payment of all Court-approved claims against the assets (except for the claims of individual Doukhobor creditors). The $142,111.07 is now being held in trust in Regina and is subject to disposition by Court order.

In one respect the simplest and most obvious line of policy would be to assign this money to the Land Settlement Board and thus reduce the Government's claim from the present $268,482.89 to $126,371.82, plus the other items, including unpaid taxes and costs of administration. The land and buildings could then be sold to the present occupants and to other qualified Doukhobors at reduced prices which would, *in toto,* net the Provincial Government the reduced amount and also would make it easier for lower-income Doukhobors to take advantage of the opportunity to buy.

On the other hand, it might be better if the land were sold at an over-all price that would cover the present claims of the Provincial Government plus estimated additional expenses of the land allotment programme as noted above. The surplus $142,111.07 might then be held as a contingency fund to cover any extra or unforeseen expenses incurred in the process of carrying out the programme. Any surplus left over after the initial transfer of the land and buildings to the individual purchasers had been completed could be used to contribute to the cost of such facilities as irrigation.

3. The claims held by a number of individual Doukhobors against the assets of the former CCUB by reason of loans made to the CCUB or its executive during the late 1920's and early 1930's. Some $290,000 of such claims was recognized by Court judgment in 1938, when the CCUB was going into bankruptcy and receivership.

If the individual Doukhobor claimants are to be repaid, presumably they would have to get their money from the proceeds of the proposed sale of lands and buildings to the present occupants and other qualified Doukhobors. This would require setting an over-all price on the lands some $290,000 higher, to cover not only the estimated claims and expenses of the Provincial Government, but of the individual Doukhobor claimants as well.

It should be pointed out that to meet the claims of the individual Doukhobor creditors of the CCUB would involve all sorts of administrative difficulties, and would cause widespread friction among the Doukhobors themselves. A number of the latter have expressed the opinion that the creditors happened to be among the more fortunate members of the CCUB who were able to earn money at business or employment outside the Community itself. Other Doukhobors who were equally industrious members of the CCUB did not have the money to lend because they were working for it at nominal wages or for payment in kind. They feel strongly that the creditors should not now receive special consideration from the Provincial Government in any final settlement of the land problem.

Moreover, the creditors whose claims were reduced to Court judgment do not represent *all* individual Doukhobors who lent money to the CCUB. The Court judgments were rendered in the name of trustees in a number of villages, who submitted the claims to the Court on behalf of individual creditors residing in the village. In a number of other villages, however, the trustees did not take such action.

THE CRITERIA FOR DETERMINING ENTITLEMENT TO PURCHASE LAND

1. Membership in good standing in the CCUB up to the time that it went into receivership. The family of a deceased member should receive full consideration. Most of the adult occupants were members in good standing of the CCUB and are now members of the Union of Spiritual Communities of Christ.

A considerable number of the present occupants are Sons of Freedom, some of whom may nevertheless have been paid-up CCUB members at the time of bankruptcy. A useful criterion for determining eligibility would be the record of rental payment to the Land

Settlement Board since 1942. Any occupant who had consistently refused to pay rents to the Land Settlement Board should be disqualified from opportunity to purchase an individual tract. On the other hand, a person who had been delinquent in payments for one or two years might be allowed to qualify if he paid up the back rent.

A number of Doukhobors who have since become Independents, and moved away from the Community lands, might be qualified, as paid-up members of the CCUB in 1938.

2. In basing the main qualification for purchase of land on paid-up membership in the CCUB up to the time it went into bankruptcy in 1938, a question of equity arises, as to whether it is entirely satisfactory to take the year 1938 as the critical one. Again, a number of CCUB members during the depression were willing but unable to pay their membership assessments due to unemployment and indigency. Should these people or their legitimate heirs be denied the opportunity to buy land, in favour of those who were more fortunate during the 1930's? The whole question of membership in good standing will bear more investigation by the land allotment organization. Perhaps the most feasible policy would be to keep a proportion of land out of the market until all claims could be dealt with.

<h2>ADDITIONAL POINTS</h2>

By and large, the most feasible policy would require the minimum displacement of the present occupants. That is, as far as possible each qualified individual should be enabled to purchase an individual tract, including house and other buildings, on land he now occupies and uses.

A major difficulty in this regard lies in the location and distribution of houses and other buildings. These, in many cases, are clustered close together in villages. Each family has the use of scattered plots or strips of land lying outside the village. How can the houses and buildings be sold to their occupants or to others having qualified claims and at the same time the land be sold to them in usable parcels?

Three or four alternative methods for meeting this problem seem to present themselves:—

1. Villages might be broken up and dispersed, and the occupants moved to the tracts which they have bought. In many cases the houses and other buildings, particularly the large community houses and adjoining flats, are in such a bad state of disrepair that this would seem to be the most economical action. The houses and buildings could be torn down and dismantled, and the salvageable materials either sold or given to the present occupants. Buildings worth keeping could be moved to new locations at a nominal cost in most cases, for most Doukhobor houses (apart from the communal dwellings) are fairly small and simple in structure.

2. In a few villages, however, some houses and other buildings are sound, but moving them would not be feasible. Perhaps the most appropriate policy would be to divide the village into individual dwellings and lots for purposes of establishing ownership. Each occupant would be allowed to buy the house he occupies and the lot on which it is located. Where the occupant has built and paid for his own house and other buildings, he need buy only the lot. In addition, each such occupant should be given opportunity to buy a holding in the land around the village, the total amount of land available to him amounting to one full share.

3. In certain communities such as Raspberry Village the buildings are of fairly recent construction (*circa* 1930) and in excellent condition. The communal houses are of brick construction and have been divided into self-contained apartment suites, and the occupants have spent a considerable amount of time and money putting in new fixtures and improvements.

Here it would obviously be impossible to divide up the land and buildings into individual holdings. In a case like this the most feasible policy would be for the occupants to form a local cooperative to purchase the assets. This could be carried out along the lines customary for cooperative apartment projects common in many cities.

IV

CHILDHOOD AND FAMILY LIFE

Claudia Lewis

INTRODUCTORY STATEMENT

THIS STUDY of Doukhobor child-rearing and family life was carried on during the summers of 1950 and 1951, through the method of participant observation. The main body of this chapter consists of analysis and generalization. Excerpts from the field notes on which they are based are included in the Appendix.

During the summer of 1950 I had the invaluable assistance of Gerry Kanigan, a graduate student at the University of British Columbia, and herself a granddaughter of Doukhobors. Because of her kinship with the Doukhobors, she was welcomed everywhere, and homes were opened to us. She had a fluent knowledge of Russian, which made it possible for us to enter these homes with a feeling of ease in communication and participation. We lived not so much as guests but as members of the family, doing our share of the household work and participating in all aspects of the daily life. Our connection with the Research Committee was made clear. I explained my purpose to the people as a desire to contribute to a better understanding of what Doukhobors are really like; it was important for me to be able to tell others, I said, how Doukhobors really lived in their homes and how they brought up their children. In general, the Doukhobors seemed to me to welcome this attempt to help straighten out their situation. There undoubtedly was suspicion in some quarters, but the families with whom we lived and had the majority of our contacts were most hospitable, friendly, and accepting of our presence. In no instance would any Doukhobor receive us as paying guests. We had to find ways to repay the hospitality as best we could, through gifts and helpful sharing of work.

During these two summers—1950 with Miss Kanigan and 1951 by myself—I lived in five different Doukhobor households, varying from a period of a few days to several weeks in each household. There were a number of overnight visits with additional families. The localities in which I made my observations included Krestova, Appledale, Winlaw, Claybrick, Glade, Blewett, Nelson, Brilliant, Ooteshenie, Pass Creek, Raspberry Village, Castlegar, Robson and Grand Forks. There were Sons of Freedom, Independents and USCC Doukhobors among those I lived with, and some who were in the process of transition from the USCC to the Sons of Freedom.

ANALYSIS OF THE NATURE OF DOUKHOBOR CHILDHOOD EXPERIENCE AS IT
PERTAINS TO THE SONS OF FREEDOM PROBLEM

One of the strongest impressions that emerged from my two summers with the Doukhobors was of the diversity of personality among adults and children alike. I did not find it possible to put my finger on any one pattern of personality characteristics which could clearly and reliably distinguish "the Doukhobor" from anyone else.

I was acquainted with children within the same sect, the same village, the same neighbourhood, who were poles apart in their personality development. That is, some were outgoing, friendly, unafraid, expansive in their natures, healthy, and beautiful to look at. Such children were extremely pleasant to get along with because they seemed at peace with their world, untroubled by strong needs to resist, defy, destroy, and yet by no means intimidated or too submissive. They seemed to be off to a very good start.

On the other hand, at the other end of the pole there were children so shy, fearful and constricted that they seemed to have lost all belief in themselves, all ability to function under their own steam. One felt in such children the possibility that severe personality damage might already have taken place—damage that would reveal itself in many devious ways throughout life.

The fact that such disparate personalities can exist within the same tight-knit group and under the aegis of an ideology as single-minded and as clear-cut as, say, the Sons of Freedom ideology only emphasizes the truth that people are not moulded by ideology alone. No matter what set of beliefs or values a culture tries to impress upon its children, these must always filter down to the children—who have diverse hereditary endowments to begin with—through a particular pair of parents, a particular set of family-life experiences.

Thus, though I believe that in general there is a mode of child-rearing among the Doukhobors, of all sects, which is looked upon as the more or less accepted one, "the way to bring up children," it is crucial to realize that what has been transmitted to the children must have been done with varying degrees of severity and flexibility, lenience and love, according to the particular households involved, and all the constellations of circumstances that can qualify the relationship between parents and children.

In fact, broadly speaking, a "way" of child-rearing among any group of people cannot be thought of apart from the impact of the total life experience of the group on the children. A "way" of child-rearing is conditioned by the whole web of experience making up the culture of the group. It does not consist solely of parental "practices"—of methods of weaning, methods of enforcing obedience, etc. It consists, rather, of the quality of experience that impinges upon the child. The way he is brought up has to do with the amount of love and security he feels, the kind of value he learns to put upon himself, the quality of his exposure to fears and frustrations and stresses, the attitude he learns to take toward authority. And all of these things are conditioned by the structure and vicissitudes of the social and economic life of the group of which he is a part and, most particularly, as his own parents are affected by this life.

Nor is child-rearing something that takes place between birth and, say, the age of six. Though many of the most crucial experiences for the child are those that he undergoes in his early years, life undoubtedly continues to "rear" him as he progresses along toward adulthood. The experiences of late childhood and adolescence may run counter to those of the earliest years, to some extent modifying their influence; on the other hand, later experiences may but implement the earlier ones, in a continuing stream that carves deeper with the years.

The "web of experience," then, has two dimensions. It is the totality of life impinging upon the child at any given moment, and it extends upward in time, as year follows year.

Obviously, this web of experience for many Doukhobors here in Canada throughout the past fifty years has been made up of continuous and consistent stress and strain.

I think the stresses impinging upon any one individual have poured in from different directions, all contributing to a totality of difficulties over a period of years: For many children there have probably been home lives too full of harshness, strictness, restraint, and a climate of anxiety; jail has taken parents away from children; there have been the restrictions, upon adults and children alike, demanded by the religious and moral tenets of the Doukhobor ideology; for young people there have been the difficulties attendant upon making a way in Canada where they felt themselves "different," and where "making a way" has been both an attractive and a guilt-producing pursuit; at all times there have been the economic difficulties, the land problem, the clash of ideologies, the social frictions within the group itself.

It is a likely hypothesis that this life of conflict and stress is what has led many individual Doukhobors straight to the Sons of Freedom, as I shall indicate in more detail later.

What I should like to concern myself with now are those aspects of childhood experience—early home-life experience—which may bring the Doukhobor child into his first encounter with serious stress. These are perhaps the most crucial stress experiences he will have. For if his home and his relationships within his family cannot give him an underpinning of belief in himself, emotional resilience, assertiveness, he is poorly equipped at the very outset to handle the conflicts he will meet as a member of the Doukhobor group in Canada.

Let us return now to my earlier statement that among the Doukhobors there is a "way to bring up children" which seems to be the more or less accepted way among all sects. Seen in historical perspective, and in terms of the experience of the group, it would be better to say that in the course of their history the Doukhobors have developed a set of feelings about the way children should be treated, their place in relation to adults, their obligations as new young members of the Doukhobor society learning its traditions and way of life. It is possible to see this set of values in action among many Sons of Freedom families today, where the application of them is probably almost as rigid as it was in the days of the grandparents in the early communities under Peter Lordly. In USCC families the framework is considerably loosened, yet the traces of it are still to be seen.

Let us look back briefly to the days of the grandparents, where we can see some of the child-rearing attitudes operating in relation to the social necessities of the group. From the early literature, and from accounts of the older people today, it is possible to build up a picture of the early Doukhobor community life in Canada as one where children were considered important members of the society, working and living along with the adults. ("At the age of nine I began a man's work. And I didn't even own a pair of trousers. Just wore a long shirt.") Indeed, in such close quarters and under such difficult pioneering circumstances, any other arrangement would have been extraordinary. It appears that there may not have been the dichotomy between child life and adult life that is familiar to us in our culture. Children in the Doukhobor communities were looked upon as little adults. This means that they experienced both restraints and privileges—restraints imposed by the need for adult Doukhobor decorum (remember, in this connection, the austerity of the Doukhobor religious and moral code) and the privileges of important participation in adult life.

In spite of this democratic element of participation, the relationship of parents to children was of an authoritarian nature. ("Oh, we had strict grandfathers in those days. I guess we really were afraid of them. If we didn't listen to them we certainly got our ears bent back!")

To understand this authoritarian relationship, we have only to remind ourselves of the kind of relationship that has always held between adult Doukhobors and their leader. It is not surprising that in their own households Doukhobor parents would mirror with their children the kind of control and discipline which they in turn look for and want from someone stronger than themselves. The Doukhobor dependence on the leader is well known. The attitude toward him, now as fifty years ago, is that of submissive children to all-powerful parent. The leader will tell them what to do, will lay down the laws for conduct, will grant permissions. ("We asked Peter

Lordly's permission to move away from the Community when my father was ill, and it was granted.")

The term "authoritarian," in fact, when applied to child-rearing, implies an attitude on the part of parents that they are the undisputed authorities, with powers that they may exercise over children solely by virtue of the authority vested in them; in such a system of relationships the "good" child is the one who has learned immediate obedience. This can often involve a very early moulding of the child to adult standards of behaviour, frequently through the medium of physical punishment. It is easy to see that in Doukhobor life, where the adult code involves so much strict control, the repressions and restraints demanded of children, in the name of obedience and conformity to the social mores of the group, may have been of a manifold nature.

"Authoritarianism" in parent-child relations, whether in Doukhobor society or as found in other cultural groups, is perhaps best clarified if one keeps in mind the opposite kind of relationship, which is finding great favour on this continent today. In this kind of parent-child relationship, "authority" indeed has not gone by the board, but has become more democratic in nature; there is recognition of the need of young children to acquire slowly the ways of the adult world; there is tolerance for childish impulses and mistakes and an emphasis on gradual growth in *self*-control rather than on an arbitrary control imposed by external authority *per se*. Initiative and independence are more valued than submission.

The danger in the authoritarian way of bringing up children, psychologists believe, is just this: Too often the results are submissiveness, emotional repression, and constriction of the manipulative and adaptive powers, with the fomenting of underlying hostile drives that may break out in indirect ways, throughout life, particularly if crisis situations arise to threaten what balance the individual may have achieved with his social environment.

It is easy to see that the dangers are particularly great where authoritarian parents have exercised their "rights" with a great deal of harshness, severity and repressiveness. On the other hand, where the feeling that flows through from parent to child is benevolent, the results in terms of personality formation may be quite different.

It is my impression that within this general authoritarian framework among the Doukhobors, there have been both kinds of parents—the benevolent and the harsh. Indeed, it is highly improbable that children such as I described in my opening paragraphs—expansive, outgoing, self-confident—could grow in these directions except in a benevolent atmosphere.

However, the likelihood is very great that in many Doukhobor households over the past fifty years the quality of feeling that has

101

come through from parent to child has been fraught with irritation, severity, impatience, harshness, repression. Many such cases were brought to light by Dr. Shulman's interviews with imprisoned Sons of Freedom. It is not hard to understand how this could be the case among a group of people so exposed to stressful circumstance.

Let us look now at some of the specific Doukhobor expectations relative to the behaviour of children in the early years of home life, keeping in mind that what I am sketching here is the traditional framework, with its set of practices through which parents transmit feelings. Though the experiences of childhood in Doukhobor life must be seen in their totality—the restraints imbedded in the privileges, it may be simpler for us to focus first upon the restrictive potential in the framework. Indeed, the basic attitude underlying this framework, privileges notwithstanding, has strong leanings in the direction of restraint for children. Where the particular parents involved have used the framework to the full as an outlet for their own hostilities, irritations and insecurities, it seems very likely that the groundwork is being laid for the kind of personality structure that may be strongly attracted to the Sons of Freedom, as a way of resolution of conflict.

This is not to suggest that all members of the Sons of Freedom have been drawn to the sect solely on the strength of their individual personality needs. Many—like the young people in Krestova—have grown up with the Sons, and have taken on the Sons' beliefs and ways because they were taught to do so. The code of their own social group has been strongly impressed upon them.

However, the rapid increase of the sect, as it has drawn in members from the ranks of the other Doukhobors, raises the question: Why do some Doukhobors go over to the Sons, and others not? This is one of the phenomena which makes it important to look into the matter of personality structure, and the possible contribution of childhood experiences to the constellation of needs activated in Doukhobor life today and satisfied with the Sons.

ADULTS COME FIRST, CHILDREN SECOND. CHILDREN MUST SHOW RESPECT, DEFERENCE, OBEDIENCE; MUST KNOW THEIR PLACE

A Doukhobor child is not expected to show any resistance or dawdling when an adult asks him to bring in the wood, go draw a pail of water, go pick some peas, go look after the baby, etc. The alacrity with which Doukhobor children jump up to do the adult's bidding, generally speaking, is a very noticeable aspect of their relation to their parents. I frequently had the feeling, when I was listening to these parental commands, that I was witnessing the exercise of arbitrary power.

The deference which children must show to adult authority has an institutionalized, or ceremonialized form. There is a custom still in existence—though I was told that it was commoner a generation ago than today—which requires children to bow down low before the parent, touching the forehead to the ground, to ask for forgiveness when there has been misbehaviour (breaking a glass, etc.). A child as young as one and a half years may be expected to execute this bow. (Compare with the ceremonial practice among adult Doukhobors of bowing to the ground. This is found even out of ceremonial context at times. I recall seeing an old grandmother bowing to the floor before me and several other members of the Research Committee, when she was asking for help, "in the name of Jesus Christ.")

That Doukhobor children have learned well the deference to adults, the sitting back and taking second place, is very noticeable whenever children and adults are gathered together. The children are present but they do not interrupt; if food is served and there are not enough places at the table, it is always the children who will eat at the second round. A wedding and funeral feasts the children will be fed *after* the adults—it is immaterial how many hours pass. (Of course, the children may nibble in the kitchen. No one wants them to go hungry). If neighbours are gathered together to sing in the evening, and the children who are present begin to get sleepy, there is no hurrying off to put them to bed. They will just have to be sleepy, that's all, while the parents have their evening out. It is an adult-centred world.

CHILDREN MUST NOT BOTHER ADULTS WITH NOISE. IT IS A PARENT'S RIGHT TO SILENCE A CHILD NO MATTER WHAT HE IS THINKING, DOING, TRYING TO COMMUNICATE

This is of course closely allied to the point just made about the expectation that children shall show deference to adults, and that adults may command at will. I have separated it out because the command for silence is indicative of the kind of restraint upon childlike impulses that is so often part and parcel of the authoritarian attitude. Very young children find it extremely difficult either to keep still or to sit still for long, and unreasonable demands for quiet can be felt by them as a severe restriction. (However, it seems quite possible that in some instances the necessity to keep still may seem to Doukhobor children a small price to pay for the privileges their good behaviour will buy for them—attendance at weddings, funerals, and other important adult functions; inclusion when guests are present, etc.)

There is, of course, tremendous variation among Doukhobor parents in the amount of noise they are willing to put up with from their children. Some seemed to me very tolerant of the "normal" noise of childhood; others tended to hush up the children whenever their play, even if it might be in an adjoining room, became the least bit boisterous. This was perhaps more true of parents in Krestova than elsewhere.

A few parents had a tendency to hush up their children's talking, if it became a trial to them to listen to, in a way which seemed to me simply to wash the children aside as individuals with feelings and needs. They might interrupt them with "Keep still, you talk too much, go play." Though this is certainly not the lot of all Doukhobor children, I repeat that the important point for us to remember is that where parents feel they have this prerogative, culturally sanctioned so to speak, there are bound to be some parents who will make use of it in over-severe abusing ways.

Allied to this expectation that young children can and should restrain their noise is the expectation that children should stand or sit quietly for long periods of time. The children at Krestova, ages approximately six to twelve, who were brought to the meeting-house to sing for our Committee members on Sunday, were required to stand quietly, in traditional formation, for a period close to two hours. Restless hands of the little fellows were tucked into overall fronts by the teacher standing near; wiggling bodies were gently turned to straight-front positions.

Along with the quiet standing goes the rigorous discipline of "Russian School," held during the winter months for the purpose of teaching the children the long graces, prayers, psalms. It is true that the Doukhobor children—today particularly among the Sons of Freedom —accomplish this memorization remarkably, beginning as young as age four or five. It is certainly possible that for some children this is pleasurable and easy learning, imbued as it is with ceremonial significance, and the sense it may convey of meaningful participation in the ceremonial life of the group. It also seems possible that for others this kind of drill may carry with it heavy burdens.

BABIES MAY BE EXPECTED TO LEARN TO CONTROL THEIR ELIMINATION PROCESSES IN THE FIRST FEW MONTHS OF LIFE

This is another of the restrictions on natural physiological impulse. Possibly the feeling prompting it is related to the general Doukhobor stress upon cleanliness. (The majority of Doukhobor homes are spotlessly scrubbed, and the Saturday bath in the steaming hot bath-house is a widespread institution. Children and adults alike are generally very clean in appearance).

Child psychologists are for the most part agreed today that a very early training process forces the child to controls that run counter to his biological needs, which should have expansive outlet in the years of infancy. The dangers are particularly great if the training is enforced rigidly and inflexibly, with accompanying harshness and punishment.

I did not actually see this training process in enough Doukhobor families to make me feel that I can generalize as to the way it is usually handled. It was my impression, however, that the training aims to teach the baby to be able, eventually, to give some sort of signal when he needs to eliminate, so that the mother can take him to the proper place. In one home I observed a baby of fourteen months well able to give this signal (a grunting sound) for both urination and defecation. She was never placed upon a potty and asked to perform. The time of elimination was left up to her, which gave her a good measure of autonomy in the matter. In fact, this seemed to be generally true of all the young children I knew. Once toilet-trained, there was no pressure upon them to have a bowel movement at any one specific time of the day.

In the case of this fourteen-month-old baby, the mother had begun the training at two months. I do not have information about what happened between two and fourteen months, how early the "signal" was mastered, and at what price in punishment or strain for the baby. Such areas as these need amplification in further study. I am inclined to feel, however, that there is usually lenience and gentleness on the part of the mothers, since Doukhobors are generally very tender with their infants.

Another mitigating factor may be the circumstance that while he is undergoing this training the Doukhobor baby is still enjoying all the comforting pleasures of sucking and of being warmly mothered.

The fact remains, however, that a very early control of a natural physiological process is expected.

CHILDREN SHOULD NOT BE GIVEN ANY SEXUAL INFORMATION. SEXUAL CURIOSITY IS SHAMEFUL

Everywhere I felt among Doukhobors a heavy taboo surrounding everything connected with sex. I was told by one informant that no sexual information is given to young people in preparation for marriage, and that girls are not prepared for menstruation. In the old days, children used to be told that "babies came from the river." This myth is still in use among present-day mothers. Even where it is not, there is general reluctance to open up the subject with children, or to accept their natural curiosities and explorations as anything but shocking and shameful. Thus very early another restriction is introduced into one of the areas of life where unrestriction and easy acceptance in childhood are crucial for healthy development.

One mother expressed to me the feeling of "shock" when some young children in the neighbourhood were discovered examining each other, and when one little girl was found "with her panties down, patting herself, obviously something she had been taught." This incident reveals the fact that Doukhobor children do masturbate. Indeed, I occasionally observed a furtive masturbation on the part of little boys, aged five to nine (hands in trousers pockets), as they stood on the outskirts of meetings or hung about watching older children's activities. A baby, who has not yet learned to be furtive about it, will get his hand smartly slapped for touching his genitals. Through punishment and taboo, a sense of guilt is built into children for activities which they do, nevertheless, engage in. This holds true of adolescents, likewise. I knew of a few illegitimate children among both the Sons and USCC, yet Doukhobor statements given to Dr. Shulman about the sexual code uniformly emphasize the "purity" of the ideal and the belief that Doukhobor youth are "more pure than English youth." Where there are transgressions of such a code, there must be room for great guilt.

The attitude toward sex as it pertains to childhood, among the Doukhobors, is but one axis of the total moral code—a code which favours abstinence and strict control of "the impulses of the flesh." Growing up as they do, under the muffled silence of this code, it is unlikely that Doukhobor children often witness intercourse in their homes, even though parents and children frequently sleep in the same room. One feels that parents would go to any lengths to prevent detection, ashamed as they are apt to be of sexual contact with each other. And if we are to believe the statements of many Doukhobors obtained by Dr. Shulman, this shame really does often culminate in a policy of abstinence or infrequent contact.

Ignorance, silence, shame, avoidance and guilt are the ingredients of the sex taboo as it operates in everyday life. With the Sons of Freedom, who insist upon the spirituality of their nude displays, and who explain their former brief practice of husband and wife exchange as a spiritual exercise, carried on without benefit of sexual relations, the avoidance becomes an active attempt at denial.

CHILDREN MAY BE SCOLDED AND PUNISHED HARSHLY

I did not often actually witness severe physical punishment, such as striking or beating, among the Doukhobors. On the other hand, many parents gave ready admission to the belief that "the best way to punish a child is to hit him. He understands that."

It can be seen that where there are no sanctions against physically laying hands on children, the door is wide open for irritable parents to abuse their children, in fact, this is exactly what had happened in the case of one of the timid, submissive children I described at the beginning of this chapter. His mother seemed very easily annoyed that summer, with her husband in jail and all the burdens of the house, children, garden and hayfield on her hands. This child was

106

subjected to a constant unpredictable volley of smacks, cuffs, yank-ings-around, which had succeeded in almost totally immobilizing him.

I repeat emphatically that I do not think such violent treatment as this is everyday practice in Doukhobor homes, yet the possibilities of its occurrence must not be minimized.

Much more common as a means of keeping children "in line" is a scolding tone of voice which I would call typically Doukhobor. I heard this lashing, whipping tone of voice used by mothers wherever I went, no matter whether they were Sons of Freedom living a marginal Krestova existence or USCC Doukhobors whose ways of life were much closer to those of their non-Doukhobor neighbours. It is a fierceness of voice that almost defies description, as though the mother has transformed her voice into a horsewhip, to secure instant obedience whenever she needs to. The very next moment she can be speaking in normal, pleasant tones again.

Also common as a means of punishing children and training them to obey is "bending the ears back." When I actually saw this done, it happened to be done mildly, without really inflicting pain on the child, and without a vicious or vengeful feeling on the part of the mother. However, here again, one must realize that the possibili-ties for abuse are legion.

In summary, let me emphasize again, I have been sketching here a framework of parent-child expectations within which the child can experience a great deal of restriction on natural impulse, including restriction on emotional expression (there is little room in the Doukho-bor child-rearing code for impudence, annoyance, anger, rebellion to parents); a framework within which parents who are themselves filled with bitterness or hostility, conscious or unconscious, can easily let out these emotions on their children, through all the doors open to them, under the guise of acceptable child-training. Serious person-ality damage to children may result from such repressions and emo-tional exposure.

Let us go on now to look briefly at some of the other kinds of stresses the Doukhobor child can encounter as he progresses through childhood.

If the Doukhobor child is allowed to go to school, there are pos-sibilities—not inevitable, to be sure—that he may suffer from his feeling of difference from other children. ("Oh, I suffered when I went to school, I can tell you. We Doukhobor children were made to feel *so* inferior. We wouldn't march, of course, and the others would taunt us so"—and spoken by one who grew up in a USCC community).

For large numbers of children, home life has been disrupted by the absence of parents in jail. In such cases, children are left in the care of one parent, or the babushka, or older sisters or other relatives.

107

That they have suffered material neglect is extremely unlikely, but the damage done when the fabric of home life is torn apart like this is hard to estimate, in terms of feelings of loss and the threat to emotional security suffered by the child. There is also the possibility that jailing of parents has had strong fear elements connected with it for some children. The statement of one mother about her young seven-year-old son who was suffering from nightmares and fears of "lions" should give us pause: "The night my husband was taken away, P. just wouldn't go to bed. He kept hanging around, all evening, till midnight. Finally, when I asked him why he wouldn't go to bed, he told me that he was afraid he'd dream of his daddy in jail. He was so scared of the idea of jail. Finally I took him in to Nelson to see his daddy, so he'd know that things weren't really so bad there."

Of course, for scores of Doukhobor children of all ages there was the disrupting Piers Island experience of twenty years ago, when the solid structure of home life was completely shattered by the removal not only of parents but of the children themselves from all their familiar associates and anchorings. The bitterness engendered by this experience, for children and parents alike, is still feeding into the resentful tide among the Sons of Freedom.

The Piers Island experience was, of course, a special circumstance, affecting only Sons of Freedom families. Other stresses which the growing Doukhobor child of any sect may encounter have to do with the language barrier, which may make him feel different from the outsiders he is thrown with at school and later at work; the restrictions which parents who are most loyal to the ideology may place upon dancing, amusement, adornment—all of which again emphasize the *difference* of the Doukhobor child. The adolescent Doukhobor girl learns how to embroider exquisitely, and piles up for herself a fine hope chest, yet at the same time she is taught that she must not attach too much importance to pretty things. The adolescent Doukhobor boy soon discovers that he is a pacifist, and must bear the brunt of this unpopular situation as best he can. Meanwhile he is making good money in the sawmills, and buying clothes and cars, while his conscience tells him this is materialistic and sinful.

The whole constellation of stressful circumstance in Doukhobor life in Canada is being fully presented elsewhere in this *Report*, and it is not my province to spell out all its details here. What I should like to do now is take hold of the threads I have introduced and tie them together, indicating briefly how these various strands lead to the Sons of Freedom.

It is my hypothesis that the Doukhobor who is attracted to the Sons of Freedom is driven there by his inability to deal with the conflicts of his life in Canada. It is likely that for him childhood experiences all along the line have fed strongly into the emotional current of values, beliefs, needs, which make it difficult for the Doukhobor to try new Canadian ways, break off independently and assertively, enjoy success without guilt. The Sons of Freedom offer an institutionalized way for a Doukhobor to build up a sense of self-esteem, or moral superiority and righteousness. The Sons of Freedom, in fact, can be thought of as an institution providing the only channel for drawing off those Doukhobors who have not been able to adjust to the direction of the main stream in Canada.

As we shall see now, the satisfactions that life as a Son of Freedom can provide are many for people who may have strong needs to express hostility, to protest and destroy, to suffer, to lean on a leader, to atone for guilt. And it is just such needs as these which can be activated in individuals who have been exposed, from earliest days, to emotional deprivation, restriction, parental severity, denials from within and from without.

Let us look first at this need to suffer, to atone for guilt, which can be so fully gratified with the Sons by the voluntary march to jail, or by burning one's home and possessions.

We know that the breaking of his moral and religious code can constitute one of the most common conflicts for the Doukhobor, as he comes in contact with Canadian life. Deserting the teachings of his people, as they pertain to the accumulation of material possessions and the taking up of worldly ways, must be fraught with a certain degree of guilt for almost any Doukhobor, under almost any circumstances. Adherence to his code is what brings him the sense of acceptance by a group. Moreover, the impress of the creed has been a strong one, sharpened by the Doukhobor's sense of difference from the outside world, and the prejudice and discrimination that he meets in the outside world.

But consider what the need for atonement may be for the Doukhobor who as a child was harshly punished for failures to live up to the expectations of conduct—failure, perhaps, to keep as quiet as he should during the long prayers or failure to repress sexual curiosity. Psychologists point out that harsh punishments for such transgressions can make a sensitive child feel so guilty that he may attempt to spend years of later life in the process of vicarious atonement.

The Doukhobor who slips over to the Sons may be one who is atoning not only for the transgressions of his adult life, but for those of his childhood. With the Sons, his conscience can be pacified somewhat by the return to the strict way of life of his fathers.

Another need that can be met by life with the Sons is the need to protest, to challenge authority. Of course, the need to protest against the Government may very well be felt to some degree by almost any Doukhobor, since this kind of behaviour has been built into the ideology through several centuries of economic and social circumstance. However, the truth remains that among the USCC there are some who are ready to grant that the Canadian Government has treated them well, except for the land situation. The USCC Doukhobors are never out camping on the highway, in "protest." It is the Sons of Freedom who are the challengers and protesters *par excellence*.

One cannot escape the assumption that among the Sons are those whose protest behaviour is the expression of more than the impress of an ideology. One suspects the presence of a drive stemming from a deeper source, such as experience with severe authority-figures in childhood. We know that a rigid exercise of authority can stir up in children not only guilt but also resentment, which may show itself in constant attempts to challenge anyone and everyone encountered in positions of authority throughout life.

It seems likely, too, that the hostility and destructiveness underlying the nude parading and arson among the Sons may not be entirely unrelated to repressive, restrictive authoritarian childhood experiences, which can set in motion hostile drives, deep below the inhibited surface behaviour. The fact that the destructive acts of the Sons are not sanctioned as a part of the ideology by any Doukhobor group except the Sons suggests the hypothesis that such practices have developed out of the hostile needs of individuals. It seems quite possible that among the burners and destroyers in the Sons are a number who would be considered delinquents in our society. The Sons have drawn them off and given them a "legitimate" way to function in society.

The outsider who has lived in Krestova has surely felt the impact of hostility on the part of certain individuals. When the older women approach in a nude parade, surround one, question, demand, affirm their beliefs, with mounting excitement, it is easy to detect the presence of a hard, unbending hostility in some of the faces. (Others, to be sure, reflect merely the enjoyment of a ceremony).

It is easy to believe, likewise, that the presence of Sorokin among the Sons at the time of which I am writing was another factor responsible for drawing in the other Doukhobors, relatively leaderless and unorganized as they were. The Sons, of course, did not look upon Sorokin as their hereditary leader, yet many of them called him "Uncle," looked to him for spiritual guidance, and took their numerous personal problems to him. His presence helped to hold the group together, to give it some cohesiveness and structure. The Doukhobors, as we know, have always leaned heavily upon the presence of a leader for support and direction. Is it possible that among those who are strongly drawn to the Sons at this time are those whose life experiences, from early childhood on, have moulded the very dependent adult? We have seen that the Doukhobor child-rearing code tends to encourage obedient, deferential behaviour. Under certain circumstances,

110

this kind of behaviour can become extreme submissiveness. The timid, passive, constricted child may become the adult who is lost without the directing hand of authority. He may seek support both where there is a leader and where there is a group strong enough to sustain him.

Lastly, it seems likely that the Sons of Freedom may exert a strong appeal for those Doukhobors whose lives have held too little opportunity for emotional expression, recreation, relaxation. Remember the long hours of prayers and psalms required even of little children by those Doukhobor parents of the most strictly religious convictions; remember, also, the restrictions on amusements such as dancing and movie-going encountered by many young adolescents in such families. ("At one time I remember they used to drag us out of bed on Sunday mornings to a meeting place where we'd have to pray and pray for hours. Oh, that was hard on children! Why, you can't sing and pray all the time. . . .")

Life with the Sons of Freedom in a stronghold like Krestova can be lived with a good deal of colour and pageantry of a sort. There is no doubt that the large ceremonial meetings, the huge feasts, the mass singing, the nude demonstrations and marches out under the sky are emotionally exciting. Life in the USCC at the present time can offer nothing comparable to this.

PRIVILEGES OF DOUKHOBOR CHILDREN

The foregoing analysis has emphasized the restrictive aspects of Doukhobor child life and the potentials for personality damage and feelings of personal failure stemming from the stressful nature of Doukhobor life. This emphasis has been made because of its bearing on the Sons of Freedom problem. It would be a grave mistake and injustice, however, to overemphasize the negative aspects of Doukhobor child-life, and before closing this section of the *Report* I want to point out again the obvious fact that many Doukhobor children have been and are being reared benevolently. Serious personality warping, as the result of early childhood experience, is not inevitably the lot of every Doukhobor child.

It is my impression that, especially among families of younger parents, in both the USCC and Sons of Freedom today there are a number where the old authoritarian parent-child framework has become considerably loosened. I was acquainted with several young mothers who were interested in newer ways of child-rearing and who, more importantly, were able to put them into practice, granting their children much more freedom to be happy, noisy, questioning children than almost any Doukhobor grandfather would approve of. It must go without saying that the stresses of Doukhobor life have been neither distributed among nor felt by all members of the population in the same degree. Those Doukhobor children who have grown up in homes where they have been able to experience dependable love and patience, protection and gentleness, have had childhoods fortunate in many respects.

Indeed, some of the experiences that Doukhobor children commonly have as they grow up should act as potent influences for good, that is, for building strength into the complicated fabric of personality. Here we can begin to speak of those "privileges" which were mentioned earlier as an important part of the total picture of Doukhobor child-life.

Though, generally speaking, the Doukhobors communicate to their children a high value on restraint, still there are large open areas where the child is free to do as he likes. This does not mean that the parents have turned turtle in their attitudes. Rather, this particular rural framework of living is one which gives everyone a certain amount of breathing room, just because it is rural, simple, non-industrialized. The parents have not developed certain of the worries that have gradually come to disturb the homes of those who are caught up in the demands of a more modern, urban, industrialized way of life. Many Doukhobor parents, for instance, allow children to stay up at night till they choose to go to bed, not because of a "permissive" feeling toward the children's wishes, but because their own comfort is not ruffled by either the idea of the late bedtime or the presence of the children.

Other areas of ease for children within the Doukhobor framework have to do with the loving care given to infants; the expectation that children shall participate in the adult affairs of the community (the children may be only passive onlookers, but their presence is always expected at funerals, weddings, meetings, etc.); the nurturance that is unfailingly provided—Doukhobor children know that any babushka in the community will feed them, look out for them.

The enjoyment of infants is a very noticeable feature of Doukhobor life. Where there is a baby, there are always people of all ages gathered around, to dandle, caress, and admire. Babies are kept sweet and clean, and are dressed daintily in a way that reflects the love showered on them. Grandmothers report that infants were swaddled in their time. I encountered no evidence that this restraining practice is in use today. There are some possible hang-overs, however. Some mothers wrap the baby very snugly in an outer blanket, in a way that pins his arms down, when he is to be carried around outdoors. And one young mother informed me that sometimes babies are still tightly wrapped, with arms down, when they are put to sleep. The older women explain the need for this, "Don't let him flutter his hands when he's asleep, or he'll scare himself." The feeling behind it is protective.

112

The acceptance of the presence of the children in all the ceremonial aspects of the adult life must give them a sense of importance, of responsible participation, very early. Children, particularly girls, share fully also in the adult life of the household. A Doukhobor girl of eleven is practically a grown woman, in the sense that she spends her day not in play but in living along with the adult women in the household, helping with the work, listening to the conversation. She is excluded from nothing. These mature little girls always impressed me as carrying their role very willingly, and not as though something unwelcome had been forced upon them.

Perhaps this important role in the home, from early childhood on, is one of the sources of the strength and dominance of the Doukhobor woman, so frequently noted by even casual observers at Doukhobor meetings. Her position fosters the growth of her self-esteem, and does not bring her so directly face to face with the conflicting situations the male is thrown into as soon as he begins to work in the outside world.

The picture for the male child today is something a little different. Because the source of livelihood in Doukhobor life is no longer exclusively in the tilling of the soil, the father in the Doukhobor home is away at work in sawmills and logging camps. It frequently happens that he cannot get home except for the weekends, if that often. The boy in the Doukhobor home has no opportunity to grow up beside his father, learning the adult skills from him, as the girl learns from her mother. He is more footloose, without function in the home. In Sons of Freedom families where the children are not sent to school, and particularly in some localities where Russian school is held only sporadically, his time is very much his own. His presence can even be felt as a nuisance, and some mothers are well aware of the drawbacks inherent for him in the present situation: "A boy has a harder time of it than a girl, because a girl can follow her mother around and learn all the work. A farm is a wonderful place for her. But these days the men aren't around on the farms, and a boy has nothing to be learning from his dad."

The boys do participate, however, in the ceremonial aspects of the life, as the girls do. They attend the meetings and funerals, and learn to recite and sing as boldly as the rest.

For boys and girls alike, one of the chief sources of ease and enjoyment is in the lack of pressure in everything that pertains to the taking in of food. This easy-going attitude is so consistent, so basic in the child-rearing pattern, and possibly has such far-reaching consequences, that it should be considered in some detail.

The infant first encounters this parental attitude when he finds that there is no pressure to give up the nursing bottle. A Doukhobor child of three with a nursing bottle is an everyday sight, everywhere. The

113

"pressure" to give it up does not come until about age four or five, when both parent and child develop some shame about it, if it is continued.

The fact that he uses a nursing bottle does not mean that the Doukhobor child is not also taking solid food. In the majority of homes where I saw these "bottle children" it was customary for them to join the family at meals, eating spottily and primitively at whatever they liked. When they had their bottles, two or three times a day, they would retire to the bedrooms, lie on the bed with the bottle, and wave their legs in the air like babies enjoying themselves, as they sucked.

Pacifiers—the store-bought nipple variety—are also used extensively. Again and again I saw an infant lying on his bed, his mouth plugged up with a large nipple. I knew one stocky two-year-old who sometimes kept his pacifier in his mouth as he ran about playing in the yard.

Of course, the mere fact that a three-year-old is still using a bottle does not tell us anything about what the significance of this is as a stage in his personality development. We have to know what the feeling of the parents is about it, what they are conveying to the child as they permit this long sucking period, what use the child himself is making of it.

For some Doukhobor children this lack of pressure to give up the sucking pleasures may imply the granting of a healthy freedom in this area to grow at the child's own pace (stemming undoubtedly from old peasant usage rather than from conscious "permissiveness"). This seemed to be the case with a child whom I shall call George, a three-and-a-half-year-old whose freedom to run and play actively all day was very unrestricted. George was alive, eager, curious, always tinkering with tools, climbing about, investigating. The atmosphere of his home gave him tremendous room for expansion. He was developing a strong personality—friendly, assertive, unafraid. His mother was one of the Doukhobor women who were not easily irritated by a child's noise, and this fortunate boy seldom met up with restrictions on his noisy play, or on the shouts and cries that came from his full-flowered baby mouth. Yet here was this active, independent child down on his bed two or three times a day with his bottle. (He ate solid food at the table, also, with freedom to take what he wanted as he wanted it.)

On the other hand, I recall an extremely submissive, passive five-year-old whose daily bottle was a symbol of something quite different. His mother was successfully making this little boy into a very dependent, constricted, quiet little fellow by her irritable and almost brutal demands that he not bother her. This child, lying on his bed with his bottle, was being the passive child whose passivity brought the reward of his mother's approval. It is scarcely to be wondered at that this child took almost no nourishment except his bottle.

114

It is not hard to believe that the Doukhobor parent—as we have seen, so ready to communicate restraint to the child—can very easily make use of the child's pleasure in sucking as a device to keep him quiet, passive, "no trouble," since the obedient child is the Doukhobor ideal. ("Why didn't you bring his pacifier?" a father asked his wife one day, when we were taking a long car ride and their two-year-old became restless and hard to handle because of the enforced inactivity.) The long sucking period, in some cases, may represent one of the passive aspects of child behaviour which is rewarded, and consequently plays a part in moulding the adult dependencies.

However, we must not overlook the positive values that can stem from the full satisfaction of the needs of the sucking or "receptive" stage in infancy—values related, biologically speaking, to the unblocked flow of the young body's dynamic energy, and, characterologically speaking, to the establishment of a basic capacity for receptive, generous, trustful expectations.

Of course, the Doukhobor child is getting his sucking gratifications from a long period of bottle feeding, not breast feeding. Yet where the mother provides the bottle with a mothering attitude, the meaning for the child can be much the same.

It is an interesting fact that during my whole two summers' time with the Doukhobors I happened to see only one baby being fed at the breast. Bottle feeding appeared to be much more common. I was told by various Doukhobor mothers that babies were nursed nowadays for only a few months and then were put on the bottle, in contrast to the "old days" when mothers nursed babies for a period of approximately three years. The reasons I was given for the change were varied, and probably should not be taken as having importance except for the mothers who expressed them. One young mother, I think with the intention of deploring the "new ways," said that mothers nowadays stopped nursing their babies after a few months so their breasts would not be pulled out of shape; another, with a hint of common Doukhobor deprecation of doctors, said that nowadays babies were often born in hospitals, and mothers were checked by doctors, and often were advised not to nurse their babies "because their milk was not very good. In the old days they didn't know whether their milk was good or not, so just kept on nursing the babies."

I do not have enough facts at my disposal to build up a sociologically accurate picture of the reasons for this shift from breast to bottle feeding. However it may be, it is clear that the Doukhobor child is not frustrated in his sucking needs. This gratification must carry with it, for almost every Doukhobor child, certain positive values, in spite of its potential as a passive refuge.

When the child has given up the bottle, somewhere between the ages of three and five, he still can look to eating as a source of gratification. Here, too, in the Doukhobor mores, there is as little pressure on the child as there is in the matter of his bottle. I rarely observed any parental concern over what a child ate or did not eat. Eating "problems," therefore, seemed practically non-existent. Children were free to eat what they liked at meal-times, and were not prohibited from extensive eating between meals. All through the summer day, on the part of both children and adults, there was a constant nibbling of sunflower seed, raw garden peas, huckleberries.

This means an enviable aura of ease for the child around the whole physiological process of eating, so often complicated with strain, resistance and struggle for children in our own culture. Such a "self-regulation" in the matter of eating can be conducive to both physiological and emotional well-being.

However, just as in the case of the bottle feeding, certain other meanings can accrue here when one looks at the total life picture, the total process of development. In short, one cannot escape the observation that the gratifications of the *mouth* become very primary gratifications in Doukhobor culture. (Think of the feasting, the singing, the talking among the adults.) One cannot help asking: Does the emphasis, all through childhood, on the pleasures of the mouth involve a fixation of the personality at an immature level? Is there a relation here between the expectation of this kind of gratification and the fact that the Doukhobor creed is a sex-negating one?

SUMMARY

In summary, let me restate the emphasis I have made. We have seen that the Doukhobor child grows up within an authoritarian framework which communicates to him, generally speaking, a value on controlled, submissive, obedient behaviour. This value may be conveyed by parents with either a benevolent or non-benevolent undertone, and with varying degrees of restriction and severity, according to the parents' personalities and the many circumstances that condition their attitudes toward their children. Where the child-training has taken place within a benevolent framework, there is considerable room for children to develop in an expansive, unconstricted way. Indeed, we have seen that the child-rearing framework, authoritarian though it is, contains a number of open spaces and privileges allowing for gratification of some of children's basic needs and encouraging a sense of participation in adult life. In spite of the fact that the Doukhobor parent may at all times communicate his value on the conforming, non-aggressive aspects of child behaviour, still the positive potential in the child's experience must not be overlooked. It is this positive potential which can give us insight into a possible source of many of the personal qualities of strength frequently encountered

116

among the Doukhobors, such as the endurance, the dignity, the tenacity, the friendliness in person-to-person relationships.

However, it has been my thesis that the Doukhobor child frequently experiences the framework of his life in a way that constricts him and lays the groundwork for a personality structure poorly suited to battle with the stresses of Doukhobor life in Canada.

The Doukhobor who grows up with repressed hostilities and a strong sense of guilt, coupled with a sense of failure, can be strongly drawn to the Sons of Freedom. Here he finds outlet and strength.

I conclude with this hypothesis, and yet here at the end I would like to return to the beginning, and to a reiteration of my first statements. It is extremely difficult to characterize "the Doukhobor" in terms of any one pattern of personality characteristics.

I would like to say, also, that I believe there is always room for the operation of unknowable—or unknown—factors.

The Doukhobor is a biological individual, as well as a creature of his social group and a product of his parents' training; there are elusive qualities of temperament in his make-up, as in anyone's, and the temperamental factors may well have something to do with the intensity of the emotional charge that draws him to the Sons of Freedom.

Likewise, the Doukhobor is a Russian peasant, trailing after him a long Russian history whose devious and multifold imprints upon character structure, values, beliefs, are largely unexplored and unknown to us.

In short, an hypothesis such as I have phrased here, and carved out of the relatively limited material available to me, needs to float upon a wide base of skeptical inquiry. Further study must implement it, enlarge it, and anchor it to a growing body of knowledge.

RECOMMENDATIONS

In the light of the foregoing analysis, it might seem on the surface that some programme of education in child-care for mothers, helping them to look at children's ways in a different light and placing an emphasis on children's great need for benevolent handling, might reach to the very core of our problem.

But child-rearing attitudes do not develop from rational persuasion. They follow upon, and are an inextricable part of, the larger structure of economic and social and religious life. If, and as, the Doukhobors can come to feel less threat to their existence, it is likely that "benevolence" will find its way into their feelings, and that new attitudes to children will evolve. Any steps the Canadian authorities can take toward ameliorating the grievances of the Doukhobors—that is, those with a factual basis—will probably ultimately ease the situation.

In the meantime there are a few large questions to consider relative to child-life among the Sons of Freedom today.

SHOULD CHILDREN OF THE SONS OF FREEDOM BE REMOVED FROM THEIR PARENTS OR FROM THE DOUKHOBOR GROUP, TEMPORARILY OR OTHERWISE?

It must be clear from the nature of my analysis of the Doukhobor situation that I would consider any removal of children from parents or relatives but an adding of fuel to the flame. The uprooting of child from home, of mother from child, is one way to start disaster in terms of personality warping. Such a policy of removal would but add grievance to grievance, protest to protest.

I believe it is generally recognized now that the removal of children from home during the time of imprisonment at Piers Island was a mistake, albeit one made with good intentions. In fact, the recognition that children need their homes is such an accepted consideration in social welfare work today that it is probably unnecessary for me to develop the point further here.

I am convinced that Doukhobor children do not suffer serious material neglect when one or both parents are away in jail. To remove them from the Doukhobor community at such times in order to provide physical care for them is the unwise way to alleviate the hardship. The sense of responsibility toward care of children among the Doukhobors is high.

WHAT ABOUT EDUCATION?

Education for Sons of Freedom children, if only through the elementary grades, would help greatly to break down the feelings of difference and inferiority that must accrue to them now through their ignorance, illiteracy, and language handicap when in contact with the "outside world."

The problem, of course, is to find a way to make schooling acceptable to them.

I know that among Sons of Freedom parents there are some who keep their children out of school, not because of their own passionate beliefs, but because of simple fear of what may happen to them if they transgress the code as it is held by the most resolute Sons of Freedom. In fact, a number of these parents would *like* to have their children in school.

Perhaps a beginning might be made in a community, not too close to Krestova (or any other strong Sons of Freedom centre), where the majority of families are Independents or members of the USCC. I can envisage a special experimental programme of education for Doukhobors which might eventually break through some of the great barriers of resistance by the Sons of Freedom. It might be necessary to call this programme something other than "school," since this word carries with it the weight of the whole Sons of Freedom struggle to disown that which makes other men successful, to abominate that which seems to threaten their own group solidarity. Acceptance of "school," too, would involve a prodigious backing-down. Possibly terms like "neighborhood centre" or "agricultural centre" could serve the purpose of sweetening the act of acceptance.

The programme of such a school might embody some of the following features:—

(1) Inclusion of Doukhobors on local School Boards.

(2) Superior teachers, specially trained in methods of conducting classes in an informal way, dispensing with the need for marching and any kind of regimentation.

(3) Dispensing with flag-saluting and the singing of patriotic songs.

(4) Teaching of the Russian language (possibly by a Doukhobor) as well as the English language, for children who want it. This, more than anything else, might break down resistance. I never encountered a Doukhobor of any sect who did not speak highly of the value of knowing many languages, and even the Sons of Freedom who decry the written word struggle at home to teach their children to read and write in Russian.

(5) A special reading programme, making as little use as possible of the standard graded school readers. It would probably not be possible to dispense with them altogether, but they might be supplemented even in early grades by excerpts or adaptations from Tolstoy, for instance, an author whom Doukhobors respect, and whose ideas they would feel to be a source of spiritual sustenance for their children.

(6) A vital social studies curriculum, which would take the children away from textbooks and the four walls of school. Sons of Freedom have a fear of books, a respect for learning in the practical areas of life; they like to see their boys learn carpentry, their girls learn housework skills. ("I had a teacher once who really knew how to make kids like school. She had us close up our books and took us out on long walks to see things and explore around.")

A social studies programme in rural Doukhobor schools would involve active studies of the local regions and their resources, trips to the neighbouring dams and mines and sawmills, special agricultural experiments. Integrated with these studies would be the children's work in carpentry, science, sewing, cooking, weaving, and other crafts. (It is possible that a well-equipped carpentry shop and a well-equipped kitchen in a school building could draw in the adults for an evening programme of adult education.)

History and geography in such a social studies programme should include history of the Doukhobors, along with study of other peoples in Canada.

(7) A rich music programme making every use of the Doukhobor child's astonishing fund of Russian songs and his ability to sing. His rich heritage could be supplemented by good folk-music from other cultures. To be acceptable to Sons of Freedom, the music programme in a school should probably not involve any learning of music from notes or song-books, at least at first, nor the introduction of any musical instruments. Use of the radio, however, would not be objectionable.

Such a school programme could have considerable value as an experiment in rural education, quite aside from its value to the Doukhobor population.

CAN OPPORTUNITIES FOR RECREATION BE PROVIDED?

There is ready acknowledgment among many of the Sons of Freedom today that their life does not provide everything they would like to give to their young people in the way of recreational activity that they consider acceptable. The trouble, they say, is that there is no longer a leader like Peter Petrovich Verigin to organize athletic games and song fests.

A recreational programme for both children and adults might help provide avenues for emotional expression, enjoyment of life, and feelings of achievement, now satisfied only through participation in Sons of Freedom ceremonies. Such a programme might be introduced as a part of the education scheme outlined above. It would probably be acceptable, however, if introduced by any agency that could come into a rural area with an athletic programme to offer. I say "athletic" advisedly. It would probably be necessary to start only with ball games, which are generally accepted by all Doukhobors, and to avoid anything else that might look like a social gathering, a party or a dance. Even folk-dancing is out of the question.

True, the Sons of Freedom population would probably also respond favourably to attempts to bring their young people, and themselves, together for singing, particularly if this involved publicity for their music. Radio broadcasts, recordings made perhaps by a Government office, invitations to folk-music specialists to come and acquaint themselves with Doukhobor music, publicity in the form of newspaper and magazine articles by qualified writers, all such efforts might help eventually to build up in the Doukhobors a little more self-esteem and legitimate pride.

Anything done to support and encourage the five-point programme of recreation and education for young people now launched among the USCC Doukhobors might be an excellent investment also. The more the USCC Doukhobors can feel their own organizational strength, and the more they can find ways to enrich their own group life, the less need will they have to look enviably toward the Sons of Freedom.

V

PERSONALITY CHARACTERISTICS AND PSYCHOLOGICAL PROBLEMS

Alfred Shulman

Basic Principles
Methodology
Parent-Child Relationships
Basic Personality Type
Stresses and Frustrations
Response to Frustration
Individual Differences
Doukhobor Personality as Related to Group Membership
Mental Illness
Recommendations

A PSYCHOLOGICAL ANALYSIS of anyone's personality, particularly those aspects of it that give rise to difficulties in living, is invariably anything but flattering. Many of the explanations that we give for our behaviour are but rationalizations, bolstering our own self-respect while at the same time serving as a facade to conceal motives not nearly as creditable. It would be an error to interpret this *Report* as being derogatory to the Doukhobors. An analysis of the motives of any group of non-Doukhobor Canadians would probably appear equally unflattering. Most of us have at least some blind spots, irrational prejudices, and infantile strivings, all of which complicate our relationships with other people, so that it is impossible for us ever to be completely healthy and happy. If these problems were to be pointed out to us, we would suffer an inevitable loss of self-esteem. Thus it must not be thought that the Doukhobors are inferior in character and morals to the other inhabitants of this country. Although such an inference would be satisfying to some people, it would be a piece of reassuring self-deception.

The purpose of this *Report* is to clarify the difficulties that the Doukhobors have had in their relationship with one another and with the non-Doukhobor population, and in consequence the emphasis has been on the more infantile and irrational components of Doukhobor personality. This must not be taken to imply that the Doukhobors are lacking in constructive, adult potentialities and assets. Many of the traits described later, which at first glance seem purely destructive, also have certain positive virtues. Take, for example, the tendency of the Doukhobor to depend on his parents, on his leaders, and on his group. Although such dependency has certain unfortunate results, it is at the same time often associated with enduring loyalty and a willingness to suffer much, rather than desert those to whom he feels obligated. His passivity and lack of self-assertiveness have pleasing aspects, too; he is likely to be warm, gentle, and compassionate. His inability to express directly his hostility often fosters the growth of a delightfully dry sense of humour. As a result of his feelings of guilt, he is likely to be extremely conscientious and hardworking. Finally, his inflexibility in the face of constant threats to the system he has built up is associated with a degree of resolution and determination that has definite utility.

Furthermore, in addition to these characteristics which have both a positive and a negative side, there are others that are definitely mature and satisfying. The zest and enthusiasm of many women; the assiduous care given to the children; the consideration that is paid to ethical goals—all of these represent stable, enduring facets of Doukhobor personality that are psychologically sound.

It is on such assets, and on many others not mentioned here, that we must rely. It can be only on the solid basis of these assets that the Doukhobors will be able to work through to a satisfactory solution of their problems. A detailed analysis of Doukhobor personality throws light on the difficulties which now prevent the achievement of this goal.

BASIC PRINCIPLES

The word "personality," as used by psychiatrists and social scientists, has a specific technical meaning. It refers to the unique ways of feeling, thinking, and behaving that each of us acquires in the course of growing up. These ways of behaving do not occur by chance or by instinct; on the contrary, they are integrated into a pattern through a process of learning that begins at birth and continues throughout the period of growth up to adulthood and beyond. These patterns of behaviour are learned in the context of the relationships of a child with his parents and with the other persons important to him, and these relationships are in turn determined by the attitudes, feelings, and beliefs of the parents themselves.

Because of the innumerable variables that can enter into a parent-child relationship, everyone's personality is unique; no two people in this world are exactly alike. Each of us has certain individual ways of feeling and thinking that he shares with no one else. Yet at the same time any group of people who have a common cultural heritage, and who have similar experiences in living, acquire as a result certain quite special modes of behaviour that show marked similarities. They bring up their children in certain characteristic ways—ways that differ from the child-rearing techniques of other groups—and as a result the members of any identifiable group have a number of personality traits in common, a "basic personality type." This will differ widely from society to society, depending upon how divergent these societies are in their child-rearing practices.

The Doukhobors are a group who share a large number of experiences. They have a special heritage of their own, and they have certain attitudes and beliefs which they transmit in a fairly consistent fashion to their children according to their own techniques. In consequence of this, it is regarded as possible to construct the basic Doukhobor personality type (or types) that exemplify the traits developed.

However, it is important to note that a person belongs to a number of different overlapping groups, and that these other groups also make some contribution to his personality. The Doukhobors are also Canadians, Russians, and heirs to the European tradition, and it is impossible to state to what extent the Doukhobor personality type is a reflection of purely Doukhobor experience, and to what extent their behaviour is a product of such factors as the Russian heritage or the Canadian way of life.

Thus, in summary:—

(1) The Doukhobors share certain traits with other Canadians because they are all heir to the European tradition.

(2) Each Doukhobor has his own unique set of needs and attitudes that make up his personality.

(3) In spite of propositions (1) and (2), it is still possible to construct a basic personality type, a way of feeling and behaviour that all, or almost all, Doukhobors have in common. It is this basic personality type and the way in which it determines Doukhobor behaviour that we are trying to elucidate in this chapter.

METHODOLOGY

Psychologists and psychiatrists have evolved a large number of techniques for studying and analyzing personality. Most of these were found to be completely inappropriate to the conditions of this project and were therefore not considered as possible tools. Originally it was planned to depend chiefly on three techniques: (1) Studies of life-histories; (2) psychiatric interviews; (3) projective tests.

The method of studying a life-history consists of getting a report from an individual of his life experiences as he recalls them, with the intention of isolating from this report the characteristic personality pattern as it emerges. The principal source of error in this procedure lies in the lack of perspective, the omissions and distortions that invariably occur when a person tells about his past. With the

Doukhobors, errors of this sort were particularly pronounced. It was rarely possible to find an informant sufficiently accurate, honest and fluent to talk about himself in a meaningful way.

Psychiatric interviewing of a formal sort consists of sitting down with a subject and getting him to talk about himself while the interviewer observes his responses and notes the picture of the man as it appears in relationship to the interviewer. Such a technique is always a matter of "participation observation." The interviewer participates in the relationship as well as observes it, although the degree of actual participation varies within wide limits. This was found to be the most profitable approach.

Projective tests (the Rorschach is possibly the best known) are based on the fact that when a person is asked to accomplish some poorly defined test, his performance will reflect, to a considerable measure, his own personality. In this investigation, Murray's Thematic Apperception Test was used. This consists of a number of cards, each of which could be used to illustrate a story. The subject is asked to invent a story about the picture that he sees. Because of the indeterminate quality of the pictures, the stories can vary widely, and will, as a rule, reflect the hidden needs and attitudes of the teller. In other words, he "projects" himself into his stories. This technique was of very limited usefulness, principally because the suspiciousness of our informants would not allow for such testing.

In the course of this project the following was done: Male subjects were interviewed by the author of this section at Oakalla Jail and the British Columbia Penitentiary. Here were obtained a few useful life-histories, and some observations made in formal interview. In addition, a considerable number of hours were spent with Mike B., a particularly deviant Son of Freedom who was at the time of this study a patient at the Provincial Mental Hospital, committed there because of the pathological behaviour he exhibited as the result of the extreme to which he carried the more maladaptive aspects of the Doukhobor personality. The bulk of the material presented here was gathered in a series of extremely informal interviews, in which both the author and his wife took part with subjects, male and female, living in the territory around Nelson. The author and his wife travelled by car with their children through the Kootenays visiting one or at most, two families a day, spending several hours in an attempt to get some awareness of the significant ways of dealing with problems that these people habitually used. The majority of subjects chosen for interview were from the Sons of Freedom group, although USCC, Independent and Sons of Freedom were all seen. With few exceptions, selections of subjects was random. Additional data were also gathered from meetings and casual encounters and from non-Doukhobor informants.

125

PARENT-CHILD RELATIONSHIPS

As indicated before, it is a thesis fundamental to both psychiatry and other social sciences that the personality of the adult is shaped predominantly by the experiences of the child with his parents and with other persons important to him. Consequently, it will be of value to review briefly some of the special characteristics of the relationship between Doukhobor parents and their children.

Miss Lewis has, in one of her reports, used the phrase "benevolent authoritarianism" to describe the behaviour of the Doukhobor adults toward their children. That phrase would seem to be a fairly accurate, terse summary of their attitude. Of course, Canadian parents are generally both benevolent and authoritarian in their handling of their children, but the Doukhobors seem to carry both facets to an extreme.

The extreme position that they take is this: Manifestations of dependence in children are indulged, encouraged and even forced, while at the same time a high degree of conformity to parental standards is exacted. It is as if the parents say to their young, "We shall give you whatever you want, provided that you do as we say and do as we do." The Doukhobor parent demonstrates this attitude to his child even in early infancy in dealing with basic biological functions. As Miss Lewis has pointed out, bottle feeding (formerly breast feeding) is allowed to continue for several years, while bowel training is commonly begun at the age of several weeks. Here on this simple gastro-intestinal level we see the encouragement of a rather infantile dependence, together with an insistence on social conformity.

The indulgence given to dependent behaviour continues throughout childhood and even into adult life, when the parental role is filled by the whole community and by the leaders. Feeding continues to be an area in which considerable gratification is allowed. The Doukhobor child is given plenty to eat; this is, of course, hardly deviant behaviour in Canada, but what is unusual is that the child is allowed to eat whenever he is hungry; commonly there is no insistence of scheduled meals. The same indulgence is given to other needs of the child. Even the poorest Doukhobor will frequently supply his young with clothes of excellent quality and at considerable expense. The children are well dressed and well cared for. With regard to play, the child (the boy more so than the girl) is allowed a generous allowance of time to enjoy himself in the company of his peers. It may be noted, too, that the child is not excluded from adult activities; he is allowed to sit in on meetings and to stay in the room while his parents are discussing adult matters.

All of this behaviour reinforces the child's basic need to be dependent on his parents. He is encouraged to believe that they will continue to supply him with the good things of life, and the continuing supply of these things becomes equated with affection, support, and love. At the same time the child must pay a price for this indulgence; he must obey his parents' stringent demands for conformity. These demands, which begin in the first few weeks of life and continue throughout the rest of childhood and into adult life, are directed principally toward curbing the child's tendency to aggression and noisy self-assertion. "Good" is equated with "quiet." The most desirable child is one that is passive, obedient, and placid; noisy, impulsive behaviour is frowned upon. While it is true that the child is indulged to the extent of being allowed to participate in adult activities, it is also true that it is insisted that he make no disturbance while he is present.

It seems that the attitude of the Doukhobor parents toward schools stems principally from their need to mould their children into a conformist pattern. An education is seen as a dangerous weapon in the hands of children, who are likely to use it to escape from parental domination. The parents are continually impressing upon the child the dangers of any way of life which they themselves do not believe in. The child is taught that he can be safe only if he continues to depend on his parents and to maintain that particular view of Doukhobor ideology that they pass on to him.

It may be noted again that parental demands of this sort are not peculiar to the Doukhobors, that other Canadians behave in a similar fashion toward their children. Yet outside Doukhobor society it is the unusual parent who curbs his child's spontaneity and assertiveness to the extent that the Doukhobor does; most parents in our society take at least some pride in the ability of their children to compete with others in a reciprocal, rowdy give-and-take, and they encourage at least some degree of independent experimentation. Still not all parents do, and in this connection it may be appropriate to point out that the core of personality that we are to designate as "Doukhobor" is not the exclusive property of the Doukhobor group; there are others in our country who possess similar traits and who exhibit behaviour that is equivalent, at least psychologically.

Thus the Doukhobor parent-child relationship may be alternatively characterized by the phrase "the giving of conditional love." The parent will continue to supply love on condition that the child is obedient. Formerly, filial obedience was frequently secured through whippings; nowadays there is no great reliance placed on corporal punishment as a means of controlling children—a harsh, scolding voice backed up with threats is sufficient. As a matter of fact, in a relationship like this, beatings are not particularly useful; one of our informants said that he was far more afraid of his father who scolded him than of his mother who beat him. The mother was merely harshly punitive; the father, at times indulgent and kind, caused the boy to feel particularly miserable and guilty when scolded. In such a relationship, a reprimand uttered in a gently reproachful tone, with an implied threat to withdraw the gratification of dependent needs, is a far worse punishment than a thrashing. In a somewhat distorted fashion, this attitude toward the children appears in the utterance of a Doukhobor parent who said: "We exact obedience through love."

A child encouraged thus to be dependent and at the same time obedient and passive has little incentive to widen his horizon by exploration and discovery. Exploratory behaviour is checked not only by the attitude of the parents toward self-assertion, but also by their fear that he may become contaminated by contact with the outside world.

The above description applies somewhat more to the rearing of boys than to that of girls, who have channels of self-expression not open to the boys. From a relatively early age, girls help their mothers with housework and with the rearing of the younger children, whom they can dominate and control just as mother does. This opportunity to play the "little mother" gives them a strength and assurance which is not available to the rather unnecessary boy. The rigidity of the household routine provides an element of safety and stability in the life of the girl which is not fostered by the rather haphazard activities of the boy.

This sort of child-rearing, though by no means confined to Doukhobors, leads to a parent-child relationship which creates a definitely characteristic personality pattern, now to be described.

BASIC PERSONALITY TYPE

PASSIVITY

Generally, the Doukhobor is noteworthy because of his quiet passivity, his lack of what we would call normal aggression and self-assertion. These characteristics are extremely apparent in all his interpersonal relationships—in his dealings with his fellows and with those outside the community. His feelings about aggressiveness are particularly pronounced with regard to its physical forms (fighting, shooting, killing, etc.), but even verbal aggression is associated with anxiety. To give an example: Bill P. came up to Krestova one Sunday morning and sauntered around casually, talking to various acquaintances. He is an apostate—the son of a loyal Sons of Freedom family; he had deserted the group and had consistently violated Doukhobor morality. At the time of his visit, he was still suffering from the effect of the alcoholic debauch of the previous night, and yet no one spoke harshly to him. When we asked him about the feelings of the community towards him, he said, "They are very angry at me but they are afraid to show it." Another example: Mike B. is a very disturbed Son of Freedom who had to be hospitalized because of the extremity to which he carried his hostility. With his intense destructiveness, he would tear his own clothes and attempt to rend those of anyone who came close to him; he frequently spat at me when I came to see him. In spite of his feelings of extreme hate, which in another patient might well have led to homicidal assault, not once did he offer direct physical violence.

This attitude toward aggression is manifest not only in day-to-day behaviour, but also in the test situation. When the Thematic Apperception Test was given to Andrew K., he proved completely incapable of giving stories in which aggression occurred. He displayed considerable ingenuity in manipulating the stories to avoid the obvious inferences of aggression (suicide, hypnosis, physical force) usually drawn from certain of the pictures. When themes of violence were suggested to him, he rejected them emphatically, saying they were impossible and they did not fit the cards. Occasionally he could not avoid such themes; in which case he would either counteract the effect by telling a "good" story after the "bad" one or place the whole situation on a fantasy level, saying that it took place in a book, or that the artist may have intended such a story but that was not really the way it was.

The quiet and passive Doukhobors are pleasant, agreeable people, easy to talk to and easy to work with. These qualities are liked by employers, by the police, in fact by all those who have dealings with them. Nevertheless, the most passive Doukhobors are severely disabled in their capacity to handle many of the problems of living. In the first place, their security and self-esteem is seriously impaired by the lack of anything that might be called a "masculine" characteristic. In our society, forthright aggression is a male prerogative, and it is customary to equate masculinity with aggressive competitiveness. The passive Doukhobor cannot do this, and there is no specifically masculine set of Doukhobor characteristics that he can adopt to delineate his sexual role. Other features of Doukhobor behaviour further undermine his concept of his sex. In our society, women not uncommonly use their bodies and their clothing in a seductive way to attract and interest men. The Sons of Freedom women use their nude bodies as desexualized objects to browbeat others. This custom of desexualized nudity, with its implication of complete indifference to the feelings of the men, further diminishes their security in their sexual role. One Son of Freedom spoke of the necessity of his wearing a beard; this distinctively masculine attribute was extremely important to him and he actually felt anxious without it. The passive Doukhobor male must cling to a number of such reassuring masculine attributes—his beard, his physical vigour and health, his capacity to do heavy manual labour. In consequence, he has a tendency to be scornful of sedentary employment or of work that women can do.

A second result of the inhibition of self-assertion is the inability of the passive Doukhobor to take any responsibility or to assume the duties of leadership. He cannot tell others what to do, he cannot oppose the wishes of the aggressive minority nor resist their direction. "I'm just a follower," he says. "I do what I am told." Very rarely a passive Doukhobor will take on some of the responsibilities of leadership, but he cannot last long because he has neither the force nor the vehemence to overcome the numerous obstacles that are set in his way. Many Sons of Freedom have an excellent appreciation of their situation, with appropriate plans of action, but when it is suggested that they convince recalcitrant members of the wisdom of their plans, they begin to back away from effective action.

Most seriously, this lack of self-assertion interferes with their comprehension of a situation and leads to bewilderment and misinterpretation; on occasion, difficulties with the English language play a subsidiary role here. Many situations arise in which they are faced with some problem that they cannot immediately understand. The most productive orientation to such a situation is to reach out for the facts, to insist on details, to analyze the data, etc., but all this implies a degree of activity impossible to most of them. Commonly, a Doukhobor in such a situation will leap blindly to any interpretation that does the faintest justice to the facts, and cling to that with a tenacious disregard for reality. This disregard for reality causes bewilderment and frustration, and leads to misinterpretation of the motives of others in a persecutory fashion.

The need to arrive at some explanation, however ill-founded, of events not fully comprehended encourages them, in dealing with experience, to use certain techniques that cause further difficulties. In concocting explanations to fit situations that are not fully understood, they must necessarily have recourse to a private, highly personal way of thinking, exclusive of reality and of the ideas of other people. This sort of thinking, which we shall call "autism," creates considerable problems in the way of communication between individuals as well as obstacles to the achievement of goals. In the course of our work we made several inquiries concerning the reasons for the burning of John Verigin's house. The instigators of this were probably actuated by motives of hostility, and one would hardly expect them to admit these motives. But at the same time there were a number of Sons of Freedom involved whose participation could be legitimately explained on the basis of their deference to others and of their allegiance to the group. This sort of motivation could fairly readily be admitted, and at times was the reason given. Yet there were some participants who insisted on giving "reasons" of a highly involved, incomprehensible sort which were obviously meaningless both to us and to the individual himself. Pete E. said, "It (Verigin's house) was a place of sacred worship and they had turned it into a den of thieves. It was a home of harlots." Upon inquiry, it was evident that Pete had not the slightest idea of what he meant or what he was trying to say.

Commonly, the Doukhobors think about government in such vague, autistic fashion. They seem to view it as "The Government," an ill-defined, all-powerful person, possessed by obscure motives generally of a hostile sort. This personification of an institution is dimly perceived and poorly comprehended, but nevertheless is quite real and quite frightening.

Their autism radically interferes with a realistic appraisal of any situation and allows them to substitute naive, wishful thinking. Thus, in spite of the completely unfavourable response from other countries to inquiries about immigration, a large number of Sons of Freedom still hold quite tenaciously to the belief that they will shortly leave Canada. Mike B., the patient in the Provincial Mental Hospital, told me that he expected to be out of the hospital "soon," although he could give no reasons of any degree of validity for this expectation.

This way of dealing with experience leads to an almost complete breakdown of meaningful communication. Non-Doukhobors are generally quite unable to understand what the needs and goals of the Doukhobors are. Even within the community all sorts of misinterpretations and misunderstandings arise. Michael Verigin sent word to Krestova that he wanted help at Hilliers with some construction work. Since there are fewer shared meanings, since a situation can be interpreted in any way according to the private needs of the individual, such a request can mean anything, and it is not too surprising that the request was taken as an invitation to come and burn down some buildings, to the ultimate distress of all concerned.

As a paradigm for the sort of difficulties that can be created by autism consequent to difficulties in self-assertion, we might mention Bill O. This man, nominally an Independent, was visited by some official in connection with the school work of Bill's oldest son. Although the man was in his house for more than an hour, Bill did not manage to find out who he was or what he wanted, and he could not be sufficiently aggressive to make the inquiries that would satisfy him. Bewildered and perplexed, he ruminated over the situation afterwards and finally developed the autistic notion that the man wanted to send the boy to the Institute for the Blind.

This mode of thinking has a counterpart in the field of action. Here we are referring to the tendency of the Doukhobors in a crisis to have recourse to behaviour that is quite inappropriate to the ends they are trying to achieve. Parades nude or otherwise, proclamations, and speeches are used to accomplish the most diverse tasks in a way that takes no cognizance of the problem involved. Nudism, as will be described later, is generally a hostile manoeuvre; however, at times it has been used for other purposes, for example, as an expression of a wish for the success of a meeting of the Consultative Committee. But disrobing in no way ensures the successful outcome of a meeting and is at best irrelevant to the job.

Nevertheless, autistic thinking and the parallel behaviour have their useful features. Primarily they allow for all sorts of clichés, sophistries, and rationalizations that would be just too transparent to anyone subject to the rigorous discipline of logical thought. Thus, Mike B., after identifying himself with Christ who was "mistreated and spat upon," could then spit on me and still maintain that in doing so he was thus showing the great love that he had for me! Mike was generally much more ingenious in his rationalizations—he said that animals, who live without "luxuries," are healthy; I reminded him of an outbreak of Newcastle disease which was then depleting flocks of chickens. This, he explained, was because they were overfed by avaricious farmers who were greedy to make a profit. Mike went to great lengths in his attempts to justify himself; in order to do so, it was frequently necessary for him to divorce cause and effect—another autistic device—in order to achieve his ends. Thus, in speaking of a woman who was burned to death as a result of arson, he disclaimed any responsibility. After all, he didn't *tell* her to run back into the house for her belongings; by her greed for material wealth she brought destruction upon herself.

Rationalizations as justification for hostile acts of arson are common, although they vary in subtlety. One Son of Freedom said that it is all right to burn community property because the Sons of Freedom as well as the USCC worked for it and, therefore, are justified in so disposing of it. Another said that no one can impute hostile motives to acts of arson, for do not the Sons of Freedom confess, repent, and suffer for these acts? Their "repenting" is itself a highly autistic manoeuvre. It is as if by saying one is sorry, all the evil is erased, the harmful effects undone, and forgiveness necessarily follows.

DEPENDENCE

The second important part of the Doukhobor basic personality type is dependence. This, too, is the perpetuation of the pattern of behaviour laid down in the parent-child relationship, in which the gratification of the infantile need for succorance is not only allowed, but actively offered. In our culture generally, we place some value on self-reliance in our children; we regard it as reasonable that they should depend upon us according to their age, but at the same time an increasing degree of self-initiated activity and autonomy is encouraged and expected. Among the Doukhobors, where there are few rewards for maturation along these lines, where deference to parental figures is almost inevitably associated with its reward—indulgence of dependent needs—there is little impetus for the development of traits of independence and self-reliance.

Consequently, the adult Doukhobor (particularly the more passive male) has virtually no capacity for self-direction and no confidence in his own ability to make decisions. Inevitably he must turn to some authoritarian figure from whom he expects support and direction in all affairs of importance.

This need for dependence appears in all his relationships with other individuals and groups. In the first place, much of the Doukhobor's attitude to his community is derived from this need. The community itself represents a larger-than-life parental figure which one can lean on. Time and time again we hear of people who left the group only to return later. Away from the group they felt lonely and lost, and longed for the shelter provided by their fellows. The participation of non-hostile individuals in arts of arson and dynamiting can be explained in the same way. "What am I to do," say many, "when they tell me that I must come along and burn so-and-so's house? I must do what the group says." Belonging to the group is such a powerful need that the individual, rather than risk expulsion, will perform acts that he regards as detrimental to himself and to the others. In the same way one can interpret the reiterated assertion that "all the Doukhobors are one people"; such statements stem from the need to believe that the society on which one depends for survival is large, strong, and stable. A second reason for the Sons of Freedom antagonism to public schools may be found here; they believe, with some justification, that a group can remain stable only if it is not subject to disturbing outside influences such as are represented by a public school education. To a considerable extent the group is held together by fear arising out of ignorance; if this state of affairs were to be altered, the group might disintegrate, and thus the individual would be deprived of this highly valued source of dependent security.

An even more striking illustration of the Doukhobors' need for dependence is their common attitude toward their leaders. The leader is to many of them a powerful god-like creature to whom they defer and submit in expectation of receiving support and direction. All responsibility rests with the leader, and the rank and file neither know nor expect to learn what is actually going on. Mr. S., a former official in the CCUB, provided an interesting commentary on this view of leader-follower relations. He asked me if the Research Committee had made any specific plans with regard to the Sons of Freedom. I told him that I thought not; his reply to this was that

133

possibly the Director of the Committee had made plans but was not telling them to me. We asked some of those who told us of the "embezzlement" which occurred during the days of the CCUB why the leaders were permitted to carry on in this fashion. "We didn't know what they were doing," was the usual reply. "We trusted our leaders and expected them to look after our interests." The good Doukhobor expected his leaders to look after him and, in turn, he would do nothing without first asking for permission.

Even more startling are manifestations of dependence on the hated governmental authorities. An interesting illustration of this occurred in the Penitentiary when a fire broke out in one of the huts. Following upon this, some of the "better" Sons of Freedom asked that the entire group be locked up and more closely supervised. "That way you will be able to keep track of everyone and prevent it from happening again," said one of them to a guard. They preferred to suffer a considerable loss of freedom and of privileges at the hands of prison authorities as long as they could continue to depend on the guards for the police functions that the group itself was unwilling to exercise. As another example, although the relocation project is a matter of considerable importance to all groups of Doukhobors, none of the groups—USCC, Independents, or Sons of Freedom—has shown any significant degree of willingness to take responsibility for the planning, for the decisions, or for the financing of the move. Similarly, much of the deterioration of Doukhobor property—the lack of irrigation, the dilapidation of the houses—results from their unwillingness to initiate activity without direction and supervision from above.

THE COROLLARIES OF PASSIVITY AND DEPENDENCE

In order to maintain their dependent status and not risk any dangerously assertive behaviour, Doukhobors must submit, in a passive, helpless fashion, to all manner of powerful forces that buffet them mercilessly. This is actually more than a figure of speech; many have had to suffer, without expressing resentment, painful beatings at the hands of leaders. The Doukhobors are constantly paying the price for the continuation of nurturance and support; they must allow themselves to be used and even to be mistreated if necessary by authoritarian and despotic figures.

The principal danger associated with such a way of life is that despotism can never be depended upon to be fair or just. The "benevolent authoritarianism" of the parents is not subject to an infinite extension; sooner or later one comes in contact with authorities who are neither kind nor well intentioned, and then one's sufferings really do begin. There is no doubt that the Doukhobors have been ill-used by certain leaders, who, for personal gain, have selfishly exploited them. Similarly, the group itself does not always act according to the best interests of the individual. Governmental representatives have not always dealt with the Doukhobors wisely. In itself this sort of mistreatment might not be too serious; but when the individual who suffers it is dependent on those who are mistreating him, and when he is compelled because of his personal motivation to submit without overt resentment, then trouble invariably follows.

The Doukhobors, like all of us, are aware of this threat, but there is nothing that they can do about it. Their dependence and passivity compel them to submit, even though they feel threatened and helpless. Frequently, notably among the USCC and Independents, these feelings of helplessness find expression in a defensive denial of sources of conflict with the non-Doukhobor population—they have nothing to hide from governmental authorities; they send their children to school; their lives are as an open book; this business about prejudice and discrimination is nonsense, etc.

Another significant result of passivity and dependence, stemming from repressive childhood experiences, is the impoverishment of spontaneity and creativeness. The free expression of emotion is dangerous; in order to control action that might sever the highly valued, dependent ties, it is necessary to control *all* spontaneous activity. The result is a narrow, rigid, stereotyped, impoverished sort of personality. This sort of damage is reflected vividly in the Doukhobor arts, which show a decided lack of truly imaginative, creative activity. Doukhobor embroidery is meticulously done and quite elaborate, but it is at the same time formal and sterile. Although the USCC have a repertory of expressive folk-songs, the Sons of Freedom abjure the use of these, nor does either group possess an extensive folk-lore.

The individual Doukhobor usually displays very little expressive movement, with few of those spontaneous gestures and grimaces by which less inhibited people give vent to their feelings. His thinking proceeds along narrow, rigid, concrete lines; he is unimaginative. This was particularly noticeable on those occasions on which it was possible to administer the Thematic Apperception Test. Commonly the stories given were full of empty clichés and shop-worn ideas, with little originality and inventiveness.

This ascetic impoverishment and lack of exuberance spreads through all areas of living. Certainly the biological pleasures do not escape. We have little information on their sexual experience, but the evidence would indicate that it is generally guilty and joyless.

In this way, vast areas of possible satisfaction are denied to them, so that their lives are rendered barren and futile. Under any circumstances, this sort of frustration is extremely damaging; for the Doukhobors it is of particular importance in that it closes off many possible avenues of release for tensions arising from so many other causes.

A further consequence of Doukhobor passivity and dependence, with resulting impoverishment and feelings of helplessness, is that they feel inferior and their self-esteem is markedly impaired. They are aware, at least dimly, of the damage they have suffered and of their incapacity for living, and under the circumstances it is impossible for them to have any true sense of personal worth or of self-confidence. Rarely, if ever, will a Doukhobor confess to such feelings of inferiority in dealing with outsiders, but indirectly such attitudes find expression in claims to moral superiority. It is as if they say, "We know that we are inadequate in most respects, but at least we are better Christians than you are." Some of the Doukhobor preoccupation with morality stems from this source; it is productive of considerable comfort to believe that one is at least in some respects superior to one's fellows. There are other twists that can be given to feelings of this sort in order to bolster self-esteem; Fred H., an extremely hostile man, obviously very much disturbed by feelings of inferiority with respect to me, laid stress upon the fact that I could not possibly understand "spiritual matters." This was one area in which he could feel immensely superior to me, and he made the most of it. But generally speaking, this sort of defence is productive of only limited satisfaction, and marked feelings of personal inadequacy remain.

HOSTILITY

The efforts of the parents to create passive, obedient children are not wholly successful. For one thing, the majority of the women evade the full consequences of their training in the outlet that is offered to them in caring for and dominating younger siblings. Some men escape, too, possibly as a result of their having ample constitutional reservoirs of energy and motility. These men do not fare well in the narrow, restricting confines of the Doukhobor community, and tend to leave the group to try to make their way in the outside world. Here, if they are successful, they gradually lose their Doukhobor identity and more or less blend into the Canadian population, as many have done in Saskatchewan. If, on the other hand, they fail to make a success of this venture, they are faced with the necessity of either drifting, rootless, or of returning to the Doukhobor fold. During the depression the policy of the CCUB was to preclude their return to that group, and they were consequently forced into the Sons of Freedom. Within the Sons of Freedom, these men are the most bitter and destructive of all; the resources of energy and initiative which provided the impetus for their experiment in non-Doukhobor living are now put to the service of the violent hostility resulting from the frustrations that they suffered.

Consequently, among the men of the community at least, there are no "normally" aggressive individuals. The majority have repressed all aggression; a minority are capable of expressing such feelings, but only in a hostile, destructive fashion.

Actually, although the direct manifestations of them are rare, hostile feelings and attitudes characterize most of the Doukhobors to a marked degree. The various frustrations imposed upon them by the stress of community living, and by the difficulties they have with the general population, feed and sustain this hostility. Basically, however, it arises out of the parent-child relationship. The parents can control the outward display of assertiveness and aggressiveness by threats of punishment; they can also force their children to repress hostile feelings by threats of withdrawing love. Yet this does not eliminate such feelings; these restrictions and controls generate rebellion. Although through fear of the consequences this rebellion must be kept beneath the surface, it cannot be eliminated; it grows and feeds upon itself and provides the impetus for much of the behaviour of the Sons of Freedom.

Through fear of the disapproval of his parents, the Doukhobor child cannot expresses directly the considerable hostility that he feels for them. There are a number of consequences to this state of affairs.

In the first place, in order to conceal from himself these dangerous feelings, the Doukhobor must keep up a continuous pretence—for his own benefit rather than to deceive others—that he feels not hate but love. He continually and constantly reiterates how much he loves everyone, how generous and kind his motives are. Mike B., one of the most hostile men I have ever met, reiterated innumerable times that he was "full of love for the whole world." It is probable that the compulsive hospitality of the Doukhobors—their inability to allow anyone to visit without offering food and drink—has its source partly in the need to deny hostile feelings. It is as if they say, "We do not hate you, we love you. See, we offer to share our bread with you to prove it."

Secondly, the hostile feelings are displaced; that is, directed away from the objects to which they were originally directed—the parents —and on to a series of objects further removed and, therefore, less threatening. It is a little safer to hate other people in the community than one's own parents. Thus the leader in his role of parental substitute receives a good measure of this hostility, quite apart from anything he does to merit such antagonism. This antagonism to leaders, as well as hostility directed to other members of the community, is still dangerous; in a tightly knit community it is too easy to see how closely others resemble one's parents. It is still safer to hate people outside the community, or a rival faction within it. And it is safest of all to direct this hostility toward inanimate objects. This is the solution the Sons of Freedom have finally arrived at. By burning houses, by dynamiting bridges, they are expressing destructive feel-

PERSONALITY CHARACTERISTICS AND PSYCHOLOGICAL PROBLEMS

ings that they can give vent to in no other way. Their violent diatribes against the Government are also understandable in that light; it is perfectly safe to get angry at a vaguely and autistically perceived Government.

It is impossible to satiate displaced destructiveness, and in its most extreme forms such destructiveness amounts to complete nihilism. Many of the attitudes of the Sons of Freedom toward education, toward property, toward industry and commerce, are products of this intense urge to destroy everything. According to Mike B., the only way for man to live is to dwell in the forest without shelter or clothes, subsisting on roots and berries. But even the less deviant Sons of Freedom have a similar problem. As we shall see later, the Doukhobors have a great need for material success, for property and for education. At the same time the intense hostility that they feel to their successful rivals, to the educated leader, to their employer, inevitably drives them on toward the extreme position in which not only the men but also their characteristic attributes are derogated, so that finally all personal striving and accomplishment in the direction of education and material success is regarded as selfish and worldly. Although in reaching this conclusion they deprive themselves of what they need most, still in doing so they preserve their position of dependence upon their parents, who, in order to perpetuate their own authority, continue to foster such a nihilistic faith.

A third result of the repression of hostility is the eruption of hostile behaviour in a disguised form, through devious channels. The most outstanding behaviour illustrating this is nudism. Removing one's clothes is a remarkably effective device for making other people uncomfortable and angry; such behaviour can be easily rationalized and made to appear something other than the hostile act it actually is. It must be emphasized that in these situations, as in most of the situations described in this section, the Sons of Freedom are themselves usually unaware of the hostility that they are expressing, and that the principal utility of such devices is that they allow the expression of these feelings quite outside of awareness.

Nudism and arson are not the only devious methods employed by the Doukhobors to express hostility. There are a number of marginal Independents, overtly owing no allegiance to the Sons of Freedom, but sympathetic to them, who derive considerable satisfaction from manipulating the various forces that beset them, and playing one group against another. Charlie O. is one such man; he has enjoyed the respect of the non-Doukhobor population for many years. In a highly successful fashion, he has manipulated the police and other authorities so as to obtain the maximum number of concessions, while at the same time has covertly laughed at them for the ease with which they were taken in.

Much of the Doukhobor ideology as verbalized by the Sons of Freedom is not so much a statement of faith as a cloak to conceal from themselves their own hostile motivation. The various clichés, such as "we are protesting against the Third World War" and the like, are actual rationalizations intended to disguise underlying destructiveness.

A fourth way of dealing with repressed but powerful hostile feelings is to project them, that is, to attribute these qualities to others, denying them in oneself. The most marked manifestations of this tendency are those of persecutory delusions. Less striking forms of the same mechanism are those by which one's own faults are seen in others or one's own mistakes blamed on others.

There is no doubt that the Doukhobors project their own hostility. Suspicion and mistrustful apprehension characterize their attitudes to one another, to other factions, to the leaders, and to the non-Doukhobor population. In this connection we would refer to the sentiment prevailing among the Sons of Freedom that they were betrayed by the leaders who had supposedly embezzled community funds. There is skepticism with regard to the motives of Sorokin; some Sons of Freedom still suspect that he has come to destroy them. Many members of the various communities distrust one another, and there is a fairly widespread, although unjustified, fear of spies and informers.

However, most of their hostile feelings are projected on to the non-Doukhobor population and the Government, whose malice, vindictiveness, and venom are, according to Doukhobor belief, boundless. They continually see themselves surrounded by enemies who are bent on their destruction, and the wildest and most improbable tales of persecution gain ready acceptance. It is still widely believed among Sons of Freedom and others that Peter Vasilivich Verigin was actually murdered by the Government; that babies were killed at the time of the imprisonment on Piers Island; that railroads have been dynamited by Government agents so that the Doukhobors might be blamed, etc. Some USCC members believe that the Government encourages the Sons of Freedom in their depredations in order to destroy the entire group.

This suspiciousness continually intrudes upon and complicates their dealing with one another and even more with outsiders. One of our informants expressed his disbelief of our assertion that we spoke no Russian. "Would the Government send spies who could not speak the language?" he scornfully asked. On one occasion we were told that it was generally believed that I, a psychiatrist, was sent in to "prove" that the Doukhobors were all insane and consequently not deserving of any consideration. Miss Lewis suffered a similar fate—it was considered at one time that she was attempting in a disguised way to educate the children of the Sons of Freedom. This tendency to attribute their own hostile motives to others who are actually desirous of being helpful automatically excludes the possibility of help being given.

It must be pointed out that persecutory ideas have a basis in past experience; prejudice and discrimination have been the daily fare of the Doukhobor population; they have been mistreated, exploited, and misunderstood. At the same time it is also true that on this framework they have hung a tissue of fantasies whose purpose it is to prove that it is not the Doukhobors who are angry, hostile and destructive, but the outside world.

It may be relevant at this point to make reference to the antagonism of the Doukhobors to registration and to taxes. This antagonism undoubtedly results from a combination of a number of motives. Basically, the situation in regard to both of these is seen by Doukhobors as one in which there is an encroachment on the sovereignty of the group. In the first place, such an encroachment must be resisted, because anything implying that the group is not the completely self-sufficient, stable unit on which one can depend must be resisted. Secondly, as a result of the hostility that they have displaced on the autistically perceived Government, any interference of this hated object must be blocked. Thirdly, as a result of the hostility that they have projected on to the Government and its agents, it is completely impossible for them to have any confidence in governmental officials, and any attempt to obtain statistical data is regarded as the precursor to conscription into the army.

NEEDS AND ASPIRATIONS

With this sort of basic personality structure, what is it then that the Doukhobors want? In the first place, they want approval and love. The passive, dependent person needs to be shown that there is some reward for relinquishing active assertiveness. He wants people to recognize his sacrifices and to love him for them. Annie B. gives up one of her two rooms to some homeless relatives, but it is very important to her that they be grateful and admiring. Andrew K. did some work for Government officials and refused payment, but he expected them to think that was rather wonderful, and he became resentful when they seemed to take his gesture as a matter of course. It is very important to be loved by the leaders and by the other members of the community; even at the present time, Sons of Freedom flock around Sorokin as if to ask for his blessing, and K.'s chief reward for a life of considerable self-sacrifice is that "everyone regards me as a friend." Furthermore, it is not enough to be liked only by the members of one's own community; the approval of the rest of the world is longed for. A frequent complaint of the Sons of Free-

140

dom is that they do not receive from non-Doukhobors the love that they deserve. On occasion, the Sons of Freedom are in a position similar to that of a child who creates mischief in order to get some sign of recognition from his parents; it is better to be punished than to be ignored. From remarks made by certain Sons of Freedom, one might infer that a number of acts of arson were attention-getting devices of this sort.

A second major need is for the material manifestations of love. Recognition and approval are not enough; concrete objects are required. We might view this as another aspect of a passive dependency in which the gift is the only unmistakable sign of affection. The Doukhobors are forced by lack of sophistication and social skills to express needs for love in such a material fashion. It is not enough for Sons of Freedom to know that Sorokin loves them; they must have a photograph of him. It is probable that the importance of photographs in the Doukhobor material culture is related to this need for the concrete assurance of affection. It is also highly significant that there is little mention of rewards in an after-life, and generally rewards on earth are expected. Similarly, physicians in the Kootenays comment that the Doukhobors derive little support from their religion in times of illness; all their faith must be put in the concrete form of the doctor himself in spite of the inevitable mistrust. The Doukhobors want the same comforts and luxuries that most other people do—refrigerators, automobiles, radios, good housing. It is not really far-fetched to say that these objects are tokens of affection from a loving God. Obviously this need comes into sharp conflict with the nihilistic destructiveness described in a previous section.

A third strong need is for knowledge and education. We have already commented on the all-pervading feelings of inferiority and the lack of self-esteem that disturb the majority of the Doukhobors. It is not surprising that they should feel that if they knew more and if they were better educated, they would be able to compete on more favourable terms with their repressive parents, their autocratic leaders and the outside world. For them, as for others, ignorance is the chain that keeps them subservient to the parental figures on whom they must depend. Consequently, they have a marked drive to enhance their self-esteem by education. Here, too, their nihilism sets up an insurmountable barrier to the achievement of their desires.

It may be noted that a similar drive is commonly found in the children of other immigrant groups with a similar family structure. However, in the Doukhobors this drive does not always find clear expression. Among the Independents and some of the USCC members it is possible to find the same thirst for knowledge and training that is found in these other immigrant groups, and we frequently encountered Doukhobors who did emphasize the security and satis-

141

faction that could be obtained by thorough schooling. Even among the Sons of Freedom, this need finds expression; here, however, the emphasis is on a knowledge of Doukhobor history and religion, but the motivation is the same. Even then the Sons of Freedom cannot themselves achieve such distinction; they derive considerable satisfaction from identifying themselves with a leader who has achieved it. Sorokin, his proud followers tell us, knows the Bible backwards. Many USCC members note the merit in John Verigin's high-school education, and hence his capacity for dealing with outsiders.

STRESSES AND FRUSTRATIONS

The three major needs described in the previous section are almost invariably frustrated. The Doukhobors want love, but they are not loved, neither by the other members of the community nor by the leaders nor by the outside world. One woman complains, in a meeting of the Sons of Freedom during which they are discussing the acceptance of financial assistance, that there are many in the community who are "rich" and yet will not give assistance to their poorer brethren. In the days of the CCUB this feeling of being deprived of love and support must have been particularly pronounced; a large number of members were expelled because of non-payment of dues, such expulsion representing, of course, a complete rejection. Nor have all leaders been more generous with their love; at times they have threatened their followers, beaten them, embezzled funds, and betrayed their trust. The non-Doukhobor world does not deal with them any more kindly; at best they suffer from prejudice and discrimination, at worst they are thrust into jail for offences that they themselves do not see as crimes.

Not only is it impossible for the individual Doukhobor to feel secure in the love of his fellows, but his marked need for dependency on the community is thwarted also by the very structure and function of the community itself, in the following ways:—

(1) The lack of social stability, the incomplete social organization, the difficulties in communication between autistic people, the lack of set roles, all prevent the individual from feeling secure within the framework of his society.

(2) The ever-present despotic authority of the leader, with his continual threats of expulsion, has stimulated anxiety in the past.

(3) In a community which requires combined, cooperative effort to achieve anything, it is necessary to have some system of workable rewards and punishments to disci-

142

pline the lazy and the selfish; these have always been lacking.

(4) There is injustice in the allotment of duties and privileges. This, and the previous point, had force particularly in the days of the CCUB. Many believe that a factor contributing largely to the collapse of the CCUB was the sense of unfairness that people felt with regard to the kinds and amounts of work that were done, and the rewards given. Today among the Sons of Freedom, in the absence of an economic community, these conditions no longer apply, but the same jealous rivalry persists and the "rich" Sons of Freedom are regarded as a threat.

(5) The repression of hostility does not abolish it; it merely directs it into devious channels. Indirect expressions of hostility appear in the form of rumour and scandal-mongering and in marked inquisitiveness. No one can feel that either his reputation or his privacy will be respected.

(6) The lack of adequate social organization and responsibility allows for the entry and free activity of pathological individuals who exploit the group to their own ends. Some of these individuals seem to be suffering from schizophrenic illnesses, and they use the group to try to work out their own problems. Related to this is the effect of certain other sects on the lunatic fringe, who have endeavoured to complicate Doukhobor existence. Bizarre communications and advice are continually arriving from these weird groups, most of which are located in California. In addition, damage to the group has been done, directly or indirectly, by psychopathic criminals, among who might be included Nick Bryan, who had a formidable police record before he committed arson, and who later claimed that he was just a "good Doukhobor."

(7) There are the apostates, those who manage to leave the community and to strike out successfully on their own, forsaking the traditions and yet not suffering. These present a problem in that their desertion acts as a temptation to others to do likewise and, in addition, leaves extra burdens and responsibilities on those who remain behind. With all this, it is no wonder that the individual Doukhobor cannot feel safe in his dependency on the community.

The Sons of Freedom are frustrated, not only in their needs for love and dependent satisfaction, but also in their need for the material gratifications representative of such love—they cannot obtain the money, the automobiles and the washing-machines that they want. In the first place, their parents, transmitting to them the Doukhobor ideology, tell them in their childhood that they are bad for wanting these things, and the excessively dependent children accept this dictum. Later on they do not have to be told; their conscience carries out this function. But even when they can escape from parental admonitions and a guilty conscience, few of them can achieve what they want. During the 1930's, debt and depression prevented them from reaching any degree of financial security. Nowadays, lack of specialized skills and training constantly stand in the way of most of them. Furthermore, without specialized skills they are particularly vulnerable to the insecurities of physical ill-health and old age, both of which render them incapable of the manual labour by which they make their livelihood. Finally, their nihilistic, sour-grapes rationalizations (property is bad and only the selfish materialists are comfortable) get in the way of their satisfying such wants.

To cap it all, they are also unable to achieve any satisfaction through education either for their economic betterment or simply for the enhancement of their self-esteem. Here, too, the parents pass on an ideology that forbids this solution, and the children, dependent on their parents for approval, accept their prohibition. Later on, the adult himself regards schooling as a threat to the integrity of the group to which he turns for support. The desire of the Sons of Freedom for an education comes in conflict also with the need to deny his own inferiority in this regard. At the same time, there are definite barriers to satisfaction even for those who escape the tyranny of their parents, their own dependency, and a bad conscience. Schools are few and often of poor quality, and are not set up to accommodate their needs. Since they are a rural population, both distance and farm work habits also militate against regular attendance at school.

In these ways the needs of the Doukhobors for love, dependence, material success and education all meet with repeated frustration.

RESPONSE TO FRUSTRATION

There is a universal tendency of the human organism to respond to frustration with aggression. The infant displays the most elementary form of this behaviour by thrashing his arms and legs when his movements are restricted. It is a basic reaction of all mankind, although the form this behaviour takes is shaped by the teachings of the society in which a child is reared. The Doukhobors are no exception; they, too, become angry and strike out when their needs are not met. They begin adult life with a potential reservoir of hostile destructiveness built up through their childhood experiences, to which there is constantly added a flood of aggressive feelings stemming from numerous frustrations. These feelings are handled in the devious fashion described earlier in this chapter.

The manifestations of hostility of most concern to the non-Doukhobor population are nudism and the depredations of arson and dynamiting. There is no doubt that this behaviour occurs practically always in a setting of frustration, and that it is resorted to more or less unconsciously as a way of retaliating. Some of the more sophisticated Sons of Freedom are aware of these motives, although they may attempt to justify their anger and the means of expressing it on the basis of the wrongs done to them. The majority, however, rationalize these acts (just as much to preserve their own peace of mind as to deceive others) and firmly state that they behave in this way "in order to warn people against the coming Third World War."

Nudism is the more favoured weapon of the Sons of Freedom; arson and dynamiting, with their obvious hostile implications, are disturbing to a considerable portion of them. However, under the stress of marked frustration, the more hostile Sons of Freedom will find relief in arson and dynamiting and compel their more passive brethren to participate. There need be no specific problem that gives rise to this form of retaliation; as has been indicated elsewhere, an increase in such depredations coincided with periods of economic depression. Sometimes it is possible to relate the burning of a Doukhobor's barn with his having made unfavourable remarks about the Sons of Freedom. Someone's increasing prosperity may be a sufficient threat. At other times, such acts arise from the stresses of group living that have been described in the previous section. Undoubtedly many of the large community houses went up in flames simply as a result of the frustration induced by the lack of social organization necessary to maintain such a cooperative enterprise. The reasons for burning one's own home are to be described later.

Although arson is not readily resorted to as a device for expressing hostility, nudism is very useful to a majority of the Sons of Freedom. Nudity among the Doukhobors in Russia had little of the emotional loading that it has for non-Doukhobors of this country. It must have been with some astonishment that the Doukhobors discovered the shocked horror with which people here responded to the sight of a completely nude body. Apparently it was not very long before the Sons of Freedom took advantage of that horror and used disrobing as a way of discomfiting people to whom they were antagonistic.

As a weapon, it has a number of advantages:—

(1) In its use there is little danger of releasing disruptive forces within the group.

(2) They need have no fear of retaliation in kind—no non-Doukhobor is ever going to take his clothes off in order to annoy a Doukhobor, and even if he did the effect would be simply ludicrous.

(3) This hostile manoeuvre is also useful because of its extreme simplicity. We have commented on the lack of well-developed social organization among the Doukhobors; as a result of this deficiency, organized, planned group-behaviour of a complex sort is impossible. Nudism is different; no detailed plans need be made, no capable leader nor structured social organization is required; it is applicable to all situations and can be resorted to without any difficulty. One has only to take off a few clothes and the enemy is demoralized, if not routed. As a hostile device, it is simple and very effective.

(4) Most important, however, is the fact that this way of acting out hostility enables them to maintain the fiction that they are neither hostile nor aggressive. Since to them, as to others, destructiveness is only destructiveness when it finds expression in physical or verbal abuse, they can deceive themselves as to what their true motives are and thus avoid guilt.

There is, however, one alternative to that of externally directed hostility. The anger that arises in response to frustration may be turned in on one's self, and this internally directed hostility results in feelings of depression. Although manifestations of this sort are found among the Sons of Freedom, as evidenced by their pessimism and their feeling that nothing good will ever happen to them, more substantial signs of this reaction are to be found among USCC members, a large number of whom are demoralized and discouraged. Their unwillingness to maintain and improve their farms springs partially from feelings of this sort, although they actually phrase the problem in terms of the uselessness of improving property that no longer belongs to them. This is one of the major distinctions between the Sons of Freedom and the USCC (to the extent that one can make such distinction); the Sons of Freedom direct their hostility more outwardly and the USCC direct theirs more inwardly.

But even the Sons of Freedom do not escape without considerable psychological discomfort. As has been pointed out before, basically they are "protesting" against their parents, and this rebellion leads to strong feelings of anxiety and guilt. In addition, they (and the USCC and Independents as well) feel guilty because their strong desire for "luxuries" and material success (the concrete manifestations of love and affection) is met with the knowledge that such a desire is frowned upon by their parents, who have inculcated into them an awareness that only the "bad" Doukhobor wants such things. Similarly, with regard to education, their strivings come up against the disapprobation of the elders who see in education the tool that will wean the children away from their parents and allow the group to disintegrate.

Consequently, the Doukhobors are, generally speaking, an anxious and apprehensive group of people. Physicians who treat them confirm the fact of their fearfulness and uncertainty. From a medical point of view, it would appear (although statistics are lacking) that there is an increased incidence of the psychosomatic disorders, those physical illnesses to which anxiety makes a significant contribution. One doctor stated that he found many cases of high blood pressure, and another spoke of numerous cases of dyspepsia and peptic ulcer. These findings are of interest because, according to many psychiatric observations, the former illness is often related to powerful feelings of hostility and the latter to strong needs for dependency, both of which characteristics we have commented upon as being of importance in the Doukhobor personality.

Physicians say also that they have been impressed by the inability of the Doukhobors to endure pain or illness. When subjected to either, they become extremely frightened. In this connection, it may be pointed out that the Doukhobors are generally intolerant of any frustration. They very rapidly become restless and impatient; when it was decided to release the more co-operative Sons of Freedom from jail, their relatives at home continued to remain in an agitated state while the necessary details were being attended to. They simply cannot wait or postpone the gratification of their needs. This low frustration tolerance may also stem from their marked anxiety and insecurity. Manifestations of guilt, as well as those of anxiety, are readily at hand. Within the medical frame of reference, this conclusion is supported by the prevalence of hypochondriacal complaints among them. Complaints of ill-health, without associated physical findings, are extremely common, and the psychiatric interpretation of this behaviour is that it arises in unconscious feeling of guilt. But it is not necessary to go to the psychiatrist for evidence of guilt—vegetarianism, the taboos against drinking and smoking are supported, at least partially, by such feelings. The overt behaviour of the Sons of Freedom is particularly impressive: they are extremely masochistic, that is to say, they are constantly inflicting pain and suffering upon themselves. A considerable number of Sons of Freedom abandoned prosperous farms in Saskatchewan to come to a barren life of poverty in Krestova. Here they burn their own homes; they go on prolonged fasts; they deny themselves sexual satisfaction;

they continually undergo all manner of futile and painful deprivations. The ones who feel most guilty go so far as to deny the validity of any personal strivings and tend to obliterate themselves as separate individuals.

The dynamics of this masochistic behaviour are these: in the first place, it represents a compromise in that it involves suffering a lesser punishment in order to avoid a greater. The Doukhobors, dependent on their parents and on the despotic leaders who succeed them, fear more than anything the loss of parental love and ostracism from the group. Consequently, they feel that it is better to suffer the lesser evil of, say, allowing one's house to be burned down than to risk being cast out into the limbo of disapprobation by the parental figures. Not only is it a way of avoiding loss of love and attention, but it can also be a means of getting attention. Mike B. speaks of going on prolonged fasts while he was in the Penitentiary in order to force the prison physician to pay greater attention to him. In another way, suffering pain can be a means of obtaining satisfaction from a powerful, authoritarian, parental figure, particularly when the pain is inflicted by the authority. Under these circumstances, punishment represents a way of recapturing the safe parent-child relationship, and, at the same time, by identifying with the source of power that is carrying out the punishment, one feels an enhancement of one's own power and self-esteem. Possibly this was the reason that Charlie K. did not sound at all resentful when he spoke of the numerous beatings he suffered at the hands of Peter Petrovich Verigin.

Masochistic behaviour also represents an anticipation of what is feared, as if by practising chastising one's self one can avoid the pain that otherwise would be suffered in the inevitable beating that is to come. The Sons of Freedom know that they will be punished by their fellows if they become too wealthy or successful; possibly it hurts less to burn one's own house down than to wait for someone else to do it.

But even hurting one's self can be a way of expressing hostility. Charlie O. made it quite clear that if anyone ever attempted to take his comfortable house away from him, he himself would burn it down rather than let it fall into another's hands. The prisoners in the Penitentiary who burned their own clothes undoubtedly did so with similar spiteful motives. More subtly, the act of doing one's self harm is an accusation flung in the face of an enemy, as if to say, "See what you have made me do." Mike B. refused to eat, to wear clothes, or to sleep other than on the cold floor for weeks at a time, but nevertheless he indicated that it was not really he who was responsible for his discomfort. If people didn't want him to suffer in jail or in the mental hospital, they would let him go home

148

Grandmother and grandchild

Community house and orchard

Farm equipment is generally outmoded

Present farm buildings are scanty and run-down

The few remaining orchards are dilapidated

Courtyard of a community house

Pumps irrigate a few gardens

Pacifiers are used extensively

Preserving

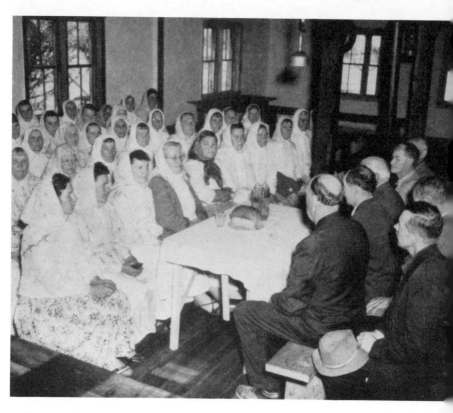

In the meeting

After the meeting

Cemetery

The often-bombed tomb of Peter the Lordly

School near Krestova

The house was fired by Sons of Freedom engaged to build it.
The school is provided with sentry-box and floodlighting.

The president of this student council is a Doukhobor

R.C.M.P. Constable seeks information on the burning of their home

Most Doukhobor men work outside the communities

At a burning

Remains of Doukhobor-owned mill

Dynamited bridge

This man guards two bridges

A protest parade halted

Young people enter a variety of jobs

to live the life he wanted. This way of thinking was particularly convenient as it served as a justification for his own hostility. The complete argument, had he been capable of being aware of it and of verbalizing it, would have run this way: "I suffer. You have made me suffer. It is no wonder then that I hate you." Approaching this device from a slightly different angle, we see that masochism serves as a means of denying one's own hostility. Pete E. argues that no one can say that the Sons of Freedom are actuated by destructive motives, since they burn down their own houses as well as those belonging to others.

However, the satisfactions to be obtained from such behaviour are indeed very limited. The Sons of Freedom continually inflict suffering upon themselves in order to get love and approval, but, of course, they do not get it. This in turn creates more anxiety, more hostility, more guilt, and more masochistic behaviour; and so it keeps on.

INDIVIDUAL DIFFERENCES

ACTIVE AND PASSIVE MEN

The Doukhobor male has been delineated in this chapter in such a manner as to emphasize the passive, dependent traits that are generally characteristic of him, but that is not to say that there are no dominant, aggressive males in Doukhobor society. In the first place, as has been indicated before, there are a number of men who are deviant in that their constitutional endowment does not allow them to assimilate readily the prescribed passive behaviour. Such individuals tend to leave the group and to pass out into the larger culture where there are fewer impediments to individual activity. There are a large number of merchants, artisans, and business-men who have become acculturated to a Canadian way of life, and are gradually drifting further and further from their parent culture. Ever since 1908, the tendency has been for the more "conservative" Doukhobors to flock to British Columbia; so that the majority of these assimilated or semi-assimilated Independents are found in Saskatchewan.

Those who were successful in this endeavour are of particular interest to us in this study. However, it must be remembered that a rewarding life outside the group was not readily achieved. Even if a man did not show the characteristic Doukhobor traits of passivity and dependence, his way was obstructed by his lack of knowledge of the English language and Canadian customs, by his deficiencies in special training and skills, and by the prejudice of the non-Doukhobor population. If he did have, in some measure, the typical difficulties in individual self-assertion, he would be extremely handicapped in the competitive give-and-take of the market.

149

Consequently, there were a number of men who, although sufficiently aggressive to venture out into the non-Doukhobor world, were not adequate to its demands, and who thereby met with frustration and failure. With this there followed a resurgence of whatever dependent needs lay latent within them, and back they came to the protective figure, the Doukhobor group. However, as indicated previously, the CCUB and the USCC did not open their doors to prodigal sons, and these dispossessed children had to choose between the Sons of Freedom and complete isolation. Naturally they chose the former. The same aggressiveness which carried them out of the group was now put to the service of the extreme hostility that they felt as a result of their frustrations in the outside world. To these hostile men are added a number of others of similar disposition and temperament who have not at any time left the Doukhobor group.

Within the Sons of Freedom, all of these men constitute a hard core of scornful bitterness and paranoid resentment. Since they lack the characteristic Doukhobor passivity, dependence, anxiety and guilt and are relatively free from uncertainty and self-doubt, they are capable of organizing others and of giving commands. Yet at the same time they are undone by their own hostility. In the first place it renders them unfit for positive leadership; they can and do instigate depredatory acts of arson and dynamiting (and probably most of such acts could be traced back to these individuals), but they cannot lead the community in constructive activities. Furthermore, they are constantly in cut-throat, competitive rivalry with each other for the prestige and the privileges of leadership. When not in a position of dominance, they will deny that the Doukhobors have any leaders and insist that all are equal. No leader of the Doukhobors can ever feel secure in his relationship with the community because of the machinations of his rivals who manipulate the more passive groups by playing on the negative side of its ambivalence to him. Finally, their destructiveness leads them to exploit their followers, whose anxiety and retaliatory hostility gradually mount until some explosion takes place.

MEN AND WOMEN

In a somewhat oversimplified fashion, we might say that the women resemble the more aggressive Doukhobor men. As indicated earlier, girls are deputized in childhood by their mothers to take care of the younger siblings. This gives them a sanctioned opportunity for the satisfaction of whatever aggressive needs they possess, so that they can develop a fair amount of self-assertiveness. We were told by one informant that more women than men leave the community; this fact could be explained on the basis of their greater

150

aggressiveness and self-assurance. Of course, a large number of such healthy, assertive women remain within the group because of marital and family ties. A few of these women were interviewed by both Miss Lewis and ourselves, and we were impressed by their enthusiasm and spontaneity. However, their family responsibilities do not allow them to make any great contribution to the community, so that although they are potentially useful to the group, this usefulness cannot readily be exploited.

At the same time there is a large number of women who have suffered from the same restrictions and frustrations at the hands of their parents as have the men. With them, too, the aggressiveness that they have been allowed to develop in relation to their younger siblings is then used to provide the fuel for the hostility that they feel. These women, possibly as a result of their childhood training, can express their hostility in an even more direct fashion than the aggressive men. In this connection we might mention their proclivity to tear the clothes from the back of anyone who annoys them. It seems that their anger is directed not only at outsiders, but also at the men of the community, whom they attempt to depreciate. Yet all these satisfactions do not seem to solve their problem; frequently the women are tense, obsessive and perfectionistic and suffer from headaches and like ailments.

DOUKHOBOR PERSONALITY AS RELATED TO GROUP MEMBERSHIP

It must be pointed out that the description of the basic personality type is intended to apply to all Doukhobors regardless of affiliation. Yet the three groups—USCC, Independents and Sons of Freedom—do show some fairly distinct differences in the personalities and attitudes of their members. As was recognized very early in this project, there are no hard and fast lines that can be drawn between the groups, and it seems that an individual can move from one to another, more or less at will, in accordance with the needs and attitudes that are at any time predominant. Here it might be of value to attempt to sort out the kinds of people that tend to congregate in each of these groups.

The USCC.—This group might be characterized briefly as being composed of relatively well-adjusted Doukhobors of the typical sort. Ideally, the USCC Doukhobor is fairly happy in his dependency and finds considerable comfort in the religious and social meetings of his community. He is passive, but finds additional strength in virtue of his group membership. Because of a fairly happy childhood he does not have to contend with an excessive amount of hostility, and he is relatively free from anxiety. When frustrated, he cannot deal with

151

the hostility that is engendered and tends to become depressed and demoralized instead of directing his anger at external objects.

The Independents.—Actually, there are two kinds of people within this group. On the one hand, there is the fairly aggressive, dominant man who has left the community because of its restricting demands and who is in the process of being acculturated. On the other hand, there is the crypto-Son of Freedom, also aggressive but less successful and more hostile. He, too, has left the community to make his own way but has not found such a life entirely satisfactory. Outwardly conforming to the demands of non-Doukhobor society, he is inwardly rebellious and suspicious, and is in fundamental agreement with the Sons of Freedom in their attitude toward nudism, arson, government, and education. Under ordinary circumstances, he will refrain from throwing in his lot with the Sons of Freedom because of his recognition of the sacrifices he would have to make in doing so. This has particular relevance to the situation in which one member of a family is a Son of Freedom and another is not, a phenomenon that was at first rather bewildering. We encountered a family in which the husband was Independent and the wife a Son of Freedom; actually both were Sons of Freedom within the framework of their attitudes and beliefs, but the husband was not sufficiently masochistic to give up the comforts he had acquired.

The Sons of Freedom.—It is probably apparent by now that the Sons of Freedom are an extremely heterogeneous group; although bound together by certain common attitudes and beliefs, they nevertheless are actuated by varying needs and motives. The Sons of Freedom group is the refuge of those who fit nowhere else.

In the first place, as has been described earlier, we find there individuals of ambitious, aggressive bent who have failed to satisfy their needs, either in the USCC or among the Independents. If they are ambitious and without great talent, they welcome the opportunity that is afforded them within the Sons of Freedom to acquire positions of prestige and dominance. If they are hostile for any reason at all, they have the opportunity here to vent their hostility in acts of arson and nudism. In this connection, we might mention the people who were discharged from the CCUB for failure to pay their dues. Whether such failure occurred because of lack of initiative, antagonism to the leaders, or financial reverses, the effect of expulsion was to engender considerable hostility, later to be expressed in the activities of the Sons of Freedom.

Secondly, we find a larger number of passive, lonely, guilty men who seek to submerge themselves in the formless mass of the Sons of Freedom and to atone for their wrong-doings, real or fantasied, in the masochistic self-denial of this way of life. Independents who have found that their striving for success did not satisfy their needs for dependency, and who eventually become aware of an intolerable isolation, flock to this group. Here, too, may be found those who are crippled by feelings of inferiority with respect to the non-Doukhobor population, and who find ego-enhancement in the exalted Sons of Freedom ideology with its messianic flavour.

Thirdly, there are a few pathological characters who would not be tolerated in any society not so poorly integrated as the Sons of Freedom. Some are frank criminals, exploiting the others for personal gain. Some are autistic, schizoid people who find satisfaction in mystic, high-flown Sons of Freedom philosophy.

Fourthly, the Sons of Freedom have a special attraction for the aged Doukhobors. Those who lack special training and skills inevitably suffer a loss of self-esteem as they grow older and are no longer capable of the manual labour by which they supported themselves in their youth. Among the Independents the aged have little status. In the USCC some prestige may be owing to them in virtue of their knowledge of Doukhobor tradition. But it is within the Sons of Freedom group that they find full recognition. After all, it is the Sons of Freedom particularly who have displaced the hostility they feel to their parents on to other objects, and the elders enjoy the benefit to be derived from this. Outwardly, at least, the Sons of Freedom are deferential to their parents, who take advantage of this to stimulate hostility toward the out-group. By instigating acts of arson and dynamiting they compel the younger members to remain in a position of dependency on and subservience to them.

Finally, there are special satisfactions to be obtained within the Sons of Freedom by those who are particularly emotionally impoverished and constricted. Deprived of any constructive outlets or channels of expression, they find a gratifying emotional release in nudism and arson. Several of our informants have commented upon the orgiastic nature of some of this communal behaviour and have likened it to the dancing of the Molokans and to the hysterical seizures occurring in the meetings of certain evangelical sects.

MENTAL ILLNESS

Many people, baffled by the illogical contradictions of Doukhobor behaviour, have sought an explanation for it in the hypothesis that the Doukhobors, more particularly the Sons of Freedom, are "insane." From time to time it has been suggested that it would be well for a psychiatrist to examine the Doukhobor population in the hope of ferreting out those members, obviously deranged, who were responsible for various acts of arson and dynamiting. Some of the people who theorize in this way start from the premise that anyone

153

who behaves according to an alien set of beliefs and principles is, *ipso facto,* mentally disturbed. This sort of thinking is indulged in by both Doukhobor and non-Doukhobor.

One rather simple definition of mental illness is that it is the state in which a person fails to find the satisfactions and security that he requires because of characteristics of his own personality that lie outside his awareness. A person is mentally ill when he is unhappy because of the frustrations that he suffers, not from the mistreatment of a hostile environment, but his own unrecognized conflicting needs. The symptoms of mental illness arise through his futile attempts to deal with this impossible situation. It must be pointed out that here we are not dealing with a separation into the completely healthy and the mentally ill; there is a continuum extending from the hypothetical completely healthy individual to the completely disintegrated psychotic. Furthermore, people with the same degree of personality disturbance vary in the success with which they solve the problems created by their illness.

By now, it must be clear that the Doukhobors are continually being thwarted in their strivings because of certain inconsistent, competing drives, and that, furthermore, they are completely unaware of the origin and nature of these drives and of the way in which they inevitably defeat themselves. This report is, in essence, an elaboration and documentation of this thesis. The majority of Doukhobors are partially sick and unhappy through causes that lie largely within themselves. It must be pointed out that this statement has little or no reference to breaches of the peace; a depressed and demoralized, but law-abiding, USCC Doukhobor is, psychiatrically speaking, at least as sick as a hostile, destructive Son of Freedom who turns outward the violence of his feeling.

This statement must not be construed as an attempted justification for various acts of unfairness from which the Doukhobors have really suffered. The evidence is quite conclusive that in many ways they have been unjustly treated. The point is that the Doukhobors have not dealt in an integrated, productive fashion with the stresses (real or illusory) impinging upon them.

It must not be thought that the Doukhobors are radically different from the rest of Canadian society with regard to the incidence of mental illness defined in this way. A large number of non-Doukhobors have comparable personality problems occasionally of a similar nature and frequently equally severe. It has been estimated that one-third of the patients of any general practitioner suffer primarily from psychological illnesses. This estimate is, if anything, conservative and does not take into consideration the patients suffering from psychosomatic disorders, those illnesses to which psychological problems make a significant contribution. Nor does this estimate take into account the vast number of people who are considered by their fellows to be "normal" in spite of the presence of interfering, neurotic difficulties.

There is no really satisfactory diagnostic label that can be applied to this sort of mental illness. Some psychiatrists say that such individuals, so common in our own culture as well as in the Doukhobor society, suffer from a "character neurosis." But this name adds little to our understanding.

It is also true that the Doukhobors develop the graver personality disorders as well. Doukhobors can and do suffer from manic-depressive and schizophrenic illnesses just as other Canadians, but a review of the records at the Provincial Mental Hospital does not indicate that the incidence or nature of these disorders differs to any significant degree from that of the general population.

Aside from illnesses of this sort, a few Doukhobors, some three or four in number, have suffered from severe personality disorders that defy classification. In essence, these individuals show a gross exaggeration of those maladaptive traits which are to some degree characteristic of all Doukhobors. Mike B., who lay nude for weeks in a completely bare seclusion room at the Provincial Mental Hospital, is one such person. He refused to take food or water by mouth and was kept alive only through tube feedings. It was completely impossible to supply him with either furniture or bedding, because he would demolish anything that was destructible. His hostility was insatiable, and yet, in spite of his hatred of everyone and everything (which he denied), he continued to expect and require unceasing love and support from those whom he wished to destroy.

RECOMMENDATIONS

There are no panaceas or magically effective solutions that can be derived from the material presented in this chapter. Many of the contributions made by the press and by individuals whom one might expect to be well informed and rational are as illogical as the paranoid beliefs of the most die-hard Sons of Freedom and are similarly based on personal motives and private fantasy rather than on the facts. Take, for example, the recommendation that the Sons of Freedom be scattered in small groups throughout Canada. We shall not discuss the more obvious objections to this plan—the opposition of the communities in which Doukhobor families would be placed and the accusation of genocide that would surely follow. Quite apart from such objections, there would be serious difficulties in carrying out such a project—difficulties which could be readily deduced from the data presented here.

First of all, the distinction between the Sons of Freedom and the other Doukhobor groups is not a rigid one; a man may switch allegiance in accordance with his prevailing needs. More than that, a number of Doukhobors do not themselves know where their loyalty lies; they may belong, say, to the USCC and yet have the sort of personality that would find the Sons of Freedom group congenial. Such individuals can be readily precipitated into the Sons of Freedom by some slight shift in the forces impinging upon them. Any punitive solution would certainly create such a shift of forces, so that the final result would be that practically all of the Doukhobors would have to be scattered.

In the second place, action which deprived Doukhobors of the support of the group would create an intolerable degree of anxiety, leading certainly either to complete demoralization and personality disintegration or to violent displays of destructiveness such as we have not seen heretofore.

Of course, no responsible administrator is likely to consider seriously such a plan as the one described. The purpose of the above discussion is to point out that any attempted solution must be based on a thorough knowledge of Doukhobor needs, attitudes and beliefs and of the way these variables are integrated within the Doukhobor personality. Even with such precautions, it seems likely that the very best of well-laid plans will achieve little against the operation of those psychological processes that have been discussed. It is impossible to satisfy any individual or group suffering from conflicting motives; gratify one of the opposing needs and the other is thereby frustrated. Thus, if it were possible to meet the Doukhobors' need for dependent satisfaction, difficulties would then arise through the frustration of their need to be independent of such crippling paternalism. Accept at face value the refusal of the Sons of Freedom to send their children to school, and you deny them the possibility of ever satisfying their strong but unconscious need for an education. Wherever we turn, we are faced with dilemmas of this kind.

Thus there are two good reasons for being wary of panaceas: in the first place, such apparent solutions only too often are not based on the facts of the situation; and, secondly, the facts of the situation simply do not permit any ready-made answer because of the conflicting motives of the Doukhobors themselves.

It would actually seem that a final solution will be achieved only when the Doukhobors make certain changes in their own personality type, much as the patients and clients of psychiatrists, clinical psychologists, and social workers achieve favourable personality changes through therapy. It is almost always very difficult to help a single individual make significant alterations in his ways of seeing and doing things, and rarely is it possible to help him unless he himself has some willingness to change. In dealing with the Doukhobors,

156

then, the problem is infinitely greater; here we are concerned not with one individual, but with several thousand; furthermore, they are people who do not recognize that their habitual attitudes and beliefs are such as to lead them into difficulties, and, therefore, they are not willing to examine their own behaviour. They have projected the blame, and, consequently, they feel no need to evaluate their own position.

Thus there are no encouraging prospects of a mutually satisfying relationship with the Doukhobors, energetically directed toward the clarification and amelioration of their difficulties in living. We cannot reasonably expect that there are any techniques that can be employed to assist them in the modification of their personalities. Yet at the same time an attitude of nihilistic despair is not indicated. We can avoid acting in such a way as to compound the problem; more positively than that, there are a number of measures that can be taken by administrative authorities that will at least facilitate the growth of the Doukhobors to political and social maturity.

The ideal would be, of course, that only administrators adequately trained in the sciences of human behaviour be appointed to positions of importance. This is probably an unattainable ideal; the Doukhobors come in contact with many governmental authorities with diverse responsibilities, so that it is impossible to ask that all of these be trained in the social sciences. Nevertheless, when filling in the future positions whose functions lie purely in the realm of Doukhobor affairs this ideal should be kept in view. However, because of practical considerations, it would be useful to work with those now in authority in formulating both the profitable and unprofitable attitudes that one can adopt in dealing with the Doukhobors. The following are some of the principles that seem particularly relevant:—

> (1) We must avoid the error of accepting Doukhobor rationalizations at face value. The Doukhobors offer arguments in support of their position and we offer counter-arguments. This is always a complete waste of time, since the source of difficulty does not arise in a rational frame of reference in which logic and clear thinking suffice. We must be alert to the feeling underlying the actual words, and often in contradiction to those words, in order to avoid complete confusion. We are dealing with the data of the emotional life which are not subject to the dicta of logic. In a similar vein, the Doukhobors say that theirs is a "religious" problem, and we obligingly send to them religious leaders who vainly try to thrash out the religious and philosophical themes of Doukhobor ideology. We do not wish to depreciate the efforts of those courageous and idealistic men who

157

have attempted to convince the Sons of Freedom that from a religious point of view they might better achieve their ends in other ways. Yet it must be admitted that many such missionaries, although acting from the highest motives, have tended to misinterpret Doukhobor behaviour in the light of their own attitudes and beliefs, so that any sort of reciprocal understanding becomes impossible and both they and the Doukhobors are thereby frustrated.

(2) Without cutting them off from the support and assistance that they require, we must avoid the trap of encouraging the Doukhobors to be dependent on paternal authority. It is essential that they develop some measure of independence and personal responsibility if they are to be able to guide themselves. The word "trap" was used, because at times, the Doukhobors themselves try to lure administrators into accepting responsibility for Doukhobor behaviour, and then resent those same administrators afterwards, regardless of the outcome. In a number of connections the Doukhobors can be encouraged to be independent. With regard to relocation, they show a strong desire to make as few decisions as possible themselves, and to leave as many as they can to the Consultative Committee and to the Government; some attempt must be made to discourage this tendency. Of course, we cannot expect miracles; as the evidence clearly indicates, passivity and dependence are deeply rooted in Doukhobor character, and it would not do to deny completely their demands for help.

(3) We must not reward the Doukhobors for their passivity. Here again there is a temptation; passive people are pleasant people, and it is satisfying to one's own self-esteem to dominate them. Many employers and policemen play a kindly, dominating role in their dealings with the Doukhobors. By behaving in this way they give the Doukhobors friendliness and warmth, but at the same time these rewards only perpetuate the passivity which is responsible for many of their difficulties. We wish them to state their needs and attitudes in a clear, forthright fashion. Similarly, if they do not understand something that we are trying to communicate to them, we must encourage them to ask rather than to sink back into bewildered resentment and autistic reverie.

(4) Accepting the fact that passivity is a trait difficult to

alter, we should ourselves take active steps to improve communication with the Doukhobors. It is wrong to assume that they understand what is being told them simply because they do not ask questions. At all times it is necessary to be certain, through repetition and inquiry, that the communication has been comprehended. Communication both within the group and between the group and outside is poor, and this deficiency, coupled with the anxiety and hostility that they all feel, leads to an excessive reliance on vague rumour and gossip. It might be possible to use various media—the radio, the press and pamphlets—in order to present statements of fact and of governmental policy and intention so as to clarify many perplexing problems.

(5) We have commented on the various satisfactions that the Doukhobors obtain through their masochistic behaviour. It is exceedingly unwise for the administrator to enter into neurotic arrangements of this sort, perpetuating them by his own attitude. This is just another way of saying that it is bad to make martyrs of those who invite martyrdom. At times it is difficult to avoid this; in the first place, it is sometimes necessary to impose restrictions upon the Sons of Freedom for the protection of both themselves and others, and secondly, they are singularly skilful in eliciting hostile responses from those who try to deal with them, so that many people are trapped into adopting a punitive, rejecting attitude. We must be aware of this danger and avoid it when possible.

(6) In attempting to deal with anxious, insecure people, it is always necessary to be relatively non-threatening, even though it is neither possible nor desirable to avoid inducing all increments of anxiety. The Doukhobors can make favourable changes in their own attitudes and responses only if they are at least relatively secure. If they are greeted with rigid, uncompromising demands, or if administrative measures are adopted that markedly increase the general level of anxiety, then further hostility and social disintegration will follow. In introducing changes, it is necessary to do so gradually, in steps that will be tolerated. Thus, an immediate insistence, for example, that all Sons of Freedom send their children to public schools would undoubtedly have disastrous results.

(7) The Doukhobors' narrowness, rigidity, and lack of satisfying emotional and creative outlets have been described. It has been pointed out that these aspects of Doukho-

bor personality result from their repressive childhood training, and are therefore not readily amenable to change. However, whenever there is an opportunity to enrich Doukhobor existence with culture and artistic means of expression, such an opportunity should be seized.

(8) The Doukhobors want knowledge and material success in order to satisfy certain needs that have arisen in the course of their development. In spite of the fact that they also deny the existence of these wants and resist those people who try to fulfil them, the wants are still present and strong. Any measures that can be taken to provide the Doukhobors, in ways that are acceptable to them, with further education, special skills, and job-training will have a salutary effect. Similarly, the economic hardships from which many Doukhobors suffer might also at times be ameliorated by judicious action, although it is necessary to be wary of encouraging their dependent strivings. Any steps that can be taken to foster economic achievement will be beneficial.

(9) There are a number of other stresses operating on the group from both within and without so as to perpetuate the sort of behaviour that must be changed. Coming from outside, there is prejudice and discrimination; from within, there are the factors of poor social organization, inadequate leadership, and the dominance of psychopathic, excessively hostile, or delinquent individuals. None of these stresses is readily eliminated, but at the same time there are opportunities for appropriate action. What, for example, are the possibilities of educating the public toward a greater understanding of the Doukhobor problem? What help can we be to the group in developing a more stable social structure? What possibility is there of removing from the group those exploitative individuals who are continually acting out their own hostile impulses?

It may be seen that these nine principles constitute a guide to remedial action rather than a solution of the problem. Yet this is the way it must be. We cannot give the Doukhobors all they want because their needs are hopelessly conflicting. All that we can do is to be patient, understanding, and alert, with the idea that, if only by avoiding blunders, we can help the Doukhobors to a true awareness of what it is that they need, and to a maturity in which responsibility and equality find full expression.

EDITOR'S NOTE.—Mr. Herbison, member of the Wider Quaker Fellowship, who was employed by the Consultative Committee and living near Krestova in constant contact with Sons of Freedom for two years, accepted the invitation to write a section on Doukhobor religion. In approaching this he faced a choice of reporting with external objectivity or of attempting to share their religious experience, and reporting it largely from the standpoint of their own assumptions, values and beliefs. The second method of operation seemed to promise a contribution all the more distinctive because the studies of economics, personality and other aspects of Doukhobor life had been written largely from an external point of view. The following chapter differs, therefore, from most of the Report in that the nature and meaning of religious experience is often seen through Doukhobor (more especially Sons of Freedom) eyes.

SUBJECTIVE EXPERIENCE

DOUKHOBORISM, like Christianity itself, has upon it the mark of time and place. The time is here limited to three hundred years, the place to areas where Doukhobors have grouped together and clung tenaciously to their sectarianism. This arbitrarily excludes the beliefs of those Doukhobors who have individually escaped the cohesive whirl of communalism and now live unobtrusively amongst other people.

Doukhobor religion has been built and shattered on three rocks: group mysticism, perfectionist ideology, and an internal church-state fusion. These will be discussed in relation to subjective experience, interpreted in the perspective of religious history as a form of mysticism, to ideology, considered in relation to Biblical religion and Christian theology, and to outward demonstration of inner conviction, involving Doukhobor faith in themselves as a people chosen of God to fulfil a special destiny in the world.

Doukhobors in their beginnings and throughout most of their existence have been primarily a religious sect. An understanding of their religion, therefore, is a vital part of any comprehensive body of knowledge about them. That such understanding is difficult to obtain is commonly explained by saying that the Doukhobors have always been on the defensive, suspicious of investigation, and masters in the art of double-talk and subterfuge. This is true, but a more profound reason is that their religion is based on insight, intuition, and mystic states of consciousness, relies much on a belief in unseen, mysterious forces, and possesses little thought-content.

To explore the world beyond the finite is harder than to recite logically articulated dogma worded by theologians with literacy and intellectual power whose art lies in their ability to capture in neat and telling phrase the longing of men for assurance that the spiritual world is safe and orderly. The mystic values this doctrinal assurance less than the reality of a vision he has had and cannot enunciate.

Doukhobors do at various times attempt to explain themselves, either in the ponderous and flowery English of a Declaration or in conversation, with catch-phrases and bits of scripture out of context. These efforts do them no justice. The essence of their faith is, in fact, so simple it can easily be stated. They believe in the capacity of every man to know the spirit of God within him, and in the duty of every man to follow the guidance of that spirit in all life. But for all its simplicity, this creed is hard to explain.

At the outset it would seem necessary in a study of this kind to approach the subject in a sympathetic and receptive mood. Doukhobors often claim that an outsider cannot understand their ideas without first agreeing with them. This is hardly true, yet little will be learned of Doukhobor religious life unless the tendency toward disparagement, condescension, and scepticism be held in abeyance. Also necessary here is the assumption that divinity may exist, that men may honestly seek it, and that something worthwhile may be found.

Many religious movements have in their origins the intimate personal experience of seeming to be in the presence of divinity, with visions, ecstasies, and direct contact with the world "beyond." Later, in the interests of preservation, organization and control, the first-hand man-to-god experiences are often absorbed into ritual or limited to shaman and priest. Some sects, however, have always tried to preserve, rather than obliterate, the right of each believer to approach God intimately on his own initiative and be guided by his own experience as superior to any other authority. Such a sect is Doukhoborism. It recognizes that the human mind is impressed by forces other than schooling, thinking, and visible authority. It supports the commonplace sayings that a man's first duty is to God, that he should follow his own conscience, and that the human spirit cannot forcibly be channeled into religious conviction.

The mystic is, then, invulnerable. His guidance being "sudden, penetrating, coercive," no human authority can shake it or alter it. We may by physical compulsion only attach him more stubbornly to his belief.

Mystical religion bears certain marks of identification. The indescribableness of the intuitive experience handicaps the visionary. The literature of religion is enhanced by vast amounts of heightened prose and poetry trying, but never with full success, to capture in words the spiritual exaltation. Such accounts may thrill the reader of similar temperament, and leave others cold. Most sects as old as Doukhoborism have developed an approved phraseology, contained in simple creed and systemized theology, by which on various levels of intellectual discernment any adherent may declare the prevailing views of the group. But Doukhoborism has persistently avoided developing a theology to define its outlook. Those pet mottoes heard so frequently—"All for one and one for all," "Toil and peaceful life," "Sons of Freedom cannot be slaves of corruption"—are slogans for battle rather than reasoned enunciations of belief. The eventual result of this refusal to probe the intellectual content of religion, and by studied system educate the mind of rank-and-file, are topics for consideration. The tendency is to be recognized as a natural sequence of the basic type of religious experience espoused by the group.

The intensity of conviction engendered by mysticism needs no external confirmation. The content of revelation seems to bear an overwhelming sense of truth and reality, the irrefutable witness of direct experience. Also a characteristic of mysticism is exclusive individualness. So vivid is the feeling of personal communion, so real the awareness of a spiritual presence, the impression ensues that nothing quite the same has ever happened before, and nothing else is quite so important. Confident in his own knowledge of divine nature and divine will, the mystic may not feel the need for the outward forms and disciplines of organized social and religious life. It is the conviction of some that the spiritual catharsis has given release from bondage to ordinary laws and customs of men, now that there exists "the glorious liberty of the children of God." This is a point of faith with Doukhobors.

What is the effect of mysticism on personal life and conduct? First there is a calm, blissful confidence, rooted in the surety of divine companionship. No words can quite convey the joyous sense of nearness to Christ, which is part of the lives of elderly Doukhobors. They touch their heart, then yours, saying, "Christ here—inside."

For mystics, there seems to be efficacy, in paring down the superfluous appendages of existence, so that in outward simplicity of living there is little to interfere with the development of inner spirituality. It is apparent that Doukhobors as a people have exemplified this trait to a remarkable degree, from earliest times, when it was forced upon them by necessity, up to present times, when with means to do otherwise most still choose austerity. What outsiders do not discern is the warm, thrilling appeal of the simple life, even when practised to the point of voluntary poverty. The Sons of Freedom, home-burning and all, are the inevitable out-cropping of an obsession with the simple-life ideal conceived in negative terms.

Going far beyond the desire merely to rid life of its complexities is the yearning for saintliness, or perfection in character and conduct, which is inherent in the thinking of those who feel personally acquainted with eternity. Doukhobors list among their numbers many individuals who possess the beauty and dignity of personality which results from this. Deeply rooted still today in the hearts of Doukhobors is a discontent which makes them ill at ease in the midst of a civilization based on materialism tempting in its manifold attractions to youth. Unlike most Canadians and unaccustomed to a culture aggressive in its demand for possession, Doukhobors have not made their peace with this world. Many of them this very day would walk off and leave the amenities of civilization if the call to do so were to come according to their expectation. For whereas most people do not seriously contemplate the Perfect Life as an immediate possibility (they just keep the idea wistfully in the back of their minds), Doukhobors, despite a certain trend toward pessimism, conceive of the Perfect Life as an ever real and attainable prospect.

In many cultures, mysticism has a place of high regard. Our own culture does not favour it. This is partly on account of certain pitfalls which are particularly dangerous for this type of religious life. These hazards emanate from the very features which give mysticism its power and effectiveness. In the first place, the elusive, intangible, other-worldliness of the experience leaves the way open to gullibility and emotionalism. When the very purpose of religious aspiration is the annihilation of the ordinary bounds and limits of existence—an escape from the confines of the five senses—illusion and excess are possible. If it is allowed that the invisible world cannot be probed by intellect and reason, and if man's duty is to obey the dictates of that unseen world, the way is open to sudden inexplicable changes in mood and action, and all sorts of vagaries in thought. The wonder is not that Doukhoborism today displays such eccentricities, but that throughout most of its history it has been sober in the expression of its religious life.

In the effort to force the mystic experience, to get feeling right, irrational practice of theopathic absorption, self-torment and scrupulosity may be entered into. The sensitive conscience is easily led to believe that any suggestion that seems unpleasant or difficult must come from God. In Doukhobors this has led to a bleakness of cultural expression and to poverty for its own sake, to negativeness as the standard of godliness. Goodness is no smoking, no drinking, no meat eating, no owning, no voting, and, with extremists, no clothing and no schooling.

The refusal to accept intellectually formed criteria has left Doukhobors open to misguidance by anyone cunning enough to play upon their partiality for anything mysterious, secret, and unofficial. And it has led them to attach undue significance to nightly dreams, premonitions, unfounded rumours, and hidden meanings. Their "spiritual" interpretation of all words and events means a search for implications not apparent to the ordinary mind and ordinary processes of reasoning.

From the intensity of conviction engendered by mysticism there can arise self-righteousness and intolerance, often disguised in Doukhobors by apparent meekness and sincerity. If God is within me, and I speak earnestly, how can I be wrong? Doukhobors kneeling before judges and officials may feel not humility, but pride and conceit. And no one was ever more smug and self-righteous than defiant nudes displaying outward flesh to advertise inward sanctity—for all that, they may themselves believe they are naked to reveal the pompousness and hypocrisy in others. Doukhobors in their sectarianism are self-contained and self-assured. Their mental isolation makes this particularly evident in public utterances. Their "Declaration" says, "We triumphantly declare that we do not allow any force whatever by men over men. . . . We have obtained perfect freedom by egressing from the slavery of corruption into the glorious liberty of the children of God." Many Doukhobors individually confess that they are not living up to their ideals, but few question the validity of the main tenets and expressions of their faith, such as pacifism. It is common to hear the incredibly naive statement, "Doukhobors have never made a mistake," even from worldly-wise men who are not fanatics. In the back of their minds is the thought that God has pre-destined everything, anl what apparently is misadventure is divine intention. Leader Peter Petrovich Verigin fell short of being a chaste ascetic, but his vices and escapades are seen by some as tricks necessary for fooling the Government, or high policy based on his knowledge of spiritual cosmography.

The exclusive individualness of mysticism can also lead to many forms of aberration. The mystic may be tempted to exalt his own experience over historical revelation and any counsels of men. Such a man feels personally released from worldly law and order, since he now enjoys the "glorious liberty" of heavenly jurisdiction. A Doukhobor Declaration says that "they have never given nor will they ever give their votes during elections, thereby are free from any responsibility before God or man for the acts of any government established by men," and that Doukhobor members are "essentially above party politics," having given prior allegiance to Christ. Their self-sufficient "building all inward" has created amongst them a disrespect for religious and social institutions and the functions of government. And further, it has kept them from consistent development of their own religious knowledge, and prevented reasonable regulation of their own community affairs. In both personal and community life, the seeming adequacy of theocracy has made many of them Utopian and escapist, obsessed with short cuts to perfection, and incapable of facing the real world. Recognition of defeat is fended off, in the case of extremists, by various forms of irrational conduct, like chiliastic pilgrimages, a search for martyrdom, and defiance of properties.

Many different types and organizations of people appreciate that heightened sensitivity by which man, by-passing the outward forms of logic, may gain direct knowledge of goodness and truth, through insight, inspiration, or sheer genius. Among artists, musicians and scientists the intuitive perception of beauty and the inexplicable flash of insight are common enough. The most matter-of-fact people know what it is to "have a hunch" or in a superior moment outdo themselves in moral decision or act of heroism. But Doukhobors have in the past glorified this aspect of life beyond all reason, denying themselves citizenship in this world so they may be free to adhere to the invisible, magical world.

Some likeness to the Doukhobor position is seen in other persuasions where common sense and scientific curiosity are considered appropriate to the ordinary walks of life, but in the sphere of religion, implicit faith is the rule. Doukhobors simply widen this area of unreasoning trust and submission to powers beyond question and forever unfathomable—so that for Doukhobors it includes every part of existence. Here is the full meaning of the statement that Doukhobors are a religious people. They are not departmentalized, having never grasped the significant difference between secular and religious. Meat-eating, communalism, the full skirt and pacifism are all of religious importance; and the intellectual, scientific method, denied in the field of faith, is similarly denied in the realm of social and economic life. This disregard for the application of human intelligence to their own problems has in the past obstructed progress, social and economic as well as spiritual, and today is the underlying cause of confusion and unrest.

Doukhobors are proud of their practical skills, and have ingenuous confidence in their ability to tackle any project in farming, logging, or building. But they have shown no talent for operating on the plane of policy making, social strategy or religious organization unless they have had a directive from above; and for Sons of Freedom, the directive has had to be surreptitious.

All the hazards of mysticism converge at this point, where the other-world demands such complete submission, the human being becomes a passive recipient, utterly submissive to the in-flooding of impulse and ecstasy. All laws, institutions, and inventions of men are extraneous to this single principle of living. Not only formal education, but all seeking after those elusive treasures of wisdom and beauty by which life is enlightened and enhanced—all this can be summed up for traditional Doukhobors in the words of Ecclesiastes: "In much wisdom is much grief." Doukhobors have been taught that they are effective in the divine scheme to the extent that they subordinate personality and human faculty to a superior, supposedly divine power. Personality counts for little, reason is discredited, thinking is evil. The breaking away from accepted forms, political and religious, the cutting loose from stabilization by scripture and other authority, the denying of thought, law and civil authority has created an unbalance in the development of Doukhoborism. The Sons of Freedom unrest is no foreign scourge imposed on other Doukhobors. It is a turmoil at the very heart of Doukhoborism, its violence a witness to an unreasoning faith whose growth was started long ago by honoured forebears. Those within the turmoil know that they are helplessly in the power of something beyond themselves, but they will not, indeed it seems they cannot, do anything about it. "We know we are crazy," says one man, "just like birds sitting on a wire. When one goes, we all go."

"I met at the place where he said. Six of us got in the car. I didn't know where we were going or what we would do. But soon I found out we were going to Brilliant, then I knew we were going to burn."

"Oh, it was awful the first time we took our clothes off, with all those people looking. Something just made us do it."

"We can't promise what we might do to-morrow, or next week. We don't know what God might tell us to do."

The unbalance in Doukhoborism must have started a long time ago, perhaps in the Russian village when the conservative peasants, secure in their local communes and church affiliation, suddenly found themselves outside the mother church and driven away from their homes, harried from place to place and persecuted because they wanted to live as they always had. They did not break away from the old faith like the Western Protestants did, with new and daring doctrines to shake the old church to her roots; they just wanted to live and believe as they always did—the sign of the cross with three fingers, religious processions moving from east toward the west. And no sooner were they excommunicated by ritual-reformer Nikon than Peter the Great thrust westernism upon them, making the men cut their beards, wear foreign clothing, and answer the census. Thousands of peasants committed suicide, many were tortured, and others spent years hiding from the authorities. Out of this confusion arose many sects, including the Clubbers, the Jumpers, the Chokers, the Self-burners, and a peaceful little group called the Spirit-wrestlers. Under the guidance of extraordinarily wise and strong leaders, scattered families gathered together in mutual dependence, and before long they developed a way of their own and became their own tradition. Con-

167

tinuing hostility from outside turned them ever more in upon themselves. Children were taught that they must depend on God alone, and He was within them. In time a group called Molokans separated themselves out, and went their own way steadied by Holy Scripture. A number of released convicts moved in, and some serfs joined to escape bondage. Later a third of the people moved out from the circle and accepted the controls of civil law. The remaining members revolved around the person of Peter Verigin, and moved like the spokes of a wheel when, from exile and without use or threat of force, he bade them forswear meat, tobacco, alcohol, military service, and sex.

In Canada the developments in community life quickened. A third of the immigrants moved out into independence, and at the centre the pilgrimages, the nudism and the arson began. The community moved to British Coumbia, but it was troubled by the torment in its midst. It became so bad that community members disowned the central hubbub and tried to find peace apart from it. But even today unwary independents may be sucked in from the outer fringe, and the inner contours of the peaceful Union of Spiritual Communities of Christ are dangerously close.

One of the most important institutions in Doukhobor life is the community meeting, the sobranya. Here is the church, the school, the fraternal society, and the government. The character of the sobranya is completely alien to political system, man-made legalities, and democratic procedure. The underlying principle is that God is present and available; and it is His will, not rules nor order and majorities of men, which is expected to influence decision. Moreover, it is assumed that as the same God is in every heart, the desired unanimity depends upon each person's giving up his own individuality so that the God within him may merge with the God in others, and in this corporate union is found the consensus of the meeting. In Sons of Freedom meetings there may be talk, there may be speeches, there may be anything unpredictable as well; but in the end, if there are decisions, they are not important—what remains impressed upon the people is a unanimity of mood, a shared attitude which provides the sense of belonging, which unites the people as strongly as any voting aye or nay. Its vague indefinability is of no concern. The effectiveness of the sobranya lies not in a building, which is unnecessary; not in ritual, which is minimal; not in the preaching, which is incidental; not in personal communions and prayer, for which there is no provision; and not in the heightened sensivity of mind and heart reaching for truth, because this is not characteristic. The sobranya is a settling-down into the past, an immersion of self into the group. The singing at a sobranya is monotonous, persistent, inescapable; it is vocal magic which takes the place of other forms and determinants of unity.

In Sons of Freedomism, corporate action is the rule. No nude is ever alone in her nakedness; no action in the name of religion is taken without group stimulus or confirmation. The technique of solidarity has been mastered. "Take one, take all," is the theme for arresting time. Delegations of protest and complaint are preferably large, and they may come wheedling, "We are simple ignorant folk, not wise and influential like you." (Aha, but foxy. We know our own power, and use it—the power of many acting as one.) When personal decision is unavoidable, the situation is pitiful. Faced with an apparently simple matter to settle on behalf of the group, a woman says, "This is the hardest thing I have ever had to do." She muffs the opportunity, fails to decide, and in distress fasts for a week and blames everything on the Government. Aylmer Maude found that the delegates sent from Russia to help him choose land in Canada were of little service because they would not make decisions, though empowered to do so.

Moral responsibility for anything that happens in times of religious zeal never falls on the shoulders of the individual. "I am not responsible," says the accused, because he acts believing he obeys the will of the group. His interpretation of the group will is not questioned. Indeed, who can presume to question it? How does anyone know what God told him to do?

It would seem evident that if the individual is not responsible for his actions, the group must be. This is true only in the general sense, that the group is responsible only to itself. God is within, an integral part of the group, so there is perfect autonomy of action in the moral sphere. The danger implicit in this belief is readily seen. To the individual, the advantages of corporateness are that it offers security and the sense of belonging, while at the same time it allows him by the process of submission to share in a freedom and magnitude of action such as he could never enjoy by himself.

On the other hand, there is a basic inhumanity in the corporate Doukhobor community. Individuality is crushed, private rights and personal desires ignored. An individual will give up everything—his home, his health, his honour—for the preservation of the group as an entity. No government persecution or codified law was so harsh and restrictive as the unwritten law of this enduring mobilization. Among fanatics, the technique of incitement and control is based upon the religious predilection of the people for the divine and the mysterious, understood not by observation and reasoning, but by spiritual insight. The man wielding power must use the I-know-something-you-don't-know lure, pretending to be in contact with secret sources, probably divine. His directions must never go forth by straight talk, but by implication and hidden meanings. Puzzling through such veiled statements is a favourite pastime, a challenge to religious capacity. The more a schemer can keep the people guessing, the more power he has.

169

The people will always be watching those who are influential, looking for some sly indication, a subtle hint, unwilling to believe that anything is said without a double meaning.

The final topic for consideration in this section on subjective experience is the fact of human leadership as an integral part of Doukhobor religious life. In the days of persecution in Russia, Doukhobors would claim that they had no leader, that all were equal, as brothers and sisters in Christ. The same denials of leadership were sometimes made in Canada, and it has always been difficult to distinguish and evaluate the position of the leader in relation to other factors affecting the group.

Leadership in a democracy, with all its levels of representation and authorization, is a mere physical mixture in comparison with the Doukhobor concept which is akin to chemical fusion. The God-in-every-man conviction makes possible a mystical concept of union of every member with every other, and vital to this union is a rallying centre without which corporate living could not exist. At their most effusive moments, Peter Verigin's followers called him "Czar of heaven," and the terminology is significant when evaluated seriously. To the people, his position was a spiritual one. The God in one man was exalted as symbol of the God in all.

Of Sorokin, a present leader of a section of the Sons of Freedom, followers say, "We willingly give our souls to him, our One and Only Divine Leader. . . " But divinity and leadership were not sufficient to hush these words at a meeting of his adherents: "It doesn't matter what Sorokin says. We are the people and we say. . . ." The people know their power is paramount. Their apparent submissiveness is deceptive. Their power is personified, and subtle, and the subtle balance of control, between leader and conglomerate will, may sway this way, then that. First, the personification has the ascendency, then the mood of the mass moves him. It is an endless interweaving of forces, never quite distinguishable one from the other.

In so far as the sense of religious unity disappears from Doukhobor life, the leadership, symbolic incarnation of group oneness with God, loses its historic character and becomes petty tyranny. To the extent that Doukhobors lose their insularity and merge with other ideologies, the old concept of leadership becomes untenable. It was an act of faith, and for many Doukhobors that part of the old faith has gone.

IDEOLOGY

Doukhoborism as a religious phenomenon in history will not be understood without being placed in relation to the basic doctrines of the Christian church and the contemporary thought of the larger denominations. Moreover, because the Bible has had such an authoritative place in determining orthodox faith, and also because certain Doukhobors in recent years have conducted Bible burning ceremonies, considerable reference will be made to the Bible in connection with Doukhobor belief.

Even the briefest definition of theology, as aiming to give systematic expression to the doctrines of the Christian faith, indicates how little intellectual analysis Doukhoborism has applied to its own beliefs. The chief sources of Christian theology are the Bible, the creeds of the church, and the works of leading Christian theologians. Of these sources, Doukhobors traditionally have belittled the first, refuted the second, and been unaware of the third.

Confident in the profound simplicity of their own religion, they are prone to criticize many idiosyncracies of other religions. The truth is, that on account of their non-intellectual approach, they are even more susceptible than most religious people to the fascinations of theurgic mysticism and magic. For the Doukhobor ancestors who were separated from the Orthodox Church, there was occult meaning in the number 1666, the date of their excommunication. In Church Slavonic every letter has numerical significance, and the number 666 which was "the number of the Beast" also yielded a suitable initial letter, so the state-church persecutor was clearly antichrist, and revealed as the chief enemy. Members of the Russian Church, despite priestly admonitions, used to visit shamans and take part in pagan festivals. Belief in supernatural healing was widespread, and it was common amongst Doukhobors—so much so that Peter Verigin had to warn that any person caught engaged in it would be refused permission to come to Canada. The practice came, nevertheless, and is still used by many a solicitous babushka who mumbles words over the body of a sick child. Parents often change the names of their children for a change of luck. Itinerant faith-healers can count upon a large Doukhobor following, and medical practitioners are familiar with the trend to "shop around" for a doctor with the efficacious formula. Magic is particularly useful to the Sons of Freedom, as when an old woman, seeing her home on fire, walked thrice around it, saying an incantation, and the flames stopped.

Doukhobor leaders were considered able to cause the death of a person by saying words. It is said that Peter Petrovich Verigin evoked a tornado to show some people at Kamsack the wrongfulness of not following him. Near Brilliant, Peter Vasilivich Verigin met a man who doubted his divinity, so, according to a witness, he magically changed some strawberries into cherries. He often referred to the event himself. Concerning the tragic railway explosion which took his life, it is now said that he seemed to have foreknowledge, because before departing on that fateful trip he asked that peanuts and raisins be distributed amongst all the children who had come to say good-bye. This

171

is he of whom it is said that at the moment of his birth a great star fell from the sky upon the roof of the house where he was and crashed into many pieces.

Among the fanatics, the threats of supernatural figures have been used skilfully to terrorize and control. Many children have trembled at the thought of Black Cat, the school bogey; and householders have lived in fear of the Red Rooster. Supernatural power has been personified and made to hide threateningly in the nearby darkness.

Insecurity, increased by social unrest, has left many Doukhobors susceptible to influences which deliberately or unintentionally play upon their longing and despair. Many of them, especially Sons of Freedom, being confused, frustrated, and often frightened, may grasp at hopes such as a white horse to Mexico, an archangel's heaven-on-earth, tickets to Turkey. And more recently, a deranged old man, after a week spent fasting at a hill-top graveyard, delivered to attentive gatherings of people irrational, obscene, but mysterious messages, which were submissively accepted as oracular, and which caused many Sons of Freedom families to leave homes and belongings to embark on a brief and futile pilgrimage. His ravings possessed enough of a combination of earnestness and cunning to play upon the Sons of Freedom weaknesses and confuse the unsympathetic.

RELIGIOUS AUTHORITY IN DOUKHOBOR LIFE

All denominations recognize some authority which is, for them, the source of truth. Doukhobors from earliest times have claimed for their authority none other than God Himself, and to this day bespeak a disconcerting familiarity with Him. Traditionally they disclaimed any hierarchy or contemporary leadership, repudiated all written codes, and scorned all outward symbols, sacraments and ceremonies.

Plainly, this complete negation of worldly authority was not realistic. Through three centuries of denial, Doukhobors have, with meekness peculiar to themselves, been submissive to forms of authority rather more subtle, but none the less demanding, than Bible, state, or church; in their stead they have been submissive to the directives of revelation, prophecy, religious leaders, and tradition.

In the Bible, the primary purpose and content of revelation is practical rather than doctrinal, its object being not the satisfaction of man's curiosity or even his mystical aspiration, but guidance in a way of life. This also for Doukhobors is the true intent of revelation. It means a clear, steady insight rather than particular revelations disclosing metaphysical truth, in which the Doukhobors are not interested. For them, revelation has taken place very much as it did throughout Biblical history. There is in the Bible only one case of "automatic trance," and this is rare also in Doukhobor history. There are in the Bible and in

Doukhoborism many examples of "audition" where the speaker commences "thus saith . . ." and speaks as though by direct quotation the words of the Lord. In both Bible and Doukhobor history there are a number of other forms of revelation, anthropomorphic theophanies, dream-interpreting, and angel voices. Doukhobors have given much credence to prophetic utterance and "spiritual" words with hidden meanings, in which they are probably close to Biblical and Christian tradition.

The importance of prophecy as a form of authority in Doukhobor life was shown a few years ago when the Sons of Freedom took violent measures to make a supposed prophecy (about leaving Canada) come true. It cannot be said that Doukhobors have been influenced by the predictive elements in prophecy any more than most Christians, but it has had undue bearing on the well-being of the sect because it has been used in recent times for practical politics more than for religious assurance. In the earlier years of Doukhoborism, comfort was derived from the prediction that God, being with them, would protect them through all tribulation until their promised reward, when all their hopes and their faith would be vindicated. Sons of Freedom find it handy to use the Bible for prophetic purposes sometimes, as when a verse in Revelation is used to prove that schooling is wrong: "And I took the little book out of the angel's hand, and ate it up; and it was in my mouth sweet as honey; and as soon as I had eaten it, my belly was bitter."

Doukhobor leaders gave assurance that God would some day bless His people with justification for all their trust and faithfulness; that theirs was a special destiny, following a divine plan known, in part at least, by the leaders. The words were often symbolic and allegorical, giving rise today to whatever interpretation suits the occasion. Members of the Union of Spiritual Communities of Christ shudder at some meanings which some of the Sons of Freedom read into sayings of deceased leaders. The deranged old man already referred to was brought into the scheme of things by some followers who claimed a prophecy which predicted that one day Doukhobors would be led by an insane person. Some believe in prophecies stating that Doukhobors will go back to Russia, live on an island, and move south of the Equator; that for Sons of Freedom a bridge-to-paradise will conveniently appear, for the Union of Spiritual Communities of Christ the way will be more difficult, and the Independents will be doomed to stay in Canada. Some claim there are prophecies about the Great White King, the yellow races, and North America flowing in rivers of blood.

The Bible is highly esteemed by some Doukhobors, who value it especially for its portrayal of Jesus. But as authority it has none of the preeminence given to it by every other Christian sect. The Bible was not read, of course, by the illiterate Russian peasants who left the

Orthodox Church, and after the schism in Russia, the Doukhobors denounced the Bible as printed word along with other man-made formalities invented to enslave the free spirit of man. It was regarded as the bulwark of corrupt organized religion, the cause of profitless disputation and division in the eternal and invisible church. Public Bible reading is not used in any Doukhobor meetings, and from Sons of Freedom gatherings, itinerant Bible reading evangelists are likely to be ejected by force.

The prevailing attitude of Doukhobors toward the Bible is that it is part of progressive revelation continuing throughout history. Subsequent revelation, especially from the lips of Doukhobor leaders, is for them also valid for religious living. It follows that if God's will is discernible in the immediate present, such contemporary revelation is more authentic than that of two thousand years ago, especially if the old revelation, perhaps appropriate to its time, has been reduced to writing and may have suffered manipulation. And further, it seems to them evident that the inspired words of contemporary leadership are more truthful, more complete, and more authoritative than the words of dead and gone prophets and apostles. The ultimate conclusion, of course, is that Doukhobor leaders have revelation and are superior to the historic Christ. This view has been held throughout the history of Doukhoborism. Human leadership, centralized in one contemporary person, is the form of authority which has appeared to be most influential.

The entry of arbitrary man-rule into the life of a sect denying such things happened when scattered and harried peasants required a centre around which to gather and unite for social and economic self-preservation. There appeared as leaders a succession of men who were strong, benevolent, imaginative, and intellectually superior to their followers. These were men of sufficient stature to meet a second need of the people, the need for some objective manifestation of their religious aspiration. Excommunication of the Doukhobors from the church left a great emptiness. Take away priest, take away icons, take away two hundred church holidays, take away formal observances and home rituals, the signs-of-the-cross and all the hourly gestures of inherited piety; more vital still, tear down the mental images, desecrate the sentimental furbelows of faith, shame reverence, and mock devoutness: then there is emptiness indeed. The person of the leader was in part a substitution for what was lost.

There is more significance to this than meets the eye. Doukhoborism is remarkable in that its symbols are neither numerous nor sanctified. They are simply bread, salt and water, placed at every meeting on a plain table covered with a white cloth—a big golden loaf of homemade bread, a simple shaker or carton or dish of salt, and a jug of water accompanied usually by a drinking cup or glass. The non-

Doukhobor observer who has a respect for sacred symbols will be shocked by an incident which is likely to take place during any so-branya. A thirsty child may go to the table and have an older person pour a drink of water from the jug. If a few drops remain unwanted, they are likely to be thrown out on the rough floor. This simple act of drinking at the homely altar expresses much of what is charming and significant in Doukhoborism.

The mode of religious leadership is part and parcel of this talent for unpretentiousness in thought and practice. It is true that when the people used to play circle-ball at Ooteshenie, and Peter Verigin, really wanting to share the fun, would get inside the circle, the others would hardly dare to aim the ball at him. Yet the religious leader had taken divinity down out of the clouds and made it warmly human, close and available. Doukhoborism regarded God's being on a throne in heaven as an illusion. With a leap of faith they perceived godliness and virtue in the daily life around them. The human soul became the boundary of heaven and hell. God dwelt in man. Religious yearning fastened on to something earth-bound—a man divine because the people made him so.

In most sects, tradition wields a powerful authority. This is so with Doukhobors, even though in their fear of legalism they have sought to keep their traditions free from formality. Their position with its ambivalence is stated by a competent Doukhobor writer who has done much to explain the favourable aspect of Doukhoborism. He says, ". . . one of the outstanding fundamentals of Doukhoborism is its re-fusal to be fettered to any given set of dogmas. . . The surest way of measuring the given trend of any undertaking is always to compare whether it runs parallel with all our past . . . if contrary to all our worthy achievements of the past, there is no justification for such a course."

The avoidance of written dogma has made the unwritten traditions supremely important. These traditions, together with all the accumu-lated teachings and "worthy achievements," are embodied in "The Living Book," an unorganized collection of oral tradition passed on by rote learning from parent to child. Memorization of this material, which includes psalms spoken or chanted, hymns, and varieties of catechism, starts when a child is four, and continues with increasing emphasis throughout life. The self-centred rural simplicity of Doukhobor exist-ence, with its deliberate avoidance of the extraneous diversions of commerce, citizenship, and education, left for the memorized inherit-ance a place of unusual influence.

"The Living Book" theoretically is ever growing and changing, re-cent revelation and experience supposedly being as valuable as contri-butions from the distant past. A few songs and legends are, in fact, being added, chiefly on account of Sons of Freedom dramatization of their sufferings in jail, but the main body of material was provided by a few early leaders— Kolesnikoff, Pobirohin, and Kapustin—who gave the illiterate peasants a heterogeneous mixture of Bible quotations, personal opinions, and bits of piety derived from sources as varied as French literature, Oriental theosophy, and mediæval heresy.

All the material of Doukhobor tradition, as handed down from generation to generation in "The Living Book," is, in the Doukhobor view, understandable only by spiritual insight and only by a living demonstration of the contents. "The Living Book" has been deliberately concealed from the world at large. From earliest times, Doukhobors have been secretive about their religious belief. Parts of "The Living Book" were sung in the form of chants intentionally difficult and obscure, words sometimes being turned into endless successions of vowels. Any person unable to keep up with the chant would then be revealed as an alien intruder.

There are four points of interest in the content of the oral tradition.

First, there are no "personal psalms" like the Biblical Twenty-third. Rather, there is joint assertion and exhortation, addressed not so much to divinity as to the people:

> All the cannons we will forge into plowshares,
> All the swords we will beat into hoes . . .
> Let truth in our hearts be established,
> Let our faith never waver nor cease.
> Sleep on, you brave fighting eagles,
> Sleep on in the arms of the Lord. . . .

Second, much of the oral tradition is practical advice in the nature of the Biblical Book of Proverbs, and is not so much religious as social, advising prudence rather than piety.

> Be kind and do not sin. Be wise. Do not consume food if you are not hungry. Avoid alcoholic drinks as you would hell. Abstainers lead a happier and longer life. Be attentive . . . obey your orders. Shun all vice, be prudent. Be not tardy. Do not believe all you hear. If you love your fellow-men, they will love you. With good deeds, you will please everyone. You will have many friends and your enemies cannot hate you. Always speak the truth. Never lie. Observe all this and your life will be long and happy.

Third, the catechism is geared to defence against questioning from outside. There are questions and answers which have to do with belief, but there are some of recent vintage like:—

> Q.—Why do you not go to English school and learn?
> A.—Your school teaches children to participate in war and kill one another. Educated children do not live with their parents and do not obey them. We are trying to learn from God's nature, which teaches us to love one another as brothers.

Fourth, considering the apparent meekness of Doukhobors, there is a startling amount of class-struggle ideology:

In this wide world of all there is plenty;
But what misery depths do we reach. . . .
For possessions we rob one another—
Ever slaving to surfeit the rich.
'Tis unfair for the poor men to labour,
And the rich men to reap the reward;
Enough of this; arise; end this evil—
Break these chains, and let Truth be restored.

There is in existence a group of three short essays—two of them by Count Leo Tolstoy—which certain Sons of Freedom have called their "Bible." The first of these, printed under the name of one Tikhon Zadonsky, was actually written by the Russian radical Stepniak. It conceives of man's progress as a struggle against three enemies—the priesthood, land-owners, and the merchant class—and advocates a holy crusade against the enslaving forces. Tolstoy's espousal of mutual love as the sole regulator of human relations, and his teaching against the use of force of any kind, even law enforcement, have combined with the turbulent class-struggle hatreds to produce considerable confusion in many minds.

DOUKHOBOR BELIEF REGARDING GOD, CHRIST, AND SALVATION

Doukhobors offer no metaphysical analysis of God. Their implicit faith can suffer no intellectual disillusionment and never leads to agnosticism. God is never repudiated, though sometimes obscured by neglect or materialism. Doukhobors sometimes toy with atheism, but this is merely for purposes of opposing scripturalism and established theology.

Doukhobor religion is theistic, in common with Biblical and ecclesiastical theology. Its God is creator and sustainer of the universe, ordering all affairs in wisdom, holiness, and love, but having narrow national limitations. The ancient Hebrew sense of God as a person, loving his people as a shepherd loves his sheep, or a husband his wife —this yearning love of God toward his peoples is lacking in Doukhoborism. Rather, there is a static blood-brother relationship, an assumed intimacy saved from pantheism only by being unphilosophical. "God is a Holy Spirit . . . His soul is an eternal body . . . not born and not created . . . ever present in itself . . . its foremost feature unending eternity . . . God is a spirit, God is word; God is power; God is love and God is man. . . ."

There was a complete revulsion from the transcendent God of Russian orthodoxy, wherein God was distant and inaccessible except by miracle or intermediary. God became immanent, a spiritual presence dwelling in the heart of the faithful, providing for the Doukhobor peasant an intimacy with his God ensured by simple piety. Strangely, however, God's very immanence seemed to rob him of his being a person. He was so close to them, so much subject to personal fancy, so little studied by trained intellects, he became vague and inseparable from man himself and from nature. This is noticeable in religious meetings of Doukhobors. They meet with God and bow to the God in each other, but they do not reverently worship. "A Doukhobor acknowledges with soul and mind the spirit—God—within his own temple." They feel His strength in times of trouble; they do not address prayer to Him as to a separate being. They seek to know Him and feel His presence; they do not praise and offer thanks to Him. Their association with Him is corporate and assumptive rather than individual and suppliant.

Doukhobors speak blandly about the brotherhood of man and have exemplified this in a cautious and passive scene. They view the universal fatherhood of God and brotherhood of man as part of the nature of things. They believe that all men are born children of God and need only to appreciate and nurture this kinship. They think of themselves as a chosen people only in the sense that they are blessed with more enlightenment and have lived more than others as men should live, and thus have a superior claim to divine consideration. This is a reason why an evangelist finds it almost impossible to proselytize Doukhobors. Redemption by an act of divine grace is simply not recognized as being necessary or helpful.

Doukhobors, like all theists, face the problem of explaining the existence of evil in a world ruled by love and omnipotence. They do not accept the patently easy explanation of a dualistic war in the cosmos, being waged by good against evil. They never have put much stock in a personal devil. They have preferred the explanation that "evil is an unreality caused by lust and greed, conquerable by purity and faith." Yet this belief can lead to frustration and pessimism when evil in self and in environment cannot be mastered by personal effort; moreover, it readily leads to religious monism, which in recent years has allowed the intrusion of "black work" into the conception some Sons of Freedom have of God's plan for his chosen people. This "black work" or destructive violence and demonstration in a sect based on "toil and peaceful life" dismays Doukhobor and non-Doukhobor alike. From the religious point of view, the breakdown of ethical standards and established patterns of behaviour among the Sons of Freedom may be partly explained by the very conception of God which has been outlined. There have been in history other sects who believed that everything they were moved by impulse to do was the bidding of the Holy Spirit. The final and infallible authority, therefore, was the individual in himself revealing divine will. The "allness of God" was a sort of blanket coverage and sanctioning of all acts men were moved to perform.

Doukhoborism is unusual in its social cohesiveness; through this corporateness the individual can be led to assume that whatever the group wills is God's will, because God is all-in-all, and whatever is done is God's doing. Dynamiting and arson, perversions of an end-justifies-the-means rationalization alien to Doukhobor principles but unfortunately characteristic of Doukhoborism throughout its history, have both been blessed in this way at times. Disrobing also is readily attributable to the stirrings of divine will acting within an individual, and the Holy Spirit pervading a mob.

The Doukhobor concept of Christ was expressed by Peter Verigin: "By our Doukhobor understanding, Christ was a person living two thousand years ago and we consider that He only opened the door to Truth and gave us the privilege to freely progress further." The historical Jesus has little significance in Doukhoborism. Doukhobors scoff at the virgin birth and cast doubt upon the miracles; for them, Jesus' earthly life was that of an ordinary mortal of unusual wisdom and virtue. As for most people, confusion of terms exists between the words "Jesus," "Christ," and "God." "Jesus" is a once-upon-a-time prototype of all virtue; "Christ" is a gentle, patient quality of inward life; "God" is used in connection with moral duty and conscience.

Doukhobors interpret Christ "spiritually," by which they mean that he is a spiritual experience, or quality of being, which is born within a believer, develops, and suffers crucifixion in the person of his faithful followers, as revealed in their time-honoured ritual, "Christ is risen," and the response "Christ is risen in the hearts of the faithful." In this the Doukhobors come very close to the sense of mystical union with Christ, which is central not only to the teaching of Paul but to the historic evangel of the Christian church. However scanty their theological understanding, Doukhobors have, in their sharing with Christ, come close to the essential meaning of Paul's teaching.

The Trinity has remained in Doukhoborism from Russian orthodoxy. As Novitsky noted earlier, Doukhobors explain away rather than explain the idea of the Trinity, though expectedly they give it a human connotation: "The Holy Trinity is the Divine body. In human beings it proclaims itself in: Father, God, as memory, Son of God as wisdom, Holy Ghost as will-power." The triune concept has a place in ritual forms (Doukhobors bow thrice in observance of it), but it has little real significance in the content of their faith.

The theological concepts of sin, judgment, and salvation in Doukhobor religion reveal nothing that is new, but it is here that Doukhobor ideas clash most sharply with prevailing theology. This realm of belief contains some of Christendom's most ardently held doctrines, actively used in evangelism and proselytization, but Doukhobors respond to these only with casual disregard or peasant logic. Doukhoborism does not accept the doctrine of the fall of man as necessitating redemption. Adam, in fact, appears to Doukhobors as a prototype of

179

original bliss, a Biblical natural man, his only sin being (in the eyes of some Sons of Freedom) that he clothes his nakedness. In this rejection of the doctrine of the fall of man, they are in accord with the Old Testament prophets and their various ideas as to the source or cause of sin—selfishness, materialism, and secularism. Sin as being instigated by Satan is alien to Doukhobor belief. Their ideas and attitudes with regard to sin are practical rather than theoretical, as with Jesus, who never speaks of sin in the abstract, always of specific sins, and not simply of the act, but of the purpose.

Doukhoborism quite clearly regards a newborn child as a creature of natural life of which God is inherently a part. There is present the idea of warring aspects in man, the sensual impulses always trying to undermine the spiritual disciplines; but this is not conceived in the Pauline way, as though evil were an alien power attacking from within, rather the enemy is mere laziness or weakness, to be overcome not with supernatural intervention but renewed dedication.

Doukhobors often declare that the doctrine of having Christ bear the sins of man is the main reason for the breakdown of Christianity as a moral force in the world, and the promulgation of the doctrine they hold up to ridicule. They believe that by having Christ bear the sins of man, responsibility for one's own actions is removed. Their conviction in this regard is supported by their traditions of a corrupt clergy linked with civic officials, conspiring to oppress the poor and absolve the rich. They make fun of the idea that personal salvation can come about simply by "being saved" in the revivalist sense without any real change of conduct. Their deep-rooted scepticism regarding this doctrine explains again why Doukhobors are so hard to "convert," despite all the prevailing despair in regard to their own faith.

The only meeting-place for Doukhobor and non-Doukhobor Christians in respect to these vital matters is in Paul's distinctive conception of dying with Christ and rising to new life with Him. Doukhobors commonly conceive of martyrdom in this way. The mystical bent of the Doukhobor mind embraces such a spiritual union as quite realistic, with the result that Doukhobors may thus feel the significance of the Atonement more truly than many who believe it.

As to death and the after-life, Doukhoborism differs considerably from traditional and prevailing theology. Doukhobors do not believe in resurrection of the body, eternal punishment, or any other-worldly heaven. Their ideas concerning the after-life have remained calmly earth-bound. A dying elder might say simply: "I go to my Father."

A Doukhobor leader, Kapoustin, preached transmigration of souls, and reincarnation is allowed by many as a possibility. But these theories are not put forward as assumptions or articles of faith. There is in Doukhoborism no idea of personal immortality, with continuance of this life's character and associations. Death is simply the gateway to the Unknown, and because of their unquestioning faith, Doukhobors face the future life with equanimity.

Funerals are community affairs, often drawn out for days, with special meals, continuous vigil beside the body (open to public view), and unabashed display of grief. Burial is in the earth, the deceased person having been lovingly dressed and placed in a plain home-made casket. Bread, salt and water are left at the graveside, and perhaps a photograph of the departed. After six weeks, relatives observe "Memorial Day," when the "soul" is supposed to leave the body. This occasion has special significance after the death of a leader, because it is at this time the new leader is to be announced. These are moments of historic importance, when the people are in a state of expectancy, anticipating revelations and miracles. For Peter Vasilivich Verigin the memorial service was at his tomb in the darkness of the night, in an atmosphere thick with mystery. A community director and loyal friend of Verigin died next morning, and another leading man declared a fast to the death.

Perfection means different things to different people. Doukhobors, together with other sects having their origin and belief rooted in the Christian tradition, look to the brand of perfection taught and lived by Jesus of Nazareth. But his counsel, "Be ye also perfect," is not very specific as to conduct. Yet Doukhobors have always believed, and the Christian church has always taught, that Jesus' ideas were for putting into practice now. "For us," said Doukhobor prisoners long ago, "the time has come."

The difficulty for them here is that Jesus left no code of ethics or set of regulations applicable to every situation. The saying, often quoted by Doukhobors, "Render unto Caesar . . .", was not a rule on which to base Christian polity. What Jesus did bequeath was a basic attitude and an ideal; in their interpretation and use of the teachings of Jesus, certain fundamental errors have been made, and it is not surprising that Doukhobors fail in some ways to make the ideal applicable to complex modern society.

First, they cannot make the Christ ideal work to accomplish ends which it was never intended to accomplish; for instance, the attainment of any good by individual or group at the expense of others. And Jesus never did claim life would be a bed of roses for his followers. A large number of Doukhobors have never seemed to live in the realization of this. Their very real record of suffering is blamed on malevolent civilization sadistically obstructing innocent children of God. "The Government took away our land, killed our leaders . . ."

Second, Doukhobor philosophy in the past has not been broad enough to include those who are not Doukhobors. Their religion proposes just a simple cure-all for the world's ills; accept the way advocated by Jesus and automatically and overnight the world will

181

become the Kingdom of God. The reason this elixir appeals to Doukhobors, and to many others, is that they fail to realize that in practice its expression is relative to social environment and individual capacity, and never can be standardized so as to provide fool-proof systems for harmonious living for all people, or even one country or one community. Nor can society at large, and governments in particular, ever be "Christian" even if all people are to become virtuous. Doukhobors have imagined that religion can suddenly replace politics, economics, road-building, health services, law and order. They have blamed many of their ills on a three-headed ogre called government, church, and school system, and yet have consistently refused to apply their religious acumen to the human needs which are the concern of these institutions. By claiming they are not necessary, they put themselves in the position of self-righteous isolation, with martyrdom as the only approved technique of adjustment to a hostile environment.

Third, the "love" which Jesus advocated as the basis of human relationship is much more than is indicated by the pious claim by which Doukhobors tend to discharge their debt to society—when they say they "love" the Canadian people and "forgive" the Government. To "love" one's neighbour is not to feel affection for him, but to wish and seek his good. A hundred hollow-eyed, naked Sons of Freedom may stand on the cold floor of a penitentiary saying they have no hard feelings against the Canadian people, but the Canadian people do not receive much benefit from this. A Doukhobor community may go peacefully about its daily work, living the ideal of toil and peaceful life, causing no harm and no trouble, but unless they offer more than this, they will be less than Christian and far from perfect. To the extent that Doukhobors have been self-contained and self-centred, their aspirations have been fruitless. An indication of a possible new development here is the holding of a collection by the Union of Spiritual Communities of Christ for the benefit of European flood relief.

In the field of comparative religion, Doukhoborism takes its place as a sect which has the philosophical stature but not the techniques necessary for survival in the modern world. In theology and in practice it shows lack of adaptability and failure to come to grips with the real world. Other faiths provide for their adherents the means of release from feelings of guilt and sin. Doukhobor religion lacks adequate techniques like atonement, absolution and sacraments for the socially acceptable release of these and other feelings generated by it. And where religion is a matter of ultimate ideals and impossible goals—a reaching for absolutes—then failure and frustration, and shame on account of unworthiness, are inevitable. But Doukhobors lack the religious techniques for relieving themselves of guilt feelings. Their religion urgently demands perfection, perfection eludes them, and there falls upon the individual conscience an unbearable load of guilt, which cannot be absolved by priestly act, or placed on any divine Saviour, or cured by miraculous ceremony. The more conservatively religious a Doukhobor is, the more oppressive may be the inner consciousness of sinfulness, and with Sons of Freedom the pressure may become so intense, it may cause dramatic attempts at self-punishment and self-purifying, such as home-burning, disrobing, disregard for personal interest, and irrational striking-out at the encroachment of the civilization which is blamed for their failure to find Utopia.

Doukhobors say, "This life is all we know and live for. Heaven and hell are within us." They deny the efficacy of the sacraments and say, "Perfection is our duty here and now, and it is possible, if only we live pure lives." The pressure of religious obligation is intense, and relief from failure is not provided. Moreover, it is Doukhobor teaching that to make any rite essential to salvation is contrary to the whole spirit and teaching of Jesus.

The craving for immediate realization of their ultimate goals is nowhere shown more vividly than in a recent attempt to establish a heaven-on-earth on Vancouver Island. Under the guidance of Michael (the Archangel) Verigin, whose "role and mission was proclaimed in Doukhobor psalms and prophecies long before his time, and also confirmed by the Scriptures," seventy people moved from troubled Krestova and started a new community on the Coast, living at Hilliers with the determination to give up "private ownership," which they considered the root of all evils in society. These seventy people declared, "The elders, messengers, and constituents of this Spiritual Community of Christ, having knowledge of the world and prophecy, draw aside these black curtains and open the white gates into the kingdom on Earth, where it shall be as it is in Heaven; without orphans and widows, without rich or poor, where they do not marry nor are given in marriage, and where reigns full equality and freedom in everything." In this community, all possessions were shared, because private ownership was considered the root of all evil, the cause of strife and wars. Even husband, wife, and child—possession of which was "the most penetrating of all human temptations"—were to be no longer subject to the claims of personal ownership. This was, it was felt, the supreme test of unselfishness and lack of "envy and lust." The inevitable failure can be viewed in the light of their faulty understanding of themselves and their inspiration, but a fuller evaluation would also take heed of the manifestations of bravery and willingness to follow the goal they saw.

VII

PUBLIC ADMINISTRATION AND THE COMMUNITY

William G. Dixon

IT IS THE purpose of this chapter to analyse the relationship between government and the Doukhobors in British Columbia; to see what has transpired under past administrations and what is happening under existing policies in areas of education, vital statistics and registration, social welfare and public health, franchise and eligibility for office, criminal law, and administrative structure.

EDUCATIONAL PROBLEMS

Earlier chapters have given a detailed statement of Doukhobor attitudes to public education. Generally, the Sons of Freedom express violent opposition to schooling. This is not confined to a refusal to send children to school. In addition, the Kootenay region has witnessed the destruction or attempted destruction of scores of school buildings. The protection of existing schools necessitates the expenditure of thousands of dollars a year for the hiring of guards.

Among the reasons for pressing toward a fuller and more effective educational programme in spite of Doukhobor opposition is that lack of education increases the helplessness and dependency of the Sons of Freedom and compounds their present conflict within themselves and with the non-Doukhobor community.

THE LEGAL BASIS OF COMPULSORY EDUCATION

Primary and secondary education in British Columbia is governed by the Public Schools Act. In addition, the Protection of Children Act has relevance.

Section 157 of the Public Schools Act specifies that "every child over the age of seven years and under the age of fifteen years shall attend some public school during the regular school hours every school day"; and further, that "every parent or guardian who fails or neglects to cause any such child under his care to attend public school during the regular school hours every school day . . . shall be guilty of an offence, and shall be liable, on summary conviction, to a fine not exceeding ten dollars; and each day's continuance of such failure or neglect shall constitute a separate offence." *

* R.S.B.C. 1948, chap. 297, sec. 157.

There are some exemptions to compulsory attendance. Exemption may be granted if the child is being educated by some other means satisfactory to the Justice or tribunal before whom the prosecution takes place. And where the Board of School Trustees has made no provision for conveyance, there must be a public school open which the child can attend within a distance of three miles, measured according to the nearest passable road from the residence of the child.

With reference to the bringing of charges, "no person shall be prosecuted for an offence under this section without the consent of the Board of School Trustees of the school district in which the offence was committed, or of some person appointed by the Board of School Trustees to represent the Board for the purpose of this section, or of the Superintendent of Education."†

The Public Schools Act is not the only statute to deal with failure to attend school. The Protection of Children Act, under Section 7, sub-section (m), provides for apprehension of any child "who, by reason of the action of his parents or otherwise, is habitually truant from school and is liable to grow up without proper education."§

Under the latter Act, the judge may make an order "that the child be delivered into the safe custody and control of his parents, subject to such regulations as the circumstances render just"; or "that the child be committed to the care and custody of a children's aid society or of the Superintendent (of Child Welfare)." In other words, he may set very definite conditions if the child remain with the parents, or he may remove the child from the home altogether until the child is twenty-one, or, if a female, is married.

ENFORCEMENT POLICIES

At the 1920 Legislative Session, the Honourable J. D. MacLean, Minister of Education, told the House that the Government was going to introduce a new Bill to amend the Public Schools Act in order to enforce compulsory education for Doukhobors. The legislation would not provide for imprisonment as this had proved ineffective with the Doukhobors. The Government would seek power to enter upon Doukhobor lands and build and maintain schools there. Alternatively, aid would be granted to community people who wished to build schools themselves. Costs were to be charged against the lands of the sect with the idea that it would cost the Doukhobors just as much whether they were in or out of school.‡

Twenty-five years later, however, in his report on education finance in British Columbia, M. A. Cameron stated the principles which have

† R.S.B.C. 1948, chap. 297, sec. 157(4).
§ R.S.B.C. 1948, chap. 47, sec. 7(m)
‡ The Daily Colonist of Victoria, March 26th, 1920, pp. 6 and 9.

come to be followed in the erection of larger school districts and the incorporation of Doukhobor communities into them.

> The report makes no special provision regarding Doukhobor schools, treating them in the same way as the other schools of the Province. It is possible that this is an error, and the Commission is quite prepared to defer to the judgment of those with longer experience in the matter.
>
> However, the decision to make no differentiation between community and other school districts has behind it some good reasons. First there is the belief that every effort should be made to get them into the ordinary scheme of things. Then there is the fact that the Doukhobor population is becoming gradually diffused, so that some school districts, particularly those in the Slocan Valley, are finding their Doukhobor enrolments steadily growing. It is, of course, quite impracticable to create new community school districts wherever Doukhobor children attend.

IMMEDIATE PROBLEMS OF EDUCATION

Through the years there have been sporadic prosecutions of parents under the Public Schools Act. Generally, they have chosen to go to jail rather than pay nominal fines, or they have moved into areas where compulsory education was not being enforced.

When a large number of adults were sent to prison in 1953, their children were committed to the care of the Superintendent of Child Welfare and placed in a former hospital at New Denver. Many have since been released, though others have been apprehended; in the institution they are sent to a special school.

There has been no opportunity of evaluating this. It can be added that no movement has yet been made against the large concentration of children in the Sons of Freedom communities of Krestova and Gilpin, and that many factors make it unlikely that the children will be held for the length of time needed to test such a venture.

Doukhobor children are largely located in the Slocan Valley, Castlegar, Grand Forks and Kettle Valley School Districts. The Sons of Freedom communities of Gilpin and Krestova, where hardly any children attend school, are of course the real problem communities.

Basic to any plan of improved education for Doukhobor children is a decision on consolidated schools. In the most recent inquiry into Doukhobor affairs, Judge Sullivan recommended that Doukhobor children should be taken into larger schools so that they would mix with ordinary children. Many Kootenay people agree with him. They contend that since many Doukhobor communities are adjacent to main highways following the rivers, they lend themselves to fairly easy transportation. They point out also that where completion of Grade VI is the dividing line for entry into a consolidated school, Doukhobor parents take this as the sign that the child has had enough education for rural living.

There is no doubt that consolidation has great merit and has a role in this programme, but there are several arguments for supplementing it by the retention and in some cases expansion of a community school programme. Consolidation is good for those who believe in schools, but probably has some adverse effect on those who do not—the very group which presents the problem. It is hardly likely that a resistant Son of Freedom who feels that education is bad because it persuades the child to depart from traditional beliefs will be encouraged to send his young child to school in a bus which whisks him off daily to a somewhat distant centre largely dominated by non-Doukhobors.

A further point is that education must not abdicate from the community; if anything, it must enter more into it. It is more likely to be accepted if intelligent, skilled teachers who realize that their function involves more than classroom instruction operate in the community. They must have the time, training, and talent to break down the community prejudice against education, and must be willing and able to participate in community life.

It is understandably difficult to get good teachers to go to schools predominantly Doukhobor, and that when they do, they often do not stay long. When the salary is equal, they are likely to go to other areas involving less difficulty. The situation will probably deteriorate in the immediate future as the wartime birth rate now brings a great influx of youngsters into the schools with a consequent increased demand for teachers.

There are two ways of meeting the need for improved teachers. One is for dedicated persons, probably as representatives of a religious group, to go into resistant Doukhobor communities and engage in an educational programme. But such people are by definition strict proponents of their own personal and religious values, and on this account they, more than others, are precluded from reaching the necessary understanding of Doukhobor values. In their wish to remake the Doukhobors in their own model, regardless of Doukhobor needs, they can cause a great deal of harm.

The second and preferable alternative is that a bonus above regular salary scales be offered for professional teachers to enter and remain in the Doukhobor communities. Such a course of action would have to be taken by the Provincial Government, as the majority of the troubled local areas are in no mood to pay for additional Doukhobor services. A recommendation is made in this *Report* with regard to administration of Doukhobor affairs that if an appropriate body is established, its budget includes an item for this purpose.

If possible, three-year terms of appointment should be drawn up, as any shorter term would make it nearly impossible to do a good community job. Needless to say, special attention should be given to teacherages or other arrangements for housing, so that the teacher

187

will have privacy and generally good living conditions. In troubled areas, it may be necessary to have two teachers in what would normally be a one-room school. Not only would each give the other support in a hostile situation, but both would have sufficient time to visit homes in the community, participate in an adult education programme and generally be available for community activities. Nor should the possibility of individual instruction in the home be neglected.

In an educational programme involving such difficulties, new personnel should undoubtedly have a period of orientation to Doukhobor culture and the community organization process. It is recommended that any continuing administration give serious consideration to short-term training of teachers going into Doukhobor communities.

There is also a possibility of separate schools for Doukhobor children. Doukhobors are at liberty to establish them at their own expense, as long as the children are being educated in a satisfactory fashion. However, there has been no concerted attempt by the USCC Doukhobors to establish separate schools, and the children should be encouraged to continue at the public schools. As for the Sons of Freedom, it would seem that such a move of encouragement would be inappropriate at this time. Their communities are disorganized, and it is hard to see how they could at present conduct a school satisfactory to the educational authorities. Some USCC communities are conducting after-hours instruction in Doukhobor history and religion; this programme should receive reasonable cooperation and support.

No attempt has been made to assess the quality of guidance services in the Kootenay area, but it should be clear that the task of counselling is a demanding one. There have been instances of Doukhobor high-school students taking part in demonstrations. For adolescents in conflict because of the clash with parental philosophy and the ideas and treatment they encounter in the non-Doukhobor community, this is not really so surprising. Such conflict can perhaps be resolved by skilled counselling, which might be provided in the larger centres through cooperation of the schools and local social welfare services.

Some departure from the usual programme of studies is necessary to ensure any effective education. If an administrative organization is created, it should work closely with the Department of Education in developing educational material acceptable to the Doukhobors.

VITAL STATISTICS AND NATIONAL REGISTRATION

Many Sons of Freedom and some others are still reluctant to record information on births, deaths and marriages, and continue to be wary of the census. National registration in World War II was often regarded as another form of conscription.

This resistance stems from a number of sources. Part of it is a carry-over from early hostility to the Russian Orthodox Church, which historically was responsible to the state for registration of vital statistics. Some Doukhobors fail to see the value of accumulating such data; they are not impressed with government concern over the birth rate, marriage trends, causes of death and movement of population. Fanatics looking forward to migration claim that since they are only temporary residents in Canada, nobody should be concerned about their affairs. Others see a sinister motive; they regard the collection of all statistics other than death registrations as but a prelude to military service.

REGISTRATION OF MARRIAGES

The Legal Character of Marriage.—Most Doukhobors would acclaim what is acknowledged to be the most authoritative definition in British law: "Marriage as understood in Christendom is the voluntary union for life of one man and woman to the exclusion of all others," because this emphasizes the emotional quality of the relationship itself rather than the role of the state.

The term "contract" is often applied to the marriage relationship because of the essential element of consent and agreement in the transaction. But marriage differs from some contracts in that the rights, obligations or duties arising from it are not left entirely to be regulated by the agreement of parties, but are to a certain extent matters of state regulation. Doukhobors reject this concept, preferring to regard marriage as a contract in which the Government should have no interest.

Marriage Law in British Columbia.—The solemnization of marriage in British Columbia is governed by the Marriage Act. Apparently the Marriage Act is designed to require public notice prior to the ceremony in order to control the marriage of minors and those under other disabilities. Moreover, it provides for registration of the fact of marriage and ensures that a certain solemnity attaches to the contract. These ends are achieved by requiring a licence or the calling of the banns before a religious ceremony, or, alternatively, a Marriage Commissioner's certificate in advance of a civil ceremony. Further, solemnization can be performed only by persons officially empowered to do so, and they bear the responsibility for registration.

The Doukhobor Marriage Ceremony.—A Doukhobor couple planning marriage advise their parents of their intention. Should the latter be dead, they inform their next of kin and call upon their close acquaintances with the news.

The groom's parents visit those of the bride, and ask if they will consent to the proposed marriage. When consent is given, they set the date for the wedding, which customarily takes place in the bride's home. The event is preceded by a betrothal ceremony to which relatives and close friends are invited.

At the marriage ceremony the groom's father declares to the bride's parents that they wish to become relatives-in-law and inquires if there are any objections. If none, the groom's mother, who has brought bread and salt, places them on the table on which there is also water. Then the groom's father tells him to bring in the bride.

The groom takes his bride-to-be by the hand and they stand in the centre of the room. His parents stand before them and beg the bride's parents to do the same. The bride's parents interrogate the couple and ask them what they want. The groom replies that he loves their daughter, wants her for his wife and begs their benediction. They ask him if he sincerely loves their daughter and wants her for his wife, and he answers, "Yes." After they have put the same question to their daughter, the groom's parents follow with the interrogations and replies.

The parents of the bride and groom give their benediction. The newly wedded couple kiss each other, bow to the parents' feet, stand and kiss the bride's parents first, then repeat the procedure with the groom's parents. The groom's parents then express their gratitude to the bride's parents for their efforts in bringing up their daughter and for their consent.

The foregoing description was submitted to the Sullivan Commission as the ritual which Doukhobors are expected to follow. Claudia Lewis is of the opinion that the ritual is not to the Doukhobors the most important part of the wedding. "The wedding itself goes on all day, and its importance is in the sum total, not in this brief ritual."

The Doukhobor Attitude to Marriage Laws.—Under present circumstances, the Doukhobor form of marriage is not recognized as being legal in this Province. One of the many complications of this is that all children born of such unions are classed as illegitimate.

In the main, the Doukhobor objection to complying with the law in this instance is that marriage is a sacred relationship and it is undesirable that any third party, in the form of government, should intrude upon this relationship. There is a distinct objection to any application for a licence involving a fee. Presumably, they do not object to the amount of payment, but say that a solemn ritual in itself should be sufficient to meet any legal requirement.

A major difficulty arises from the fact that the Doukhobor religion does not recognize any person as a minister or a clergyman. The marriage ceremony involves only family and community approval. Absence of a minister or clergyman means that even if a Doukhobor couple comply with the licensing procedure, no person at the ceremony has official authority to solemnize and register the marriage.

Actually, several steps have been taken to provide for the recognition of Doukhobor marriage without changing the Act in any fundamental way. The most notable experiment was carried on from October 17th, 1941, to April 26th, 1945, when the Russian-speaking District Registrar of Vital Statistics stationed at Nelson was designated as an official witness of Doukhobor marriages. He attended the marriage ceremony and was then able to give assurance to the Director of Vital Statistics that the parties concerned had duly married according to the Doukhobor custom. Although this procedure was apparently initially acceptable to the Doukhobors, hostility gradually developed toward the incumbent, and his status as an official witness was terminated. The Legislature has assured the validity of these marriages by inserting a new section in the Marriage Act.

Another development occurred in the Fraser Valley, where a group of Doukhobors approached the Provincial Government and requested that one of their number be designated as a minister within the meaning of the Act. This was done, and he now attends their weddings. However, this procedure is not acceptable to Doukhobors living in the Kootenay area.

One other device has been suggested to the Doukhobors as an answer to their particular dilemma. It has been proposed that, in addition to the usual Doukhobor ceremony, the principals should be legally married by civil contract by a Marriage Commissioner. It should be pointed out that the Provincial Government has encouraged this procedure, but because it involved the role of government in marriage, it has met with little success.

In Saskatchewan the Provincial Government has since 1909 recognized the Doukhobor marriage ceremony. Responsibility for registration rests with the groom. But under Saskatchewan law, Doukhobors are still required to comply with the procedure regarding a marriage licence or its equivalent. Actually they often fail to do so, but this does not in any way alter the legality of the subsequent ceremony.

The Case for Recognition of Doukhobor Marriages.—The essence of the Doukhobor marriage ceremony is that it is a form of marriage by consent, conducted by the parents of the principals, and witnessed by a host of relatives and friends. The question is whether this ceremony should be afforded legal recognition in British Columbia.

In some ways, Doukhobor marriage parallels historical British custom, where for a thousand years the church recognized consent as the main requisite to a valid marriage. Moreover, until 1940 in Scotland marriages involving consent even without witnesses were legal.

Thus, while the Doukhobor form of marriage lags in recognition of the role of the state, it is not markedly different from these other concepts of marriage.

Neither the Marriage Act nor any policies enunciated by the Provincial Government prevent religious groups from conducting marriage ceremonies according to their views. The only concerns of the law are that certain preliminary requirements be met and that there be registration of ministers performing ceremonies and of the marriages which are solemnized.

It is possible to see how public notice of an intended Doukhobor marriage could come within the spirit of the Act. The real issue then narrows down to recognition of a marriage ceremony conducted by the families of the principals. Absence of ministers in the Doukhobor community makes for administrative difficulty because, while the Act does not tell a minister what to do or what to say in the ceremony, it holds him responsible for making certain that all legal requirements are observed. Should then the state deny the validity of marriage within a group which does not have a minister, simply because the usual mechanics of registration revolve around a minister or clergyman?

It is submitted that the Doukhobor custom conforms to the spirit of the law. It is a public acknowledgment of relationship. It is not merely a marriage by consent, but involves an interrogation of the bride and groom similar to that made by a minister.

While the law cannot, of course, specify any degree of solemnity for a marriage ceremony, there is always a concern that solemnity pervade the ritual. There are probably as many variations of solemnity among Doukhobor marriages as there are among other religious marriage ceremonies. Perfectionist qualities not required of the general population should not be demanded of Doukhobors. At the very least, the Doukhobor ceremony is just as impressive as that prescribed for the civil celebration by the Marriage Act.

But, in addition to the possibility of compliance with existing legislation, there are other fundamental reasons why the Doukhobor marriage ceremony should be recognized. The point has already been made that children of a Doukhobor union are classed as illegitimate. In addition, it should be noted that failure to recognize the Doukhobor ceremony involves a threat to family life within the community. It can be readily realized that an unscrupulous person can involve a partner in a marriage ceremony which has no legal status. A Doukhobor woman marrying in good faith has no claim upon a man if he should desert her. If there are children, her only recourse is to try to get support for them in the Courts as an unmarried mother. Moreover, the common-law relationship complicates matters such as a widow's eligibility for workmen's compensation.

Other groups obtain recognition similar to that which is here asked. The Marriage Act already provides special recognition to Quaker and Jewish marriage ceremonies, and presumably the same privilege is open to other groups which comply with the spirit of the Act.*

Means of Legalizing Doukhobor Customary Marriage.—Under the Marriage Act the state, through its system of marriage licensing, endeavours to determine if the potential partners are legally eligible to marry. Many Doukhobors object to obtaining a licence or certificate. However, the alternative of reading the banns involves no payment of money. The pertinent part of the Act reads as follows:—

> Publication of banns shall be made by proclaiming the intended marriage openly, in an audible voice, during service, in some church, chapel, or place of public worship of the religious body to which the minister or clergyman who is to solemnize the marriage belongs, situate within the local municipality, parish, circuit, or pastoral charge where at least one of the parties to the intended marriage has resided for the period of eight days immediately preceding, at one or more services on each of two consecutive Sundays; or where the practice or faith of any religious body substitutes Sunday, or any other day, as the usual and principal day of the week for the celebration of Divine service, then on two consecutive Saturdays, or such other days.†

Due to the objection of Doukhobors to obtaining a licence, a variation of the reading of the banns might be introduced. Thus there might be an additional clause to section 9, subsection (2), reading as follows:—

> In those instances where the principals to the marriage intend to follow the Doukhobor custom of marriage, then a parent of one of the principals shall read an announcement of the marriage at two successive religious meetings or gatherings. In the absence or refusal of parents to perform this function, the announcement may be read by some other person.

This procedure is dependent on the regularity of religious gatherings. One way to overcome this difficulty would be for a public notice in a regularly published newspaper to be considered as a reading of the banns. An appropriate subsection might read as follows:—

> Alternatively, the intended bridegroom shall cause to be placed on two occasions in a daily or weekly newspaper published in English or Russian in British Columbia, a public notice of the proposed marriage, including the full name and address of the intended bride and bridegroom and the time and place of the proposed marriage ceremony. The two notices shall be inserted in the daily or weekly newspaper published nearest to the residence of the bride, and the second notice shall be published not sooner than three days after and not later than seven days after the first notice.

Subsection (5) of section 9, which makes the minister reading the banns responsible for submitting a notice to the District Registrar of

* R.S.B.C. 1948, chap. 201, sec. 9(4).
† R.S.B.C. 1948, chap. 201, sec. 9(2).

Vital Statistics during the week intervening between the first and second proclamation, might be expanded to read as follows:—

> Every person who publishes the banns of marriage either by reading at a religious gathering or publication of notice in a daily or weekly newspaper prior to the solemnization of a marriage abiding by Doukhobor custom shall, during the time intervening between the first and second proclamation, mail to the District Registrar of Births, Deaths, and Marriages, of the registration district as constituted pursuant to the Vital Statistics Act in which it is intended that the marriage shall be solemnized, a certificate of publication of banns in Form M11, and the notice shall state upon which date the banns have been and are to be published.

The Marriage Act provides that no person under twenty-one shall be married unless consent in writing is given by both parents or by a guardian. Moreover, no marriage of any person under sixteen is to be solemnized without the consent of a Judge of the Supreme or County Court. In cases where the marriage is to be solemnized by a minister or clergyman after publication of banns, the consent of the parents or declaration of a Judge is to be filed with the minister or clergyman. Moreover, a birth certificate or other satisfactory proof of age must also be filed with the minister or clergyman.

These provisions do not seem to present great difficulties as far as marriages by Doukhobor custom are concerned. While it is probably true that consent in writing is not given for those under twenty-one, Doukhobor parents do give consent by actual participation in the marriage ceremony. The provision with regard to marriage of persons under sixteen should remain.

The final issue to be discussed is the method of registration of Doukhobor marriages, provided they are given legal recognition. The Marriage Act deals with the question as follows:—

> Every minister or clergyman and every Marriage Commissioner authorized to solemnize marriages shall at the time of each marriage solemnized by him register the marriage by entering a memorandum thereof in a book kept for that purpose pursuant to this section by him or by the religious body to which the minister or clergyman belongs; and the memorandum shall be signed by each of the parties to the marriage, and by at least two credible witnesses, and by the minister or clergyman or the Marriage Commissioner by whom the marriage was solemnized.*

Some other arrangement would need to be made. It is suggested that both the bride and groom complete a suitable certificate and that it include the signatures of two witnesses. Responsibility should be placed on the groom for filing the registration.

Finally, the mechanics of registration must not be forgotten. One question revolves around the maintenance of a marriage registration book by someone taking the usual place of a minister or clergyman. The Union of Spiritual Communities of Christ might designate rep-

* R.S.B.C. 1948, chap. 201, sec. 24.

resentatives for certain areas, such as Grand Forks and Castlegar, to carry responsibility for this function.

Subsequent to the presentation of the Report of the Doukhobor Research Committee, the Government introduced an amendment to the Marriage Act relating to Doukhobors.‡

The changes follow the above recommendations. Subject to the following requirements "nothing in this Act shall be construed as in any way preventing Doukhobors from solemnizing, according to the rites and ceremonies of the Doukhobor religion, a marriage between any two persons, neither of whom is under any legal disqualification to contract such marriage and either or both of whom are Doukhobors."

The suggested adaptation of the banns precedure has been followed, in that a parent of one of the principals is to proclaim the intended marriage at two successive meetings or gatherings of Doukhobors within the registration district as constituted under the Vital Statistics Act where at least one of the parties has resided for a period of eight days. The proclamation may be made by a next-of-kin if there is no parent willing and able to do it, or by any other person.

Seven days before the marriage the declaration of the proclamation is to be mailed to the District Registrar. Flexibility in filing is assured in that the declaration may be in a specified form "or to a like effect."

Immediately after solemnization one of the parties to the marriage is required to submit a written record to the District Registrar. It is to be signed by both the principals and two adult witnesses.

REGISTRATION OF BIRTHS

The registration of births in British Columbia is governed by the Vital Statistics Act.*

The Provincial Government takes many precautions to assure birth registration. Every doctor attending a birth must mail a notice to the District Registrar within forty-eight hours. Hospitals must submit a monthly summary. Schools are required to give information of children attending for the first time.

Of course, the father or mother of the child carries major responsibility for registration. Most USCC members do not now object to registration *per se,* but there is conflict on two points:—

In the first place, section 9 of the form for registration of a live birth asks for the citizenship of both parents of the child. The explanatory note attached to the interrogation is as follows:—

Citizenship (Nationality) is defined in terms of the country to which the person owes allegiance. The term "Canadian" should be used as descriptive of a person who was born in Canada or who has rights of citizenship in Canada, unless he or she has subsequently become the citizen of another country.

Many Doukhobors, of course, object to any profession of allegiance. The Divison of Vital Statistics has suggested that the word "Doukho-

‡ S.B.C. 2 Elizabeth II, 1953 (second session), chap. 15.
* R.S.B.C. 1948, chap. 357.

bor" be added after "Canadian" for members of this group, but this is unacceptable to the USCC. The situation might be resolved by removing the words "to which the person owes allegiance" from the explanatory note and substituting the phrase "of which the person is a national." The first sentence would then read:—

> Citizenship is defined in terms of the country of which the person is a national.

Another way of dealing with this issue of citizenship would be to insert a special clause:—

> Any person objecting to a profession of allegiance on religious grounds is permitted to answer the following questions instead of the above interrogation: Were you born in Canada? If not, where were you born? Have you ever been naturalized? By own paper? By parents' papers? By marriage?

The second point of conflict centres on the requirement in respect to the registration of illegitimate births.

The Vital Statistics Act states:—

> In registering the birth of an illegitimate child, it shall not be lawful for the name of any person to be entered as the father, unless at the joint request of the mother and of the person acknowledging himself to be the father as evidenced by their signatures to the statement prepared for the purpose of registration of the birth.*

Normally, either the father or the mother registers the birth of a legitimate child, but only one signs the form. The demand that both parents sign in the case of an illegitimate child is regarded by the Doukhobors as an affront to the sanctity of their marriage. A District Registrar does not routinely question the legality of a marriage in birth registration procedure. Some Doukhobors are aware of this and offer only one signature.

This problem cannot be resolved as long as Doukhobor marriages are not recognized under the Marriage Act. Existing legislation is designed to prevent the naming of a man as the father of a child of an unmarried mother when he actually denies paternity. Moreover, even if some formula could be devised to make it possible for one Doukhobor parent to do the registration, that still does not alter the fact that the child is illegitimate under the law.

Finally, a word should be said about legitimization. Should the Doukhobor custom of marriage be legalized, and any parents repeat their marriage vows, their children born earlier would then be legitimate.†

REGISTRATION OF DEATHS

The registration of deaths in British Columbia is governed by the Vital Statistics Act.

* R.S.B.C. 1948, chap. 357, sec. 8(1).
† R.S.B.C. 1948, chap. 183.

Under the Act the undertaker is held responsible for the completion of a death registration and its delivery to the District Registrar. However, the term "undertaker" is not restricted to a professionally qualified person. It "includes any person who has charge of the body of a deceased person for the purpose of burial or cremation or other disposal." Thus, a member of the family in a remote area, if in charge of the body, has the responsibility for registration.

Apparently there is little need to consider specified provisions in the law to cover Doukhobor deaths. The Doukhobor is not opposed to medical care, and the increasing use of hospitals by Doukhobors means that there is then a medical ascertainment of the causes of death. Moreover, undertakers experience little difficulty in getting information from Doukhobors who come to them for burial of relatives. Finally, the Royal Canadian Mounted Police have such a knowledge of the people in the rural areas of the Province that they usually know who has died, and the matter is reported to the District Registrar.

It is important to note two aspects of death registration. One is that there is no charge for registration. The other is that the state is not concerned about the form of burial service, or even if there is one, for that matter. It only requires registration of the death.†

Generally speaking, the issue revolves around cases of aged persons who suddenly die in the community and are buried there without registration. There is no cause for changing the law; the solution is to be found in compliance, which should be obtained by a programme of education.

The foregoing suggestions are made with a view, not only to strengthen vital statistics registration but also to bring Doukhobors within the workings of this branch of provincial life as another step toward a better relationship between government and the Doukhobors. However, changes in the law will not settle all the relevant problems. Difficulties and misunderstandings are bound to arise, and it is therefore suggested that legislative revisions might be accompanied by the strengthening of vital statistics administration in the Kootenay area. An additional staff member could render valuable service in explaining the workings of the law and could assist in the correction of improper registration. He might also explore the possibility of expediting the delayed registration of Doukhobor births, something which is provided for in the present Act.

NATIONAL REGISTRATION

Under the Order in Council of 1898, Doukhobors settling in Canada were declared exempt from military service. This, however, did

† R.S.B.C. 1948, chap. 357, secs. 14, 15, 16, 17.

not mean that they were exempt from national registration, which involves assessment of a person's capacities for either military service or labour. As carried out in Canada, national registration was actually little more than a prelude to military call-up, as very little of the voluminous information collected was put to use.

Doukhobor registration was discussed in the House of Commons on many occasions during World War II. An Order in Council of September, 1940, extended the exemption to "the descendants of such immigrants who have continued without interruption to be members . . . of the aforesaid community of Doukhobors . . ."*

The Honourable J. T. Thorson, Minister of National War Services, made the position of the Government clear in the following quotation from the National War Service Regulations:—

> Members of the denominations of Christians called Mennonites and members of the community of Doukhobors who immigrated to Canada pursuant to the arrangements evidenced by the Order in Council of August 17, 1873, and by the Order in Council of December 6, 1898, respectively, or the descendants of such immigrants who have continued without interruption to be members of the aforesaid sect or denomination of Christians or of the aforesaid community of Doukhobors and who have resided without interruption in Canada, shall be entitled, subject as provided in these regulations, to the postponement of their military training.†

Generally speaking, conscientious objectors were supposed to perform alternative service on Provincial projects or in National parks, at the rate of 50 cents a day and board. The operation of this provision is described by Dr. Jamieson.

The original Order in Council of December 6th, 1898, granted exemption to the Doukhobors settling permanently in Canada. This exemption was repeated in the National War Service Regulations in the recent conflict. This discussion of the difficulties associated with future planning is based on the presumption that this procedure will be repeated in any future mobilization.

There are separate problems associated with USCC members, Independents and Sons of Freedom. With reference to the USCC group, the suggestion has been made that each male child should have issued for him a certificate of Doukhobor membership soon after birth. Upon reaching military age, he would exchange this for an exemption card bearing his picture. This would provide him with advance proof of exemption, so that in case of general mobilization the official interrogation productive of trouble in the past would not be repeated.

This plan has a number of defects. In the first place, no government can commit any future government on a policy of exemptions. Secondly, the plan might be interpreted as official encouragement of

* Canada, Parliament, House of Commons, Official Report of Debates, 1941-42, p. 3955.
† Ibid., pp. 4309-43, 10.

exemption-seeking. Also important is the impact on the non-Doukhobor community. There would be resentment at any flashing about of exemption cards, even in peacetime.

In identifying bona fide Doukhobors for exemption, USCC leaders act at present as an administrative arm of the Government. As decentralization continues, it will be increasingly difficult for this function to be carried out, to say nothing of the problem of deciding who is actually a descendant of a Doukhobor.

Independents pose a problem because their breaking away from communal living does not necessarily mean that they have forsaken pacifist views. In time of war they may feel impelled to apply for USCC membership for certification of exemption rather than simply to apply for exemption as individual conscientious objectors.

The question of what to do with resistant Sons of Freedom in time of war would confound a Solomon. The distinction between national registration and registration for military service is at the present time unrecognized by them. Many are good workers who certainly contribute nothing to a war effort when languishing in jail. They would probably be nothing but a hindrance in an alternative service camp.

It seems impossible to devise any administrative arrangement in advance for this perplexing problem. The main hope is that in any further measure the Federal Government will act constructively on the whole issue of conscientious objectors, including Doukhobors. This means not only good administrative structure, but, even more important, the use of appropriate personnel.

CENSUS ENUMERATION

It is refreshing to note that there is one problem relating to resistant Doukhobors which does not occur more than once every ten years. That is census enumeration.

In the past, enumeration of Doukhobors presented real difficulties. On one occasion, Sons of Freedom not only staged a nudist demonstration but threatened to strip the officials. The 1951 Census featured no such demonstrations, and was a credit to all of the directing officials.

No difficulty was experienced with the USCC members. Many of them were used as enumerators, and their employment did much to facilitate the whole process. On the other hand, the concentrated areas of Sons of Freedom presented real difficulty. In spite of meetings arranged with their leaders, very little information was gained in the usual way. Government records had to be used to arrive at estimates.

Administratively, there seems no way to improve upon this system. The gathering of census statistics can be made easier only by the success of the total programme.

199

"LICENSE FORFEITURE AND CANCELLATION ACT"

A peculiar piece of legislation called the Licence Forfeiture and Cancellation Act* has especial bearing on the Doukhobor registration problems. This law, passed in 1940 and obviously directed at Doukhobors, provides that anyone who fails to comply with the Vital Statistics Act and school attendance laws may be refused or deprived of a licence by any public body. An appeal is allowed "on the question only whether he is a person who is subject to be deprived of licence within the meaning of this Act."

This Act invokes a double penalty. That is, in addition to the usual imposition of fine or imprisonment for the offence itself, a licence of an unrelated nature can be refused or lifted.

Inquiry has revealed that the Licence Forfeiture and Cancellation Act is used only by the Forest Service, which refers an applicant for clearance to the police before issuing any licence. As no record has been kept of applicants, the impact of this policy cannot be assessed. If application of the law were extended, it probably would be felt most in refusal of trade, motor-vehicle and driver's licences.

It can be said in favour of this legislation that it is not the same as the franchise restriction which hit out at all Doukhobors indiscriminately. This is directed only at those who refuse to comply with certain requirements.

Extraordinary measures are sometimes needed to deal with extraordinary situations. But even apart from the issue of double penalty, this legislation has two bad features. It is directed at refusal to educate and the refusal to register, which are not demonstration offences against the community but represent a stubborn resistance based at least partially on religious persuasion. The other point, of course, is that failure to have a licence may cost a man his usual means of livelihood.

An examination of the Public Schools Act and the Vital Statistics Act shows that the usual penalty is a fine, although no mention is made of what happens when the offender refuses to pay the fine. Presumably the Summary Convictions Act would prevail in such cases, and a Doukhobor, like anyone else, might find his possessions attached if he refused to pay the fine.

This issue has been discussed with many authorities, some of whom think that the Licence Forfeiture and Cancellation Act should be repealed outright, and others that it should be enforced rigorously. If there is any option, this Act should not be applied administratively until it has been demonstrated that both educational measures and repeated application of the usual penalties fail in effect.

* R.S.B.C. 1948, chap. 186.

Doukhobors present comparatively few problems for the Provincial health and welfare programme. They give good care to their children, have a lower than average incidence of crime and delinquency in other than demonstration offences, and many of them live independently of social assistance. To be considered here are social assistance, child welfare services, planning for an adequate corrections programme, and the need for strengthening recreation and public health services in the Kootenay area.

SOCIAL ASSISTANCE

The Social Assistance Act.—Social assistance in British Columbia is governed by the "Social Assistance Act" and Social Assistance Regulations.*

The Act itself is very broad in its provisions, as indicated by section 3, which reads as follows:—

> Social assistance may be granted out of funds appropriated by the Legislature for the purpose to individuals, whether adult or minor, or to families who through mental or physical illness or other exigency are unable to provide in whole or in part by their own effort, through other security measures, or from income and other resources, necessities essential to maintain or assist in maintaining a reasonably normal and healthy existence.

Of interest in assessment of the Doukhobor situation is a clause forbidding discrimination, which reads as follows:—

> In the administration of social assistance there shall be no discrimination based on race, colour, creed, or political affiliation.

The Director of Welfare is charged with the general administration of the Act. Subject to the approval of the Minister of Health and Welfare, he has power "to establish regulations and formulate policies" not inconsistent with the Act.

Policy on Assistance to Doukhobors.—Whether Doukhobors who fail to comply with the law on school attendance and on vital statistics should be granted social welfare is one of the thorniest problems faced by the Social Welfare Branch of the Department of Health and Welfare. According to available sources, the issue first arose in 1937 when J. W. Smiley, Relief Investigator at Nelson, stated that Doukhobors without marriage certificates and birth certificates for their children were no longer eligible for unemployment relief.† However, a Government spokesman in Victoria quickly denied this announcement. He said that the Government's edict applied particularly to criminal acts. Failure of Doukhobors to register marriages

* R.S.B.C. 1948, chap. 310.
† Vancouver Sun, April 30th, 1937, p. 7.

and births would not alone make them ineligible to receive government assistance.†

During the depression years the Government evidently felt that it could not deny assistance at a time of great need, regardless of the views of recipients. In the 1940's the policy was changed. The position of the Department was made clear in 1948 in a memorandum from the Deputy Minister's office to the Director of Welfare. It read in part:—

> . . . There has been no change in the policy laid down by the Minister several years ago to the effect that no person is eligible for any form of social assistance who does not comply with the requirements of Provincial and Dominion legislation.‡

There is evidence, however, that this ruling was not always rigidly applied through the years.

A major change in policy was made on July 28th, 1950, when it was decided that since there was no law demanding mandatory application for family allowances, the requirements would be met if births were registered and children attended school regularly.§ For some time it had been a ruling of the Department that a necessary step toward qualification for social assistance was to register for family allowances.

With the committal of hundreds of Sons of Freedom in the spring of 1950, there arose the question of the support of remaining members of the families, as the Provincial Government decided not to apprehend the children of offenders. In effect, the representatives of the Sons of Freedom were allowed to be responsible for investigation and certification. No individual was required to sign the simplified form, as long as the representative committee of Sons of Freedom handled it. In order to remove fears about giving information on the children, the Minister of Health and Welfare even agreed to allow the group to retain the forms for a period of two years subject to a possible Provincial audit.

It is necessary to explore the validity of the former denial of assistance to Doukhobors who refused to comply with the law. Admittedly, the policy has recently been changed, but this is no guarantee that the change will continue indefinitely. The issue is of such importance that the policy should be settled.

The case for social assistance to resistant Doukhobors or to their dependents rests in the first instance on a principle recognized in the case of the sick, the mentally ill and the delinquent of whatever creed, that however resistant, useless, depraved or criminal an indi-

† Victoria Times, May 1st, 1937, p. 9.
‡ Memorandum from E. W. Griffith, Deputy Minister of Welfare, to C. W. Lundy, Director of Welfare, dated June 2nd, 1948.
§ Memorandum from Marie Riddell, Supervisor, Family Division, to J. W. Smith, Regional Administrator, Social Welfare Branch, Nelson, B.C., dated July 28th, 1950.

vidual may become, he has the right to expect the necessities of life simply because of the fact that he is a human being. Recognition of such a principle appears to refute any suggestion that needy persons should be denied food, shelter, and clothing because of refusal to comply with a law which conflicts with scruples that derive from their religion.

Both the Vital Statistics Act and the Public Schools Act provide penalties for non-compliance. Failure or difficulty of enforcement provides no reason for subjecting a certain category of offenders to other measures, unless specified by Statute; such treatment of a low-income offender singles out the potential social assistance recipient for punitive action, while a similar offender with sufficient income escapes.

There is also a definite propaganda value in providing assistance. It is one of the ways of demonstrating to the Sons of Freedom that the Government is not the malevolent giant they think it is. The recent action of the Social Welfare Branch in proffering assistance with minimum registration requirements is a case in point; the Sons of Freedom refused the assistance but many must have been impressed by the offer.

Further, any plan that forces impoverished Sons of Freedom to look to their own community for all support is at variance with the generally accepted idea of aiding those who wish to loosen community ties to do so. This will not be achieved if the community is forced into becoming a bitter, ingrown group because of lack of outside interest.

Finally, while it is true that, under section 13 of the Social Assistance Act the Director of Welfare, "subject to the approval of the Minister, is empowered to establish regulations and formulate policies not inconsistent with this Act . . .", insistence on registration and school attendance as qualifying conditions appears inconsistent with the spirit of the Act in its emphasis on the meeting of need where it exists.

In any event, it is doubtful whether such a fundamental right as eligibility for assistance should be subject to administrative discretion. No such important policy as the denial of assistance to a religious minority should be laid down without a full examination by the Provincial Legislature.

The Community Doukhobor Social Assistance Rate.[*]—Until recently all social assistance recipients who were members of a Doukhobor community generally received less than other persons of that category in the Province. This was presumably a local decision; no such policy appears to have been laid down by the Victoria office. The

---

[*] Memorandum of J. W. Smith, Regional Administrator, Social Welfare Branch, Nelson, B.C., to District Supervisor, Nelson and Trail, dated May 22nd, 1951.

policy has now been revised to give greater flexibility. Doukhobors now receive the same basic food allowance as everyone else, and shelter and sundries are provided as circumstances require.

RECREATION SERVICES

This review relates only to public provision of recreation services. Public recreation in British Columbia depends a great deal on the stimulation provided by the Physical Education and Recreation Branch of the Department of Education. The policy of the Branch is to enter a community only after there is an appreciable demand for its services. Even then its contribution is usually limited to the payment of $50 a month toward the salary of a qualified director.

Although there is a part-time programme at Grand Forks, there is a good deal of complaint that young Doukhobors drift into town in the evenings and hang about the streets with nothing to do. The same may be said of Castlegar. The construction of new schools in these two communities raises the question of further development of evening recreation programmes. The suggestion has been made that school buses could be hired in the evening to bring people in from the surrounding areas.

The proposed Commission on Doukhobor Affairs should give close attention to this question. If a representative of the Commission were stationed in Grand Forks, for instance, he should be concerned with making it a community effort of both Doukhobors and non-Doukhobors. There certainly should be no thought of confining the programme to any one group. It is suggested that the Physical Education and Recreation Branch, the City of Grand Forks, the USCC, the proposed Commission, and Castlegar might well consider a joint effort which would at least provide one full-time person.

PUBLIC HEALTH SERVICES

The effectiveness of public health work in Doukhobor districts in the West Kootenay tends to vary with the nature of the communities themselves. The response is better from the scattered, more diffused population than from the isolated, tightly knit villages. Very little progress has been made at Krestova with public health services. Even the response to well-baby clinics was so discouraging that they were discontinued.

It is generally true that home-visits are more effective than formal clinics. Home-visiting by its individual attention is pleasing to the family and avoids any active move or acceptance of a government service which attendance at an official clinic might be taken to imply. Home-visiting is also more effective from an administrative point of view because the nurse can see the home and advise the mother about her particular problems. Through home-visiting, the Doukhobor families in the more remote areas come to recognize in the public health nurse an unprejudiced person doing a job which they can appreciate.

In USCC areas most babies are now born in hospital. Birth notifications given to the health unit provide a ready-made reason for a visit by the public health nurse, and the mother with a new-born child is more ready to receive advice than at any other time. Such a contact can lead to an established relationship.

Readiness to accept medical advice varies with the group. Referrals for X-ray are often refused when it is found that the individual's name and identity will be photographed on the plate. Requests for sputum are usually refused if the individual has not had sanatorium treatment. Several tuberculous cases have failed to respect advice regarding isolation; in this matter the Doukhobors are similar to many non-Doukhobors.

In all areas the Doukhobors accept immunization, particularly when it can be done in the home. They are especially eager to receive smallpox immunization; instances have been reported in which Doukhobors have vaccinated their own children by the "arm to arm" method. There does not appear to be any aversion to having blood Kahns done, but requests for stool samples are usually refused. There are no comprehensive figures on blood donors, but one small community of Doukhobors recently made a much better response than other Canadians.

Health films have met with mixed receptions. They were reasonably well received at Pass Creek, Ooteshenie and Champion, and after a difficult start at Glade there was moderate enthusiasm but little cooperation. No such films have been shown at Krestova, where they are equated with the commercial movies and regarded as evil.

Since home-visiting offers the best means of health education among the Doukhobors, this service needs to be strengthened. Dr. L. S. Anderson, Director of the West Kootenay Health Unit, who cooperated in preparing this review, feels that additional personnel are required in the Lower Slocan Valley, Castlegar and Grand Forks.

CORRECTIONS SERVICES

The record of the Sons of Freedom in British Columbia includes an excessive history of imprisonment. The greatest problems of prison administration occurred during the detention of several hundreds of them on Piers Island from 1932 to 1935, and in the 1950 disturbances when hundreds more were committed to the Federal Penitentiary. It is the purpose of this section to indicate an approach to any repetition of large-scale disturbances.

The Need for Planning.—Future difficulties should be expected, even if the best possible programme is devised; a good programme in itself may initially stimulate some trouble. There is good reason for planning in advance to meet the likelihood of future need for detention. Some Sons of Freedom leaders have abetted disturbances by claiming that the Government cannot possibly deal with hundreds of offenders and, to some degree, they have made their point.

Penal Programmes in British Columbia.—The Canadian penal system divides responsibility on the basis of sentence; persons sentenced to two years or more are committed to a Federal penitentiary while those with a lesser penalty go to a Provincial jail.

With few exceptions, Canadian penal institutions are unprepared for the additional complications of Sons of Freedom inmates. Neither Federal nor Provincial institutions are equipped to do a rehabilitation job with them. They disrupt the whole routine of any institution and the programme for other prisoners. Inevitably, because of their tactics, they create in the prison staff an antagonism which leads to treatment reinforcing their conviction that all government is bad.

Responsibility for Detention.—Should a Commission on Doukhobor Affairs, if such is established, be responsible for the detention of Doukhobors? Such a plan is hardly advisable; the Commission should be a coordinating body rather than an administrative one. Again, there is a great deal of technical knowledge required for successful prison management.

The best answer is probably to be found in the close cooperation of the Commission with an existing department in order to assure an effective programme. The Commission should be able to supplement the usual institutional budget with its own funds so that special services necessary for rehabilitation of Sons of Freedom may be available.

Specifically, it is proposed that the Department of the Attorney-General assume responsibility for the detention of Sons of Freedom guilty of demonstration offences. All such offenders, whether a Federal or a Provincial responsibility, should be concentrated in one unit guided by one policy. The basic reason for this suggestion is that a programme of rehabilitation is more likely to be effective and economical if made a specific responsibility of one department than if offenders are scattered through different institutions where they would be regarded merely as a nuisance. A flexible programme, especially desirable in this case, might be more easily achieved through Provincial administration.

The Location of the Unit.—A unit might be located in the Kootenay area, somewhere on the Coast, or on a site adjacent to an existing institution. A major argument for the Kootenay District is that Doukhobor offenders could easily be visited by their families and friends. However, the creation of a Kootenay unit might become a shrine for Sunday afternoon rallies and have a regressive influence on the rest of the population, while die-hards from the community might try to instigate offenders into precipitating incidents. A further argument against a Kootenay location is the difficulty of recruiting appropriate staff. Persons familiar with prison problems are not to be found in the area in any numbers, and established members of the Provincial service would probably not rejoice in having to leave their homes for such an assignment.

This means that the detention site should be in the coastal area. Location in the vicinity of Vancouver would facilitate the use of personnel from existing institutions which are all situated in the Lower Mainland, and consultation with top officials or the appropriate Minister would be readily available.

One scheme might be for the Provincial Government to have an arrangement with a farmer in the Fraser Valley whereby a portion of his land would be immediately available if required. Another would be for the use of land adjacent to Oakalla Prison Farm or the proposed unit at Haney. Either suggestion implies that a site be selected in advance. Prefabricated steel buildings insulated with asbestos are readily available in the Vancouver area and can be quickly erected. Of these two suggestions, probably the better plan would be to have the site close to Oakalla. A prison can always use another building; the proposed Commission on Doukhobor Affairs might buy some prefabricated buildings and make them available to the Oakalla authorities. The buildings would be put to good purpose in relieving present overcrowding at Oakalla and would be quickly available if Sons of Freedom should arrive in numbers.

In any planning, provision should be made for women offenders. At the present time the majority are confined to the Kingston Penitentiary. Their care also should come under the scrutiny of the Commission on Doukhobor Affairs.

Administrative Structure.—If it is important to plan in advance for buildings for Sons of Freedom offenders, it is even more pressing to devise an administrative structure appropriate for this particular situation. The top administration should consist of a Director, a Consultant on Programme, and a Security Officer. The duties of each will be evident as the total programme is described.

In its present stage of transition, the Provincial corrections service would be reluctant to release its key personnel for such administration. A "stand-by" administration, therefore, should be formed in advance from the staff of various institutions. Such agencies as the Vancouver Detention Home, the Boys' Industrial School, New Haven, the Young Offenders' Unit, and Oakalla might each be willing to release one official for the sake of a challenging rehabilitation job. Agreements could be made in advance that, when required, leave of absence be granted for a year or until such time as new staff be adequately trained. The location of the proposed unit in the Vancouver area would mean that an official could still keep in touch with his own agency.

This "stand-by" administration should be formed immediately, so as to acquaint itself fully with the problem. In cooperation with the proposed Commission on Doukhobor Affairs, they should map detailed plans for a programme.

For additional staff, there can be some recruiting immediately the necessity arises, and this task will be facilitated by the location of the unit in the Lower Mainland area. However, a core of experienced personnel should also be drawn from existing institutions. In addition to Provincial agencies, the Federal Penitentiary might make a contribution by seconding some of its better staff members to the unit.

The Programme.—The outlook for a programme is not completely bleak, even for such an uncooperative group as resistant Sons of Freedom. They at least like to talk, and discussion is the main avenue for treatment of problems such as theirs.

The heart of the programme should be the relationship of individual staff members with specific groups, and a staff training programme should emphasize the fundamentals of group therapy. Building units should be planned so as to support the rehabilitative work.

Of course, all these treatment aspects should come under the direction of the Consultant on Programme. In addition to group leaders, he may find it necessary to have one or more psychiatric social workers attached to his staff. Under the direction of a consulting psychiatrist, they should be available for the treatment of disturbed inmates amenable to such an approach.

Release Procedures.—Remission, parole and ticket of leave are the means by which an offender in a Canadian prison may secure his release before the end of his stated sentence. Ticket of leave is the usual device for the release of an offender on a conditional basis. It has recently been applied to large numbers of Sons of Freedom, who, like anyone else, are required to meet the condition, among others, that they shall abstain from any further violation of the law.

If pledges are to be used at all, they should be signed only by those who are emotionally prepared to sign them, and who feel that they can accept their implications and live up to them. Further conditions may be imposed. One possibility is that, as a form of

208

dispersal, the released person should be required to live elsewhere than in the Kootenay area. To facilitate such a plan, the proposed Commission on Doukhobor Affairs might make funds available for rehabilitation, particularly if movement of a family is involved.

The Federal Government does not have a follow-up staff for supervision after release, but depends on the services of private agencies. There are none in the Kootenay area. The Provincial Government has a Probation Officer stationed at Nelson, but he cannot be expected to devote himself to this problem.

The Ticket of Leave Act requires reporting once a month to the local chief of police, but that does not constitute good supervision. Most released offenders benefit from guidance, and in this instance there is a case for demonstrating that conditional release involves such supervision. In the event of the recurrence of a large-scale problem, the proposed Commission on Doukhobor Affairs should seek the cooperation of the Provincial Probation Service in providing additional personnel and should be prepared to meet most of the cost.

FRANCHISE AND ELIGIBILITY FOR OFFICE

Doukhobors constitute the sole minority group excluded from the Provincial franchise in this Province, now that Chinese, Japanese, and Indians have been granted the right. As will be noted, the Federal franchise is in principle based on the Provincial Statute, and consequently Doukhobors residing in British Columbia are excluded. On the other hand, there is no bar to Doukhobors participating in municipal elections, nor does there appear to have been a restriction at any time.

The Provincial Franchise.—Since the Federal franchise for Doukhobors is dependent on Provincial action, it is necessary to examine the provisions of the Provincial Elections Act.*

In the main, everyone is entitled to be registered as a voter in a British Columbia Provincial election if he is 21 years of age, is a natural-born Canadian citizen or British subject, has lived in Canada for a year and in British Columbia for six months immediately preceding application for registration as a voter, and is a resident of the electoral district in which he wants to vote.†

Among those disqualified from voting at a Provincial election is "every Doukhobor," with the exception of anyone who "has served in the Naval, Military, or Air Force of any member of the British Commonwealth of Nations in any war, and who produces a discharge from such Naval, Military, or Air Force to the Registrar upon apply-

* R.S.B.C. 1984, chap. 106.
† R.S.B.C. 1948, chap. 106, sec. 3.

ing for registration under this Act and to the Deputy Returning Officer at the time of polling"‡; or who "is the wife or descendant of a person who comes under the scope of this clause."§

The Act defines a Doukhobor as follows: "'Doukhobor' means a person, male or female, exempted or entitled to claim exemption or who on production of any certificate might have become or would now be entitled to claim exemption from military service by reason of the Order of the Governor in Council of December sixth, 1898, and every descendant of any such person, whether born in the Province or elsewhere."*

The most pertinent sections of the Order in Council referred to are:—

> The Minister submits that Sub-section 3 of Section 21 of the Militia Act, Chapter 41 of the Revised Statutes of Canada, contains the following provision: "Every person bearing a Certificate from the Society of Quakers, Mennonites or Tunkers, and every inhabitant of Canada of any religious denomination, otherwise subject to military duty, who, from the doctrines of his religion, is averse to bearing arms and refuses personal military service, shall be exempt from such service when ballotted, in time of peace or war upon such conditions and under such regulations as the Governor in Council, from time to time prescribes."
>
> The Minister recommends that under the power vested in Your Excellency in Council, by the above Provision, the Doukhobors settling permanently in Canada be exempted unconditionally from service in the Militia, upon the production in each case of a certificate of membership from the proper authorities of their Community.†

The Dominion Franchise.—The Dominion Elections Act, 1938, governs the Federal franchise. Section 14 excludes from voting ". . . in any province, every person exempted or entitled to claim exemption or who on production of any certificate might have become or would now be entitled to claim exemption from military service by reason of the Order-in-Council of December 6, 1898, because the doctrines of his religion make him averse to bearing arms, and who is by the law of that province disqualified from voting at an election of a member of the Legislative Assembly of that province."**

It should be noted that entitlement to exemption is not the only factor for disqualification under the Federal law. Thus, Doukhobors in Saskatchewan may vote in the Federal election because they are included in the Provincial franchise. The Federal Government, however, is under no constitutional compulsion to follow the Provincial election legislation. It may go beyond the Provincial law if it wishes.

‡ R.S.B.C. 1948, chap. 106, sec. 4 (1)(e).
§ R.S.B.C. 1948, chap. 106, sec. 4 (1)(f).
* R.S.B.C. 1948, chap. 106, sec. 2(1).
† Minute of a meeting of the Committee of the Privy Council, approved by his Excellency the Governor-General on December 6th, 1898. P.C. 2747, signed by A. D. P. Heeney, Clerk of the Privy Council.
** Statutes of Canada, 1938, chap. 46, sec. 14 (2)(j).

The Municipal Franchise.—The right to vote for municipal candidates is covered by the Municipal Elections Act,* and the Municipal Act.†

In these Statutes there does not appear to be any exclusion of Doukhobors from the right to vote. The Municipal Elections Act applies to any city other than Vancouver, and to any township or district municipality. All prospective voters must be British subjects.‡ Within cities, any person twenty-one years of age owning land may vote. So may any person holding a trade licence with a fee not less than five dollars. Another qualification is that of being a householder within the municipality, a "householder" under the Act being any person who pays two dollars a year to the municipality in the form of a poll tax or its equivalent. The one difficulty that a Doukhobor might meet would be in reference to the statutory declaration that a householder or the holder of a trade licence must make to prove his status. However, a perusal of the forms shows no demand for allegiance.§

The qualifications of voters in district municipalities are broadly the same as above.||

Election of School Trustees.—The election of school trustees is governed by the "Public Schools Act."¶

Within municipal school districts and large municipal school districts, the qualifications of voters are the same as those for the election of the Mayor or Reeve.

Persons living in a part of a large municipal school district not within the limits of a municipality must have qualifications equal to those of voters in a rural school district.**

Where the Council of a municipality has levied a special tax for school purposes on parents and other persons who are not liable for school taxes, they are eligible to participate in an election. However, they cannot vote on money by-laws.††

The qualified voters of a rural school district are generally as described above and include ratepayers in the district who are British subjects 21 years of age and their wives or husbands.‡‡

A candidate for office in a Provincial election in British Columbia must be able to qualify as a voter and be registered as such. This automatically excludes anyone defined as a Doukhobor. A search of pertinent Federal legislation does not reveal any similar requirement.

* R.S.B.C. 1948, chap. 105.
† R.S.B.C. 1948, chap. 232.
‡ R.S.B.C. 1948, chap. 105, sec. 5.
§ See Forms 1 and 2 in Schedule to "Municipal Elections Act," R.S.B.C. 1948, chap. 105.
|| R.S.B.C. 1948, chap. 105, sec. 12.
¶ R.S.B.C. 1948, chap. 297.
** R.S.B.C. 1948, chap. 297, sec. 38(3).
†† R.S.B.C. 1948, chap. 297, sec. 38(4'.
‡‡ R.S.B.C. 1948, chap. 297, sec. 93(1).

Evidently a Doukhobor finds himself in the strange position of not being able to vote in a Federal election, but able to take a seat in the House of Commons as a result of that election. There does not appear to be anything in the Municipal Elections Act which would bar a Doukhobor from office as long as he is 21, a British subject, and has the necessary property qualifications. The same is true of candidates for School Board. However, there is a provision in each instance —Federal, Provincial and Municipal—that an elected candidate must take an oath of allegiance.

In this section the legal aspects of franchise and eligibility for office in the case of Doukhobors have been reviewed. In drawing conclusions from this material, an interpretation of the implications of the actual legislation will first be made.

The Legislature chose to define a Doukhobor by descent rather than as a person who upholds a particular religion. Thus, it would seem that a person now integrated in the Canadian community who might be a convert to another religion, but who possessed Doukhobor ancestors, is denied the vote.

There are other peculiar features of the definition. For example, a person "entitled to claim exemption" may not want exemption, but the entitlement is sufficient to deny him the vote. His only hope is to waive exemption by enlistment, as there is no provision for a statutory declaration of renouncement of exemption.

Probably the most unfortunate part of the definition relates to descendants. Specifically, children of Doukhobor parents are denied the vote on the basis of their parents' belief, not on their own, and without reference to their degree of integration into the community. This not only poses a moral problem but raises almost insuperable administrative difficulties. One might well ask, with W. R. Motherwell, in 1934, "How many crosses will it take to get the Doukhobor blood out of them . . . ?" Does the law really mean that, in spite of intermarriage between Doukhobors and non-Doukhobors, children and grandchildren *ad infinitum* will be denied the vote because somewhere in the family tree there was a Doukhobor ancestor? In practice, the answer depends on the factors of geography and surname. In the Kootenay districts, any known Doukhobor, or any descendant of a Doukhobor, is likely to be challenged if he tries to get on the voters list. Elsewhere in the Province it probably does not occur to the clerks to challenge each prospective elector as a Doukhobor, and so the franchise could be exercised quite illegally. Doukhobor women who marry men with non-Doukhobor names have the greatest opportunity of evading the law, if they wish to do so.

The section on eligibility through military service also challenges common sense. The individual must have participated in a war; he may have served for years in the peace-time forces, but that does not qualify him. Moreover, he must have a discharge; current members of the armed forces are not eligible.

The case for extension of the franchise to Doukhobors is a simple one. In British Columbia no perfectionist qualities are demanded of the voter. A criminal may vote if not in prison at the time of the election. Treason is not a barrier to voting. The voter released from prison need offer no evidence of reformation, no testimony that he is in favour of education, display no marriage certificate, offer no proof of loyalty, nor need he explain his views on military service.

While it is true that the great majority of Doukhobors in British Columbia today state that they do not want to take responsibility for electing a government, this is not a fixed and static situation. A growing number do want to vote, and at present they feel the discriminatory nature of the denial.

The final issue to be considered is eligibility for office. A Doukhobor is excluded only from the British Columbia Legislature, and that bar would be automatically removed if Doukhobors were granted the Provincial vote.

It is true that many Doukhobors would feel unable to accept office because of the oath or affirmation of allegiance. In spite of an appreciation of the moral dilemma of those who wish to take part in community affairs, it is difficult to see how there can be any departure from the swearing of allegiance, which is one of the basic tenets of organized government in the Commonwealth.

Since the presentation of the Report of the Research Committee a new "Elections Act" has been introduced, making no mention of exclusion of Doukhobors from the franchise. Consequently Doukhobors in British Columbia are now eligible to vote in both provincial and federal elections.‡

THE CRIMINAL CODE AND DEMONSTRATION OFFENCES

Probably the most widely known fact of Doukhobor life is that members of a sub-group, the Sons of Freedom, are frequently imprisoned for offences under the Criminal Code. These are not usual criminal offences; they may be termed demonstration offences in that they are claimed to be protests against warlike trends, government policy, incarceration of offenders, and in some instances divergent behaviour of certain members of the group. The common offences of the Sons of Freedom are nude parading, the bombing and burning of schools, and destruction of railroad and other private property. It is the purpose of this section to review the legislation pertinent to these offences.

Section 205A of the Criminal Code of Canada provides that:—

Everyone is guilty of an offense and liable upon summary conviction to three years' imprisonment who, while nude,

‡ S.B.C., 2 Elizabeth II, 1953 (second session), chap. 5.

(a) is found in any public place whether alone or in company with one or more other persons who are parading or have assembled with intent to parade or have paraded in such public place while nude, or

(b) is found in any public place whether alone or in company with one or more other persons, or

(c) is found without lawful excuse for being nude upon any private property not his own, so as to be exposed to the public view, whether alone or in company with other persons, or

(a) appears upon his own property so as to be exposed to the public view, whether alone or in company with other persons.*

For the purpose of this section, anyone is regarded as being nude "who is so scantily clad as to offend against public decency or order."

No action or prosecution for violation of the section is to be taken without the consent of the Attorney-General for the Province in which the offence is alleged to have been committed.†

This legislation was passed in 1931. In his contribution to the debate in the legislature, Mr. Esling, member for Kootenay West, seemed to make it clear that the new section had financial overtones:—

> We realize that the Provincial Government is responsible for enforcement of law. But there are circumstances beyond which it is impossible for a Provincial Government to go. The costs are too great, and if the truth must be told—and I say this advisedly—these people are numerically too strong for this Government or the Provincial Government to keep them within bounds. I have always contended and still contend that the Federal Government, having brought them here, must share the responsibility for their conduct and the cost of their maintenance while here.‡

Under Section 205A a Son of Freedom participating in a nude parade, or even appearing nude in a public place by himself, is liable to three years' imprisonment. If he or anybody else is guilty of an intentionally indecent act (such as accosting a woman), the maximum penalty provided is a fine of $50 and six months' imprisonment.

Nude parading would seem to fall within the definition of unlawful assembly, which is described in the Criminal Code as follows:—

> An unlawful assembly is an assembly of three or more persons who, with intent to carry out any common purpose, assembled in such a manner or so conduct themselves when assembled as to cause persons in the neighbourhood of such assembly to fear on reasonable grounds, that the persons so assembled will disturb the peace tumultuously, or will by such assembly needlessly and without any reasonable occasion provoke other persons to disturb the peace tumultuously.§

The maximum punishment provided for unlawful assembly is one year's imprisonment.

* Criminal Code of Canada, sec. 205A.
† Ibid.
‡ Canada, Parliament, House of Commons, Official Report of Debates, 1931, p. 4132.
§ Criminal Code of Canada, sec. 87.

The contention of the Sons of Freedom that there is nothing wrong with nudism except in the minds of the observers has been seconded by some authorities who argue that, while Doukhobor nudism is exposure, it is not indecent exposure, and the state should ignore it by repealing the existing legislation and not prosecuting at all. In point of fact, nudism is often ignored. In many instances, the police simply warn the offenders and send them home. But there is a difference between this highly desirable administrative discretion and full repeal of the law on nudism. Without any doubt, the non-Doukhobor public cannot accept Sons of Freedom nudity with any complaisance.

The best action in connection with nudism will be a comprehensive programme which removes its causes. But there is a case for the application of a penalty, the threat of which will deter many Sons of Freedom. The problem is to provide punishment which deters but which does not create martyrs.

One year after the imposition of the increased penalty in 1931, the Sons of Freedom responded by disrobing by the hundreds and constituting such a problem of imprisonment that the expedient of Piers Island had to be devised. Moreover, the 1950 disturbances likewise indicated no concern with the heavy penalty. Nudism continues despite existing legislation.

The whole structure of criminal law is based on the thesis that people really do not want to go to jail, and that, if they do go, they do not want to stay there very long. Some Sons of Freedom appal the criminologist by searching for punishment. A short sentence, with its jolt of unpleasant reality, may be just as effective as a longer one, and it does not have as much status among the Sons of Freedom who seek martyrdom.

In the original debate it was claimed that the Provincial Government was not quite equal to the burden of prison maintenance, and that one way for the Federal Government to share the load would be to increase the penalty to more than two years and thus make the offenders eligible for a Federal penitentiary. The present degree of co-operation between the two Governments and the apparent willingness of the Federal Government to contribute financially to any feasible approach alter the situation. However, the Criminal Code is now (1954) under review, and the draft of Bill No. 7 provides for revision of the law relating to nudism, and includes a proposed penalty, for a summary conviction, of five hundred dollars or imprisonment or both.

With regard to the other offences commonly charged against the Sons of Freedom, the destruction of private or public property by bombing or arson, there appears to be no call for a change of the law.

CANCELLATION OF EXEMPTION OF OFFENDERS

From time to time the proposal has been made that any Doukhobor found guilty under the Criminal Code of an offence involving violence should be deprived of exemption from military service. Actually, no blanket exemption is now provided; in the event of future mobilization the Federal Government would have to decide whether to grant a broad exemption to Doukhobors born in Canada, as it did in the last war. Therefore, the real proposal is that Doukhobors guilty of violence should be denied eligibility for any future exemption.

The case for cancellation of exemption can be stated very briefly. It is that those guilty of violent acts should lose the privilege of an exemption which is based on pacifist belief. The hope of the advocates of this proposal is that the Sons of Freedom would be so fearful of losing possible exemption that they would hesitate to resort to violence. If such a proposal were adopted, the person with a record of violence would almost automatically be refused exemption in case of future war, unless he could show very good evidence of rehabilitation. In this he would be in no different position from any other conscientious objector who normally has to show that his record of behaviour is consistent with his application for exemption.

Many Independents and USCC members favour this move. Some Sons of Freedom would undoubtedly proclaim it as the final act of bad faith on the part of a punitive government, but others might see the logic of the argument that violent behaviour is inconsistent with the claim for exemption as a pacifist.

The main argument against the proposal is that it presupposes a logical assessment of reward and punishment by an essentially confused group. It must also be recognized that no matter how valid the proposal, it would affect mainly the young men of the Sons of Freedom, as the women, older people and physically unfit would not be likely to find themselves in uniform. Nor would the young men necessarily be deterred by the thought of the penalty. As has occurred before, others might volunteer as the culprits in order to shield them, or ineligibles might be instigated to do the "black work." The zealous Son of Freedom, moreover, might believe that he would not actually find himself in the armed services, but that his only concern would be involvement in a long battle with officialdom over his military status.

The proposal, finally, may be at odds with one of the tenets of discipline; namely, that punishment to be most effective should quickly follow the offence. The threat of being a participant in a future war may have little impact on the Sons of Freedom. The proposal might have more merit in countries where draft procedure would immediately follow release from imprisonment; from this particular point of view it has little to offer in Canada, where compulsory service is a hesitant step taken only during a period of actual war.

After much consideration the recommendation is made that, in the event of future mobilization, exemptions should not be granted to persons with a record of crimes of violence. Should it be decided that this proposal is to be accepted, there is a question as to the timing of the move. While information might be given out that the move is being considered, it is suggested that good strategy calls for the Government to be engaged in a positive programme of rehabilitation before introducing the measure. In other words, it should not be an isolated punitive move.

THE ADMINISTRATION OF DOUKHOBOR AFFAIRS

There never has been a defined programme for the relationship of government agencies to the Doukhobors. In the main, the policy in time of trouble has been to rely upon police action without extending clear guidance as to its operation. Until disturbances recur, the situation is dismissed from mind. Day-to-day incidents which add up to hostility are often ignored. Moreover, until cooperation was elicited by the Consultative Committee, there was little evidence of coordination between government agencies offering services to the Doukhobor community.

Many of the things that should be done have already been indicated. It is the purpose of this section to outline the administrative structure necessary to implement these recommendations.

ADMINISTRATIVE STRUCTURE

It is submitted that the situation calls for a new type of organization. The main point revolves around function. As the programme moves into the action stage, its direction will call for a small group chosen for administrative and judicial qualities and the ability to contribute a considerable portion of time.

FORM OF ADMINISTRATION

Specifically, it is proposed that a Commission on Doukhobor Affairs, responsible to a Minister, be appointed by the Lieutenant-Governor in Council. A chart of the proposed administrative structure is shown at the end of this chapter. The function of the Commission would be to co-ordinate the services of all levels of government as they relate to the Doukhobors, and to give leadership in new approaches toward promoting better relations between the group and other Canadian people. The Commission should be a body of five or seven representatives, from the Kootenay area and interested organizations and specialists.

The choice of the Commission form of organization for a task such as this one is suggested by a distinguished student of public administration. He has stated that the need to discover policy and formulate it, to exercise wide discretionary or controlling powers affecting private interests of persons or property, to exercise coercive power in controversial areas, to protect administrative integrity against hostile outside pressure, can best be met by a Commission.

A suggestion was made by Blakemore in 1912 that the administration of Doukhobors be separated from the ordinary process of government and that they be treated as a special group. In other words, it was suggested that the Indian Affairs formula be applied. Nothing could be less desirable. Any administrative device that contributes to the impression that the Doukhobor is a person apart is to be avoided. Wherever suitable, he should be eligible for and should receive the same treatment as any other Canadian.

The proposed arrangement would not invade the responsibility of existing departments. Rather, it would serve as a coordinating body and offer stimulation in some neglected areas of operation. For example, there is no suggestion that there be any interference with the functions of the Department of Education or the local School Boards in reference to education of Doukhobor children. But there is a case for a coordinating body, having broad responsibility for improvements in the situation, to work closely with existing authorities to give aid and guidance wherever it is possible to do so.

The Commission should have a budget of its own. To cite again the example of education: If the Commission feels that there is a need to offer bonuses to teachers in a certain problem area, it might co-ordinate its efforts with those of the local School Board so as to obtain the best available personnel. Other examples might be mentioned. The release of offenders from the penitentiary may mean that an additional social worker should be added to the staff of the Social Welfare Branch at Nelson or Grand Forks. The Commission might "buy" this service, although the supervision of the social worker would still rest with the Social Welfare Branch.

The role of chief executive officer of the Commission is described by the suggested title "Coordinator of Doukhobor Affairs." In the main, he should coordinate and not administer. It should not be necessary to give him any statutory power; what he accomplishes should depend on the desire for aid and the will to cooperate among the Doukhobors and public officials. However, it should be made clear in the Statute creating the Commission that it represented the

218

administrative arm of the Government in its approach to the Doukhobor problem, and that the various government departments would be expected to confer with the Co-ordinator on relevant issues.

A staff is needed. An executive assistant should be in charge of central office management and also carry responsibility for community relations in the Nelson-Castlegar area. The resident representative of the Consultative Committee at Krestova should continue his activities under the direction of the Coordinator and be responsible for community relations in the Slocan Valley. The appointment of a resident representative at Grand Forks is vitally necessary. He would have a triple function—community relations in Grand Forks and district, liaison with the USCC members there, and the building-up of a relationship with the Sons of Freedom at Gilpin.

Normally there is a strong case for the integration of an affected group by the appointment of a representative to such a Commission. In this particular situation, the Doukhobor leaders should not at first be attached to the administration, lest they be accused of "selling out." They can probably function better if it is clear to other Doukhobors that they have an independent role.

THE ROLE OF ADVISORY SERVICES

There is much controversy in public administration about the value of advisory boards, but it seems clear that these are necessary in the administration of Doukhobor affairs. Certainly it is desirable that the Consultative Committee be continued. Its role in public relations is invaluable, and, moreover, it can act as an auditor of the planning and programme of the Commission. Semi-annual meetings should be held so that the work of the Commission may be properly analysed and interpreted.

THE FINANCING OF THE COMMISSION

The proposed Commission does not call for a costly structure. Its role will largely be one of stimulation and coordination, but funds will be required for personnel and the strengthening of certain services when required.

A detailed budget is not appropriate here, but it is estimated that a comprehensive programme can be conducted at a cost of approximately $96,000 per annum. Of course, this does not include the cost of any relocation project. Nor does it include the cost of the construction of a detention unit at Oakalla for possible Doukhobor occupancy, but which would be used for other purposes as long as there were no demand for it.

The Government has now made an advance in the administration of Doukhobor affairs, setting up a cabinet committee composed of the Attorney-General and two ministers representing constituencies having a large population of Doukhobors. In addition, an inter-departmental committee of deputy ministers has been organized as the advisory and administrative arm of the government, and a sub-committee of regional civil servants is now functioning in the Kootenay-Boundary area.

These are forward moves, but there is a need for reviewing their appropriateness. This is particularly true of the inter-departmental committee. It is not conceivable that the deputy ministers in Victoria can attain the necessary understanding, nor that the Doukhobors can achieve it on their side. Traditional hostility, lack of real interest, and geography will combine to maintain ineffectiveness. The regional sub-committee is not remote, but it too is composed of people who are already busy with other concerns. The case for a Commission on Doukhobor Affairs is still clear.

PROPOSED ADMINISTRATIVE STRUCTURE OF DOUKHOBOR AFFAIRS

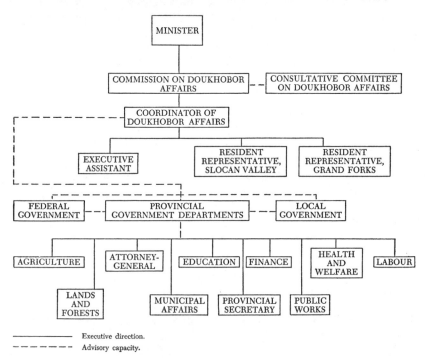

———————— Executive direction.
— — — — — — Advisory capacity.

VIII

SOIL, AGRICULTURE, AND REHABILITATION

Charles A. Rowles

INTRODUCTION

IN BRITISH COLUMBIA the Doukhobor story began with the purchase of lands intended for agricultural use in the West Kootenay region of the Province, along the Kootenay, Slocan, and Columbia Rivers and in the Boundary region along the Kettle River; since then it has centred around the ownership and use of these lands. To a considerable degree the lands hold the key to what may be ahead. The Research Committee, therefore, decided to undertake a study of these lands, which are now held in trust by the Land Settlement Board.

A preliminary examination of the land showed that the study would require considerable transportation and equipment for field parties. It appeared that the expense involved would be beyond the resources of the Research Committee, and the work was planned as a cooperative project between the Department of Lands and Forests of the Government of British Columbia on the one hand and the Doukhobor Research Committee on the other. One of the main objects of the study was to classify and map the soils of the former CCUB lands with a view to determining how they might best be utilized. It was also intended to report on their present use and on the condition of the irrigation systems and buildings and other factors of production.

Field operations were begun in July, 1951, with a field party consisting of A. L. Van Ryswyk, employed by the Research Committee, and Neil T. Drewry and W. P. F. Green of the Department of Lands. During the season the party covered thirteen blocks of land along the Kootenay, Columbia and Slocan Rivers and in 1952 the work was continued in the area of Grand Forks, with E. Gordon replacing Mr. Green.

When the work was planned, it was hoped that a party would be provided by the Department of Lands to study the engineering aspects of irrigation on the CCUB lands. Under the direction of G. Lake, this work was completed in 1953. Until their results are available, a final report on the former CCUB lands is not possible.

FIELD METHODS

The area was covered by car and foot traverse. One party classified and mapped the soils, taking profile descriptions of each soil type recognized, recording the depth, texture, structure, consistency, colour, and reaction of each soil horizon. For the more important soil types, field tests were made to determine their field moisture storage capacity, and undisturbed soil core samples and bulk samples were taken for study by Mr. Van Ryswyk at the Soils Laboratory at the University of British Columbia. The present condition and use of the land was noted, along with information respecting the condition and value of the buildings and equipment. The soil and land-use boundaries were plotted on aerial photographs of a scale approximately twelve inches to a mile. Acreage values were calculated later from the photographs.

The field boundaries and roads on the Community lands have no relationship to the original legal land-survey boundaries and monuments, which, for the most part, have completely disappeared. As a consequence, some difficulty was encountered in establishing locations and positions of soil boundaries, and the aerial photographs proved to be of great assistance for this purpose.

The engineering party, beginning its field work in 1952, determined levels and collected other information of importance for the designing of an irrigation scheme.

Although the field surveys and supporting laboratory and design work is not complete, a great deal of information regarding the former CCUB lands is now available. It is anticipated that a detailed technical report will be prepared when the work has been finished, and in the sections following only a preliminary and general report dealing with soils and agriculture will be presented.

GENERAL DESCRIPTION OF THE AREA

The soils of the former CCUB lands occur in thirteen blocks scattered over a distance of forty miles along the Slocan, Kootenay, and Columbia Rivers in the vicinity of Castlegar, Crescent Valley, and Passmore, and along the Kettle River in the vicinity of Grand Forks. In all, approximately 19,000 acres are involved, about 5,300 of which are in the Grand Forks area.

Road and railway communications through the area are good, and along the Columbia, Kootenay and Kettle Rivers they are excellent. A paved highway connects Grand Forks, Trail and Nelson, and daily passenger and freight services operate on the railway. Daily air service is available to Vancouver and Calgary, the airport being located on former CCUB land at Ooteshenie. A branch railway line and gravel highway connect the communities in the Slocan Valley with those along the Kootenay River. The service roads to such communities as Krestova and Pass Creek are in poor condition and the community of Glade is handicapped for transportation in that it lies on the east bank of the Kootenay River and can be reached from

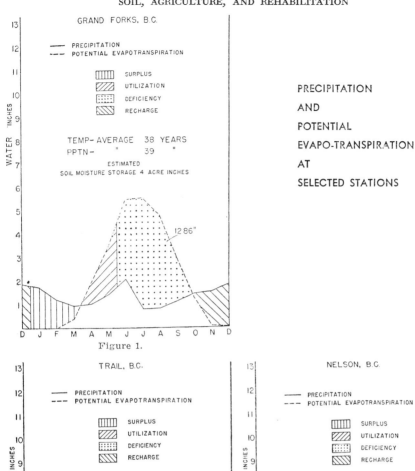

Figure 1.

PRECIPITATION

AND

POTENTIAL

EVAPO-TRANSPIRATION

AT

SELECTED STATIONS

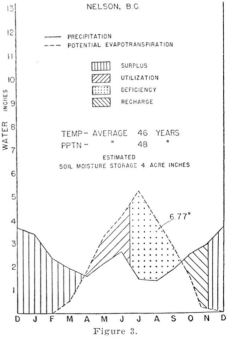

Figure 2.

Figure 3.

TABLE I.—CLIMATIC AVERAGES OF SELECTED STATIONS

LOCATION	MEAN TEMP.[1]			EXTREME HIGH	EXTREME LOW	FROST FREE[2,3]	GROWING SEASON[3]	PRECIPITATION[1]	
	JULY	JAN.	ANN.					ANN.	JUNE TO AUG.
	F.°	F.°	F.°	F.°	F.°	(Days)	(Days)	In.	In.
Trail (Warfield)	71	24	48	---	---	186	206	25.98	4.40
Castlegar	---	---	---	---	---	116	205	---	---
South Slocan	68	22	47	---	---	157	---	31.12	5.59
Nelson	67	25	46	96	−4	144	199	27.02	5.46
Crescent Valley	65	21	44	---	---	97	---	29.49	5.05
Perry Siding	---	---	---	---	---	117	195	23.82	4.02
Grand Forks	69	19	45	101	−17	130	205	16.26	3.75

[1] Climate of British Columbia, 1952, B. C. Department of Agriculture, Victoria, B. C.
[2] Connor, A. J., and staff, 1949, The Frost Free Season in British Columbia, D.O.T. Met. Div., Toronto, Ont.
[3] Brink, V. C., Climates of British Columbia for Agrologists, Part 1, Department of Agronomy, University of British Columbia, Vancouver.

224

the main highway only by boat. Champion Creek is only slightly better off, being served by a poor road running south from Ooteshenie.

The terrain is mountainous, and the agriculture and other development is confined almost exclusively to the valleys. Variations in climate are marked, but in general the area is characterized by hot summers and cool though not cold winters, the extreme temperature range being somewhat wider at Grand Forks than at the other recording stations in the area (Table I).

The frost-free period (the number of days between the last day in spring and the first day in autumn when the minimum temperature reaches 32 degrees F. and the growing period (the number of days when the average daily temperature is 43 degrees F. or above) for a number of points in the area are indicated in Table I. These statistics represent average conditions and are only indicative of the general climatic condition at the point of record. It will be noted that although there is a considerable variation in both the frost-free and growing periods, most of the areas have climates favourable for the production of tree-fruits and other sensitive crops. In some areas, notably in the Slocan Valley and along Goose and Gander Creeks at Krestova, an incidence of summer frosts is noted.

The average total annual recorded precipitation ranges from 16.1 inches at Grand Forks to 28.7 inches at Crescent Valley (Table I). About one-third of the total precipitation comes as snow. The high temperatures in summer and moderate to low summer rainfall combine to produce a marked soil moisture deficiency during the growing period. The nature and magnitude of the average moisture deficiency may be noted from Figs. 1, 2 and 3. It will be noted that these Thornthwaite evapo-transpiration curves show that the soil moisture deficiency is quite marked at Grand Forks, commencing toward the end of May and continuing on until September, and amounting to a total moisture deficiency of 12.86 inches. The soil moisture deficiency at Trail is indicated to be just slightly less than at Grand Forks. At Nelson the indicated deficiency is less, the calculations indicating that on the average the soil moisture storage is not exhausted until the latter part of June, and that the total deficiency amounts to only 6.7 inches.

The Thornthwaite calculations referred to above are based upon an available soil moisture storage capacity of four inches. However, field and laboratory tests made during the survey have shown that very few soils of the former CCUB lands have moisture storage capacities of this magnitude. In fact, many have storage capacities of less than two inches. It is evident, therefore, that for successful crop production, adequate irrigation is essential for nearly all the soils of the former CCUB lands.

In the original virgin state virtually all the soils of the Community lands along the Kootenay, Columbia and Slocan Rivers were forested. Much of this forest was commercial timber which has since been harvested. The main species harvested were reported to be fir, larch, cedar and white pine. The situation at the present time is quite different, and during the survey no mature timber was noted on the Community lands. There was some evidence of overcutting, mainly to supply the village requirements for fuel, posts, rails, etc. Regeneration generally is slow and the forested parts of the more accessible areas consist of species of no commercial value, such as hazelnut and willow.

Much of the land along the Kettle River was also forested, but in the vicinity of Grand Forks many of the southfacing slopes and terraces were open grasslands or only lightly treed when settlement took place.

SOILS

The area is mountainous, consisting mainly of acidic rocks showing much evidence of glaciation. The mountains appear rounded, polished and striated with quarried slopes. Occasional sharp peaks with remnant cirques and cirque valleys rise to above 5,500 feet elevation. The valleys where the soils of agricultural significance occur are U-shaped, with steep walls.

Most of the valley soils have been formed on glacial or post-glacial river terraces. These terraces range from about four feet to almost one thousand feet above the present river-levels and vary in texture from coarse gravels to loams. Some of the more recent lower terraces contain considerable fine material, with texture ranging from fine sandy loam to silt loam. In several places slumped and eroded terraces also occur. Formations associated with the present rivers are most evident along the Slocan, which follows a rather meandering course compared to the other rivers. These recent deposits are close to present stream level and are usually of fine texture.

In addition to the terrace formations, stream fans and alluvial deposits often occur where side valleys enter the main river valleys. These deposits are highly variable but often contain a high proportion of boulders and other coarse material. Toward their lower edges the number of boulders usually decreases, with a corresponding increase in the proportion of fine material.

The well drained upland soils of the Community's lands in the vicinity of the Kootenay, Columbia and Slocan Rivers may be classed as Brown Podsolic. In the Grand Forks area, Brown Podsolic soils also occur on the wooded northern slopes and mountains. However, Black Earth soils predominate on the exposed southern slopes and terraces.

226

TABLE II.—TENTATIVE CLASSIFICATION OF SOIL FOR GENERAL
FARMING WITHOUT IRRIGATION

(Acres estimated from aerial photographs)

LOCATION	CLASS 1	CLASS 2	CLASS 3	CLASS 4	CLASS 6	CLASS 7	TOTAL
Champion Creek	—	2	26	61	242	589	920
Ooteshenie	—	8	233	153	1,890	1,299	3,582
Brilliant	—	6	31	134	73	951	1,195
Raspberry	6	19	73	16	31	96	241
Glade	—	—	244	—	248	471	963
Shoreacres	20	—	216	—	88	307	631
Pass Creek	—	151	78	—	404	1,957	2,590
Krestova	15	82	159	199	882	774	2,111
Kochs Siding	—	39	8	—	43	102	192
Claybrick	30	50	13	87	97	24	301
Lebahdo	36	66	58	41	48	65	314
Winlaw	—	59	52	28	22	62	223
Perry Siding	—	2	32	12	102	137	285
Grand Forks	—	102	1,115	—	3,061	438	4,716
Caesar	—	—	22	89	47	17	175
Gilpin (not former CCUB land)	—	—	10	—	414	12	436
Totals	107	586	2,370	820	7,691	7,301	18,875

227

TABLE III.—TENTATIVE CLASSIFICATION OF SOIL FOR GENERAL
FARMING WITHOUT IRRIGATION

(Acres estimated from aerial photographs)

LOCATION	CLASS 1	CLASS 2[1]	CLASS 3[1]	UNCLASSIFIED	TOTAL
Champion Creek	49	166	123	582	920
Ooteshenie	214	1,201	807	1,281	3,582
Brilliant	153	88		954	1,195
Raspberry	91	46	8	96	241
Glade	113	290	89	471	963
Shoreacres	235	21	67	308	631
Pass Creek	53	314	105	2,118	2,590
Krestova	366	911	6	828	2,111
Kochs Siding	33	23	6	130	192
Claybrick	43	184		74	301
Lebahdo	36	58	30	190	314
Winlaw	27	58		138	223
Perry Siding	29	105		151	285
Grand Forks	483	897	295	3,041	4,716
Caesar	10	12	89	64	175
Gilpin (not former CCUB land)	10	18	29	379	436
Totals	1,945	4,401	1,724	10,805	18,875

[1] On account of soil porosity and topography, sprinkler irrigation is considered here.

228

Undisturbed profiles of the Brown Podsolic soils usually have distinct A_0 horizons, one-half to 1 inch in thickness with reactions ranging from pH 5.5 to 6.5. Some profiles have thin A_1 horizons ranging up to about 1 inch in thickness. Greyish white A_2 horizons are found in some profiles, but not in all, and seldom are more than one quarter of an inch thick. The B horizons range from pale brown to yellow-brown in colour and often have weakly blocky structure. In reaction they range from pH 6 to 7. The parent materials consist mainly of rather coarse alluvial materials or glacial till with slightly acid or neutral reaction.

The Black Earth soils have A_1 horizons, ranging in thickness from 12 to 20 inches. These horizons are usually very dark grey-brown in the upper portion and grey-brown below. They are high in organic matter and slightly acid in reaction, pH 6.2 to 7. The B horizons are usually brown in colour and have blocky structure. Accumulations of lime are usually found in the lower portions. The parent materials usually consist either of alluvial sediments or glacial till. Some are quite compact, and they usually contain lime.

In addition to zonal Brown Podsolic and Black Earth soils, many scattered areas of Recent Alluvial, Gliezolic, High Lime, and other types of Intrazonal soils occur. The largest areas of recent alluvial soils are found adjacent to the Slocan River and along Goose and Gander Creeks at Krestova, where they are used very intensively for gardens. Areas of Peat, Muck, Gliezolic, and other Intrazonal soils are also found along the Slocan River and at Pass Creek. A number of small areas of High Lime soils are found in the Grand Forks area.

The soils of the former CCUB lands have been further classified into series on the basis of parent material and type on the basis of texture. Laboratory tests are now under way to evaluate further their physical and chemical properties; this information is intended for use in assigning water and suggesting how the lands might best be distributed and utilized. Two tables have been prepared to indicate the quality of the soil in the different communities. These tables are very general, and the classification of the soils may be changed when the laboratory studies are complete.

In Table II the lands have been classified according to their usefulness without irrigation. The classification is patterned after that used by the United States Soil Conservation Service and the various land classes are defined below:

Class 1: Very good arable land suitable for general farming and intensive cultivation. Comprises the medium textured soils which receive some moisture by natural sub-irrigation.

Class 2: Fair arable land suitable for general farming but having some limitations, such as imperfect drainage, which makes tillage or cropping difficult.

Class 3: Poor arable land too droughty for optimum crop growth but suitable for extensive cultivation of cereals and forages. Consists mainly of medium textured soils of glacial river terraces.

Class 4: Land not suitable for regular cultivation but which may be utilized for planted pasture and forage crops.

Class 6: Non-arable land suitable for cultivation because of such factors as excessively coarse soil texture, unfavourable topography, stoniness or erosion. It has limited use as pasture.

Class 7: Non-arable land, such as steep slopes, rock outcrops, barren areas and sand dunes.

It may be noted from Table II that a total of 3,063 acres or 16.1 per cent of the former CCUB land is classed as arable without irrigation. Of this, 2,370 acres or 12.4 per cent of the total is placed in the category of poor arable and only 105 acres or 0.5 per cent is classed as very good and arable without irrigation. It is apparent, therefore, that without irrigation the productivity of the soils of the former CCUB lands would be very low and the agriculture limited. Table II also shows that there are 7,301 acres or 38.7 per cent of Class 7 land, consisting of steep mountain slopes, rock outcrops, and sand dune areas of very little use, and a further 7,691 acres or 40.7 per cent of Class 6 land, which is also completely non-arable and of only limited use as pasture.

The former CCUB lands have been classified in Table III according to their suitability for cultivation with irrigation. The classes included in this table are based on soil properties without regard to the availability of water or cost of irrigation. When the information from the engineering surveys is available, it will be combined with that in Table III to develop a further classification. At the present, Table III is included simply to indicate the extent of soil suitable for irrigation on the former CCUB land.

The classification in Table III is general and will be adjusted when the laboratory information is available. A brief description of each class is given below. It should be noted that although Class 1 land could be irrigated either by field or sprinkler methods, Class 2 and 3 land would require sprinkler irrigation in most instances.

Class 1: Good land well suited to intensive cultivation under irrigation. It comprises the well drained, medium textured soils with favourable topography.

Class 2: Fair land for cultivation with irrigation but having some limitation, such as coarse texture, unfavourable topography, or excessive stoniness.

Class 3: Poor land for cultivation with irrigation and only recommended for this purpose when very favourably located and when irrigation water is cheap and plentiful.

Unclassified: Land which has not been classified for irrigation because it is completely unsuitable for irrigation or because irrigation is not required.

It is apparent from Table III that the former CCUB land includes a comparatively large acreage of soil suitable for irrigation, i.e., 1,945 acres of Class 1 and 4,802 acres of Class 2 soil. However, at the present time only 532 acres are being irrigated and some of this very inadequately (Table IV). The former CCUB land, therefore, includes a rather large acreage of undeveloped soil suitable for irrigation; in fact, it includes the great majority of the undeveloped irrigable soils of the entire area. When the engineering surveys are complete, it will be possible to estimate the cost and feasibility of developing this land. However, it is clear that in the best interests of the resident Doukhobors, and of the Province as a whole, every possible effort should be made to irrigate as large a proportion as is possible and feasible.

On the basis of present knowledge it appears that the largest acreage of good soil where irrigation would be practical is at Grand Forks. There is also favourable opportunity for considerable expansion of irrigation at Shoreacres and Glade and on the lower terraces at Brilliant and Ooteshenie. Some expansion of irrigation also seems possible on the Class 1 soil at Krestova, although water cost would not permit consideration of the Class 2 land at that community. It seems likely, too, that much of the Class 1 soil and some of the Class 2 soils at the other communities would also justify proper irrigation.

When considering the utilization of the soils of the former CCUB lands, it should not be overlooked that some of them are ideally suited for urban and industrial development. The importance of this fact is likely to increase in the future and in some locations will determine the soils' ultimate utilization. The importance of domestic water supply as well as water for irrigation is bound to increase and therefore all lands adjacent to the former CCUB lands should be included in the surveys at present under way so that the development of the entire area may be fully integrated.

AGRICULTURE OF THE FORMER CCUB LANDS

The agriculture of the former CCUB land varies somewhat from community to community, as does the condition of the buildings, irrigation and equipment. However, in the sections that follow, the villages will not be considered separately, and only a general over-all picture of the area will be attempted.

The acreages of soil being used for various purposes were estimated during the field work, and these acreages are summarized in Table IV. Probably the most significant figures in this table are those indicating the extent of present irrigation. It will be noted

TABLE IV.—UTILIZATION OF CCUB LANDS IN WEST KOOTENAYS
AND GRAND FORKS, 1951-52

(Acreages Estimated from Aerial Photographs)

LOCATION	IRRIGATED	CULTIVATION	PASTURE (FORMERLY CULTIVATED)	PASTURE (ROUGH)	BUILDINGS	FOREST AND WILD LAND	TOTAL
Champion Creek	34	69	188	–	4	625	920
Ooteshenie	75	185	1,275	230	30	1,787	3,582
Brilliant	30	20	100	75	11	959	1,195
Raspberry	57	14	89	–	3	78	241
Glade	81	237	97	183	15	350	963
Shoreacres	7	210	40	45	6	323	631
Pass Creek	31	211	199	64	14	2,071	2,590
Krestova	40	210	390	50	45	1,376	2,111
Kochs Siding	5	25	16	40	4	102	192
Claybrick	1	50	100	16	7	127	301
Lebahdo	–	18	5	145	1	145	314
Winlaw	3	64	33	23	4	96	223
Perry Siding	13	60	53	11	5	143	285
Grand Forks	130	685	930	1,550	100	1,321	4,716
Caesar	–	20	25	–	–	130	175
Gilpin (not former CCUB land)	25	–	45	–	–	366	436
Totals	532	2,078	3,585	2,432	249	9,999	18,875

that in each community only a very limited acreage is irrigated, and that for all the community lands the total irrigated acreage was only 532 acres. This means that for the community land as a whole there is less than one acre of irrigated land per family. In some communities the area is even less. For example, at Krestova, there is about one-fifth of an acre of irrigated land per family. It should also be noted that the total figure of 532 acres includes a number of areas where the soil was receiving insufficient amounts of water and areas where the methods of application were inadequate. Recalling that without irrigation most of the soils of the community lands are quite unproductive, it is apparent that their agriculture is extremely limited.

When considering the present very limited and inadequate irrigation on the former CCUB lands, it should be noted that in the earlier history of the lands very large sums of money were devoted to irrigation development. Thus by 1930 it was estimated by Harry Trevor that a total of $438,000 had been expended for this purpose. For one reason or another, the elaborate schemes have failed completely or are now in various stages of disrepair. One of the main reasons for this was their apparent construction without technical advice and proper design. For example, some $230,000 was devoted to an irrigation system to pipe water from Pass Creek to the villages at Brilliant and across the Kootenay River to ten villages at Ooteshenie. The scheme was of unsound design and got no water to Ooteshenie, a costly and tragic failure which could have been avoided had competent advice been sought. Other important systems, such as West Grand Forks ($100,000) and Krestova ($25,000), were also failures. Some of the smaller systems proved more successful. The one at Shoreacres operated until 1948, when the irrigation pipe under the Kootenay River broke. It has not been repaired, and the water for the seven acres now under irrigation is pumped from the river. In other systems, failure has been due to deterioration of the wood pipes used in construction. Breaks are becoming more numerous, and it seems just a matter of time until the small acreage now receiving water will be reduced still further. One exception to this general situation is the Raspberry Village scheme, which is adequately designed and operating well.

Another important factor that has led to the present condition of irrigation has been the lack of authority and co-operation in the maintenance and repair of systems. Successful community irrigation is possible only when there is adequately assumed responsibility for the control and maintenance of the system. It is evident that this has been lacking on the former CCUB lands. In some instances when a scheme or portion of a scheme has failed, individuals from that area have even attempted to prevent irrigation water from reaching others more fortunately situated.

Referring again to Table IV, it will be noted that 2,078 acres are classed as cultivated. This class includes all the unirrigated land on which a crop was being harvested. In most areas the crop was hay, cut with the scythe and racked by hand. Two types of pasture land are included in Table IV—pasture that was formerly cultivated land, 3,585 acres, and rough pasture that apparently had never been cultivated, 2,432 acres. In both types of pasture the forage yields were very low.

The largest acreage of the land was classed as Forest and Wild land and comprises the steep mountain and valley crops. For the most part, this land has been logged and regeneration is slow. The cover is largely composed of wood plants and young trees of no commercial value. Firewood, posts, rails, and so on are still being cut from some areas, but in its present condition this land has little use.

Only a few pieces of farm machinery were seen, such as walking-ploughs and drag-harrows, very old and of little value. Not a single farm tractor, large or small, was seen in the villages of the entire West Kootenay area. The farm equipment in the West Grand Forks villages was slightly better than in the other communities. Trucks and cars were noted at all villages, but these are not primarily used in connection with agriculture.

The types and numbers of buildings on the former CCUB land are

TABLE V.—TYPE AND NUMBER OF BUILDINGS ON FORMER
CCUB LANDS

COMMUNITY	DWELLINGS	OUT-BUILDINGS
Champion Creek	15	48
Ooteshenie	133	330
Brilliant	31	79
Raspberry—(old village)	11	21
(new village)	9	17
Glade	53	200
Shoreacres	47	95
Pass Creek	32	116
Krestova	103	347
Kochs Siding	15	25
Claybrick	14	32
Lebahdo	1	5
Winlaw	8	18
Perry Siding	15	52
Grand Forks	158	725
Caesar	6	25
Gilpin (not former CCUB land)	54	79
Totals	705	2,214

summarized in Table V. It will be noted from this table that there are a total of 705 occupied dwellings, the largest numbers being at Grand Forks (158), Ooteshenie (133), Krestova (103), and Gilpin (54). Many of these dwellings are very poor, as is indicated by their appraisal value, estimated by Mr. Green in the West Kootenay and Mr. Gordon in the Grand Forks region. Thus the average appraised value of the dwelling in the West Kootenay communities was $385, and for the Grand Forks, Caesar, and Gilpin communities, $545. The number of outbuildings on the former CCUB lands totalled 2,214. These too had a low appraisal value, the average for the West Kootenay areas being $16, and the Grand Forks, Caesar, and Gilpin communities, $55.

From what has been recorded it is evident that the agriculture of the former CCUB land is limited and very inefficient by modern standards. It consists principally of gardening by the women and old men with hand tools on small and sometimes indifferently irrigated plots. Some hay is cut on the non-irrigated areas, and cattle and a few horses graze over areas once cultivated. The cattle are kept to supply milk, and the horses are used to haul wagons and also for logging. There is one producing orchard of twenty-six acres at Raspberry, but in most other communities the products of the soil are scarcely sufficient to keep the inhabitants supplied with vegetables, fruit and milk. Cash income comes almost exclusively from wages earned away from the Community lands.

The present agricultural situation on the CCUB lands is in strong contrast with the reputation established by these lands before the company went into receivership. In the 1920's when the CCUB was operating two fruit packing plants, a jam factory, and two canning factories, the popular opinion of its agricultural development may be summed up by the following quotation from Maurice Hindus, cited by Trevor:

> One gazes down upon endless rows of orchards and gardens, superbly cultivated. It has the aspect of a modern, progressive, prosperous community whose inhabitants are quick to make use of the discoveries of science, and spare no pains to woo the precious crop from a stubborn soil.

Yet the comprehensive study made by Trevor himself a few years later revealed very different conditions. The agriculture of the Community lands from 1928 to 1931 was examined by him from the standpoint of its efficiency and the proportion of the total individual village income derived from agriculture. During the study, Mr. Trevor had access to the CCUB books and records and lived at the community villages. Some of his findings for 1929 are summarized in Table VI.

For this table the number of human units in each village was calculated by Mr. Trevor on the basis that a man or woman under 55 years of age was one human unit, a child under 15 as one-third unit,

TABLE VI.—LEVEL OF TOTAL INCOME AND INCOME FROM
AGRICULTURE FOR COMMUNITY VILLAGES, 1929

VILLAGE	NUMBER OF HUMAN UNITS	INCOME PER HUMAN UNIT	FARM DIVERSITY INDEX	FARM CREDIT DIVERSITY INDEX	CROP INDEX
Brilliant, No 1	82.33	$157.13	53.7	26.6	37.0
Brilliant, No. 2	74.33	91.77	34.4	28.7	19.0
Kamennoe	90.00	56.36	49.1	36.9	65.5
Ostrov	54.66	74.06	39.7	30.9	30.8
Ooteshenie (Posdniakoff)	60.33	70.81	38.8	33.1	9.7
Ooteshenie, No. 14	55.66	28.80	41.5	38.9	12.7
Ooteshenie, No. 15	67.66	30.60	39.9	35.7	5.1
Malinovoe	74.33	52.09	39.5	37.6	21.7
Prekrasnoe (Kalmikoff)	70.66	102.17	43.0	35.9	57.6
Prekrasnoe (Riasantzeff)	72.33	99.49	45.2	37.9	31.1
Plodorodnoe (Vasilenkoff)	67.99	39.45	40.4	36.9	31.4
Plodorodnoe (Storozeff)	58.83	88.37	20.4	24.8	69.4
Fruitova (Gorkoff)	86.20	84.20	22.0	21.1	44.8
Fruitova (Stoochnoff)	58.74	58.74	24.6	13.8	43.6
Krestova (Mahortoff)	73.20	73.20	36.9	28.3	26.8
Krestova (Lazareff)	54.20	69.87	31.3	28.0	57.0
Average	—	$73.63	37.4	30.9	35.2

and a man or woman over 55 was one-half unit. The income per human unit he found by dividing the "income" for the village by the number of human units it contained. The "income" for the village represented the sum of the receipts of the village from wages earned and from agricultural products sold and consumed. It will be noted from the table that the income per human unit varied greatly from village to village, and that for the years under study the income per human unit was highest at Brilliant Village No. 1 ($157) and lowest at Ooteshenie No. 14 ($28.80).

The Farm Diversity Index shows the percentage of the total village income that was derived from farm operations. Thus Mr. Trevor's figure of 53.7 per cent for the Farm Diversity Index of Brilliant Village No. 1 indicates that 53.7 per cent of the total village income came from farming, including shelter, food, and wood, the remaining 46.3 per cent from wages earned by its members at the central office or outside the colony. The Farm Diversity Index values included in Table V show clearly that even before the CCUB went into receivership, the products of the farms accounted for less than half of the total village income, the average contribution for communities studied being 37 per cent.

Mr. Trevor's definition of the Farm Credit Diversity Index is that "it is the percentage of the income from products produced and consumed on the farm to the total income of the village." Thus the Farm Credit Diversity Index of 26.6 per cent for Brilliant Village No. 1, in Table VI, indicates that 26.6 per cent of the total income was from food and shelter provided by the village for its inhabitants. Mr. Trevor also points out that "the difference between Farm Diversity Index and Farm Credit Diversity Index shows the percentage of the total village income derived from sales of agricultural products in the village." It will be noted from Table VI that the two indices differ but little in most cases and that the difference between the averages for all villages is only 6.9 per cent. Mr. Trevor's figures show clearly, therefore, that even in 1929 the main value of the farming operations at the villages was to provide food and shelter for the inhabitants. Only at Brilliant Village No. 1 did the sale of agricultural products contribute substantially to the total average income. From the villages studied, an average of only 6.9 per cent of the total village income was derived from the sale of farm products. This is very low. Yet, were Mr. Trevor's studies repeated today, certainly an even lower figure would be obtained. It seems evident, therefore, that neither in the period before the company went into receivership nor afterward was the sale of agricultural produce by the villages a major source of income for them.

Referring again to Table VI, the Crop Index values are based on the yields of grain, hay, potatoes, peas, carrots, mangels and turnips,

237

and represent the ratio, expressed as a percentage, of the average yields of these crops on the farms of the CCUB villages to the average yields of the same crops on other farms in the area. Mr. Trevor points out that "the Crop Index of 37 indicates that the yields of Brilliant No. 1 were about one-third of the yields of the same crops from the farms included in the University of British Columbia Farm Survey (1929)." It can be seen from the table that Mr. Trevor found, on the average, the yields in the CCUB villages were only 35.2 per cent as high as they were on other farms in the same area. It is also of interest to note that in the case of seven independent Doukhobor farms Mr. Trevor studied in the same areas, the Independents obtained average yields 50 per cent higher than the Community villages. Comparisons of the same type made today would probably show even greater differences in favour of the Independents and others not located on the former CCUB lands. This strongly suggests that to get most from the CCUB land it should be subdivided so that each operator is on his own.

In 1931 Mr. Trevor found that 3,446.6 acres of land were in orchards and 9,776.3 acres were otherwise cultivated on the CCUB lands. After examining the Community village farms on which these orchards and crops were growing, he reported as follows:—

> They [the farms] are neglected, their soil is deprived of its fertility, the water is not brought where it is most needed; the many varieties of fruit are not marketable, most of the fruit is spoiled by insect pests and fungus.

On the methods used in handling the orchards on the Community farms, he commented as follows:—

> The spraying of the orchards is inefficient and seldom is it done more than twice in one season. Often an orchard is only sprayed once, and sometimes not at all. The orchards are infected with scab, slugs, aphis, and especially coddling-moth. A great portion of the orchards do not bear fruit, and much of the fruit which matures in the good sections of the orchards is spoiled by coddling-moth or ruined in some other way. The average return from one acre has been ridiculously low.

Much of this orchard area was seen during the summer of 1951. It has no commercial value as orchard and appears largely abandoned. With the exception of the one at Raspberry Village, all the orchards noted were planted with poorly chosen varieties arranged in a very haphazard and unsatisfactory manner, which alone must have made them very inefficient.

From these considerations it seems that the change in the condition of the agriculture on the CCUB lands since they went into receivership is not as great as the present appearance of the land might indicate. What essentially has taken place is that the orchards and fields that were bringing little cash return to the villages have been turned over to grass and used for hay and pasture. The villages did, and still do, have fine gardens produced by hand on small plots. However, apart from these small intensely cultivated gardens, the land was not, and is not, being utilized effectively. Many factors would be involved in an attempt to improve this situation, and several bearing directly upon the soil and agriculture are mentioned in the recommendations which follow.

RECOMMENDATIONS

DEVELOPMENT OF IRRIGATION

Since without irrigation the effective utilization of most of the soil is not possible, one of the first requirements is that water should be brought to as large an acreage of Class 1 and Class 2 soil as is possible and feasible (Table IV). In any rehabilitation programme the former attempts at irrigation would be of virtually no value and completely new systems would have to be planned. To facilitate this, the soil and engineering studies at present under way should be completed.

Irrigation is expensive and if the irrigated land is expected to bear the entire cost, its irrigation cannot always be financed successfully. However, from the standpoint of the benefit to the country as a whole there is often justification for granting some capital assistance in such cases. In the present problem it is recommended that in the case of the Class 1 and 3 soils, the Prairie Farm Rehabilitation Administration of the Federal Department of Agriculture be asked to assist on a basis similar to that of irrigation projects in the Prairie Provinces.

Finally, a word of caution must be given. The successful operation and maintenance of irrigation systems depends upon recognition of authority and cooperation. At the present time, both are lacking among the residents of the former CCUB lands. Therefore, before assistance for irrigation development was provided, this authority and cooperation would have to be established through the various means discussed in other sections of the *Report*.

DIVISION OF THE LAND

For maximum utilization the land should be subdivided to encourage individual interest in the soil. This will require the detailed attention of a special authority, such as a Doukhobor land allotment organization. This authority should use all the information assembled from the soil and engineering surveys and should make the division to meet the requirements of the Doukhobors in such a way that the division is as fair as possible to all. Some of the soil and economic factors that should influence the division are suggested below. It should be the responsibility of a special authority to combine these with the psychological and sociological factors so that the most satisfactory division is obtained.

Subdivision will have to be based on such factors as the number of people who have claims, the possibility and cost of expanding irrigation, and the extent to which the individuals wish to rely on agriculture for their income. It would seem likely that in many cases outside employment will remain the chief source of income for those who purchase CCUB land. For this reason, adequate provision should be made for relatively small units suitable for intensive gardening at such points as Brilliant, Ooteshenie, Raspberry and Shoreacres. Pass Creek, West Grand Forks and areas in the Slocan Valley should be left mainly in relatively large units for those who wish to devote more time to agriculture. Krestova and Glade might be considered for the village community type of organization if it is required.

It is also recommended that, rather than dividing the Class 3 soil and unclassified and non-irrigable soil into small uneconomical units, consideration be given to the development of community pastures and wood-lots. Provision for technical control in the management of such community projects would be required.

TECHNICAL ASSISTANCE

A programme of technical extension should accompany the division of the lands as an attempt to avoid the mistakes of the past. For this purpose a specially qualified man, whose duty it would be to encourage agricultural development and the use of sound irrigation and agronomic practices, should be added to the staff of the Extension Division of the Provincial Department of Agriculture.

AGRICULTURE ASPECTS OF RELOCATION OF SONS OF FREEDOM

The suggestion that the Sons of Freedom should move from their present locations has been made both by them and by the other Doukhobors. In fact, both groups have stated that they feel this is essential. It is desirable, therefore, to consider some of the aspects of such a relocation.

One of the possibilities is that the Sons of Freedom might emigrate to another country. At the same time the possibility of relocation within the Province should be examined.

THE PRESENT SETTLEMENT PICTURE IN BRITISH COLUMBIA

Active settlement of other groups and individuals has been going on in British Columbia for a long time. At present, interest in settlement in the Province is marked, and a considerable number of agencies are actively involved in promoting and directing it. Within the Department of Lands and Forests of the Provincial Government, the Division of Land Utilization, Research, and Survey, the Land Inspection Branch and the Land Settlement Board all deal with the classification and disposal of the Government lands for settlement purposes. In the Department of Agriculture, the Land Clearing Division owns and operates machinery which clears land for settlers on a rental basis. The Department of Trade and Industry co-operates with both groups and individuals interested in settlement. In the Federal Government, the divisions most concerned are the Department of Veterans' Affairs, which supervises the Veterans' Land Act, the Department of Citizenship and Immigration, the Experimental Farms Service, and the Prairie Farm Rehabilitation Organization. The latter is very active in studying and developing reclamation and irrigation projects in cooperation with the Department of Veterans' Affairs. In private industry, both the Canadian Pacific Railway and the Canadian National Railway have colonization branches in the Province with staffs to direct and supervise settlement. In addition, real estate and other financial organizations promote settlement in various ways.

It is apparent that in attempting resettlement in British Columbia the Sons of Freedom would be entering a very competitive field, and one in which selection of settlement sites has been going on for a long time. Much time and effort has been spent on settlement projects, some of which have been very successful while others have failed. It can be anticipated that it will prove difficult to find a suitable resettlement area for the Sons of Freedom within the Province.

THE MINIMUM REQUIREMENTS FOR SUCCESSFUL GROUP SETTLEMENT

A group settlement such as is desired by the Sons of Freedom can have a chance to be successful only if it meets the minimum requirements listed below:

(1) The settlers themselves must have a determined and united will to succeed in the chosen site.

(2) A suitable area for resettlement must be available at a price which is in line with its potentialities.

(3) Employment must be available or be made available for the settler's labour, or there must be markets for the products of his labour.

(4) If the settlement is made in an undeveloped area, its development must be properly planned with respect to logging, draining, irrigating, etc., as the case may be, so that the full potential of the land is realized.

(5) The settlers must have the physical resources to carry them through to success.

The history of group settlements in British Columbia shows that failures have occurred in the past because one or more of these requirements were not met. All such failures were accompanied by much hardship and suffering, and some by considerable cost to the Government. Before any relocation is undertaken within the Province, the Government should be satisfied with regard to all five requirements. When these are considered in terms of the Sons of Freedom relocation, a number of serious problems are apparent.

The Sons of Freedom state that they wish to relocate where they can farm. At the present time they are gardeners rather than farmers, the women doing most of the work while the men are away working for wages. A garden plot and cow provide the vegetables and milk for the family. They have no farm machinery and practically no cash income derives from the farm. Generally, they have followed this way of life since their arrival in Canada, and it would be a marked change for them to become full-time farmers.

Their religious beliefs present a problem in finding a location where they could farm successfully. One of these is that they must not take life. This means that they will not raise live stock for slaughter or market, which in many parts of British Columbia is essential for successful farming. This belief also interferes with the efficient keeping of poultry.

Tomatoes, corn, sunflowers and fruits are important foods in their vegetarian diet. For a relocation site to be acceptable to them, they state it would have to allow the growing of these crops. This fact, together with their dislike for severity of climate, makes it extremely unlikely that voluntary relocation would take place in any of the northern sections of the Province where the largest areas of undeveloped soils are to be found. In any case, if the farms were to be without poultry, hogs or beef cattle, permanently successful farming in such areas would be difficult.

They also state that they wish to be isolated, where they can develop a community without conflict with others, but at the same time it is clear that they need to have access to jobs and services. There is, moreover, the aspect that non-Doukhobor communities in the Province will favour isolation. These factors would be difficult to reconcile.

They have estimated that five hundred families would be involved in the relocation, although the actual number would remain unknown until a move was made. This uncertainty would make it difficult to determine the acreage needed.

When their request for relocation was first made they wanted to move immediately but it was apparent that they had no knowledge of what the settlement opportunities or requirements were. Until they gain a better understanding of these, it cannot be anticipated that they will have an adequately realistic approach to relocation.

OTHER FACTORS TO BE CONSIDERED IN THE SELECTION OF A RELOCATION SITE

In looking for a relocation site in the Province, the choice would have to be made between land owned by the Crown and that owned privately. There are still tracts of land held by the Crown in isolated sections of the Province which might be developed for agriculture. However, they are largely in the northern sections of the Province and therefore not likely to be acceptable to the Sons of Freedom. The areas of potentially arable Crown land in the southern part of the Province are more limited and have been picked over carefully by others. Those that are left are relatively inaccessible and would be costly to clear, irrigate, or drain. On the other hand, in most cases the privately owned land is close to or within the boundaries of existing communities and unsatisfactory on that account. It is likely to be a slow and costly process to acquire such lands either by purchase or expropriation. Therefore, at least a core of Crown land would be desirable. This would provide a limited amount of land cheaply and quickly and might permit the purchase of adjacent private land at a later date, with the advantage of allowing the scheme to be a progressive one.

The area of land required for relocation could not be determined in advance because it would be impossible to find out just how many families would move. Broad limits might be set on the basis of the importance to be assigned to agriculture in the new settlement. From the information supplied by the Sons of Freedom, it would seem that either large scale, full-time farming or small scale farming with opportunity for employment elsewhere would be acceptable. The amount of land needed per family for full-time farming would depend upon the nature of the soil, but in any case, to support an agricultural community as large as the Sons of Freedom, a considerable area would be required. A further argument against full-scale farming is that they have not shown that they will accept and practise modern agricultural techniques. These factors, together with the cost involved in setting up a full scale farming community, suggest that it would be better to consider the possibility of small scale farming with additional employment away from the farms.

243

On the basis of past and present performance, it seems that farming should not be expected to yield more than subsistence and that only enough land would be needed for each family to be well provided with farm produce. This should leave an inducement for young people to find other employment and yet provide a possibility for those who were not working outside to have a reasonable standard. The acreage per family needed for this would be governed in part by the outlet for both labour and agricultural products, but an area of from five to ten acres of productive soil should suffice. Such a development would require a minimum of equipment and capital. The soil and climatic conditions for the kind of agriculture desired by the Sons of Freedom restrict the choice of site to the coastal area or to the dry interior where irrigation would be necessary.

Maximum isolation is not desirable, but the site should be far enough away from other communities to avoid conflicts and also near enough to offer some outside interest.

In a settlement such as the one outlined, opportunity for outside employment would have to be available. The settlement might be located close to existing communities and labour markets, or employment might be provided in connection with the settlement itself through the forestry industry. Many of the Sons of Freedom are experienced loggers and mill hands, and some even operate small sawmills. If the site of relocation were in a region of commercial timber, these skills would be useful. Men might find employment with private operators who are already in the area or who might be interested in moving to the area if a labour source became available. Alternatively, the Sons of Freedom might be assisted in developing a forestry enterprise of their own. This source of action would require considerable assistance to get it under way.

Before relocation could become a reality, financial and other assistance would have to be provided, the magnitude of which would depend upon the site of relocation and the type of development planned. The two major decisions to be made, once these were determined, would be the basis on which the help could be given and the proportion that would be repaid.

Generally, in the past, lands which have been reclaimed, cleared, or irrigated have borne the full cost. If such developments bring benefit to other areas and to people who are not actually cultivating the soil, there is a sound reason for not charging the full cost of development against the particular parcel of land. These arguments would seem to apply to the present problem and might well be recognized in any financial arrangement made.

Technical advice and education would be essential to the success of a relocation project with the Sons of Freedom involving either agriculture or forestry. This is evident from the condition of both of these industries on the Community lands at the present time. Unless they were given technical direction and were willing to accept instruction and modern methods of management and conservation, conditions at the relocation site might soon resemble those at Krestova and Ooteshenie.

SUMMARY

As long as the Sons of Freedom and other Doukhobors insist that the Sons of Freedom must move from their present locations, the question of relocation will require attention. In view of the difficulty that may be anticipated in finding a site where the Sons of Freedom could successfully relocate in British Columbia, it is recommended that the search for such a site in another country be intensified. At the same time, the Sons of Freedom should be encouraged to evaluate realistically the opportunities of relocation within the Province as well as rehabilitation in the areas where they are now living. These areas seem to meet most of the agriculture requirements set out in this section, although the possibilities of irrigation have not yet been ascertained. It is certain that if money were spent on these areas, the present situation of the Sons of Freedom could at least be improved. The decision to aid their relocation within the Province has to be based largely on the belief that they must be separated from other Doukhobors and on other sociological factors.

If it proves impossible to find a suitable alternative site, the Sons of Freedom should be helped to improve the condition of their agriculture where they are. For this reason, soil and water surveys should be completed as a basis for determining the cost and extent of possible agricultural rehabilitation and development in the areas they now occupy.

IX
SUMMARY OF RECOMMENDATIONS

THE BACKGROUNDS of the recommendations are examined in Chapter II and elsewhere, more specifically in Chapters III, VII, and VIII. The recommendations were drawn up chiefly by Professor Dixon, Dr. Rowles, Dr. Jamieson and the editor from the material which is summarized in these and in the other chapters. Assistance was obtained from other members of the Research Committee, but full consultation with all of them was not possible at the time the recommendations were drafted.

As is stated throughout the *Report*, these are not offered as an immediate solution to the many problems facing the Doukhobors and their neighbours. Such an aim would be absurd, and attempts to reach quickly a hypothetical state of perfection in a human situation such as this where many of the causes of conflict are anchored in the growth of centuries would be ridiculously impractical. The recommendations, like the study itself, come from the well-examined belief that while the situation can readily grow worse, with no deliberate effort on the part of anyone, it can be maintained at its present level only by conscious, and thoughtful effort. Making an actual improvement will require much knowledge, great effort, and even some good fortune in addition.

The *Report* has been an attempt to supply a factual record of Doukhobor life and its relationships in order to make the necessary knowledge available. The recommendations suggest a first application of this knowledge, and were framed by the Research group themselves because such a course promised economy of time. They aim to set out ways in which some of the tensions in the situation may be eased. They are not drawn up singly or at random, but have an integration which emerges from the integration of Doukhobor life and its relationships. The recommendations related to governmental action regarding the Sons of Freedom involve a balance of pressures and inducements and are dependent on intelligent administration. A preoccupation with only the punitive elements of the recommendations, and with the Sons of Freedom by themselves, isolated from the total programme, would not improve the situation because the seeds of their movement are in Doukhoborism itself. Benefit is unlikely to result from any fragmentary application of the recommendations; in fact, the situation could be worsened in this fashion almost as readily as in any other.

Since the presentation of the *Report* to the Government in 1952, various pieces of legislation have been introduced. They include the recommended amendments of the Marriage Act, omission of the excluding passages in the Elections Act, attempts to press on with the education of Sons of Freedom children, and new forms of administering Doukhobor affairs. The above comments must apply even to such well-intentioned action.

ALLOTMENT OF FORMER CCUB LTD. LANDS

It is recommended:—

1. That in order to settle the issues concerning the land and buildings formerly owned by the Christian Community of Universal Brotherhood Limited, and now held in trust and administered by the Land Settlement Board, a programme of selling the lands and buildings to the present occupants and other qualified Doukhobors be started immediately.

2. That an over-all price be set which would repay the Provincial Government its net mortgage investment of $268,482.89, together with unpaid taxes and administration costs that have accrued since 1942. Additional items of cost for inclusion in the over-all price would be the estimated administrative and other expenses incurred in carrying out the programme.

3. That in setting the over-all price, allowances be made for certain credits or claims on behalf of the present occupants and other qualified Doukhobors. These include:—

> (a) The annual rentals paid to the Land Settlement Board by the occupants since 1942, now totalling more than $70,000.
>
> (b) The sum of $142,111.07 now being held in trust in Regina, Sask., subject to disposition by Court order.

4. That as far as possible the land and buildings be divided up into individual allotments for sale to entitled individuals. The land should be subdivided into individual allotments of comparable value, equalized on the basis of arable soil and other factors. In some localities submarginal lands should be left as community pastures and common wood-lots.

5. That qualifications for land purchase be based upon two main criteria:—

> (a) The record of paid-up membership in the CCUB Ltd. while it was a going concern; and
>
> (b) The record of rental payments to the Land Settlement Board of those who have continued to occupy the lands and buildings.

247

6. That a Doukhobor lands allotment organization, its staff acquainted with the economic, legal and agronomic facts of the situation, be appointed by the Lieutenant-Governor in Council to administer the operation of subdivision and allotment. A start should be made on this immediately.

7. That the extension service of the Department of Agriculture be expanded to take care of the increased work which will devolve on it in the guidance of Doukhobor farmers.

8. That the survey by the Department of Lands and Forests of the soils of the former CCUB Ltd. lands continue through the summer of 1952.

9. That the Department of Lands and Forests undertake a study of the water and irrigation aspects of the former CCUB Ltd. lands in the summer of 1952.

10. That soil and water surveys be made also of surrounding non-Doukhobor lands in the area so that any development plan for the former CCUB Ltd. lands may be integrated with the best interests of the entire region.

11. That irrigation development be undertaken, based on the findings of the surveys.

12. That the Prairie Farm Rehabilitation Organization of the Federal Department of Agriculture be asked to take part in the development of irrigation in the entire region.

EDUCATION

It is recommended:—

13. That the proposed Commission on Doukhobor Affairs co-operate with local School Boards in strengthening the educational programme.

14. That the proposed Commission be prepared to supplement salaries of teachers in areas resistant to education.

15. That the work-load of teachers in selected areas be so planned that they have time to engage in community organization activities.

16. That, in situations where prosecution of parents for habitual truancy of children is considered desirable, and local School Boards will not give the necessary consent for action, the Superintendent of Education exercise his prerogative to do so.

17. That there be an expansion of personnel providing counselling and guidance service in the schools attended by Doukhobor children.

18. That a flexible programme of studies be developed for use in areas resistant to education.

248

VITAL STATISTICS

It is recommended:—

19. That, provided it meet conditions previously outlined, the Doukhobor form of marriage be recognized under the Marriage Act of British Columbia.

20. That recognition of the Doukhobor form of marriage be accompanied by a strengthening of vital statistics administration in the Kootenay area for purposes of interpretation of the requirements.

21. That section 9 of Registration of a Live Birth be revised or expanded to meet Doukhobor objections to the implied profession of allegiance.

SOCIAL WELFARE AND PUBLIC HEALTH

It is recommended:—

22. That the Social Welfare Branch of the Department of Health and Welfare continue its policy of demanding only minimum registration requirements of Sons of Freedom families who are in need.

23. That the Physical Education and Recreation Branch of the Department of Education, the Union of Spiritual Communities of Christ, the proposed Commission on Doukhobor Affairs, and the communities of Grand Forks and Castlegar consider the provision of a full-time recreation director to serve the two communities.

24. That public health nursing services in the Lower Slocan Valley, Castlegar, and Grand Forks areas be strengthened by additional personnel to meet the need for care of Doukhobor families.

25. That, because of the need for flexibility of programme and integration of detention administration with other Provincial services, the Department of the Attorney-General assume responsibility for the imprisonment of offenders apprehended in any future mass disturbances.

26. That a stand-by administration of three persons, drawn from the staff of existing correctional institutions, be formed immediately and be requested to develop plans for Sons of Freedom rehabilitation in a penal setting.

27. That a detention unit for potential Sons of Freedom offenders be constructed in the Lower Mainland area and be made available to some correctional institution until such time as it may be required. This construction should be undertaken immediately. The necessary authorization should be obtained to enable future Sons of Freedom offenders, who would otherwise be placed in a Federal penitentiary, to be confined in this unit.

28. That the Federal Government share in the cost of providing these detention services.

FRANCHISE AND ELIGIBILITY FOR OFFICE

It is recommended:—

29. That existing legislation excluding Doukhobors and their descendants from voting in Provincial and Federal elections be repealed.

CRIMINAL LAW

It is recommended:—

30. That section 205A of the Criminal Code, which deals with parading while nude, be repealed.

31. That if a nude demonstration does not actually come within the definition of an unlawful assembly, section 87 of the Criminal Code be revised to define a nude demonstration of three or more persons as an unlawful assembly. In any event, it is suggested that no action or prosecution for a nude demonstration by three or more persons be commenced without the leave of the Attorney-General of the Province in which the offence is alleged to have been committed.

32. That there be maintenance of adequate police personnel for the effective patrolling of areas of unrest.

33. That any Doukhobor convicted of a crime of violence under the Criminal Code be denied the privilege of coming under any future military exemption granted to the Doukhobor community; it to be understood that this measure should be accompanied by an appeals procedure.

SONS OF FREEDOM RESETTLEMENT

It is recommended:—

34. That the Sons of Freedom be assisted to emigrate if opportunity should arise for them to go to a nation where their conflicts would be lessened and where health and economic factors would be satisfactory. The search for such an opportunity should be continued.

35. That, failing emigration, if a site suitable in soil, climate, employment opportunities, and social factors can be found, the Sons of Freedom be assisted to relocate elsewhere in the Province.

36. That if relocation of the Sons of Freedom should take place, the operation be placed under the Land Settlement Board, and that an administrative staff, including a Director of Relocation and special-

ists in agriculture and other necessary fields, be recruited to control the relocation.

37. That, failing the location of such a site, the Sons of Freedom be assisted to rehabilitate in the areas they now occupy.

38. That the soil and water surveys recommended for the former CCUB Ltd. lands be extended to other localities occupied by the Sons of Freedom.

ADMINISTRATION OF DOUKHOBOR AFFAIRS

It is recommended:—

39. That the Lieutenant-Governor in Council, with the advice of the Consultative Committee on Doukhobors, appoint a Commission on Doukhobor Affairs to coordinate the activities of all levels of government as they relate to Doukhobors, and to give leadership in new approaches in meeting the problems of the group. An executive director, to be known as the "Coordinator of Doukhobor Affairs," should be appointed to the Commission.

40. That the Consultative Committee on Doukhobors be continued, to function in an advisory capacity to the Commission on Doukhobor Affairs.

APPENDIX

NOTES AND APPENDIX TO CHAPTERS I AND II

Harry B. Hawthorn

ACKNOWLEDGMENTS AND NOTES

The presentation of contemporary and historical fact in Chapter I leans not only on the findings of the Research Committee but also on the following works:—

Maude, Aylmer: A Peculiar People: The Doukhobors. New York, 1904.

Wright, J. F. C.: Slava Bohu, the Story of the Doukhobors. New York, 1940.

Reid, Ewart P.: The Doukhobors in Canada. M.A. Thesis, McGill University, 1932.

Zubek, John P.: A Study of the Local Attitudes of High School Students and Adults Toward the Doukhobors of British Columbia. M.A. Thesis, University of British Columbia.

Snesarev, Vladimir (Harry Trevor): The Doukhobors in British Columbia. M.S.A. Thesis, University of British Columbia.

Hooper, Ronald H. C.: Custodial Care of Doukhobor Children in British Columbia, 1929 to 1935. M.S.W. Thesis, University of British Columbia, 1947.

Soukareff, W. A.: History of the Doukhobors. Grand Forks, B.C., 1944.

Maloff, P. N.: The Doukhobors. Thrums, B.C., 1948.

The author is conscious of his indebtedness to John Dollard, Alexander Leighton, A. I. Hallowell and Ernest Beaglehole, who blazed some of the paths followed in this study. To these and to many others there are debts for the treatment they have given to comparable situations of cultural stress and change.

ESTIMATE OF POPULATION IN 1951

Given by F. Ozeroff, Registrar of Vital Statistics, Nelson

Place	U.S.C.C. Independent	Sons of Freedom	Place	U.S.C.C. Independent	Sons of Freedom
Brilliant	190	45	Krestova	..	1,600
Castlegar	500	25	Slocan Valley	1,000	350
Ooteshenie	700	75	Blewett	300	25
Pass Creek	600	25	Salmo and Ymir	250	10
Champion Creek	150	..	Creston	150	..
Burnaby	..	5	Grand Forks	3,500	384
Thrums and Tarrys	350	100			
Shoreacres	300	150	Totals	8,490	3,069
Glade	500	275	Other (unspecified)	200	

ESTIMATE OF POPULATION, 1951 CENSUS

The Census itself resulted in lower totals. The following figures on Doukhobor population are extracted from the Ninth Census of Canada, 1951:—

	Male	Female	Total		Male	Female	Total
Canada	6,830	6,345	13,175	Manitoba	37	31	68
Nova Scotia	..	1	1	Saskatchewan	2,384	2,152	4,536
New Brunswick	1	..	1	Alberta	166	157	323
Quebec	10	5	15	British Columbia	4,209	3,961	8,170
Ontario	23	38	61				

No Doukhobor population was listed in Newfoundland, Prince Edward Island, Yukon, and Northwest Territories.

253

APPENDIX

LIST OF EARLY DOUKHOBOR FIGURES AND MOVEMENTS

(After Aylmer Maude)

About 1750-75:	Sylvan Kolesnikof active.
1775-85:	Ilarion Pobirohin active.
Born 1743 (died 1820?)	Savely Kapoustin.
1801-24:	Migration of Doukhobors to Milky Waters.
1805:	Kapoustin invited to Milky Waters.
1792-1832:	Vasily Kalmikof.
1816-41:	Ilarion Kalmikof.
1841-44:	Doukhobors transported to Caucasus.
1864:	Peter Kalmikof died.
1864-86:	Loukeriya Vasilyevna Kalmikova.
1887:	Peter Verigin banished to Shenkoursk.
1893:	Peter Verigin advises vegetarianism, non-resistance, and renunciation of intoxicants and narcotics.
Winter of 1894-95:	Peter Verigin banished to Obdorsk.
June 28 (o.s.), 1895:	Burning of arms.

CHRONOLOGY OF DOUKHOBORS IN CANADA

1898: Delegates select land in Saskatchewan (N.W.T.) for homesteading.

1899: Arrival of main body of settlers.

1900: Beginning split between individual and communal ownership.
First protests against Canadian land laws.

1902: Pilgrimages and protests by forerunners of Sons of Freedom.

1903: Beginning of communal activity and prosperity in Saskatchewan.

1907: Reversion to Government of 100,000 acres of Community-occupied land through refusal to register for individual titles as required under Homestead Act.

1908: Pioneer group left to start development of land in British Columbia.

1909: Beginning of purchase of lands in British Columbia.

1909–12: Migration of more than 5,000 Doukhobors to British Columbia.
Establishment of communities in British Columbia.
Planting of orchards, construction of reservoir, general industrial and agricultural development.
Partial repayment of mortgages.

1917: Incorporation of CCUB Ltd.

1923: Beginning of arson and dynamiting of schools and Doukhobor property in British Columbia. (Individual subsequent acts of violence not listed).

1924: Group of British Columbia Doukhobors founded settlements in Alberta.
Death of Peter Verigin.

1925: Seizure and sale of Doukhobor property for failure to send children to school.

1926: Loan of $350,000 from Bank of Commerce through National Trust Company to CCUB Ltd.

1927: Arrival of Peter Petrovich Verigin.

1929–30: Loans raised by Peter P. Verigin (reportedly $500,000) from Doukhobors for migration out of Canada.

1938: Mortgage foreclosure on CCUB Ltd. lands.

1939: Sun Life, National Trust, moved toward sale of Doukhobor lands.

1939–42: Provincial Statute assuming trusteeship and meeting mortgage claims.

1940: National Registration Act.

254

1943: Man-power mobilization measures put into effect.
Burning of jam-factory at Brilliant.
1947–48: Increasing numbers (including most of Sons of Freedom) registered with National Employment Service and drawing unemployment insurance.

OUTLINE OF DEVELOPMENTS IN DOUKHOBOR ORGANIZATION

1896: Title "Christian Community of Universal Brotherhood" chosen by Peter Verigin.
1899: Migration of 7,427 Doukhobors to Canada.
1900: Beginning split between individual and communal ownership.
1902: Appearance in Saskatchewan of forerunners of Sons of Freedom.
Arrival of Peter Verigin from Siberia.
1903: Beginning of communal activity and prosperity in Saskatchewan.
1908: Pioneer group left to start development of land in British Columbia.
1914: Return of some Independents to Community under fear of conscription.
1917: Incorporation of CCUB Ltd.
1918: Formation of Society of Independent Doukhobors.
1923: Beginning of arson and dynamiting of schools and Doukhobor property in British Columbia.
1924: Group of British Columbia Doukhobors founded settlements in Alberta.
Death of Peter Verigin.
1927: Peter Petrovich Verigin arrives in Canada.
1928: "Named Doukhobors" designated—all who gave allegiance to P. P. Verigin.
1934: Formation of the Union of Spiritual Communities of Christ under the leadership of P. P. Verigin.
1939: Death of P. P. Verigin.
1941: J. J. Verigin becomes secretary of USCC.
1944: Burning of J. J. Verigin's home.
1945: Union of Doukhobors of Canada formed.
1947: Sons of Freedom considered as having expelled themselves from U.D.C.
1952: Formation within the Sons of Freedom of the Christian Community and Brotherhood of Reformed Doukhobors.

SONS OF FREEDOM DEPREDATIONS—YEARS 1923 TO 1953

Year	Number of Depredations	Year	Number of Depredations
1923	5	1941	2
1924	11	1942	5
1925	1	1943	9
1928	4	1944	13
1929	13	1945	13
1930	12	1946	35
1931	37	1947	83
1932	15	1948	13
1935	3	1949	29
1936	19	1950	42
1937	33	1951	8
1938	12	1952	55
1939	10	1953	114
1940	2		

These depredations may be grouped into the following categories:—
(1) Burning or bombing of schools 84
(2) Doukhobor owned or occupied property 390
(3) Other government or non-Doukhobor property 124

255

APPENDIX

OUTLINE OF GOVERNMENT ACTION, 1898 TO 1950

1898: Order in Council granting exemption from military service.
1906: Commission appointed by Minister of Interior to investigate Doukhobor lands.
1907: Reversion of 100,000 acres of Community land in Saskatchewan to Government through refusal to register for individual title as required under Homestead Act.
1908: Sentencing of nineteen Sons of Freedom to imprisonment for nudity at Fort William.
1909: Saskatchewan recognized Doukhobor marriage ceremony.
1912: British Columbia Royal Commission on Doukhobors (William Blakemore).
1919: British Columbia legislation barring Doukhobors and other conscientious objectors from voting in Provincial elections (but not applicable to descendants).
1920: Amendment of Public Schools Act to enforce attendance.
1925: Seizure and sale of Doukhobor property for failure to send children to school.
1929: Custodial care of eight children, 14 to 16 years old, arrested with their parents when nude parading.
1931: Criminal Code of Canada provided with three-year penalty for nude parading.
Descendants of Doukhobors barred from voting in British Columbia.
1932–35: Imprisonment of approximately 600 Sons of Freedom on Piers Island following mass outbreaks.
Placement of 365 children of prisoners. Death of three infants when mothers in Oakalla.
1934: Doukhobors barred from voting in Federal election (confirmed in 1938 Dominion Elections Act).
1939–42: Provincial Statute assuming trusteeship and meeting mortgage claims.
1940: Order in Council extended Doukhobor military exemption to descendants.
National Registration Act required registration of all Canadians.
British Columbia Licence Forfeiture and Cancellation Act aimed at Doukhobors failing to comply with school attendance and vital statistics requirements.
1943: Manpower mobilization measures put into effect.
1945: Official witness of Doukhobor marriages instituted at Nelson.
1947–48: Increasing numbers (including most of Sons of Freedom) registered with National Employment Service and drawing unemployment insurance.
Royal Commission on Doukhobors (Judge H. J. Sullivan).
1949: Cost of guards on school buildings, $77,446 in 1949.
1950: Mass disturbances and sentencing of 400 to prison.
Research and Consultative Committees brought into being at request of Provincial Government.
Provincial Government granted social assistance regardless of school attendance and birth registration of children.

ISKRA

Iskra (The Spark) is a weekly mimeographed news bulletin with a circulation in 1951 of 780 copies, published in Russian at Grand Forks under the auspices of the Union of Spiritual Communities of Christ.

The general tendency of the publication is a pacifist one. It normally contains a leading article of about one and a half foolscap pages on a pacifist, moralizing or closely related theme. This is followed by short news items from various press agencies, most of them dealing with the situation in Korea, Egypt, Iran and other current areas of trouble. The items quoted almost invariably suggest either (a) the danger of these local conflicts developing into a major war, or (b) the inherent opposition of all the peoples of the world to war in any form.

These news excerpts are in turn followed by signed articles submitted by individuals, which may be as long as two or three pages. Then come letters to the editor on all subjects, including opinions of articles published in previous numbers. These are followed by obituaries and other notices. The average length of the paper is seven or eight pages.

Iskra is widely read among the USCC and Independent groups, but is not permitted to be sent to any known Sons of Freedom lest its contents be misinterpreted, resulting in the commission of unlawful acts.

A new editor, in his first leading article, writes: "The aim of 'Iskra' is the development of the conscience of men, the bringing out of all that is good and shining within us. Its aim is also to show how to correct our general shortcomings. By no means our least aim is the carrying out of the struggle for peace in the whole world, in which we are guided by the Doukhobor 'Weltanschauung' founded on the teaching of Christ."

A. W. WAINMAN

NOTE ON THE THEMES OF DOUKHOBOR PSALMS, HYMNS AND FOLK-SONGS

The themes sung to music by the Doukhobors are divided by them into three categories—psalms, hymns and folk-songs.

The main theme of the psalms is God and his worship. They are taken from many sources. Some are from the Old Testament, including the Psalms of David and the Book of Isaiah. Others are from the New Testament, including the Gospels of St. Matthew and St. John and the Book of Revelation. But whereas the psalms from the Old Testament seem to adhere fairly closely to the Biblical text, those from the New Testament are often a very free paraphrase.

A large number of psalms, however, do not originate from the Bible at all, and many of them are obviously modern compositions, some being in verse.

The hymns are almost all modern and none is taken from the Bible. The words of the great majority are written either by I. S. Prokhanov, a man of Molokan faith, who published a book of hymns in the 1920's, or by Ivan Sysoev, of Perry Siding, the leading poet among the Doukhobors in Canada at the present time. Some of the hymns are written by other Doukhobors living, or recently deceased, in Canada, while a few are taken from Russian literature; e.g., Lermontov and Nadson. The hymns are numerous and many are being added to the collection every year. In theme, like the psalms, they are mainly religious, but they do not always take God as their main subject. Some, for example, deal with their leaders, Peter the Lordly and Chistiakov; others with the sufferings of the Doukhobors in prison. As their Russian name "stikhi" (verses) suggests, these hymns are written in rhymed verse and divided into stanzas.

The folk-songs of the Doukhobors are largely variations of the regular Russian folk-songs, both as regards work and music. Sometimes they are so different from the original as to be almost unrecognizable. They are not meant to deal with the religious side of life, and they are often sung after the psalms and hymns at religious and social gatherings by way of relief. They have not, however, anything resembling the gaiety and light-heartedness of the ordinary Russian folk-songs.

A. W. WAINMAN

Sleep on You Brave Fighting Eagles
(Commonly sung at opening of meetings)

Sleep on you brave fighting eagles,
Sleep in the arms of the Lord;
You have received from your Master
Peace and the promised reward.

Now on this hard earned pathway,
Easy for us 'tis to tread;
You paid the price they exacted,
So we could journey ahead.

Many and cruel were the tortures,
You took in Siberian plains;
In Tundrian regions you suffered.
Dreadful and sad were your days.

Today as we think of your suffering,
And of the hardships you passed,
We pray to abide by your message,
And join in the great common task.

Sleep on you brave fighting eagles,
Sleep in the arms of the Lord;
We shall o'ercome all temptation,
And follow Christ and His word.

We've Concluded Our Assembly
(Sung at close of meetings)

We've concluded our assembly
And we'll all go home.
All good lessons we have learned there,
In our hearts to assume.

Chorus:

Calm and peaceful, calm and peaceful,
We will all go home.
All good lessons we have learned there,
In our hearts to assume.

O Lord, bless us with our willing
So we'll win advance;
Let Thy teachings be an ensign
We to all announce.

We shall wish again to assemble
And we'll all be there;
To hear all the good instructions
How to lead ourselves.

The Doukhobor Anthem

Break away from the way of the old world,
Let your voices in thankfulness sing;
No creed to be known, no law recognized,
But the law of the crucified King.
We're contenders for truth and for freedom,
Trusting Love, in the struggle to win;
Soon all people shall join in one spirit;
None shall strive with one's brother again.

Chorus:

Arise ye, arise ye all lovers of peace;
Arise to the struggle for freedom.
Let your voice be resounding and fearless,
Calling onward and onward and on.

We need not the rule of kings and of crowns,
Neither mansions with splendor enhanced.
Thrones and prisons are part of a system,
That our forefathers struggled against.
They have shown us the true path and holy,
They have given their life for the cause;
Though severe were their hardships in prisons,
Clearly ring out their voices to us.

All the cannons we'll forge into plowshares,
All the swords will we beat into hoes;
Love and Reason must govern and guide us—
Men are brothers, and not mortal foes.
Higher, higher we'll lift up the banner—
Toil entwined with the emblem of peace;
Let Truth in our hearts be established,
Let our faith never waver nor cease.

All this world of deceit and corruption,
All the slaves under Satan's command;
Deeds of evil, of greed and of envy,
Soon shall come to a terrible end.
And for all the designs of the wicked,
There's no place in the heavens above;
There shall gather the pure and the thankful,
Hearts that faithfully suffered for love.

Second Chorus:

Arise ye, arise ye, the toilers of the world,
Arise ye for love and for freedom.
Let your voice be resounding and fearless,
Calling onward and onward and on.

Eli Popoff

EXTRACTS FROM MINUTES OF MEETING OF SIXTY DULY AUTHORIZED DELEGATES OF THE SOCIETY OF "NAMED DOUKHOBORS" RESIDING IN THE PROVINCE OF SASKATCHEWAN, ON JUNE 27TH, 1928.

The first question on the agenda was regarding the attitude of the members of the "Named Doukhobors" toward military service, the taking of life, and violence in general.

After due consideration it was resolved that having regard to the doctrine of the Society of "Named Doukhobors," based as it is upon the teaching of Christ and the word of our Lord the Father as revealed by Him, as well as to the nature of the resolutions passed in the several districts and read to the meeting by the respective delegates present, the meeting unanimously proclaims that the members of the Society of "Named Doukhobors" not only object to, but cannot permit, any violence, much less the taking of life under any pretense whatever. The spirit of Christ, whom the members of "Named Doukhobors" worship, is the spirit of love, forgiveness, peace, toil, and of universal brotherhood of man.

The Society of "Named Doukhobors" affirm and proclaim that the welfare of the whole world does not justify the sacrifice of one single child. Our God is a God of mercy and not sacrifice. No man who exercises violence or commits murder, though he may call himself "Doukhobor" can be a member of the "Named Doukhobors," and such a person is a hypocrite and the application of the term "Doukhobor" to such a person is nothing but an ornamental sound, for no man committing murder shall receive eternal life.

The second question on the agenda to be considered was regarding marriage, divorce, and its consequences.

According to the faith of the members of the Society of "Named Doukhobors," marriage should be lifelong. "What God has joined together let no man put asunder." The foundation of marriage is love. Without such love there can be no marriage, and members are deemed free. The divorced couple must give each other certificate of release in writing, permitting each other to remarry according to their wishes.

All questions pertaining to support and maintenance of the issue, if any, and the compensation to the damaged party, shall be left to the decision of the elders of the society, whose decision shall be final and binding upon all parties concerned.

The third question on the agenda had reference to the taking of a census of the members of the "Named Doukhobors" in the Province of Saskatchewan, and to registration in general.

It was resolved that an accurate and detailed list of members should be taken by the district registrars of the society and that the executive committee should make all necessary returns to the proper Provincial authorities.

The executive committee was directed to effect a full and final family list of members of the "Named Doukhobors" residing in the Province of Saskatchewan, not later than by July 30th, 1928.

The fourth question on the agenda had reference to Court actions generally.

Should any disagreements, quarrels, or affronts occur between members of the society, the same shall be referred to the executive committee or, at the request of one or more of the parties concerned, to the general conference of the authorized delegates for consideration and judgment.

No criminal matters shall be referred to or entertained by either of the above-mentioned bodies for the reason that any member who commits a crime automatically ceases to be a member of the Society of "Named Doukhobors" and subjects himself to the jurisdiction of the Criminal Courts.

The fifth question to be considered on the agenda had reference to the attendance of school-children of the members of "Named Doukhobors" in schools of all grades and regarding education in general.

True education should be considered not only desirable but indispensable, having regard to the present critical times, when mankind is being led to destruction by its false standards of so-called culture and education, in order that divine love, peace, brotherhood of man, light of truth, the teaching and spirit of Christ might be brought into the world on the blade of knowledge. It is necessary and desirable for our children to attend the Canadian schools, but teaching of imperialism and hatred in its various forms should not be tolerated.

DECLARATION

OF THE "NAMED DOUKHOBORS" IN CANADA

Proclaimed and accepted at the Second Convention by the authorized delegates, held at Verigin, Sask., Canada, from the 29th of July to the 7th of August, 1934, A.D.

(1) We, the "Named Doukhobors," have been, are and will be members of Christ's church, confirmed by the Lord and Saviour Jesus Christ Himself and assembled by His Apostles.

(2) The "Named Doukhobors" essentially are of the Law of God and of the Faith of Jesus. The Law of God is expounded in the Ten Commandments and the Faith is professed thus: "We believe in and profess Jesus Christ the Son of God Who came in the flesh and was crucified. He is our sole Leader, Saviour and only Hope. There is none and could be no other name under the heavens through which man could be saved. We have faith and hope through His name to attain the highest blessings, and there is no higher blessing than "Eternal Life in Unutterable Joy." This is the hope and reward in Christ Jesus and the principal aim of the "Named Doukhobors." Following in the footsteps of our Divine Teacher, we, the "Named Doukhobors" proclaim as did He: "We have come into this world not to transgress the Law of God but to fulfill it," and therefore renounce all idolatry and sacrilege and acknowledge only the law and supreme authority of God. We the "Named Doukhobors" who have acknowledged and submitted ourselves to the law and authority of God by this have liberated ourselves from the guardianship and power established by men, because "We cannot serve two masters" and the "Named Doukhobors" cannot be slaves of men, having been redeemed by the precious Blood of Jesus Christ. The "Named Doukhobors" are not slaves of corruption, but essentially are Sons of the Free Spirit of Christ and declare: "That we ought to submit more to God than to man." We triumphantly declare that we do not allow any force whatever by man over man and even more do we deny the permissibility of killing of man or of men by a man or men under any circumstances, causes or arguments whatsoever. Every individual, group of individuals, parties or governments of men and anyone whoever they may be proclaiming their struggle against war and its prohibition but at the same time agreeing and allowing to the killing of even one individual for the sake of any interests whatsoever, is a lie and a hypocrisy and nothing but a "Leaven of the Pharisees." The life of one man is of equal value to the lives of many men. The

commandment of God says: "Thou shalt not kill." Christ explains and warns: "No murderer shall inherit eternal life." War—mass slaughter is an item compiled, where the killing of one individual is allowed, there the possibility of mass murder is inevitably admitted—which is war.

(3) The modern world—mankind, has scattered and divided itself into countless numbers of groups—following the watch-words and programmes of the various political parties. Every political party struggles with another not for the welfare and benefit of the people, but for dominance over them, with all the consequences of a diabolical incitement. The "Named Doukhobors" have never recognized and do not recognize any political party. They never have entered nor will they ever enter into the ranks of any political party. They have never given nor will they ever give their votes during elections, thereby they are free from any responsibility before God or man for the acts of any government established of men. The "Named Doukhobors" essentially are above party politics—they not only gave their votes but their bodies, blood and souls to the one and unreplaceable guardian of the hearts and souls of men—the Lord and Saviour Jesus Christ, thereby attaining perfect freedom by egressing from the slavery of corruption into the freedom of glory of the Children of God. We emphatically declare to all: "KNOW YE THE TRUTH AND THE TRUTH SHALL SET YOU FREE."

(4) The "Named Doukhobors" accepted and are fulfilling the Command of Jesus Christ: "Render therefore unto Caesar the things that are Caesar's (meaning the governments of men); and unto God the things that are God's." Residing in whatever state or country in this world, we triumphantly declare that, going under the banner of "Toil and Peaceful Life"—everything demanded of us which is not contradictory to the Law of God and to the Faith of Jesus, we will accept, fulfil and execute, not through fear but by conscience.

OPEN LETTER FROM THE SONS OF FREEDOM, 1928

Dear Brothers and Sisters, the Independent Doukhobors:

We turn to you with an invitation. Unite with us, so we can together go with Christ, to save mankind and ourselves on earth! We consider it necessary to delve into the not too distant past, in order to remind you that some ten years ago the capitalistic world flamed in an imperialistic war.

The mighty power of the selfish interests of the bourgeoisie led to a war which was unheard of before and the world was dragged country after country into its bloody orbit.

After all this, revolutions, starvation and varied epidemics come about, mowing down to the right and left and taking to the grave countless numbers of unfortunate souls.

What is to blame for such a catastrophe to mankind, a catastrophe unheard of in history till now?

We, the Sons of Freedom, give a short and precise answer to the question. The cause of all this is the SCHOOL with its wrong orientation, thrusting sadism upon the youthful generation. Especially when a person partakes of higher education, or attends military academies, does he become a truly insane animal. Sometimes, through oversight on the part of a common soldier to salute a general or a lesser officer, the unfortunate is beaten half to death and oftentimes to death.

The clergy, upon graduation from the institutes of higher learning, i.e. the universities, under the pretext of religion and fanaticism, inveigle the unwary, bless them in the churches and then send the young people off to war, to kill their own brothers and themselves in the name of their fatherland.

Furthermore, heavy taxes are imposed upon the population, taking from the poor their very last penny. That is why the Sons of Freedom unreservedly declared—and now declare—not to send their children to government public schools and not to pay taxes. They wish to train their children not to be servants of dead words but of a dynamic spirit so that they may become members of a higher spiritual order.

Now we shall turn to the question of how the Doukhobors fell to the temptation of Canadian capitalism.

Upon their arrival from Russia, the Doukhobors' main concern was how to make a living. The Canadian government opened up great tracts of land, called homesteads—160 acres for 10 dollars. This land was available to them and pretty well in keeping with their religious beliefs. Upon receipt of the land the Doukhobors with their customary industry began to till the soil. When the people had settled and built homes, the government allowed itself to bring before them the question of the oath of allegiance.

Some of the Doukhobors refused to take the oath, and as a result were forced to leave their homes and to let loose their cattle. However, the proximity of winter and the arrival of Peter Lordly Verigin caused the authorities to return, by force, the people who had left their homes. Verigin's arrival brought a ray of hope to the Doukhobors and they once more began to work their lands and acquire new machinery. Once more their beliefs and hopes were shattered by the demands of the authorities for the oath of allegiance.

Again some refused, while others accepted and by so doing retrogressed to that same period in time, the way from which is paved by the sacrifices of our forefathers under the Czarist regime. These people began to hire help, grow rich and buy up land.

The Christian Community of Universal Brotherhood, after its second contact with the government concerning the oath of allegiance, was compelled to seek and invest money in land in the various provinces, mostly in British Columbia.

Then the World War broke out, and the Independent Doukhobors, who had grown wealthy by means of investments in war bonds, were asked by the government to participate in the war as soldiers, and some were even forced into the army. These acts prompted the Independent group to send delegates to Ottawa to explain to the Premier of Canada that they were true Doukhobors and the followers of Christ's teachings. Thusly, they were able to hoodwink Ottawa, but they did not succeed in hoodwinking the people they had exploited, or driven out of their homes by mortgage foreclosures. These people who were overworked, underpaid, driven out of their homes by foreclosures or otherwise, are among you and the day of reckoning is drawing near.

What happened to the Christian Community of Universal Brotherhood during these trying times?

Because the Independent Doukhobors markedly aided the government during the war, the C.C.U. Brotherhood had to meet governmental demands as well. Since their provisions were limited, they had to cut down on their diet in order to create a surplus of products to meet the demands made by the government. As a result, for a period of time the people of the community were doled out one half-pound of flour and some gruel per person per day, i.e., 24 hours.

The demands of the government continued, and it was at this time that Peter (the Lordly) Verigin announced in the newspapers that, in order to conform to the demands, he found it would be necessary to drown all the elderly people and the young children—who were essentially non-producers.

APPENDIX

Second Part

Dear Brothers and Sisters, the Independent Doukhobors:

We have just finished reviewing what we had written before, that is our open invitation to you and the short history of our past.

Please forgive us if we were over-emphatic, and forgive us for recalling to memory the pain of losing, as some of you have, your sons in the war.

We wish now, from the bottom of our hearts and with brotherly love, to say again, as we said before, about the catastrophe in the world, that it was merely the beginning, or in other words it was only the budding stage, there is yet the fruit-bearing stage ahead.

The capitalistic world is not asleep, despite the fact that bank accounts are now smaller it is not sufficient to satisfy it.

The civilized bourgeois world is not asleep, it has intensified production and concentrated its resources into the production of arms and aerodromes and submarines as well as poisonous gases. The idea is to cause a clash, whether it be on land, under it or in the air or on the sea, so long as human blood is once again tasted. However, the proletarian class, suffering through the ages, unclothed, barefoot and content with a piece of dry bread, has come to understand their chicanery.

While the capitalists prepare death-dealing weapons by day and by night, the proletariat of all countries are not asleep either, they are organizing into a union. The imperialists desire to destroy this union, but the workers wish to gain control and to destroy imperialism once and for all time.

And when these two forces clash, "HERCULES AND THE ANCIENT SERPENT," the struggle will be terrible to behold, before which brick and mortar will not stand, survivors will be few and humanity will choke itself with blood.

Dear Brothers and Sisters, this world-wide and inevitable clash is coming, it is already on our doorstep.

In order to circumvent this coming destruction, we prophetically claim and beg you to avail yourselves of an inner ticket, given freely to all and without reproach, to enter the abode of Our Father, and thusly save your children and yourselves.

Many will ask themselves, what is this "inner ticket"?

It is the words, printed in large letters on our banner:

"THE SONS OF FREEDOM CANNOT BE THE
SLAVES OF CORRUPTION "

Finally, dear Brothers and Sisters, whosoever shall pursue "CORRUPTION" shall perish.

Glory to our God.

(Signed) THE SONS OF FREEDOM.

24th June 1928.
Verigin,
Saskatchewan.

NOTES AND APPENDIX TO CHAPTER III
Stuart Jamieson

METHODS AND ACKNOWLEDGMENTS

In the study of the economic life of any group of people in a western nation a customary initial step is to draw on basic statistical data so as to get a preliminary over-all picture of numbers, age and sex distribution, areas of residence, employment by industries and trades, rates of pay and weekly or annual incomes, spending habits, ownership of property, and so on. An immediate difficulty faced in this study was the lack of accurate and comprehensive statistical information. Large numbers of Doukhobors have consistently refused to provide information to the Census Bureau and other government agencies. Such usually helpful and reliable sources as the Dominion Bureau of Statistics, therefore, were of little assistance.

To get this basic data, a painstaking study of the records and files of numerous public and private agencies in a number of different fields was required. It involved picking out Doukhobors by name from thousands of others. The author was fortunate in being assisted in this work during the summer of 1950 by C. K. Toren and P. J. Fogarty, who at that time were doing graduate work at the University of British Columbia.

Grateful acknowledgment is given of the kind assistance and co-operation provided by the officials of numerous public and private bodies. Particularly useful and comprehensive statistics were made available from the files of the district offices of the National Employment Service, the Provincial Land Settlement Board, the Motor-vehicle Licence Bureau, and local Tax Assessment Boards. Among private organizations, the Associated Boards of Trade of Eastern British Columbia were particularly helpful in circulating a prepared questionnaire on our behalf among several hundreds of their member firms, to provide information about labour-management relations and employment of Doukhobors. Personal interviews with officials of many individual firms, both large and small, yielded valuable information. Useful data about the relationships of Doukhobors with other workers in various trades and industries were provided by officers and members of numerous trade-union locals in the West Kootenay. Particularly helpful among these were the United Brotherhood of Carpenters and Joiners (TLC), the United Steelworkers of America (CCL), and the International Mine, Mill and Smelter Workers' Union.

To obtain the financial and other data about the Christian Community of Universal Brotherhood Limited, and its liquidation under receivership after 1938, required an exhaustive study of Supreme Court records in Vancouver, as well as interpretation of various financial statements provided by former officers of the CCUB Ltd. itself. In this work the author was ably assisted during the summer of 1951 by Richard Chong, graduate in Commerce of the University of British Columbia.

From such sources as these a fairly full and comprehensive picture was drawn of the current role and status of the Doukhobors in the West Kootenay region. More difficult in some respects than the job of assembling these facts, however, was the task of interpretation, which involved the always difficult question of motivation. It is generally agreed today that the incentives that influence or govern the various economic activities of men are far more numerous and complicated than the mere "rational self-interest" assumed in classical economic theory. Economic incentives and values are necessarily part of the larger society and culture with which individuals and groups identify themselves. To understand the special economic status and problems of the Doukhobors today thus requires a study of their history, unique culture, and traditional beliefs, and of the various ways in which these have been modified through a half-century of contact with the Canadian environment. This, of course, is too large an order for an economist to undertake alone, even with considerable assistance. At every stage of the investigation, therefore, the author found it necessary to compare notes with his colleagues who were concentrating on other aspects of Doukhobor life, and his chapter in the Report has had to borrow heavily from them.

The Doukhobors are in many ways a unique people who face particularly difficult problems of adjustment. In a larger sense, however, they represent merely a special case of a peasant people with a separate religious tradition facing the problems of culture survival in the secular industrial society of the North American Continent. A number of penetrating socio-economic studies have been made of other such groups, and these have helped provide the author with useful frames of reference for this work. He would like to mention E. C. Hughes: *French Canada in Transition,* as being particularly helpful.

NOTES AND APPENDIX TO CHAPTER IV
Claudia Lewis

EXCERPTS FROM FIELD-NOTES

The following incidents are taken from my field-notes of family life among the Doukhobors. It is on the basis of this material that I have built up my concept of the authoritarian nature of the traditional Doukhobor child-rearing code.

It has not seemed feasible to organize these observations into closed categories, each illustrating one point only, such as mode of punishment of children, benevolent handling, exposure to restrictions, etc. Daily life does not lay itself out so neatly, for our scrutiny.

Perhaps, however, this material can convey the general flavour of the child-life, with its mixture of freedom and restriction, its exposures to benevolence and to harshness, its privileges and the prices paid for them.

I have not disguised the name of Stefan Sorokin, but all the names and initials I have used to designate Doukhobor families and children are fictitious.

KRESTOVA

An Afternoon of Visiting

As we went from house to house on this afternoon, to make brief visits, several little children trailed along with us. Our group consisted of Gerry Kanigan and myself, two neighbour women and three of their children, one of them eating sunflower seeds steadily from her knotted handkerchief. Other small children appeared from time to time and joined us. All of these children seemed to be taken for granted wherever we went, but were very quiet, never entering into conversation, lining themselves up unobtrusively on beds and chairs. They showed little responsiveness to the babies in the households.

On the way back we stopped at a barn to see two newly born calves. Gerry and I went right in to watch a girl trying to get them to drink from a pan. The children made no move that I could see to enter the barn, and said nothing as they stood at the doorway looking in.

Invited to Dinner

Mrs. F. insisted upon cooking dinner for us when we stopped in to call on her. The nine-year-old grandson was there, but retired to the tiny bedroom adjoining the kitchen, along with his aunt, a girl of 18, while we ate. He sprawled on the bed, and his aunt sat beside him, the two of them quietly getting themselves out of the way. The table was set only for Gerry Kanigan and me. When we were through eating, a place was made for the boy. The adults in the household claimed that they had already eaten.

Punishments

During our afternoon visit with 24-year-old Mrs. T., the baby, aged one and a half, toddled around outside, and got into a plate of huckleberries. She came inside carrying the plate, with huckleberries all over her fists. Her mother took the plate away and made the child bow to her grandmother, as atonement for getting into the grandmother's berries. This was not a bow way down to the floor, but a deep nod of the head and bending at the waist, which this little tot was able to execute in pretty good form. The mother's tone of voice, as she asked the child to bow, was not harsh, and what she was conveying to the child seemed to be something in the nature of a casual form the child must learn to go through; there were no highly emotional overtones.

Mrs. T.'s older sister, who was present, spoke up regarding the trouble she has with her husky little two-year-old boy. "I try to talk reasonable to him, but he just doesn't seem to understand this. What he *does* understand is a good spanking."

Children in the House

Today a little five-year-old boy, John, has been hanging around here with his older brother most of the day. An 11-year-old neighbour girl, Tanka, has been here, too, washing out quantities of old beer-bottles for Mrs. L. The summer supply of root beer is about to be made. Tanka has taken it upon herself to keep an eye on this little neighbour boy, John, just as she does when her own little brother is around. I heard the same sharp scolding voice when the child made the slightest move that she thought he ought not. For instance, she was filling a big tub with water out in the back yard, painstakingly pumping the water from the spring up to the water "tower," whence it flowed down through a hose. John once put his finger into the stream coming from the hose and got a sharp rebuke. He also was rebuked and sharply told to move when I was helping Tanka wash the bottles, and the little boy was standing, as she thought, too near me, in my way. And how Tanka screwed up her face, like a little vixen, as the words came lashing out! The result is that John does nothing but stand around, or sit around, making few moves, acting as though he doesn't expect to be allowed anything. When I brought out my collection of little toys for the children, he didn't touch them as the older ones did. He sat back as though he took it for granted that he wouldn't be allowed to touch them. When I gave him a toy aeroplane, he handled it very gingerly.

As the four children, Tanka, John, John's eight-year-old brother, and our own eight-year-old Paul, gathered around my toys and began to giggle rather loudly with pleasure, they were hushed by Mrs. L., who was working there beside us in the kitchen. All did "hush" immediately.

Tanka has been here all day helping Mrs. L., and had dinner with us at 2:30 p.m. When Mrs. L. asks her to get the hot water or bring in the cream from the cellar under the house, she jumps right up with the quickest obedience. The little children certainly jump when Mrs. L. speaks to them, too. There is little harshness in her tone, but it conveys authority.

From a Conversation with a Doukhobor Woman

"Do parents tell their children about sex," we asked, "or just like them to find out for themselves?"

"They don't tell them. They feel a little embarrassed to talk to them about it."

"What about menstruation? Are girls prepared for it?"

"No, we let children just grow up naturally."

"Do parents tell children where babies come from?"

"Some do; some tell them they come from the river. What's the matter? You want me to tell you?" (Laughing.)

Evening in the Back Yard

Last night we were sitting a while in a back yard with a group of neighbours and their children, to chat and enjoy the cool evening air. Most of us sat on the empty apple-boxes that were kept in a pile against the wash-house. ("By God, we always have plenty of chairs," the father of the family explained.) Two of the boys, five and eight years old, began climbing in their apple-boxes, sitting in them, playing they were cars. The eight-year-old stumbled over his box in the course of this play, and his foot landed in an old empty pail near by. His father spoke sharply to him, whereupon both he and the other boy immediately put their boxes straight, turned themselves into two little adults, and sat down quietly.

Two Visits with Mrs. R.

(Husband in jail; three children, garden, hayfield to look after; also has frequent care of children of a sister who is ill.)

Tonight, while I was visiting at Mrs. R.'s house, both she and her eight-year-old daughter trounced, shoved, moved, scolded five-year-old Jimmy around. The poor little fellow just can't make a move in my presence without being told not to. Mrs. R. finally picked him up bodily and swung him out to the porch to remove him from us. He dashed right back in and she did it again. This time he stayed and cried out there.

At Mrs. R.'s in the afternoon, to sit and chat. The eight-year-old daughter gets her crocheting and sits with us in the cool green white-washed room. Children are ever-present, taking part in all the adult affairs. Jimmy pulls up his chair and sits on it, and if he starts running around is lashed right back into the chair with sharply scolding words. The child sits there at least a full hour, doing practically nothing, because he is allowed to do nothing. Mrs. R. confesses she gets awfully tired of being with children. "They make me so mad."

A Funeral

Clean little white-washed blue room filled with babushkas in shawls; two or three men; open coffin; great geranium plant. Babushkas sit about the ceremonial table and chant, chant, from noon to three o'clock. Children come in, to look, to stand a while by their own babushkas; one four-year-old climbed into his grandmother's lap and nestled there for nearly an hour. Women come in and stand by the coffin a while, not weeping much. Occasional handkerchief lifted to eyes, but the next moment, smiles and joking. "We do not feel sad when an old babushka dies. She has had her life, lived it out. With a young person, it is different."

Sorokin is sent for. He sits with the singers, stands by the coffin.

"Come, come, please stay with us; eat, eat, as we say farewell to our Mother."

We are thus cordially invited to the funeral feast prepared by the dead babushka's daughter-in-law, with many women to help.

Thirty-five people sit at the long table spread on the shady side of the house. Borsch, spaghetti in butter, kasha with raisins, bread, oranges, cheese, fruit-juice made with prunes, apricots, strawberries; platters of watermelon. Children do not join this feast. Some sit on the outskirts and look. When we are through (with traditional prayers and dirge-like monotone chants between each course), children swarm to the table and grab up the oranges and watermelon slices that are left.

Back to the cool room to stand and chant some more; children enter, too, freely, not pushed in, not pushed out.

Then the coffin is carried out to the daylight, where it is placed on top of the wooden case that is to hold it; it is opened, we all gather round—children, Sorokin, everyone. The photograph is taken. Quickly now the coffin and box are borne out to the wagon waiting in the dusty road. The daughter-in-law of the house grabs up one handle and helps along when no man is handy.

Down the road, walking behind the horse and wagon, crowd of women and children, singing. A whole community escorting the old Mother to her rest. A tiny boy holds his grandmother's hand and walks the whole mile; boys, girls troop along.

The graveyard—a place in the highest bush, unkept. A row of young boys, nine, ten years old, line themselves up on the mound of earth that has been thrown up. They remind each other to take their caps off as the coffin is opened for the last time.

The bereaved family stands facing the crowd. They speak back and forth in the traditional way: "I hope it was all done well." "Oh, yes, spasibo, spasibo." The relatives, four or five of them, break into unabashed weeping; then immediately are self-contained again. The emotion comes easily when the ceremony calls for it; goes easily.

Sorokin speaks: "Dust we are made of, we go back to dust; she lived her life well."

The women chant. There are bows down to the ground by the relatives.

The coffin is lowered, the family throwing in the first clods by hand. The men fill the grave and complete the high ground, while the women sing. The children stand quietly through it all, not singing, not bowing, not crying, but there, a part of it.

So the whole village buries its "Mother."

Green Apples

Last night, while a group of children were playing around in the yard, one of them picked some green apples, stuffing them in his pockets. When his mother discovered this, she got up from where she was sitting on the porch steps, gave him a rough smacking (I didn't see it, but heard it), and let out a volley of scolding words in Russian, her only language: "Get out of here—go far away, we don't want you around here." The child stood there for a moment silent, red-faced, taking it. Then his father came out of the house and added to the volley of scolding, also demanding that the boy "get out." At this the child turned and walked out of our sight, down the little hill toward the spring. The adults who were gathered on the steps spoke excitedly about the danger of green apples: "They are poison."

The boy could be heard sobbing down by the spring. In a few minutes his father summoned him roughly, with more yelling and scolding: "I told you to *get out!* What are you doing down there? Come on, get out of here . . . I'll outlaw you from this house. I don't want you anywhere around here!"

The boy came up from the spring, sobbing heavily, and went off around the corner of the house toward the gate. In about ten minutes, the crying over, he returned, walking slowly and quietly toward us, past his mother on the steps, and up to the porch, where he stood for a while. The adults appeared to take no notice of him. Then his father asked him to go to bed, and got the wash-pan down for him. Shortly after, his father followed him into the house.

A little later, when I stepped into the kitchen, I could see the boy leaning on his elbow in his bed in the next room. I smiled at him and he smiled back. His father was in bed, too, on the other side of the bedroom, in the dark. He was talking steadily and softly to the boy, in what sounded like gentle tones.

A Young Mother

Mable lives in a house with her four-month-old baby and two young brothers, whom she cares for. Mable must be twenty or twenty-one. Her husband, mother, and father are in jail. She has lived in Krestova only a short while, coming here from Slocan Park to be near other people while her husband is in jail. She told us that her mother was in jail earlier for a three-year period, then was out for one year, and now is in again. During that early jail period, when Mable must have been a girl in her early teens, she stayed home alone caring for the two young brothers. "Have you ever been in jail yourself?" I asked. "No, I haven't had the chance—too many children to care for."

"Would you *like* to be in jail?"

"Well, we feel that's where we should be."

Mabel was combing her hair and complaining that it was beginning to come out badly. "Because I've worried so much, I guess."

She has a big Stromberg-Carlson radio, run by batteries. She turned it on; there was music. I commented that it sounded so nice to me. She said she couldn't care about listening to music when there was so much trouble in her heart.

We sat for a while on her overstuffed davenport, talking. The baby's little potty, clean and dainty and new, had been left on the davenport, along with some baby clothes and blankets.

I got up to leave. Mabel said she would walk back with me. She wrapped the baby tightly in an outer blanket and walked along with me, holding the baby with its back against her body, its face to the road, as though it were a stocky bundle.

Ceremonial Singing

This afternoon, as the women stood singing outside the house where the local committee men were meeting with Sorokin, children of all ages were to be seen among them. They included two babies in arms (one tightly wrapped, one not), a group of girls about ten years old, a small group of boys of eight or ten, and a few straggling little children of three, four or five who hung very closely to their mothers' knees. The general impression of the children at this meeting was of considerable passivity. They stood, or sat, and watched quietly. The only one I observed singing at times was eleven-year-old Tanka.

Five-year-old Jimmy was present with his mother, Mrs. R., just standing, standing against her full skirt. When he started to climb a rail fence about two feet away, he was quickly told not to. He returned to the skirt, and continued standing, passively, meekly.

Sonya's Life

Sonya is a young married woman of twenty-four. She was in prison with her mother for a while at Piers Island and then was taken to the Alexandra Orphanage. (She proudly told me that she had still another prison experience for a few weeks when she was on a visit to Alberta. She was picked up with some of her friends for not having registration data.)

She married, and together with her husband's people bought some land down in Crescent Valley. This land has now been turned over to the Sons of Freedom, however. Sonya spoke proudly of her home down there in Crescent Valley, with its fine garden. Now that her husband is away in jail, she has come back to Krestova with her baby, to stay temporarily with her mother.

Sonya has an extraordinary singing voice. It has that Doukhobor quality, hard, metallic, loud, clear and sweet. She said she would like to have been able to study singing, to learn to read music from notes. "But how could I, when I can't even read English?"

We asked her what she believed about school, and in spite of the admission she had just made, out came the old story—schools teach war. If they'd stick to just reading, writing, arithmetic, they'd be O.K.

Now here is a girl who likes pretty things and who dresses in Doukhobor clothes that might almost be "English" clothes. I have noticed her at meetings, in her lovely silk two-piece dress. She got out her exquisite white wedding dress to show us. The apron had sequins on it, and the blouse glittered with crystal buttons. Yes, she loves pretty things and spends a lot of time fixing herself up. We met her on the street in Nelson one day. No Doukhobor shawl, hair done on top of her head in a striking braid formation; bangs curled and meticulously set in place; lots of costume jewelry—pins, brooches.

Pretty, young, exquisitely dressed. But, like all the others, she says that it is wrong to accumulate property, wrong to surround yourself with pretty things. "That is not the way to live. Sure, we like pretty things, but we should not let ourselves accumulate property. If you have no property, then you have no enemies. An enemy would have no reason to come and fight you. That's why we burn everything so we can say, 'Why should we go to war? We have nothing to defend.' If an enemy came here, we'd just invite him in, and ask him to live with us . . . No enemy would want *this* house because there's nothing nice about it."

Sonya pointed outside to a spot where a very fine house belonging to a relative had burned to the ground. She spoke proudly of the fact that absolutely every piece of furniture, even the lovely cedar hope chest had gone up in flames.

Yet Sonya let slip a little later that she had left her nice crocheting down at her own home in the valley, "because of all these burnings."

The Piers Island Days

We were walking through the dry, high village, up on what I call the plateau. Women came out to gates all along the road to talk to us. At one house three women who were sitting on their steps called to us to come rest a while with them. It was about noon; the hot, hot sun beat down, wilting the garden; the sunflowers were drooping. These people have no water to irrigate gardens. Drinking-water must be hauled in great barrels from a creek some distance away, at fifty cents a barrel. (We saw a group of boys about twelve or thirteen years old hoisting a couple of these big iron containers on to a wagon for a trip to the creek. No horse. The boys would do the pulling.)

These three women had little to do but sit, apparently. Sit and talk. One had been in the Girls' Industrial Home as a child while her parents were in Piers Island. She was full of it. Words, words poured out in Russian—the mistreatment, clothes forcibly taken from them, little to eat at first, "sometimes only a carrot and a piece of bread for a meal."

Silent children sat on the steps with us, watching and listening.

Mrs. R. mentioned one day that after she was taken from her mother and sent to a foster home, in the Piers Island days, she became afraid to go out at night. "I was afraid to be alone, too. I'd take a lot of children to bed with me for company."

The M. Family

We stopped in to visit with the M. family. Mrs. M. has four daughters, two sons. Her husband is now in jail. They have been living with their mother-in-law since they burned their house across the road. The family is very different from Mrs. R.'s, for example. The four girls and one boy who were home moved freely in and out of the house and the room where we sat; I heard no rebuking words restraining the children; the little 3-year-old girl was lively and active, biffing playfully, and sometimes not so playfully, at the brother and sisters; the little boy about nine had poise enough to come and sit for a while in the living-room with Gerry and me, though he could speak little English with us. At the dinner table the children all ate great platefuls of food, heartily. The three-year-old was not at the table. She just ran in and out playing. But when she asked for some peas, she was given a place beside her mother and ate a big bowlful.

One of these children, a girl about seven, had a bathing suit on when she came in, late in the afternoon. She got into her blouse and skirt right there in our presence, but managing very modestly.

This family was hearty, warm; the children handsome and delightful. The girl about eleven whispered a Russian "excuse me" when she had to pass my chair in the kitchen. Healthy, beautiful faces; strong-looking children.

There was much talk among the adults while dishes were being washed in the dusky kitchen about the reasons for the house burnings, the Doukhobor philosophy, the protests and nude demonstrations. Some of the children were present, sitting on a bench against the wall, solemnly listening.

I said to the mother when I left. "You have a *lovely* family." "I think so, too!" she laughed.

The Singing of the Children

At the Sunday meeting in the Krestova meeting-house about thirty girls and twenty-five boys from ages five to twelve had been brought together to sing for us, to demonstrate the fruits of "Russian school." The girls were lined up at the front of the room on one side, boys on the other, the two groups facing each other, little children in front of older and taller children. The ceremonial table stood at the head of the room, and behind it sat Sorokin, a visiting Quaker, Gerry Kanigan, a Doukhobor local committee leader, and myself.

The rest of the room is filled with close to a hundred men and women, standing in their traditional formation—men on one side, women on the other. The children sing and recite, sometimes in unison, sometimes just one child at a time, for at least an hour and a half. They recite the Doukhobor sayings in an unbroken, clear, shouting voice. The words rise and fall in a steady chant, and there is no wavering or stumbling. The singing is the same—forthright, bold. These are not feeble little childish voices, but strong, confident voices. When a child sings or recites by himself, he does it as a matter of course, with no embarrassment or giggling, no looking around afterwards to see what the effect was on others. He looks straight ahead and speaks out clearly. One very little boy, about seven, occasionally stumbles in his long recitation, and is prompted by the teacher, but this does not confound him. He keeps right on trying in a clear voice. Some of the little ones tiptoe out occasionally, probably to the toilet, and then in again to their places, falling right in with the singing.

As people entered the meeting-house in groups or individually, everyone present gave the elaborate Doukhobor greeting, with its bows. Children participated in this.

The children were dismissed a little early, after about two hours of standing in formation. There was very little wriggling about among them during that time.

When the meeting was over, we who were the guests were to be fed at a house some way up the road. As we stood in front of the meeting-house in what I thought was just an informal chatting, I suddenly became aware of the crowd pushing me to the front and asking me to start walking; a song rose up from the women, and there we were, in a ceremonial march down the road to the feast; in front, Sorokin, Gerry, and myself, and two men from the local committee. Behind us, the whole crowd of Doukhobor men and women, raising their chant to the skies, which were very blue and hot. As we walked down that road, beneath the mountains, with the whole air filled with the psalm and all the people walking, walking, I had a more "ceremonial" feeling than I have ever experienced. It is an excited rush of feeling.

A few children walked along, too, but were told by committee men to stay at the side of the road.

WINLAW, CLAYBRICK, GLADE, APPLEDALE, SLOCAN VALLEY
(Sons of Freedom families, unless otherwise indicated.)

An Evening of Singing

One evening neighbours came to our house for an evening of singing. Of course, the children came along. Picture the small living room filled with seven or eight young children (ages approximately four to nine), two adolescent girls, five adult women (some Sons of Freedom, some USCC). The children began to play with my little collection of toys, zooming around on the floor with them. A regular beehive in our midst. But we hadn't begun our singing yet, and no one raised any objections for a few moments. Shortly, however, Mrs. D. decided it was too noisy, and figured out an easy way to get the children into the adjoining kitchen. She simply picked up the lamp and carried it in there. The children did follow, like a bunch of little bugs. And there they played, crashing, banging, talking, shouting. What a clatter! The group of adults who remained rather stiffly seated in the living-room seemed to look upon this with some amusement and tolerance. It was really too noisy to talk comfortably, but no one hushed the children. I wonder if this could have happened in Krestova. I have an idea it could not. Someone would surely have said "Hush!" And I'm not sure the children would have felt so free, anyway.

Possibly the women who were our guests did not feel in a position to stop the children, and were waiting for Mrs. D. to do it? Possibly she hesitated because I had brought out the toys and she didn't want to offend me?

At any rate, I finally suggested that we start singing. "Maybe it will drown out the children!" I said.

We began one of the psalms—rich, sweet harmony in three parts. The children became instantly quiet. They dropped their toys. They stood up. One or two came right into the living-room and joined us. The rest soon followed, and there they were, packed on the couch, sitting there singing out of their serious little faces. Their own choice.

As it got close to ten o'clock, a number of these children were drooping and wilting with sleepiness, falling against their mothers. But this did not make the mothers jump up and say, "Oh, I must go home and get Verna to bed." No, they don't let the children interfere with their evening. Children will, of course, get sleepy, but they can wait. Grace and Verna went over and stood beside their mother, both attempting to lean against her for support and comfort and rest. A more uncomfortable scene of madonna seated, with two children half on lap, I never did see. Yet this was tolerated for some fifteen or twenty minutes. And other sleepy children were doing likewise, seeking out their mothers and leaning against them. The attitude of the mothers was one of casual acceptance; all in the course of the day's work. The nature of life. There were a few casual pats of affection as the children leaned on their breasts.

Supper with the Neighbours

We were all invited to the L.'s for supper. This meant feeding a total of six adults and five children. There wasn't room for all at the table. As a matter of course, the adults sat down and ate first, while the children played around outside. It was about eight o'clock in the evening when they came in for their shift. I thought to myself, how utterly different from the attitude toward children in the families I know in so many American cities. There, the whole arrangement would revolve around the children. Their regular mealtime would not be shifted at any cost, and how shocking to have supper as late as eight o'clock! Children must be in bed by that time!

Bending Back the Ears

Seven-year-old Billy's mother always knew where he was, and whenever she needed firewood for the kitchen stove, she called him and asked him to bring it. This he always did with an alacrity which amazed me. "How did you get him to do this?" I asked her. "Well, I had to bend back his ears a few times, but he has really learned it now. The stove just can't wait when wood is needed."

The Older Generation

It was easy to see that Mrs. D.'s old father (an Independent, according to his daughter) believed in a sterner way of living and rearing children than Mrs. D. does. He came and went in our household rather silently, because he was so deaf, but one day at the table he gave me quite a harangue on how young people in these days are letting the good old Doukhobor way die. People never used to let children run to the table and gobble their food and leave, the way his daughter's children do. No, they used to pray, and he proceeded to show me how.

Occasionally he barked at the children, as Mrs. D. never did, to quiet them or make them behave at the table. He could cow them to some extent when he did this.

He will not come to live permanently with Mrs. D., though he is a lonely old man, because she married a Son of Freedom.

Rough with the Children

There are three little neighbour children in this valley who seem much more constricted than Mrs. D.'s children. They run free all day, but are shy and quiet in my presence, though they have seen a great deal of me. Mrs. D. tells me that their father does not get along well with their mother, is really rough with her and often with the children, too, "though he loves them so much." I saw part of a "row" on Saturday night, when the father was home after his week of absence at work in the bush. We were all sitting quietly on our porch, after our long pea-canning day. Over at the neighbour's house we suddenly heard a crash. The door flew open, making an oblong of yellow light in the darkness. A child rushed out but was yanked in by the father with yelling words, and the door was banged shut. There was quite a commotion of banging and yelling and shouting.

"Another row," Mrs. D. remarked quietly.

Modesty

The D. children, now aged eight and nine, have absorbed quite a code of modesty. For instance, one day we were all going swimming, and a number of children were milling around in my room as I unpacked my bathing suit. I began taking off my shoes, and nine-year-old Margaret herded the whole crowd of children out. "Come on, Claudia's going to undress." The children vanished like snow melting.

Another day, the baby was bathed in the big laundry tub. We carried the tub out into the yard so I could get a picture of it in the sun. When the baby was through, Mrs. D. instructed her little six-year-old nephew, who was visiting us, to take a bath, since he was going on a trip into Nelson. From the kitchen I could hear him splashing around in the tub, and I knew the nine-year-old girl was out there scrubbing his back at her mother's request. Well, well, I thought. This doesn't sound like Doukhobor ways. But when Peter emerged from the tub, I saw that he had been wearing his swimming trunks the whole time.

Adolescents

Sunday evening, while it was still light, they congregated on the porch of the highway store and post-office. A crowd of about twenty of them, girls and boys, about ages fourteen to eighteen. Just sitting there. One boy twanged a guitar. A few walked in and out of the store, buying candy bars and pop. There was such a crowd of them and they seemed to be so idly sitting that I thought they were a picnic group waiting for the bus to come along. But no, it was explained to me that this was just the meeting place of the neighborhood Doukhobor kids.

273

APPENDIX

The Chocolate Cake

It was a pleasure to see little Verna shovelling in the food the day we were all invited to dinner at Mrs. G.'s. Verna sat there with her mouth just about at plate level, and literally did shovel and spoon in the mouthfuls from the plate. Not a word from her. Serious little brow. Shovel it all in. Have some more corn. Wipe up every bit of food from the plate with a piece of dry bread.

About an hour after that dinner, Mrs. G. decided to frost a chocolate cake she had made that day and had considered a failure. We all stood around in the kitchen doing dishes after the big meal, while she iced the cake. Children ran in and out. All right, the cake is iced, let's have some and find out whether or not it was a failure! A big piece is cut and put on a plate for each one of us, even for the tiny two-year-old niece who had supper with us, just because she was there and didn't want to go home up the road. The delicious, rich chocolate cake was handed right out to the children, though dinner was over only an hour ago and we had raspberries and cookies for dessert then. But in a Doukhobor home no one worries about that. Who would think of eating nice cake without giving the children some? Come on, eat it up, enjoy it!

Mrs. G. certainly thought nothing of feeding the little niece and taking care of her as though she were her own child—jumping up from the table and rushing to get the little toilet chair at the child's sudden cry for help. "Do you often take care of this little girl?" I asked in my outlander ignorance. "Why, that's *Polly's* little girl" was the answer, as though to say for goodness' sake, relatives always take care of each other's children. Then she went on to explain a little more, "Sometimes my girl is up there all day. It doesn't make any difference, one place or another, it's all the same." While we were eating, Polly stopped at the back door and left a big pail of milk. She had milked Mrs. G.'s cow for her as a surprise, so Mrs. G. would not have to trouble herself about it on that evening when we were there as guests.

Incidentally, there were no husbands in the picture then for all these young women. The men were in jail.

Children at Meetings

At the Slocan Valley and Glade meetings on Sunday there were numerous children of all ages: babies in arms and some babies in carriages; "knee babies" who stand or sit close to their mothers as they sing, sometimes breaking away and running around and playing near by; children of four and five, not sticking close to the crowd but playing on the outskirts, in small, loose groups; a few boys of about nine, ten, eleven years, staying by themselves at a little distance (at Glade listening when Sorokin spoke, but not listening to the singing—they wander off when this begins); girl gang of same age, also sticking more or less together on the outskirts, definitely separated from the boys. None, or very few, of these children join the singing. At Glade there were two or three teen-age boys sitting at a little distance listening, and a few teen-age girls among the women, singing.

All of the children were, on the whole, very quiet. They had learned they must not be noisy; if a little one did start to talk or shout loudly, he was promptly hushed and did hush. By and large, the children seemed rather free to join the crowd or not, as they pleased. Their presence was accepted; they were taken for granted; no one objected to the little ones running to their singing mothers occasionally and then running away again. But the children must be reasonably quiet. This they seem to understand. I saw one mother strike (not very harshly) at the year-old baby in her arms when he began making too loud noises. This gesture was as though she felt she must hush him at all costs, and the way to do it was to get her hand on his face, where the trouble was coming from.

274

Ceremonies in the House

We have spent four days in this household. The special "English" manners put on for us in the beginning are breaking down, and the Doukhobor ways are creeping back into the house. This morning, at the breakfast table, Mrs. M. suggested that her daughter Vera, twelve, say the Lord's Prayer in the traditional way (in Russian) before we sat down. ("We always say it, usually, but thought maybe you wouldn't be used to it.")

Even the three-year-old stood seriously and quietly for this long grace, his arms folded in the traditional manner. At dinner he even participated in the grace, repeating the words after his mother.

Kitchen scene this morning: One half of the big kitchen table filled with a tub of peaches; Mrs. M. and I standing there peeling and cutting for canning. At the other end of the table daughter Vera sitting with her notebook, copying Russian songs and sayings into it, asking for help from her mother on spelling; and the three of us practising one of the beautifully harmonized Doukhobor religious songs.

Bowing to the Ground

Yesterday the seven-year-old daughter broke a nice drinking-glass. Her mother had her bow down low and say "forgive me" in Russian. Also, the three-year-old boy had some trouble for which his mother made him bow down to the floor and ask forgiveness. It had to do with soiling his pants. Unfortunately, most of this happened out of our earshot.

The Whipping Tone of Voice

Yesterday I heard Mrs. M. call out to her two younger children in that stern, decisive, sharp way that Mrs. R. of Krestova used so often. The children were about to get into a big tub of cold water in the yard. Mrs. M. felt that it was too cold for them and they must be stopped. I wonder if this particular sharp tone of voice ever fails to stop children! The words are lashed out like a whip. Certainly it was very effective yesterday.

Another Meeting

We went to a large Sunday meeting held in a community hall. Doukhobors of all sects gathered to hear Sorokin. Seated across the front of the hall facing the audience was a line-up of visitors, including Sorokin, two Doukhobors from Saskatchewan, and two local committee men (Doukhobors), as well as Mr. and Mrs. O., who were hosts for this meeting. The O.'s two granddaughters, about five and six years old, felt entirely free to walk up the aisle, nestle against their grandmother up there in front, get off her lap and go to their grandfather and generally just tiptoe all around the place while the meeting was in progress. No one seemed to think they were in the way. A stocky little three-year-old also made herself completely at home at the front of the room, in the space between audience and speakers. She quietly and curiously padded around examining everybody, everything (including the glass and pitcher, bread and salt, on the ceremonial table). She was very quiet about it, and no one seemed to think this young visitor was anything amiss at the front of the room. Toward the end of the meeting, when two determined nude women stalked up the hall and planted themselves before Sorokin, this little three-year-old stood before them and quietly stared. She was clutching in her hand the improvised nursing bottle that all these children use, an old Orange Crush bottle fitted with nipple.

OOTESHENIE, BRILLIANT, PASS CREEK
(USCC Families)

Life of an 11-year-old

There was a little 11-year-old girl, Violet, living in the big frame house in the "village." She was over in our quarters most of the time helping with the work and generally hanging around because she liked to be there. Mrs. H. would constantly ask her to run errands—run find the baby, run take a bucket out to Mr. H. at the plum-tree, run out to the garden and get something. The child always jumped right up, no matter what she was doing, and executed these errands promptly and willingly. She seemed to accept this errand-girl role without resentment. She liked to be there with us adults, and I'm sure it would not have occurred to anyone to question her presence. For instance, when some people from Trail stopped one day to buy some fruit, and stayed a while in the living-room to talk with us about the Doukhobor Research Committee, little Violet was right there, kneeling on the floor by my chair, taking it all in.

She took pleasure in telling me about Doukhobor life, as though she were an adult giving me valuable information. And I daresay the things she told me about Doukhobor attitudes were pretty accurate! She told me how her mother had hated cooking in the community kitchen during the old community days. "There were only two women at a time to cook the meal for all that crowd, and in the summer it was so *hot!*"

Violet also enjoyed explaining Russian words to me, and was able to tell me which were "pure Russian, only our old people speak that way now," and which expressions were typical of the younger folks.

It was clear to see Violet's leaning toward English ways. She had attended Russian school in her village that winter, but spoke disparagingly of it. She wanted to make it entirely clear to me that young people of her generation (remember, she belongs to a USCC family) preferred the English school and the English language.

The Sex Taboo

One day we were all at the table on the porch eating lunch. The baby, age two, was through eating and was playing around on the porch behind us. He had on some pants with a loose elastic. As he played, the pants dropped down below his waist-line, exposing his genitals. Mrs. H. happened to glance around and see him standing there looking at us, all exposed in this way. She let out a little exclamation of horror, and lost no time jumping up to pull up his pants.

On another occasion, the neighbour girl, Violet, was feeding the baby in his high chair. He had on only some cotton underpants. Idly he began to finger himself, pulling aside his pants and exposing his genitals. Violet suddenly saw this, her eyes popping with horror. She let out an "Ooh," and then jumped up and smartly slapped the little boy's hand, while she covered him up again.

Boys Should Not Fight

One morning I saw two boys of about eleven begin tussling with each other out in the back region in the yard among the barns and sheds. They had no sooner begun than an old grandfather rushed out from somewhere and separated them very forcefully. It had looked like fairly innocent tussling to me.

Children Should Be Quiet

A few of the "village" children were playing in the courtyard behind the square twin houses. There were sounds of teasing, rough-housing, calling back and forth. As I sat on the porch, reading, I scarcely noticed. The sounds of children at play seem to be about the same the country over. They melt into the background.

But suddenly from the big village house came the sharp lashing words, the shrew-like voice, demanding quiet and good behaviour.

The little playing group dispersed.

The Old and the Young

I was impressed by the respect and deference young Bill J. (about twenty-five or thirty) showed to his old dad, Bill J. Sr., formerly one of the treasurers for

276

the community at Brilliant. This old dad is a widower and lives in a house very near his son. Young Mr. J. was telling us that it is easy to get along with the strict older generation if you know how to handle them. He said he never lets a day pass without stopping in to say hello to his dad, and see if he needs anything.

The day we called, Bill J. Sr. greeted us in his son's living-room. He stood there, straight and dignified, and gave me a little address on spiritual living (all translated respectfully by young Mr. J.). The old man was a beautiful picture, white-haired, ruddy-cheeked, wearing a blue shirt of a cloth and design I hadn't seen before. A man with the carriage and manner of Tolstoy.

On our ride home, Mr. H. (USCC Doukhobor from Brilliant) described this old man to us as "someone like Gandhi. But he's really too good, he isn't human." It seems that the old gentleman had taken Mr. H. aside and chastised him for getting a beautiful new Chevvy!

Young Mr. J. has some of his father's "spirituality." We sat in this young man's living-room—he works at a lumber-yard a few miles away—and listened to him talking earnestly about spiritual things. He showed me the Russian book, Biryukov's "God is in Truth, not in Strength," which he had been taking to the lumber-yard with him to read under the bright night-light when he had some time off on his shift.

USCC Wedding

We arrived at the bride's home at about 11 o'clock in the morning. Already a number of friends and relatives had gathered. The bride was dressed in her bridal gown (entirely modern, not Doukhobor), and she and the groom were walking around through the rooms of the house, followed by a best man and a bridesmaid in a satin gown. The bride and bridesmaid had on corsages of artificial flowers, so skilfully made that it didn't dawn on me for some time that they were not real. The groom and best man each wore a white artificial flower in his lapel.

In the living-room a long table was set, ready for guests, and the white-washed wall had been decorated with coloured streamers—pink, blue, and white.

The people milling around were of all ages. There were babies and young children, young boys and girls in their teens, many cousins and relatives in their thirties and forties; some old people, including a most twinkling-eyed old man who had served several years in prison in Siberia before coming to Canada, and bears on his back still the marks of the lash, so I was told. The people in this crowd looked, acted, and talked just like any Canadian citizens. The women in Doukhobor dress were decidedly in the minority. One of the guests was a neighbour who is a doctor—not a Doukhobor.

I was sitting in a small room off the living-room during all these preliminaries and pretty soon along came a man with a bottle. It is a Doukhobor custom that you take a drink at a wedding. He poured me out a small drink—it was a mixture of some kind—and from that time on these bottles were very much in evidence. (When I reported to a Son of Freedom woman later on in the Slocan Valley that there had been drinks at this wedding, and that the bride was not in Doukhobor dress, she seized upon these points avidly, as though to say, "Aha, see how wickedly those Orthodox Doukhobors live!")

The actual ceremony was held at 12 o'clock noon. "We're going to have the ceremony now," people said, and almost before you knew what was happening, the bride and groom had taken their places together at one end of the living-room and the immediate relatives had grouped themselves around them in a semi-circle. The guests clustered around the edges of the room. A rug was put down before the bride and groom, because they were going to have to bow to the floor.

The bride's mother, a very vigorous and attractive woman, came out of the kitchen and took her place in the semi-circle, still wearing her apron over her modern silk print dress.

This ceremony was extremely brief and not very impressive. It consisted of relatives stepping forth out of the semi-circle, saying traditional words to the bride and groom, then stepping up and kissing them. More than once the bride and groom knelt down and touched their heads to the floor while a prayer was being said. It was all over in about five minutes. And then we sat down to the big table.

I doubt that the actual ceremony is the most important part of the wedding to the Doukhobors. The wedding itself goes on all day, and its importance is in the sum total, not in this brief ritual. I found the day very impressive, myself, in its tremendous gathering of relatives and all the well-wishing that went on. In fact, the most impressive part began after the ceremony, when we sat down to eat. (I should not omit that a professional photograph was taken just before the ceremony. The bride and groom posed beside the three-tiered wedding cake, in the act of cutting. This cake was the kind of white-flower-iced wedding cake that you see in any bakery window.)

At the table there were the traditional prayers and songs. The bride and groom sat at the head of the table, holding each other's hands most of the time. The food was, of course, borsch, great slices of home-baked white bread, kasha with raisins, potatoes, corn, tomatoes, cucumbers, vegetable and fruit tarts served with melted butter or thick cream, watermelon, quartered oranges, cookies, cakes, bowls of fruit. There were large pitchers of an orange drink on the table, made, I am sure, by diluting certain powders with water. Quite different from the pitchers of fruit-juice at Krestova, where the fruit actually is there in the pitcher along with the juice. Also, the bottles of liquor were liberally passed around. Some of the women did not take it.

At the end of the meal we rose for the prayer and then were all told to sit down again. There was a hush in the room while it was explained to me: "At this time it is customary for everyone at the table to make a donation, along with a wish."

The bride and groom moved to the middle of the room and stood there expectantly. The first donor was, I think, the father of the bride. He pulled a great roll of bills out of his pocket and began hurling them one by one down on to a platter placed on the table for the purpose. He talked rapidly in Russian, making a wish on each bill he threw down, relative to how the bill should be spent. And as he threw each bill down, the bride and groom kissed each other on the wish that was made. There was great gaiety over this, because the bills were thrown down so rapidly!

All around the table the wishing went, everyone hurling down money and the bride and groom kissing to keep up with it. The table was set over and over again during the day for all the guests who came, and there was a smaller table in an adjoining room. The giving followed each round of eating.

Unfortunately, we had to leave about 2.30 p.m., because I didn't feel that I could be driving on the road after dark in my old car. If we could have stayed on, we would have all been taken over to the groom's home toward evening, where the whole procedure would have begun again. To me the crowd at this wedding seemed a big one—fifty to seventy-five people— but Mrs. D., whom I had brought with me, a relative of the bride, said that it was a "very small wedding" and "not so gay as some weddings." Possibly the gaiety increased as the hours passed. While we were there, certainly there was not the slightest hint of any drunkenness. The atmosphere was friendly, warm, happy.

Now for the children attending this wedding. At functions like this, the children are welcome, but they certainly take the back seat. They are not expected to sit and eat at the tables until the adults are finished. I saw Mrs. W.'s little 9-year-old girl sitting around all wilted and drooping in the shape of a question-mark. And, to my horror, we were well on our way home when "our" 9-year-old girl, Margaret, announced to her mother that she had had nothing to eat and was hungry. With all that food around! We had to stop and get her a sandwich at a roadside place.

ACKNOWLEDGMENTS

My psychological frame of reference, as it pertains to analysis of Doukhobor childhood, owes much to Dr. Alfred Shulman's thinking on the question of Doukhobor personality formation. In general, my theoretical orientation makes use of concepts developed by such anthropologists, social theorists, psychiatrists as Ruth Benedict, Abram Kardiner, Clyde Kluckhohn, Erik H. Erikson, Erich Fromm, Lawrence K. Frank, and Wilhelm Reich.

NOTES AND APPENDIX TO CHAPTER VII
William G. Dixon

CUSTODIAL CARE OF DOUKHOBOR CHILDREN

The best study of the custodial care of Doukhobor children when their parents were confined to Piers Island was written by R. H. C. Hooper in 1947 in a thesis for the master's degree at the School of Social Work of the University of British Columbia. This section is largely a summary which Mr. Hooper has kindly consented to have made of his findings.*

Apprehension of Children

The first action taken by the Provincial Government to provide Doukhobor children with custodial care came in August, 1929. At that time fifty-five women and forty-nine men were convicted at Nelson for indecent exposure and sentenced to six months' hard labour. Seven girls and one boy, ranging from fourteen to sixteen years of age, were arrested with their parents; they were later presented in Court as neglected children and committed to care as wards of the Superintendent of Neglected Children. They were then sent to the agency shelter of the Vancouver Children's Aid Society in Vancouver.

From the discontent and the passive resistance of the children, it was evident that they felt a deep resentment not only toward the authorities, but also toward the agency, whom they blamed jointly for the arrest of their parents. The children were eventually placed in the Industrial Schools on October 23rd, 1929. There was little evidence that the youngsters benefited in any way at all from their experience, and they were returned to the Interior on the subsequent release of their parents in February, 1930.

The apprehension of these eight children was but a prelude to the placing of a large number in the care of the Government. By the end of the summer of 1932 the Provincial authorities found themselves responsible for three hundred and sixty-five Doukhobor children whose parents had been committed to prison.

The legal basis for the Government's action in this instance merits scrutiny. It was quite apparent, of course, that the youngsters were a direct responsibility of the Province, since all were neglected children as defined by the Infants Act of British Columbia. Under ordinary circumstances they would be made wards of the Superintendent of Neglected Children. On release from the Penitentiary

* Ronald H. C. Hooper: Custodial Care of Doukhobor Children in British Columbia, 1929 to 1935, (unpublished master's thesis, Department of Social Work, University of British Columbia, 1947).

the parents could apply to the Court and, on giving satisfactory evidence of their ability to resume parental responsibility, would be reinstated as guardians of their children.

However, the Government chose to maintain the children on a non-ward basis, which meant that they would not be presented to the Court for committal to the Superintendent of Neglected Children. Just why the Government took this attitude is not clear. Possibly there was unwillingness on the part of the Government to break the legal relationship between the parents and their children; possibly it was thought inadvisable to subject the children to a Court experience.

The action taken was illegal because non-ward care implies parental consent to placement. Moreover, it precipitated an administrative difficulty. Since the children had not been legally committed, no surgical operations could be performed without parental consent. The majority of parents would not initially give their permission, and it was only after prolonged negotiation that an agreement was reached.

Planning of Care

Just what type of care the children should receive was, of course, a primary issue. It was originally suggested that two unoccupied construction camps in the Interior be remodelled. But it is to the credit of the child welfare personnel that they decided that the younger children, at least, were to be placed in private foster homes, where they could receive individual attention in a family environment. Infants were to remain at the jail with their mothers until they reached the age of 6 months, although this arrangement was flexible.

The final arrangement was that the Children's Aid Society of Vancouver accepted one hundred and nineteen children ranging in age from two months to twelve years; these children were all placed in approved foster homes by that agency. The Alexandra Orphanage at Vancouver, the Loyal Protestant Home at New Westminster, and the British Columbia Protestant Orphans' Home at Victoria cared for a total of seventy-five children in the age-group of three to nine years. The Provincial Industrial School for Girls and the Provincial Industrial School for Boys accepted seventy-five and ninety-two children, respectively. These children ranged in age from seven to eighteen years of age and were segregated from the regular inmates committed on authority of the Juvenile Court. Maintenance was paid to the private institutions at a rate of $4 per week per child until June, 1933, when it was reduced to $3.60 per week, or 51.42 cents per diem per child.

The Vancouver Children's Aid Society was faced with a large task in finding foster homes for so many children. But newspaper publicity was so wide that hundreds of families wrote and signified their willingness to accept Doukhobor children. This did not indicate, however, that the agency always had high-standard homes available. It was necessary in several instances, in view of the urgent need for placement and the overtaxed facilities of the receiving home, to use homes that could give only a reasonable standard of care. In some cases, foster homes were approved where living-quarters were overcrowded, or the home itself situated in a district which would not provide the most suitable environment for the children. Hooper is satisfied, however, that in no case was a child placed in a home which might prove detrimental to its welfare.

To maintain family unity, efforts were made to place brothers and sisters in the same home. However, it was often difficult to identify youngsters from the records, and there was sometimes an unintentional separation.

The foster-parents, with few exceptions, gained considerable satisfaction in caring for the children. During the period the one hundred and nineteen were in care it was necessary to change placements in only thirty instances, involving twenty-seven children. Of these changes, in eleven cases the children were moved to be with siblings and in six instances transfers were made at the request of the foster-mother; the remaining thirteen changes were necessitated by external conditions, such as the ill-health of the foster-mother.

Hooper deals at some length with the experience of the Industrial Schools with the older children. He reports:—

"Undergoing the same separation from their families, these older children were . . . resentful of the Government for its militant actions, and hostile toward the institutions to which they were sent. With adolescence they had absorbed the basic concepts of the 'Book of Life,' and played an active part in the religious, social and economic life of the Sons of Freedom colonies. Approaching maturity, the entire episode had a broader significance for them, many believing that they were actively participating in one of the many persecutions their people must undergo at the hands of the oppressor. By adopting a familiar pattern of passive resistance during the initial period, they not only lived in accord with the tenets of their church but also found an emotional outlet for the hostilities arising out of their feeling of persecution."

In September, 1932, the girls at the Industrial School were introduced to the classroom. As might be expected, there was resistance, not only to entering the classroom, but also to giving any information on past educational training. Though it was recognized that the majority had attended public schools at some time, it was impossible to grade them, and the group was arbitrarily divided into two classes on an age basis. Eventually some progress was made in inducing the children to accept some education.

It is interesting to note that the traditional Doukhobor penchant for concealed leadership was also displayed by the girls. Apparently a new leader was appointed each day, and she determined for the group whether the day's regulations or orders were acceptable or otherwise. Hooper comments that "so unobtrusive was this leadership that the staff was often unaware of the identity of the particular girls in authority."

Maintenance of Family Ties

It is to the credit of the child welfare personnel of the Provincial Government that they endeavoured to foster the maintenance of family ties of the Doukhobor children in their custody. Their task of allaying the anxiety of the parents was not made easier by those Sons of Freedom who fabricated atrocity stories.

Family friends were allowed to visit the children, but the permission of the particular institution or agency was required in advance. Their credentials were then cleared with the Provincial Police, and the parents of the children were advised of the proposed visit. If the parents consented, the visit was allowed. In the case of the Children's Aid Society, the children were interviewed in the agency offices rather than in the respective foster homes. Official delegates from the Christian Community of Universal Brotherhood were permitted to enter institutional premises on authority from the Superintendent of Neglected Children or the Attorney-General after consultation with the Provincial Police. In the case of relatives, the regulations were strictly enforced for the first two months only. Although police reports were sometimes sought, permission of the parents was not solicited after it had become apparent that they did not object to the association of their children with Community and Independent relatives. Where siblings were placed in more than one agency or institution, mutual visits were arranged at intervals. This enabled the children to retain some active part in the family relationship throughout the placement. The Children's Aid Society of Vancouver and the Girls' Industrial School were particularly active in this respect. There was no regulation to prevent the children visiting parents at Oakalla Prison before the latter were transferred to Piers Island, but only the Girls' Industrial School and the Children's Aid Society made such visits possible.

During the period of placement there was a voluminous flow of correspondence between the incarcerated parents and the children. For example, from September 18th, 1932, to April 16th, 1933, the seventy-five girls in the Provincial Industrial Schools sent out a total of 1,164 letters and received 900 in reply from friends and relatives. While this frequent correspondence was encouraged, it nevertheless placed a heavy burden on staff members. Translation and censorship of mail in itself was a heavy task, to say nothing of providing information on children unable or unwilling to write.

The first two weeks of the apprehension of the children were hectic. In the absence of a definite policy of censorship, many of the children had written of cruelties and suffering which they felt had been inflicted upon them, and the agencies were besieged with requests for information. To allay fears, an agreement was worked out whereby reports were to be sent to the parents in Oakalla of any illness, and lists made of all children slated for school attendance. Further, it was decided that when any parent requested specific information about a child on a matter of importance, a special report was to be forwarded to the prison for the parent. It was also agreed that snapshots should be taken of all children and made available to parents and relatives at a nominal charge.

On June 24th, 1932, in an effort to ease the pressure on the translator at Oakalla, all Doukhobors were instructed to write in English. The order did not prove satisfactory, as the exchange of letters began to diminish appreciably. Many, unable to write in English, had to delay corresponding until a friend agreed to write for them, or, failing this, were unable to communicate at all.

This disruption, coupled with the death of three infants, created discord in Oakalla Prison, and on July 21st, 1932, the prison authorities requested that the Doukhobors be again allowed to use Russian. Of course, there was still the problem of delay, but this was offset by a greater frequency in correspondence and a resulting diminution in parental anxieties.

The Children's Aid Society adopted a very positive policy to provide information on younger children who could not write. Foster-parents were encouraged to write to the parents every two months informing them of the children's health, habits, and activities, and enclosing, if possible, a note or drawing by the children as well as a snapshot of them. The parents, on the other hand, were requested to write the foster-parents on alternate months in English, enclosing notes for the children. They were advised not to ask for the address of the foster home, but this restriction was not enforced after February, 1933.

In January, 1933, while the major difficulties of correspondence were solved, some parents in Piers Island occasionally complained of not receiving any information about their children. The institutions and agencies agreed to send a monthly progress report on each child to the Penitentiary, in addition to the regular letters and the reports of illness.

The Issue of Medical Care

The question of medical care is important, chiefly because of the fact that many Sons of Freedom still believe some children were neglected and continually use this to discredit any current intentions of the Government. Specifically, the issue revolves around the death of three children whom the Sons of Freedom claim "rotted under the arms."

The environment in the women's section of Oakalla was not conducive to normal recovery for any sickly child, for although a matron was in attendance and additional sanitary conveniences were installed, accommodation was overcrowded. The prison surgeon became so alarmed at the situation that he recommended that the babies be removed to more suitable quarters. As a result, seventeen bottle-fed babies were transferred to the Children's Aid Society on June 25th and placed in foster homes in Vancouver. Seven breast-fed babies were allowed to remain at the prison, but their condition was not helped when their mothers went on a hunger strike. The children were then removed to hospital for feeding, but three died of gastro-enteritis.*

After the death of the children, the Sons of Freedom made appeals all across the world for relief from cruelty. In addition to the charges about the removal of the seventeen children to foster homes and the death of the three infants, they complained of improper treatment of the older children in the Industrial Schools. They alleged that the girls were beaten, lodged in "black holes," and subjected to forced feeding after a two-day hunger strike. It was claimed that the boys were strapped and placed in "black holes," received corporal punishment for bed-wetting, and were forced to stand for hours before the portrait of King George V.

The complaints were so widespread that the Canadian National Committee for Mental Hygiene made inquiries of Miss Laura Holland, Deputy Superintendent of Neglected Children. There is no record of inquiry into all the allegations, but the John Howard Society of Vancouver prepared a report for the Canadian Prisoners' Welfare Association on the death of the three children. It reported that the matron of Oakalla prison said that many babies on arrival were suffering from colds and gastro-enteritis. With one or two exceptions, all were in a very weakened condition. The report went on to say that the Oakalla Prison officials felt that the babies who died had very little chance. They were born either just before or just after the arrest of the mothers. They said that, as a whole, the babies were a sickly group, and the hunger strike of the mothers aggravated their condition.§

Termination of Custodial Care

The placement of three hundred and sixty-five children was an experiment that did not last long enough to test its possible value. In 1932, in the depths of the depression, the National Council of Canada urged the Kydd Commission to protest "the million dollar Doukhobor policy" as it pondered recommendations for government spending.† Tom Uphill complained in the Legislature that "the Government spent infinitely more on a handful of lawbreaking Doukhobors than it did to feed British Columbia's jobless army."‡ He said that the support of a Doukhobor child cost 57 cents per day, or $17.50 per month, while unemployed parents received only $2.50 per month for the support of a child. One dollar per day was provided to maintain a Doukhobor at Piers Island, while the relief allowance for a man, his wife and six children, was less than a dollar per day.**

The pressure on the Government was heavy, and when a delegation of Independent and Community Doukhobors approached Provincial Government officials, they received a sympathetic hearing. A number of terms were laid down for the release of children to Doukhobor homes. Among these, the foster-family had to agree to maintain the child without cost. The consent of the parents to the transfer had to be forthcoming, and the home was to be investigated by the Provincial Police. It was definitely laid down that the child had to attend school and be taught to respect the laws of Canada. Of course, parents then in jail were to receive their children upon release.

As events transpired, it was necessary to modify this plan. The main difficulty was that the parents were unwilling to give their written consent to the placing of the children with Independent and Community Doukhobor families, even

* The Vancouver Sun, July 15th, 1932, p. 1, and The Vancouver Province, July 29th, 1932, p. 24.
§ The Vancouver Sun, October 13th, 1932, p. 3.
† The Vancouver Daily Province, June 17th, 1932, p. 16.
‡ The Vancouver Sun, March 23rd, 1933, p. 16.
** The Vancouver Sun, March 23rd, 1933, p. 1.

though they were relatives or friends. The Department of the Attorney-General finally ruled that the children could be placed in Doukhobor homes with the legal support of the Provincial Government without parental consent.

Although it was originally planned that the Provincial Police should have the responsibility of investigating the potential foster homes, it was later decided that someone experienced in children's work should perform this function. As a result, D. B. Brankin, Superintendent of the Boys' Industrial School, was appointed and was given the assistance of the Provincial Police. By May 27th, 1932, all but four of the three hundred and sixty-five children were placed in Doukhobor foster homes. When their parents were released on parole between October, 1934, and July, 1935, the children, of course, were returned to them.

Evaluation of the Experiment

Hooper concludes his study with an evaluation of the whole experiment. He found that the physical care provided was in accordance with accepted child welfare standards of the day. The custodians respected the right of self-determination of the Sons of Freedom. While school attendance was demanded, the normal right of the parents to determine the religious faith of their children was recognized. None of the children received any religious instruction which might conflict with the faith of their sect, and the older children were allowed full freedom of religious expression.

The Government had hoped the children would gain valuable lessons in citizenship from their experience. It was believed that sympathetic treatment by other Canadians would show them that the outside world was not as hostile as they thought. However, the authorities did not realize that at best the placement experience could be only a partial compensation for the deprivation of family life.

Hooper's conclusion is:—

> The institutions and agency were successful in countering many of the negativistic feelings that resulted from the separation of the families, and in preventing the experience from becoming damaging to the children's emotional development. However, it was not within the scope of their activities to attempt a re-education programme, which, if successful, would have resulted only in emotional conflicts when the families were reunited. The children would have been torn between their desire to conform to the wishes and beliefs of their parents and their newly acquired ideologies.

He ends with a plea that if any similar action is anticipated in the future, the Government should approach it on a long-term basis and should not be deterred in its plan by illogical demands for economy.

CORRECTIONS SERVICES

The greatest problems of prison administration for Sons of Freedom occurred during the detention of several hundred on Piers Island from 1932 to 1935, and in the 1950 disturbances when scores were committed to the Federal Penitentiary. It is the purpose here to review briefly these two detention programmes and to indicate lessons for administrative structure and policy.

The Piers Island Project

In the spring of 1932 approximately six hundred men and women, in roughly equal numbers, were committed to prison for nudism. The length of their sentences made them a responsibility of the Federal Government, which decided to lease Piers Island for the purpose of confinement. Most of the following material derives from an interview with B. S. Macdonald, formerly Assistant Deputy Warden of the Piers Island project.

For administrative purposes the unit came under the direction of the Warden of the British Columbia Penitentiary at New Westminster. A senior officer was placed in charge, with a staff of approximately fifty people. Guards were not drawn from the usual Penitentiary staff, but were recruited from Vancouver Island areas and discharged at the termination of the project. The inmates prepared their own food and did the necessary housekeeping duties.

Although the unit was located on an island three miles square, and escape was not a problem, the inmates were not allowed the run of the whole area. The men and women were confined to two large compounds containing the necessary buildings. There was no incendiarism, even though the buildings were tar-paper shelters and lamps had to be used because of the lack of electricity.

Little was done to segregate the groups among the women, but the men were divided into four groups—old men, young men, special working gangs, and the extreme die-hards. Out of the total six hundred people, only about thirty refused to do work of any kind.

The project was first operated as a regular prison, but the absurdity of this was soon realized. Refusal to obey was initially punished by the use of the paddle but this technique had little effect. Similarly, putting inmates on a bread and water diet made little impact on a group which had traditionally used hunger strikes as a weapon.

Very little resistance was encountered. Evidently nudism was discouraged by the fact that the island was infested with yellow-jackets. A refusal to work in the early period of the project was quickly terminated by the rather drastic move of depriving of water those on a hunger strike. It is reported that the opposition dissolved within three hours after this action.

Indirect methods were used to maintain work. A few other prisoners were on the island; these were induced to ask the Sons of Freedom for help, in place of an official demand for work. Outdoor workers kept busy by salvaging timber from the beaches and sawing it into firewood for the dormitories.

Poverty of programme was the greatest disadvantage in the project. Apparently not much thought was given to planned rehabilitation. No psychiatric services were available, which is not surprising at that time. Other than repair work and the making of clothes and shoes, there was no work programme. The inmates were left to their own resources. Practically nothing was done by way of re-education, even in an informal way.

Releases were handled on a flexible basis. All co-operative inmates got six days "time off" per month. Others were apparently released early because they appeared to be good prospects. When the unit was closed in the spring of 1935, only about thirty men were transferred to the Penitentiary for completion of sentences.

This brief review indicates that the Piers Island group was not as difficult as the incarcerated offenders of the 1950 disturbances. This may be partially explained by the fact that they were simply nudists and thus free of the influence of the bombers and burners, but another conclusion might be that the Sons of Freedom group have become more difficult with the passage of twenty years.

The British Columbia Penitentiary Project

The British Columbia Penitentiary at New Westminster almost invariably has a few Doukhobor offenders within its walls, but the problem became acute when approximately four hundred Sons of Freedom were deposited at its gates in the early summer of 1950. The relatively few women involved were sent to Kingston Penitentiary.

Removal to an island was not repeated, but a special unit was constructed outside the Penitentiary walls. Unfortunately, it was of inflammable materials. This permitted the complete destruction of the camp by fire, with a consequent transfer of all inmates to the main prison.

Administration was the ultimate responsibility of the Warden of the Penitentiary, but a special director was put in charge of the camp. He had the advantage of a good many years of teaching experience in the Penitentiary and, in addition, had served as an army examiner and in a military detention administration.

The main lesson to be learned from this administrator's experience is that anyone in charge of a Doukhobor detention project needs help. That is, he needs at least two responsible officers—one in charge of programme and the other in charge of security measures. He needs to be freed from detailed executive direction and to have time to plan policy. The operation of such a unit is the most wearing of tasks, and no administrator should be asked to carry the load without a good team around him.

In this instance, the director's responsibility was increased by two factors. The inflammable nature of the building meant that not only was there a real element of danger, but there was also necessarily a constant preoccupation with the possibility of fire. Such generation of tension among staff or inmates led to further difficulties. Moreover, a group of intransigent offenders was transferred from the main prison, where they had been a problem to Penitentiary routine, and this compounded the difficulty of administration of the new unit.

ACKNOWLEDGMENTS

This section is a study of Government policy in a number of contentious areas. In the main, the approach has been to explore issues with appropriate members of the public service and obtain the benefit of their views in formulating an opinion. I am very grateful to all the public officials who gave me so much assistance.

Most of the historical material had to be obtained from newspaper sources. I would like to express my appreciation to W. E. Ireland, Provincial Librarian and Archivist, and Miss M. C. Holmes, Assistant Provincial Librarian, for their co-operation in making it possible for me to gather pertinent material.

I am particularly indebted to the staff of the Social Welfare Branch at Nelson. J. S. Smith, the Regional Administrator, provided me with every convenience, and Mrs. V. I. Blaney was most generous with secretarial assistance.

INDEX